# THE COMPLETE BOOK OF GHOSTS

# THE COMPLETE BOOK OF GHOSTS

## A Fascinating Exploration of the Spirit World, From Apparitions to Haunted Places

PAUL ROLAND

ISBN: 978-1-83857-171-9
AD006744UK

Printed in the UK

4 6 8 10 9 7 5 3

# CONTENTS

# INTRODUCTION

The belief in an immortal human soul or spirit and its survival after the death of the physical body is as old as humankind. It is shared by almost every culture and yet, there is still a substantial proportion of the population who doubt or deny the considerable empirical and anecdotal evidence supporting its existence.

This book provides compelling, perhaps even overwhelming, evidence of the existence of ghosts, while making an important distinction between the various manifestations of this fascinating phenomenon.

The stories collected between these covers have been drawn from three of my previous books on the subject – *The Complete Book of Ghosts*, *Hauntings* and *Ghosts and the Spirit World* – and encompass such diverse natural phenomena as out-of-body and near-death experiences, crisis apparitions, phantom forerunners, bi-location and thought forms, as well as related supernatural phenomena, including poltergeists, spirit photography, possessed possessions and of course haunted houses, hotels and even entire ghost towns.

A few examples have been drawn from my own extensive personal experience and the rest from a lifetime study of occult phenomena. This has led me to an understanding that there is nothing to fear from investigating the supernatural and exploring the paranormal, provided that we can distinguish between a genuinely objective experience and one coloured/distorted by our personal expectations, beliefs and fears.

I have collected numerous stories which illustrate the wide variety of ghostly manifestations and these can be read for pure entertainment and a pleasant shudder, or frisson as the French would have it, but the real value of these examples is what they reveal about the nature of reality and our changing perception of it.

Why, for example, would one person see a ghost in its entirety and another see only a portion of it in the same location and at the very same time? Why do some apparitions interact with the living while others seem oblivious to our presence? If ghosts are conscious disembodied souls, how is it possible for us to glimpse an entire scene from the past? And if ghosts are mere echoes in the ether, why do some manifest to warn of danger, channel their talents through the living, or come back to convey a message from the world beyond?

Humankind has a fundamental need to believe in the immortality of the soul because it validates our own existence and gives us the hope and faith to endure the trials of life and the pain of loss. But if true ghost stories were merely chilling fairy tales and myths, they would not have endured through millennia and form the core belief of 57 disparate cultures, philosophies and religions.

It is true that orthodox Christianity does not profess belief in the immortality of the individual human spirit, nor the transmigration of the soul which is common to those traditions which espouse reincarnation, but esoteric Christianity does advocate the idea. As does that branch of esoteric Judaism known as Kabbalah which teaches initiates how to rise through the various stages of spiritual awareness 'in the spirit' using the central glyph of the Tree of Life.

Further back, in prehistory before the establishment of organized religion, our ancestors honoured their dead in expectation of an afterlife and attempted to communicate with their spirits and also the spirits of animal 'guides' through shamans, tribal elders, medicine men and the high priests. Their practices for freeing the spirit survive in the rites and rituals of modern day shamans and pagans for whom the invisible world of disembodied souls and animism is as real, if not more so, than our physical world, for the other, they believe, is eternal while ours is transient.

The Ancient Egyptians were obsessively preoccupied with the afterlife to such an extent that their religion was focused on making a cult of the dead, but in secret the high priests practised what today we would call astral projection to initiate neophytes in the mysteries of life and death.

Their custom of placing a mummified corpse into a series of sarcophagi of increasing refinement symbolized their belief that there are three non-physical components within the human body – the *ka*, *ba* and *akh* – which equate with the astral body of the Western esoteric tradition, the mind and the immortal soul. The astral body (also known as the etheric or dream body) is the matrix of energy which is effectively a blueprint for the physical form we assume on entering this material dimension at birth. And it is this incorporeal projection of our physical body that we call a ghost or apparition.

# CHAPTER ONE

# BELIEF IN THE SOUL

The belief in an immortal human soul and its survival after death dates back to prehistoric times and is common to almost every culture around the world.

Evidence of a belief in immortality can be found in ancient burial customs which reveal that our ancestors had an expectation of an afterlife and a respect for the memory of the dead. This reverence for the departed, which dates back to the Stone Age and possibly beyond, is the clearest evidence that primitive man possessed self-awareness long before he had formed the means of expressing it in words. Prehistoric cave paintings from Africa to Australia support the belief that early man had a strong intuitive link with the spirit world and attempted to communicate both with his ancestors and with animals through tribal elders, shamans, medicine men and, later, the high priests of the first civilizations. Despite, by present standards, the inherent cruelty and comparative lack of sophistication of these early societies, it is evident that they all shared a belief in spirits long before the concept of good and evil found expression in orthodox religion.

## CULTS OF THE DEAD

The ancient Egyptians were so preoccupied with the prospect of an afterlife that their entire civilization was founded on the cult of the dead. Their custom of placing mummified corpses into sarcophagi of increasing refinement resulted from their belief that there are three non-physical components within the human body, (the *ka*, *ba* and *akh*) which equate with the etheric, astral or dream body of the Western esoteric tradition, the mind and the immortal soul. The etheric body is the non-physical counterpart that is effectively a blueprint for the form which our body takes on entering this material dimension.

Many believe that the pyramids may have been built not only as tombs for their pharaohs, who were venerated as living descendants of the gods, but also as the means of initiation into the mysteries of life and death. According to this interpretation, their alignment with specific constellations was chosen to provide a path through the sky for the ascending spirit of the pharaoh to journey back to the heavens,

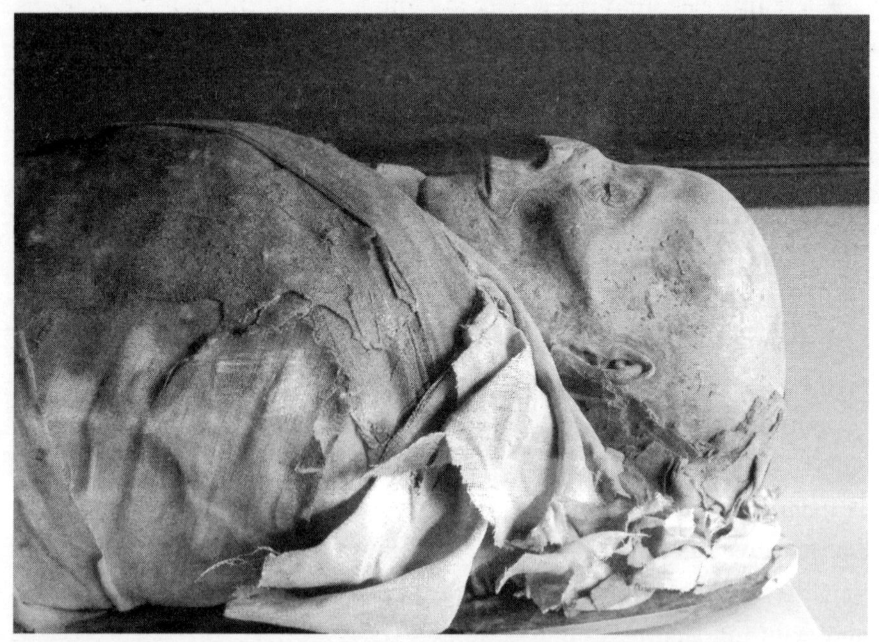

*'[The ancient Egyptians'] custom of placing mummified corpses into sarcophagi of increasing refinement resulted from their belief that there are three non-physical components within the human body . . . '*

specifically the Sirius constellation in the Milky Way whose river-like pattern of stars appeared to be a celestial reflection of the Nile. It is also feasible that the empty stone sarcophagus in the King's Chamber of the Great Pyramid at Giza was used to stimulate the conscious separation of the soul in order for the high priests to be able to commune with the gods. The structural shape of the pyramids was believed to have both a mystical significance and a practical purpose, focusing the Earth's magnetic energies to a specific point and to such effect that the initiate would be unable to resist the force drawing their etheric body out of its physical home. Earth energies are stronger near water which suggests one explanation of why the pyramids were built near the Nile. The theory was tested in the 1930s by English occultist Dr Paul Brunton who spent the night in the King's Chamber and there experienced an involuntary astral journey.

> . . . all my muscles became taut, after which a paralysing lethargy began to creep over my limbs. My entire body became heavy and numb . . . The feeling developed into a kind of iciness . . . All sensation in the lower limbs was numb. I appeared next to pass into a semi-somnolent condition . . . I felt myself sinking inwards in consciousness to some central point within my brain, while my breathing became weaker and weaker . . . There was a final mad whirl within my brain. I had the sensation of being caught up in a tropical whirlwind and seemed to pass upwards through a narrow hole; then there was the momentary dread of being launched into infinite space . . . I had gone ghost-like out of my earthly body.

The Egyptian belief in the three spirit elements is significant because it has its equivalent in many cultures around the world which are different in virtually every other respect. It cannot be coincidence that the Greeks wrote of the significance of the *psyche*, the *pneuma* and the *nous*; the Muslims spoke of the *sirr*, *ruh* and *nafs*; the Hindus acknowledged the *atman*, *jiva* and *pranamayakosha*; while the Jewish mystics contemplated the nature of the *neshamah*, the *ruah* and the *nefash* which the Christians assimilated and externalized in the concept of the Holy Trinity.

Belief in a spirit double which can free itself from the body during sleep and exist separate from the body also gave rise to the Roman *larva*, the Tibetan *delok*, the German *doppelgänger*, the English *fetch*, the Norwegian *vardoger* and the Scottish *taslach*.

Today belief in a spirit double is shared by cultures as diverse as the Azande in Africa, the Inuit of Alaska and the Bacairis in South America as well as the major religions and philosophies of the East. Clearly there must be a basis in fact for this shared belief. It seems unlikely that mere wishful thinking or the desire to deny our own mortality could account for the consistency of such beliefs.

## SACRED SPIRITS

In many parts of the world, ghosts are not considered to be a creation of local folklore, but a fact of life. In China the dead are understood to co-exist with the living, a belief which gave rise to the practice of ancestor worship, while in South America the deceased are honoured with annual festivals known as the Day of the Dead which suggests that the material world and the spirit world might not be as distinct as we might like to believe. In the Eastern and Asiatic religions it is believed that death is not the end, but simply a transition from one state of being to another. The Hindu Upanishads, for example, liken each human soul to a lump of salt taken from the ocean which must ultimately return to the source.

> All the diverse elements, in the end, go back to the source and are absorbed in it, as all waters are finally absorbed in the ocean . . . A lump of salt may be produced by separating it from the water of the ocean. But when it is dropped into the ocean, it becomes one with the ocean and cannot be separated again.

In Buddhism, the personality is believed to dissolve at the moment of death leaving only pure consciousness (*rupa*) to seek a new body unless

*All-night vigils amongst specially decorated graves are a popular way of marking the Day of the Dead in South America*

the individual was an enlightened soul (*bodhisattva*) in which case it can ascend to the higher states of being and there choose when to intervene in the lives of the living as a guiding spirit. However, those individuals who are as yet unable to free themselves from earthly attachments may descend into the realm of the hungry ghosts, the Buddhist equivalent of the Christian hell.

It is implied that the majority of discarnate souls linger in a limbo between lives, known as the *bardo*, before reincarnating. *The Tibetan Book of the Dead* was intended to act as a guidebook for the soul which found itself in this transitional state. It was to be read over the dying and the dead who, it was thought, might be disorientated by finding themselves in this unearthly environment.

> The hour has come to part with this body, composed of flesh and blood;
> May I know the body to be impermanent and illusory.

Though it was written more than 1,000 years ago, its description of the three phases of death are uncannily similar to modern accounts of the near-death experience. The first stage, called *chikai bardo*, occurs when consciousness is suspended at the point of separation from the physical body. At this moment the individual is unaware that they are dead. Only when they look down on their own lifeless body do they realize that this ethereal essence is their true self.

> . . . thine intellect hath been separated from thy body. Because of this inability to loiter, thou oft-times wilt feel perturbed and vexed and panic-stricken . . .'
>
> *The Tibetan Book of The Dead,* Evans-Wentz translation

There then follows a detailed description of the etheric body and its capabilities.

> Having a body [seemingly] fleshly [resembling] the former and that to be produced, Endowed with all sense faculties and power of unimpeded motion.

The following passages stress the importance of letting go of all emotional attachments to people and places so that the soul may ascend into the light. But some may be unwilling, or unable, to relinquish their possessions or may harbour regrets or resentment which will effectively bind them to the earthly plane. Others may be literally haunted by their own evil deeds and they will only exorcize these memories by reliving them in a succession of hells of their own making.

> O now, when the Bardo of Reality upon me is dawning!
> Abandoning all awe, fear, and terror of all phenomena,
> May I recognize whatever appears as being my own thought-forms,
> May I know them to be apparitions in the intermediate state

Having faced the consequences of his actions, the discarnate soul can then submit to the mercy of the Buddha within, his own divine essence who determines whether he can enter Nirvana or must reincarnate. Assuming that most souls will need to return to the world for further trials, the concluding prayers are intended to guide it to re-enter under the most favourable circumstances.

> O procrastinating one, who thinks not of the coming of death,
> Devoting yourself to the useless doings of this life,
> Improvident are you in dissipating your great opportunity;
> Mistaken, indeed, will your purpose be now if you return empty-handed from this life

## SPIRITS IN THE SCRIPTURES

The oldest recorded account of an encounter with a spirit in Western mythology can be traced back to the appearance of the Witch of Endor in the Old Testament who was ordered by King Saul to summon the spirit of the prophet Samuel.

Saul, the King of Israel, had condemned all occult practices as blasphemous, but when he heard that the Philistines were marching on the city of Gilboa he appealed to God for help. Receiving no answer he disguised himself and called on the witch who used a talisman to invoke the dead from the netherworld. The spirit of Samuel materialized out of the earth in the form of 'an old man . . . wrapped in a cloak' and complained of having been disturbed. Saul begged forgiveness and assured the spirit that he would not have disturbed him had his kingdom not been in peril to which Samuel replied that what is fated to befall men cannot be undone. The spirit then departed, leaving Saul to face his enemies.

The story is seen by some as a satire on the king who is forced to acknowledge forces greater than those at his command, and it also serves as a moral fable. Saul deceived the witch (by coming to her in disguise), but she proved to be the wiser. After the spirit departed she showed compassion for the humbled ruler, killing one of her animals to feed him. The story also underlines the Jewish belief that the soul of the deceased hovers near its body for 12 months after death before ascending to heaven.

Communication with spirits was forbidden by the Old Testament (Deuteronomy 18:9–14), but conscious awareness of the higher worlds for the purpose of self-realization or enlightenment had been practised since biblical times by initiates of Merkabah, a forerunner of the modern Jewish mystical teaching known as Kabbalah.

Spirits are not acknowledged explicitly in the New Testament although their existence is clearly implied, most notably in Luke 24:39, when Jesus tells his followers: 'Touch me and make sure that I am not a ghost, because ghosts don't have bodies, as you see that I do!'

Elsewhere, particularly in the 'lost' Gnostic gospels discovered at

Nag Hammadi in 1947, there are several significant references to the living spirit within every human being and to the disciples' personal experience of the astral world and altered states of awareness. In the Gospel of Philip, Jesus makes a clear distinction between 'the real realm' (i.e., the material world) and 'the realm of truth'.

> People cannot see anything in the real realm unless they become it. In the realm of truth it is not as [with] human beings in the world, who see the sun without being the sun . . . Rather, if you have seen any things there, you have become those things.

In 1 Corinthians 15:50 and 2 Peter 1:18 it is stated that flesh and blood cannot enter the celestial kingdom; in John 3:13 it is noted that heaven is for spiritual beings and that we are all spirit in essence and will return from whence we came:

> And no man hath ascended up to heaven, but he that came down from the heaven, even the Son of man which is in heaven.

According to the Gnostic gospels, Jesus appeared to his followers as a spirit to prove that the soul survives death, but due either to selective editing of the gospels or a mistranslation of the rich metaphorical language of the Gnostic gospels, this central teaching became literalized. St Paul attempted to clarify the idea that Jesus had risen physically from the tomb and in so doing made a distinction between our earthly form and our spirit:

> There are also celestial bodies, and bodies terrestrial: but the glory of the celestial is one, and the glory of the terrestrial is another . . . There is a natural body and there is a spiritual body.
>
> 1 Corinthians 15:35–44

Elsewhere, in 2 Corinthians, St Paul speaks of having attained separation of the spirit and the body at will and having ascended 'in the spirit' to the third heaven, which was a technique he may have mastered as an initiate of an aesthetic sect of Jewish mystics who practised Merkabah – an advanced form of meditation which translates as 'rising in the chariot'.

## ANCIENT APPARITIONS

In order to understand the nature of ghosts we need to accept the fact that we all possess what is often called a dream body – an etheric or spirit double composed of subatomic matter connected to our physical form by an etheric umbilical cord which is only severed upon death. Such a concept is central to the philosophies of the East, but can seem too fanciful to those Westerners who have not had an out-of-body experience (OBE), or at least have no memory of the experience, for it is likely that everyone has had an OBE during the deepest stages of sleep.

So what evidence is there for the existence of this 'true self' and how might it explain the various phenomena we categorize under the broad heading of 'ghosts'? While much of the evidence is anecdotal, there are numerous cases where an apparition was witnessed by more than one person or where an individual was later able to verify details they had observed during their astral journey. There is also solid scientific evidence for the existence of the etheric double gathered from experiments conducted in the mid-1970s by Dr Karl Osis of California, USA during which the invisible presence projected by a psychic in an adjoining room was recorded either by photosensitive instruments or sensors which could detect the tiniest movements of a feather in a sealed container.

This question of evidence occupied the ancients as intensely as it continues to occupy us today. The earliest recorded discussion on the subject can be found in the writings of the Chinese philosopher, Mo Tzu (470–391 BC).

> Since we must understand whether ghosts and spirits exist or not, how can we find out? Mo Tzu said: The way to find out whether anything exists or not is to depend on the testimony of the ears and eyes of the multitude. If some have heard it or some have seen it then we have to say it exists. If no one has heard it

> and no one has seen it then we have to say it does not exist. So, then, why not go to some village or some district and inquire? If from antiquity to the present, and since the beginning of man, there are men who have seen the bodies of ghosts and spirits and heard their voices, how can we say that they do not exist? If none have heard them and none have seen them, then how can we say they do? But those who deny the existence of the spirits say: 'Many in the world have heard and seen something of ghosts and spirits. Since they vary in testimony, who are to be accepted as really having heard and seen them? Mo Tzu said: As we are to rely on what many have jointly seen and what many have jointly heard, the case of Tu Po is to be accepted.' Tu Po was minister to the Emperor Hsuan [827–783 BC] who ignored warnings that if he executed Po on false charges he would be haunted by the minister's ghost. Three years later Hsuan was killed with an arrow fired by an apparition resembling Tu Po in front of an assembly of feudal lords.
>
> Chapter 31, Yi-pao Mei translation

## RESTLESS SPIRITS

The legend of Tu Po is clearly a moral fable and was widely accepted as such. In other parts of the world such stories became the basis for local myths, especially if there was a lesson to be learned. In South America, for example, there is the legend of the Weeping Woman who is said to have committed suicide after a handsome seducer refused to marry her as he had promised to do. She is said to haunt the highways in search of her children whom she had killed in order to be free to marry him. Her tale is told to young girls entering womanhood as a warning against believing the lies of men. In Japan there is a long tradition of apocryphal ghost stories in which wronged women return from the dead to take their revenge on those who have dishonoured them. The tale of the Tofu Seller is characteristic of this type of fable. It tells of a blind tofu vendor who is tricked into removing a charm from the door of a house by a wizened old hag who claims to be the ghost of the householder's first wife. Once the charm is removed, the ghost glides inside and a horrible scream is heard from within as the old hag frightens her husband's second wife to death.

The most persistent ghost story in Japanese culture is the legend of the *Kuchisake-onna*, the spiteful spirit of a vain young girl who was the wife or concubine of a jealous samurai in the Heian period. Fearing that she had betrayed him with another man he is said to have disfigured her and then taunted her by saying: 'Who will think you're beautiful now?' Her face covered with a mask, the *Kuchisake-onna* wanders through the fog seeking solitary children, young men and women, whom she asks: '*Watashi kirei?*' (Am I beautiful?). If they answer 'yes' she tears off the mask and asks again. If they keep their nerve and again answer 'yes' she allows them to go on their way, but if they run screaming she pursues them, brandishing a long-bladed knife or a scythe. If she catches a man she butchers him and if she catches a girl she mutilates her, turning her into another *Kuchisake-onna*. The story is so deeply rooted in the Japanese psyche that as recently as 1979 there was public panic when it was rumoured that the *Kuchisake-onna* had been seen attacking children. In 2004, cities in South Korea were rife with similar rumours.

The earliest credible account of a spectral encounter was recorded by the Greek philosopher Athenodorus who lived during the 1st century BC. Against the advice of his friends, Athenodorus agreed to rent a room in a lodging house that was reputed to be haunted because it was cheap and he wished to prove that his actions were determined by his intellect and not his emotions. At nightfall his nerves were tested by the appearance of a gaunt-faced spirit of an old man draped in the soiled vestments of the grave. The spectre was weighed down by chains and appeared to be in anguish but was unable to communicate what it was that bound him to that place.

The philosopher kept his nerve and indicated that he was willing to follow the ghost wherever he wished to lead him. It led Athenodorus along a narrow passage and out into the garden whereupon it faded into the bushes. Athenodorus noted where the spirit had disappeared and the next morning he informed the magistrates, who ordered workmen to excavate the garden. There they unearthed a skeleton weighed down

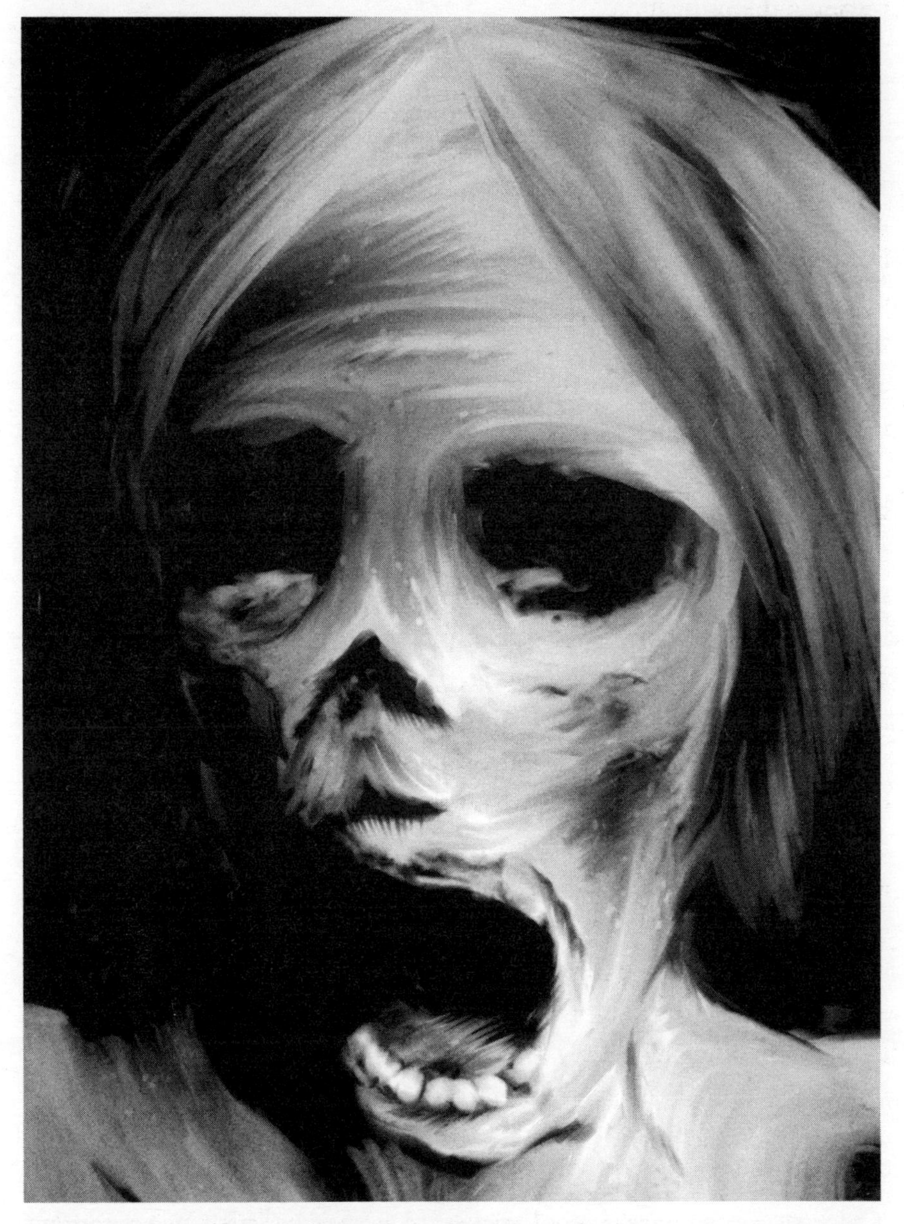

*'"*Watashi kirei?*" (Am I beautiful?)' The legend of the* Kuchisake-onna *resurfaced in South Korea as recently as 2004*

by rusted chains which they assumed was that of a murder victim. They then had the skeleton reburied according to Greek funeral rites. Such stories have their counterpart in virtually every culture from ancient times to the present day.

The English ghost story tradition can be traced back to an episode involving Lord Lyttleton who, in 1779, claimed that he was tormented by the spirit of his jilted mistress, Mrs Amphlett, whose three daughters he had also seduced. She had committed suicide in despair and had returned to foretell the day and hour of his death. His friends, fearing for his sanity, thought they would try to outwit the spook by turning all the clocks forward. When the appointed hour passed without incident his lordship retired to bed much relieved and cursing himself for being a superstitious fool. But the dead are not so easily cheated and at the appointed hour Lord Lyttleton expired in his sleep from a fit.

## WHAT IS A GHOST?

Ghosts are not a supernatural phenomenon but a purely natural one. It is generally accepted that they are either earthbound spirits or residual personal energy which lingers at a location which was significant to the individual in life or at the moment of their death.

Our fear comes from our vain attempts to deny the existence of these apparitions and not from any power that they can hold over the living.

> If we could take a material man and dissolve away his physical constituent without interfering with the sense-data by means of which we perceive him, we should be left with, exactly, an apparition.
>
> G.N.M. Tyrrell, *Apparitions*, 1953

Colorado-based parapsychologist Jeff Danelek has become something of a ghost-hunters' guru after presenting a compelling argument for the existence of spirits in his influential study, *The Case For Ghosts* (Llewellyn, 2006). In place of the usual sensationalistic stories of playful poltergeists and other paranormal phenomena, Jeff approaches the subject in an objective, down-to-earth manner that has earned him the respect of both the scientific community and other paranormal investigators.

*Jeff Danelek*

## WORKING THINGS OUT

During the course of writing this book I asked him to share his theories with me and explain how he reached his thought-provoking conclusions.

> I noticed that most of the stories I came across – especially those that dealt with interactive communications between spirits and humans – almost invariably centred around similar themes – namely, a certain over-attachment to a place or person, or a fear or uncertainty about moving on. Very few ghosts, it seems, appeared particularly happy or indifferent to their plight, forcing me to wonder if it wasn't certain mindsets that were keeping them effectively bound to our world when, by all reason, they should be moving on to the joy of the ethereal realm. Noticing that living human beings also tended to keep themselves stuck in undesirable circumstances (stress, jealousy, materialism, addiction, depression) often as a result of an unwillingness to acknowledge – much less attempt to change – their attitudes, I simply wondered what would happen to such people when they died. As such, my understanding of ghostly psychology is largely based upon what I understand about human psychology in general; I simply took it to the next level and tried to visualize how materialism, stubbornness and anger (among other attitudes) might impact on the disembodied energy of a deceased person. It really wasn't that difficult to do, especially considering that a ghost (which I define

exclusively to be the disembodied conscious energy of a once living human being) is every bit as human when dead as they were alive and, therefore, just as prone to making the same bad decisions and maintaining the same counterproductive attitudes as they did in life. This, in fact, is why I believe they are ghosts in the first place and why being an earthbound spirit is such a predicament.

Jeff has identified various categories of ghost which he believes equate with recognizable personality types.

## CATEGORIES OF GHOST

The first thing to understand about a ghost is that where human beings are concerned, not even death can change things. I believe that when a person dies, they move on to the next realm with all the personality traits, quirks, prejudices, biases, and a lifetime of accumulated wisdom – and nonsense – fully intact. Working from that premise, then, it's not difficult to imagine how some people would either choose to become a ghost or might find themselves trapped on the physical plane by their own personality flaws. As such, we might assume that the reasons for becoming a ghost may be as numerous and varied as are the types of personalities humans exhibit.

### THE UNAWARE GHOST

Many paranormal investigators believe that some entities may remain within the physical realm simply because they are not aware that they are dead. As such, they go on about their life much as they did before, completely oblivious to the fact that they are no longer a part of the physical realm and remain that way until some sudden trauma or realization goads them into either remembering that they have died or demonstrates that they are, in fact, no longer among the living. This idea has been popularized by such excellent movies as *The Sixth Sense* and

> *The Others* and is a part of many people's beliefs about ghosts (a perception Hollywood has done much to reinforce).
>
> I, however, find it extremely unlikely that ghosts don't know they're dead. Near-death experience (NDE) accounts remain remarkably consistent in their insistence that even upon sudden and unexpected death the soul invariably detaches from the body and hovers about nearby, all the while aware of its surroundings and cognizant of the fact that it is no longer attached to its physical body. If these accounts are accurate portrayals of what the human psyche experiences at the moment of death, it seems that to not be aware of the fact that one had 'passed over' would be about as hard to miss as would be the loss of a limb; some things, it seems, are just a little too obvious not to notice. Unless they died in their sleep or were so inebriated when they passed that they never knew what hit them, I should imagine the one thing they could not help but notice is their own death, especially once one started encountering deceased loved ones and, perhaps, various religious figures. As such, I seriously doubt that any recently deceased spirit would be in – or, at least, remain in – a state of ignorance for long. It simply doesn't hold together logically.

Jeff has an original explanation to explain the disproportionate number of earthbound spirits of children that have been reported.

> It is possible that children or the mentally incapacitated might not recognize the situation for what it is and remain attached to the physical plane after their death. Ghosts of children are frequent subjects of a haunting, leading to the possibility that children who are unable to comprehend death in practical terms may well be too confused to move on after their demise. Death is, after all, generally considered a 'grown-up' affair that is rarely discussed with children. As such, some may have no real understanding of what is happening to them and so remain trapped in a type of 'sleep state' until they either can finally

comprehend what has happened and move on or are rescued by other spiritual entities whose job it is to look out for these gentle souls and guide them along.

### THE DENIAL GHOST

Just as there are people who make denial a major part of their life, it is only natural to imagine that there are those personalities who will make it an integral part of their afterlife as well and so will simply refuse to accept the truth of their own earthly demise. They can be the ones who remain earthbound the longest, for human pride can be as powerful and debilitating on the other side as it often proves to be on this side of eternity, which can make it especially difficult to convince them to give up the charade and move on.

### THE ATTACHED GHOST

This type of ghost is so emotionally attached to the things of the world that it refuses to let go of them. This is often their home or some place they truly loved. And so they stay behind, always hovering on the edge of human perception, but rarely if ever able to interact with it in any meaningful way.

Such ghosts often remain around for years, or even decades, so great is their attachment to the things of the world. They tend to be the more possessive ghosts who insist that new residents leave their home, or attempt to interfere in the lives of those they left behind. Over-identification with one's profession or trade can also produce this effect – ghosts of librarians or school janitors, for instance, are examples of this – and elderly couples and shut-ins who have learned to isolate themselves from the outside world especially run this risk.

### THE JEALOUS GHOST

Though exceedingly rare, there are accounts of ghostly entities attaching themselves not to things, but to people, and interjecting themselves into earthly relationships, usually out of some misguided notion of possessiveness or outright jealousy. This could be anything from an over-possessive spouse that can't accept the thought of their mate remarrying, to a spurned lover who took his or her own life only to come back and attach themselves to the source of their unrequited affections later. Active only around the source of their possessiveness and then usually only when in the presence of that source's new-found affections, the jealous ghost can be among the most tenacious and frightening ghosts of all.

## THE FEARFUL GHOST

Due to cultural or religious conditioning, some personalities are simply too afraid to find out what fate has in store for them and so prefer the mundane existence of a haunting to the potential punishment a final judgement might portend. Often these are individuals who did considerable harm – or believe they did – to others and so fear being held to account for their offences and punished. To them, then, remaining within the comparative safety of the physical realm is their only means of avoiding this judgement and the punishment they believe they so richly deserve, and so they cling to the material world the way a frightened child might cling to its mother's leg on the first day of school.

*Due to cultural and religious conditioning, certain personalities are simply too afraid to find out what fate has in store for them*

It's not just evil-doers who

find themselves in this state, however, but ordinary people who have had strong religious beliefs drilled into them from childhood and feel they have not lived up to them are good candidates to become fearful ghosts, especially if they believe God is angry with them and they have not had a chance to 'repent' or had their sins absolved by a priest before they died. Fear is almost as strong an emotion as love, and can keep one tied to the earth plane as completely as denial, possessiveness and jealousy can, and is easily capable of making us our own worst enemy and more adroit at inadvertently torturing ourselves than any external foe – or Deity – could ever be.

## THE MELANCHOLY OR SAD GHOST

Perhaps the most depressing type of entity one can encounter, the 'sad' ghost is someone who is so overwhelmed by some tragedy that they continue to wander the physical realm as if in a state of shock that they seem unable to recover from.

Suicides often end up as 'sad' ghosts, for the same factors that drove them to take their own lives frequently keep them bound to the very physical realm they took such pains to rid themselves of. As such, they can also be among the most difficult to 'rescue', for they are often too self-absorbed in their own pain to either recognize the need for salvation or care about it. They truly are the most lost of all souls and may require significant intervention on both the part of the living and other spiritual entities to pull them towards the light.

*They continue to wander the physical realm as if in a state of shock*

### THE MISSION GHOST

This type of ghost stays around in order to take care of some unfinished business that was cut short by their unexpected death. This 'mission' can be as simple as revealing the location of a hidden will, or as major as trying to find justice for a life cut short by murder, but in either case mission ghosts seem intent upon achieving some goal they've set before themselves and feel they cannot rest until they have succeeded.

### THE GOODBYE OR COMFORT GHOST

The goodbye ghost is a manifestation that appears – often only once – to either say goodbye to a loved one bereaved by their loss or to simply assure them that they are well and have passed over successfully. These can manifest as electrical phenomena or something as dramatic as a full-body manifestation. Tales of widows seeing their late husbands sitting on the foot of their bed or children encountering the manifestation of their dead sibling in their bedroom are legion, and even recently-departed family pets have been occasionally reported. Trauma and excessive grief may account for some cases, but certainly not for all of them.

### THE CURIOUS GHOST

I'd imagine that those personalities who in life demonstrated a curiosity about the afterlife or were of a scientific bent might find the chance to manipulate matter and energy from the other side to be too good an opportunity to pass up. I'd suspect such personalities, however, to be fairly rare and frequently frustrated in their efforts to get through to us 'thick mortals', and so wonder if they might not be prone to tiring of the game and move on to explore other realms of the spirit.

### THE MISCHIEVOUS GHOST

Similar to the curious ghost but of a somewhat more menacing vein is that which we call the mischievous or 'playful' ghost.

*It is as though haunting is great amusement, and it will spend any amount of energy to play the game for as long as it can*

It is different from the curious ghost in that it isn't as interested in demonstrating the reality of the supernatural realm as it is in simply frightening the still living. It is as though haunting is one great amusement to it, and it will spend any amount of energy necessary to play the game for as long as it can. Such ghosts are immature and childish (like the personalities behind them) and are comparable to the practical joker who thinks everything he does is hilarious and can't understand why others can't see the humour.

This can manifest itself in something as innocent as moving furniture, hiding a piece of jewellery or pulling the sheets off a bed, to physical assault! They want to make a nuisance of themselves and, in fact, go out of their way to make living with them almost impossible.

They may be the source of at least some poltergeist activity. A nervous teenage girl may simply be the perfect conduit for a mischievous entity to manifest or do its mischief.

## THE ANGRY GHOST

People have been willing to endure tremendous hardship and great personal loss in the quest for revenge, so the thought that an angry personality might be willing to endure the personal hell of an earthly wandering in search of vengeance is not difficult to imagine.

Fortunately such entities are relatively rare, but even so they present the greatest challenge to the ghost-hunter. Anger is a destructive force that grows more powerful with time and can only be dissipated through the power of love and compassion.

# ANGELS AND APPARITIONS

The vengeful ghost has become a cliché of graphic horror fiction and films. But in reality it seems that a restless spirit can do little more than appear looking melancholic and hope that it will prick the conscience of the guilty party into making a full confession, or persuade a kindly soul to restore its reputation. Ghosts have also been known to warn of danger and even to take control of endangered ships and aircraft, guiding their pilots and passengers to safety.

## ACCUSED FROM BEYOND THE GRAVE

The murdered do haunt their murderers, I believe.

Emily Brontë, *Wuthering Heights*

In January 1897 Mary Jane Heaster of Greenbrier, West Virginia was grieving for her daughter Zona who had died in mysterious circumstances earlier that month at the age of 23.

The official cause of death was recorded as being 'complications resulting from childbirth', but Mary Jane was adamant that her daughter had not been pregnant. Zona had, in fact, given birth to an illegitimate child two years earlier, but it was preposterous to suggest that her health had been compromised to such an extent that she could have succumbed as a result.

Mary Jane was not satisfied. Her suspicions had been further aroused by the testimony of the attending physician, Dr Knapp, who was also, coincidentally, the coroner. He had been summoned to Zona's home on the fateful night to find that her husband of just three months, Edward (Erasmus) Shue, had moved the body to an upstairs bedroom and had re-dressed her in her finest Sunday clothes.

He was in a severely agitated state, cradling his new bride's lifeless body in his arms and wailing as melodramatically as a music hall villain.

He refused to allow the doctor to examine her closely, insisting that he be left in peace to grieve. He claimed to know nothing of the circumstances that had led to her death as the body had been discovered by a young boy whom he had sent to the house on an errand. It was the boy who had found her lying lifeless downstairs and had run for help.

All Edward would say was that she had succumbed to an 'everlasting fit'. Under the circumstances Dr Knapp could do nothing more than catch a cursory glimpse of the dead woman's face which he observed had a marked discoloration on the right cheek and on the neck consistent with a blow and strangulation.

At the wake Edward's erratic behaviour aroused further suspicion. He refused to allow any of the mourners to approach the casket and had covered the marks on her neck with a scarf which he claimed had been her favourite.

It was quite by chance that her mother happened to remove a white sheet from the coffin just before the burial. Perhaps it was female intuition or a whisper from beyond the grave. Whatever compelled her to recover the sheet it was to prove a defining moment in the case.

## The Indelible Stain

The first thing Mary Jane noticed was the odd odour which she had initially attributed to embalming fluid, but the more familiar she became with that smell, the more convinced she became that it was something else, something indefinable. When she tried to rinse the sheet the water turned the colour of blood. Scooping some of it out with a jug she was astonished to see it was as clear as drinking water, yet the water in the bowl remained crimson red. The sheet was no longer white, but pink, the colour of diluted blood.

No matter how hard she scrubbed the sheet and no matter how long she soaked it, the stubborn stain remained. The only thing Mary Jane could do now was pray. She demanded answers, for if denied she knew she would lose her mind from grief. In the following days when the dying light of day had receded and the shadows lengthened her prayers were answered.

On four successive nights Zona's earthbound spirit manifested in her mother's house and revealed how she had suffered at the hands of her abusive husband. On the night of 22 January he had flown into a rage when he learned that she hadn't cooked meat for his dinner. He beat her and broke her neck. And to prove it, the apparition turned its head around 360 degrees! Had anyone inspected the body they would have seen the incriminating bruising and felt the dislocated vertebra in the neck. But as no post-mortem had been performed there was no evidence to support the mother's suspicions, other than the accusation of a ghost.

*On four successive nights Zona's earthbound spirit manifested in her mother's house*

## Exhumation

Nevertheless, Mary Jane marched over to the office of the local prosecutor, John Alfred Preston, and demanded that he put the question to her former son-in-law. Preston couldn't order Edward's arrest on hearsay evidence at the best of times and certainly not on that allegedly provided by a ghost. But he had his doubts concerning Edward's version of events and was only too willing to have Zona's body exhumed for an autopsy. Edward's evident distress at the news seemed to confirm what everyone in the town had been saying for weeks – that he had taken her life and, therefore, he couldn't be permitted to get away with it.

The autopsy confirmed that the real cause of death was strangulation, which was all the prosecutor needed to instigate proceedings. Edward was immediately arrested and while he paced up and down his tiny cell in the county jail further investigations unearthed his chequered past. Proof was obtained of two earlier marriages, one of which ended in divorce and the other with the 'accidental' death of the second wife who had been killed by a blow to the head. Apparently three wives were not enough for Edward who boasted to his fellow inmates that he intended to chalk up seven marriage partners before he settled down to an ignominious old age. He was confident that no jury would convict him. After all, what evidence could they have? No one had actually seen him murder his wife. An intruder could have done it. All he needed to do was sow sufficient reasonable doubt and he'd walk out of the courtroom a free man.

He had heard rumours of Zona's ghost, but dismissed it out of hand as the ravings of a grief-stricken mother. Unfortunately for the prosecution, testimony pertaining to the ghost was ruled inadmissible by the judge even before the trial got under way. When Edward walked into the courtroom on the first day of the trial it was all he could do to suppress a smug grin.

## The Trial

Edward's attorney shared his client's over-confidence and that was his undoing. He thought he would have some fun at Mary Jane's expense by asking her to repeat her ghost story in the belief that it would discredit her in the eyes of the jury. But she remained calm throughout the questioning, impressing both the jury and the judge. Nothing the defence could say seemed to sway her. It was not her imagination, she assured the court, that had told her that her daughter had been killed by having her breath choked out of her and her neck 'squeezed off at the first vertebra'. That was the first time that the precise cause of death had been mentioned during the proceedings and when it was subsequently confirmed by the physician who had written the autopsy report there was a hushed silence in the courtroom. Edward was caught in a web of deceit and subsequently convicted of murder. The only reason he escaped execution was the fact that he had been convicted on circumstantial evidence and not the word of an eyewitness. He died in prison on 13 March 1900 and is the only man to have been convicted of murder in the United States on the testimony of a ghost.

## SPINNING IN HIS GRAVE

In the autumn of 1916 a flight training school in Montrose, Scotland was the scene of a series of hauntings which seem to support the belief that a spirit will return from the world beyond if it feels compelled to right a wrong or seek recognition it believes it deserves.

For several months a vaguely discernible figure attired in a pilot's uniform was seen outside the mess hall by senior members of staff. It would approach the door of the hut then vanish. Inside meanwhile, pilots and staff would describe having sensed a presence. One even swore that he saw the spectre standing at the foot of his bed. Subsequent research concluded that the ghost must have been that of flight instructor Desmond Arthur, who had been killed during a routine flight in 1913 as the result of a botched repair to his biplane. The error had apparently been covered up and the accident attributed to pilot error which must have had Arthur spinning in his grave for as soon as the true facts came to light, the haunting ceased and Arthur presumably returned to his rightful resting place.

## THE DOOMED U-BOAT

On a darker note, the crew of German submarine UB-65 appear to have been doomed from the moment their U-boat was built. During its first voyage a torpedo exploded while being loaded aboard, killing six men and the second officer. But this was not the last time the officer was seen aboard. While it was on its first patrol the crew reported seeing the officer standing on deck with his arms folded and looking up into the clouds. He was seen again the day the captain was killed and thereafter whenever some disaster struck the vessel. The mere appearance of the phantom was sufficient to drive one sailor into committing suicide by jumping into the sea although nothing untoward had actually occurred that day. On its final fateful voyage in 1918 it was sighted apparently abandoned on the surface by a US submarine, L-2, whose captain ordered his crew to action stations in the belief that it was a trap. But before he could fire on it the U-boat exploded and sank beneath the waves. The last thing the American captain noted in his log was the appearance of a German officer standing motionless on the hull, his arms folded and looking upwards into the sky.

## GHOST SHIPS

Such incidents are often attributed to echoes in the ether, but there have been many cases where ghosts have actively intervened to save the living. In 1949 the captain of the passenger liner *Port Pirie* was on shore in Sydney, Australia awaiting orders while the crew were giving the ship a last look over in preparation for their next voyage.

One of the engineers filled the boiler and turned the pumps off when the gauge indicated that the boiler was full. But as he walked away the pumps started up by themselves. After double-checking the gauge he turned the pumps off again and turned away, but again the pumps turned themselves back on. Now that his curiosity had been aroused he stripped down the boiler and gave it a thorough overhaul. He discovered that the gauge was faulty and had been registering that the boiler was full when it was almost empty.

Had the ship been allowed to sail with this fault undetected it could have resulted in a fatal explosion at sea with the loss of all hands. When the engineer told his crewmates about this one of them remembered that it had happened before. The ship's first chief engineer had been killed after the boiler had run dry and blown up. With his last breath he had vowed that he would never let it happen again. Could he have been responsible for turning the boiler pump back on to warn his successor of the potentially fatal fault?

A similar story surrounds the sinking of the sailing ship the *Pamir* which went down in the Atlantic in 1957 with very few survivors. Since then this modern Flying Dutchman has been sighted by several ships in distress whose crews reported being saved from certain death by the phantom ship.

Although the *Pamir* does not appear to have taken an active part in the rescue of the stricken ships, the grateful survivors swear that it exerted a 'mysterious force' which pulled them out of a squall into calmer seas while remaining unaffected by the bad weather itself. Such seamen's

*Ghost ship the* Pamir *– grateful survivors swear it exerted a 'mysterious force' which pulled them into calmer seas*

stories may seem far-fetched, but it is worth noting that the rescued seamen mentioned that one of the phantom ship's crew could clearly be seen with his arm in a sling – a fact that was only later confirmed by one of the *Pamir*'s surviving crew members.

An interesting footnote to the *Pamir* case is that every time it has been sighted its crew are fewer in number, suggesting that with every rescue the curse is lifted for one or more of its doomed sailors.

## GUARDIAN ANGEL IN DISGUISE

By no means all ghosts are out for revenge or to right an injustice. Some appear to be guardian angels in disguise. One of the most remarkable cases was that reported by British pilot Bill Corfield, who flew into a terrible thunderstorm en route to Athens in 1947. As the plane and its crew were buffeted by high winds and visibility was severely reduced

Bill had little choice but to take them down to 20 metres above sea level and fly blind in the hope of breaking through the clouds.

Just then his navigator spotted the Corinth Canal, an extremely narrow passage only 5 metres wider than the wing of the plane. Instinctively Bill banked into the mouth of the canal and levelled off, flying in the pitch dark for 7 kilometres, a manoeuvre Bill later admitted was 'suicidal'.

But no one panicked. In fact, the crew were overwhelmed by a sense of serenity that one compared to being in a cathedral. Bill admitted, 'I knew – absolutely and without doubt – that my brother [Jimmy who had been killed in World War Two] was with me in the aircraft. There was nothing physical [to see] but he was there.'

So convinced was he of his brother's presence that Bill took his hands off the steering controls and let his brother pilot the plane. It was only when they were clear of the canal and in clear skies that Bill took back control and delivered the plane and its grateful crew to their destination.

## THE LAST FLIGHT

Ghost ships have long been a staple ingredient of salty sea tales and ghost trains are said to have been sighted on more than one abandoned railway line, but phantom planes are a distinct rarity.

Early on the morning of 13 June 1993 air traffic controllers at John Wayne airport, in Orange County south of Los Angeles, were besieged by calls from pilots complaining that a private plane was invading their airspace, posing a serious risk to both inbound and outgoing aircraft.

Its shrill engine sent three noise monitors into the red and annoyed the ground staff who noted its FAA (Federal Aviation Administration) number so they could lodge a formal complaint. People living in the exclusive properties surrounding the airport had also been driven to distraction. They'd been phoning the authorities all morning to voice their anger that a maverick pilot was being allowed to disrupt their breakfast, buzzing their homes and performing aerobatics too near to a residential area.

In fact, he had been flying so low that several irate citizens had noted the FAA number painted on the distinctive red fuselage, N21X.

Within the hour, the registered owner had been identified. It was Donald 'Deke' Slayton, a former Mercury astronaut, captain of the 1975 Apollo-Soyuz mission who was known to have an insatiable appetite for speed.

## Nobody's Hero

But he was nobody's hero that morning. As his plane finally climbed into the clouds and faded from the radar screens muttered curses and annoyance was all that trailed in his wake. It was not only a damn nuisance, it was a highly irresponsible stunt and more than a few residents were determined to pursue their complaint through the FAA until they got a result. It wasn't long in coming.

Two weeks later a letter of censure against 'Deke' Slayton was approved and three weeks after that it was finally delivered to his wife Bobbie. Only she wasn't his wife any longer. When she called the FAA to ask them what kind of sick joke they thought they were playing, she made it very clear indeed that she was Deke's widow and she was angry with good reason. She had been with him that morning at his bedside hundreds of miles away in Texas as he lay dying from brain cancer.

And no, no one else could have borrowed the plane as it was on display in an aeronautics museum in Nevada on the day in question, stripped of its engine.

# CHAPTER TWO

# THE NIGHT SIDE OF NATURE

The modern preoccupation with the paranormal could be said to have begun in 1848 with the publication of *The Night Side of Nature*. The Victorians were avid readers of ghost stories, but they bought this collection in unprecedented quantities because its author, Scottish novelist Catherine Crowe, appealed both to their romanticism and their reason. Her obvious delight in describing Gothic horrors was balanced with rigorous research. Each episode was backed up by witness statements, documents and dates to reinforce the author's belief that the supernatural was as worthy of serious investigation as the natural sciences. Her view was that the scientific establishment was arrogant and presumptuous in stating that all paranormal phenomena were the result of hysteria. It was her contention that the majority of scientists 'arrange the facts to their theory, not their theory to the facts'.

Crowe's timing was opportune. The belief in the infallibility of science was beginning to be questioned, yet the literate classes were also losing their faith in religion. Neither science nor religion appeared to have all the answers, but it seemed that a commonsense approach to the supernatural – and specifically to the question of life after death – might finally reconcile the two. By insisting that at least two independent witnesses corroborate each sighting, she laid down the ground rules for conducting paranormal research which was to change little over the next 100 years.

## WILLINGTON MILL

Her most thorough and intriguing investigation concerned Willington Mill, near Newcastle upon Tyne, England, which was a haunted mill house owned by an industrialist, Joshua Proctor, who provided a sworn statement which Mrs Crowe included as a preface to her account. The property was only 40 years old when Proctor moved in during the spring of 1840, so it did not conform to the traditional idea of a house haunted by the spirits of previous owners. Moreover, Proctor was a devout Quaker, a God-fearing Christian not given to belief in spooks. And neither was Dr Edward Drury, a hardened sceptic and amateur ghostbuster who was the first on the scene when rumours of the haunting circulated around the region. It was Dr Drury who was to bring the facts to the attention of Mrs Crowe. In July, Drury and his trusted friend Mr Hudson inquired if they could spend the night in the mill house in order to 'unravel the mystery', implying that they expected to expose a hoax. On meeting Mr Proctor they were immediately struck by his honesty and candour and so decided that they would not need the brace of loaded pistols with which they had intended to frighten the trickster. Proctor clearly believed that something was amiss and had even sent his family away so that the investigators could have a clear field.

At 11 pm on the night of 3 July 1840, Dr Drury and his companion made themselves comfortable on a third floor landing outside the haunted room and settled down for an all-night vigil. At midnight they heard the sound of bare feet running across the floor, then knocking sounds as if someone was rapping with their knuckles on the bare boards. Other noises followed in quick succession – a hollow cough and a rustling – suggesting that a presence was making itself known. By 12.45 am, Dr

Drury assumed that the show was over and was planning to retire to bed leaving Mr Hudson on the landing, but before he could do so Dr Drury saw a sight that was to haunt him for the rest of his life. A closet door swung open and 'the figure of a female, attired in greyish garments, with the head inclining downwards, and one hand pressed upon the chest as if in pain', strode slowly towards him. The spectre advanced towards Mr Hudson at which point the doctor found the courage to charge at it but he passed right through the apparition, knocking over his companion. Drury confesses that he recollected nothing for three hours afterwards and was assured by Hudson and Proctor that he was 'carried down stairs in an agony of fear and terror'. The good doctor was so traumatized by his experience that he required ten days to calm his nerves before writing his account. He ended it by stating that he had gone there as a devout disbeliever but had emerged convinced of the reality of the supernatural.

Not content with relying on Dr Drury's account and Proctor's verification, Mrs Crowe dug deeper, unearthing accounts of earlier and subsequent sightings at Willington Mill given by four other people, plus a local newspaper proprietor and a historian who discovered that ghosts had been seen in a house that had occupied the same site 200 years earlier. Mrs Crowe wrote:

> The following more recent case of an apparition seen in the window of the same house from the outside, by four credible witnesses, who had the opportunity of scrutinising it for more than ten minutes, is given on most unquestionable authority. One of these witnesses is a young lady, a near connection of the family, who for obvious reasons, did not sleep in the house; another, a respectable man . . . his daughter . . . and his wife who first saw the object and called out the others to view it. The appearance presented was that of a bare-headed man in a flowing robe like a surplice, who glided backward and forward about three feet from the floor, or level with the bottom of the second storey window seeming to enter the wall on each side and thus

> present a side view in passing. It then stood still in the window and a part of the body came through both the blind which was close down and the window, as its luminous body intercepted the framework of the window. It was semi-transparent and as bright as a star, diffusing a radiance all around. As it grew more dim it assumed a blue tinge and gradually faded away from the head downward. Had any magic lantern been used it could not possibly have escaped detection . . .

Mrs Crowe then travelled to Willington Mill to question the witnesses herself and found them to be entirely credible.

> They spoke of the facts above detailed with the simple earnestness of people who had no doubts whatever on the subject.

But although *The Night Side of Nature* can be credited with raising public awareness of paranormal phenomena and making a case for having the subject taken seriously, it was an event on the other side of the Atlantic which raised belief in the afterlife to such an extent that it became the foundation for a new religion – spiritualism.

## THE FOX SISTERS

The event that led to the birth of the spiritualist movement occurred in Hydesville, near Rochester, New York in the spring of 1848.

On 31 March, a Methodist farmer named James Fox, his wife Margaret and their two daughters, Margaretta aged 14 and Kate aged 12, retired early in the hope of catching up on their sleep. They had suffered several disturbed nights due to noises which they assumed were caused by the wind rattling the shutters of their wooden-framed house. But the wind was not to blame. Before coming to bed Mrs Fox tried the sashes to see if they were loose and was answered by bangs for which there was no obvious explanation. Puzzled, she put the children to bed then prepared to retire herself. The family all slept in the same room and so Mrs Fox was a witness to what happened next. The rapping noises began again. Kate reminded them all that the next day was April Fool's Day and assumed that someone was playing a practical joke. She thought it might be fun to test them and challenged whoever was making the noises to copy her. She snapped her fingers and was immediately answered by the same number of raps. Then Margaret clapped and was answered in the same way. By now Mrs Fox was concerned as she knew that no one else but her husband could be in the house and he would not indulge in such frivolous games. She was also aware that a previous tenant had moved out after complaining of inexplicable noises. She later wrote:

*The Fox sisters (l to r) Margaretta, Kate and Leah*

> I then thought I could put a test that no one in the place could answer. I asked the noise to rap my different children's ages, successively. Instantly, each one of my children's ages was given correctly, pausing between them sufficiently long to individualize them until the seventh [child], at which a longer pause was made, and then three more emphatic little raps were given corresponding to the age of the little one that died . . .

Mrs Fox kept her composure, but she was increasingly anxious. She asked out loud if it was a human being making the noises. There was no reply. 'Is it a spirit?' she asked. 'If it is make two raps.' She was answered emphatically with two bangs that shook the house. In later weeks, disbelievers accused the children of making the noises by cracking their joints but it is reported that anyone who had heard the loud reports which shook the walls that first night would have dismissed such explanations out of hand.

Emboldened by her ability to converse with the other side, she then asked if it was an 'injured spirit' to which she received two loud raps in reply. Using an impromptu code, Mrs Fox elicited the following information from the intruder. It was the spirit of a 31-year-old man who had been murdered in the house and had left behind a widow and five children. Mrs Fox obtained permission from the spirit to invite the neighbours in to witness their exchange, but many were too frightened to enter the bedroom. They waited outside while a hard-headed pragmatist by the name of William Duesler sat on the end of the bed and quizzed the spirit with more personal questions. Duesler's cynicism melted the moment the bed vibrated in response to the strength of the rapping sounds.

Duesler managed to draw out more information including the fact that the murdered man was a peddler by the name of Charles Rosma and that he had been killed five years earlier by a previous tenant of the house, a Mr Bell, for the $500 that he had saved and carried with him. Subsequent inquiries confirmed that a maid had been sent away on the evening a peddler had been invited to spend the night, and that when she returned the next morning the peddler had gone.

By Sunday, 2 April, rumours of what was taking place in the Fox family home were the topic of conversation around every breakfast and dinner table in the town. Hundreds of people converged on the house hoping to hear the raps and learn the latest news from the spirit world. Interest intensified when it was learnt that the murdered man had informed the family that his body had been buried in their cellar. Without delay James Fox and a number of men picked up picks and shovels and started digging up the dirt floor. The excavation had to be interrupted when they struck an underground stream, but a couple of months later the water had drained away and digging was resumed. Five feet down they struck a plank.

Underneath they discovered human bone fragments and tufts of hair in a bed of quicklime.

Meanwhile, the previous owner, Mr Bell, had been traced to nearby Lyon, New York, but in anticipation of being accused of murder he had petitioned his neighbours to provide written testimony as to his good character. There was little that the law could do at this stage other than wait for more damning evidence to be unearthed – or for Mr Bell to be forced into making a confession by his conscience or by the persistent phantom. Curiously, the murdered man had predicted that his killer would never be brought to trial and it proved to be so.

But then, in November 1904, the cellar wall collapsed revealing the original wall behind it and between the two, a skeleton. Someone had evidently exhumed the body from its initial grave beneath the cellar floor and re-interred it behind a hastily built partition. It was all reminiscent of a scene from Edgar Allan Poe. But who was the victim? Those who looked upon it were in no doubt, for next to the grisly find lay a peddler's tin box.

## The Birth of Spiritualism

The Fox family were the first people to become national celebrities in the field of spiritualism, simply by being in the right place at the right time. Not surprisingly, there were those who resented the attention they had attracted, specifically the Church authorities who were suspicious of anyone claiming direct communication with the dead. Under pressure from the Church and puritan elements within the Rochester community, three separate committees were set up in the following months to investigate the phenomena. They subjected the children to strip searches and tests in which they tied their ankles together and made them stand on pillows to isolate them from the floor, but still the rappings continued. All three committees concluded that the children attracted the anomalous activity even if they were not the cause of it. When the children were absent from the house, nothing happened. To save them from becoming a freak show attraction they were separated by their parents and sent away to stay with relatives. Kate went to live with her older sister Leah in Rochester and Margaretta lived with her brother in Auburn. Yet still the noises continued.

However, before anyone could claim that this proved that the children had somehow manufactured the sounds, the spirits raised the stakes. Leah's sceptical lodger, Calvin Brown, was pelted with objects by an invisible assailant while invisible hands prodded and pulled at guests in brother David's boarding house.

More incredibly, a 16-year-old girl, Harriet Bebee, who visited the boarding house, was disturbed to discover that the spirits followed her home to plague her and her family in a similar fashion. The Fox family were finally forced to abandon their besieged home and move to Rochester, but to their dismay the spirits pursued them to their new house where the rappings persisted. Some were so loud that they could be heard at the other end of town.

Such an epidemic of poltergeist ('noisy ghost') activity suggests that at least some of the phenomena might have been produced by the children themselves – teenage girls have subsequently been found to be the origin of much psychokinetic activity (physical phenomena caused by involuntary discharges of psychic energy) due to physiological changes at puberty – rather than by the sudden incursion of angry spirits into one region of the country.

However, it seems some of the mischievous antics can only be explained in terms of spirits. One such identified himself through decoded communications with Kate as a dead relative by the name of Jacob Smith. The deceased were evidently keen to communicate, but were limited to creating loud reports and throwing objects across a room. Attempts were made to create a more sophisticated alphabetical code using different knocks to identify specific letters but any form of communication which relied on a crude form of Morse code was laborious and unreliable. A new and more direct way had to be found. The answer lay in allowing the spirits to take over the body of a willing individual so that the spirit could speak through their voice boxes or guide their hand to write a message from the world beyond. This development was foreseen by an anonymous spirit in a message dictated to Isaac Post, a visitor to the Fox home in 1849.

'Dear friends, you must proclaim this truth to the world. This is the dawning of a new era; you must not try to conceal it any longer. God will protect you and good spirits will watch over you.'

The age of the medium was at hand.

## A SURPLUS OF SPIRITS

Mediums were nothing new. Since prehistoric times shamans, witch doctors, holy men and priests had claimed to be able to commune with their ancestors and the gods. In some cases it is clear from the nature of their messages that they were expressing ideas from their own subconscious and that the gods from whom they channelled their laws and edicts could be seen to have been universal archetypes personifying aspects of their own psyche. Many however, appeared to be genuine channels for discarnate entities whose predictions and insights were later verified by subsequent events. But psychic sensitivity and its various manifestations – clairvoyance ('clear seeing'), clairaudience ('clear hearing') and clairsentience ('sensing an unseen presence') – are not the exclusive preserve of 'gifted' mystics. Everyone, to a greater or lesser degree, has the ability to attune to the presence of spirits.

In the wake of the Fox sisters' experience, hundreds of ordinary people across the United States and Europe began holding séances and many were shocked to discover that they too could produce loud reports and automatic writing, and move objects. More than 100 'mediums' appeared in Rochester alone in a single year. Newspaper reporters across the country were run off their feet chasing stories of spectral manifestations and levitating tables. One journalist scooped his rivals when he learnt that the Fox sisters were not the first to have experienced such phenomena.

Two brothers and a sister named Davenport who lived in Buffalo, New York, had been disturbed by loud reports and vibrations in 1846, but they did not understand their significance until they attended a séance held by the Fox family four years later. During one of their own séances, Ira Davenport was told by a spirit to fire a pistol. In the flare of the discharge, witnesses swore they saw the ghostly figure of a man with his finger wrapped around the trigger. After the shot, the pistol was snatched out of Ira's hand and it fell to the floor. The spectre, who identified himself as 'John King', subsequently entered the bodies of each of the brothers and spoke through them for all in the room to hear.

*Séances were the natural off-shoot of the rise of spiritualism, and were often taken part in by way of a diverting after-dinner parlour game*

Soon spirits across the country were performing all manner of 'tricks' for the amusement of spellbound onlookers: playing musical instruments, moving furniture, producing ectoplasm (a gelatinous substance drawn from the living essence of matter), manifesting objects in mid-air (apports) and even superimposing their faces on that of the medium – a phenomenon known as transfiguration. It was as if the disembodied had suddenly discovered a way to tear the veil between their world and this and were as excited and uninhibited as children who had just learned to ride a bike.

Spiritualism swiftly became a recognized religion. In spiritualist meetings a medium would deliver a sermon dictated from the spirit world and then pass on messages from the departed to the eager congregation. However, the more serious-minded members voiced concerns that nothing of a profound nature was ever communicated. The mysteries of life and death and the nature of the world beyond were rarely alluded to in anything other than the vaguest of terms. The spirits seemed preoccupied with mundane matters and 'unfinished business' on earth. It was as if they were trapped in a limbo between the worlds, unable to move on so long as their loved ones refused to let them go. For the bereaved it was undoubtedly comforting to be given indisputable evidence of survival in the form of personal information that no one else but the deceased could have known, but for those seeking answers to life's mysteries it was ultimately unsatisfying. Perhaps spiritualism wasn't the breakthrough it had promised to be.

Needless to say, the Church was outraged and condemned all communication with the beyond as dabbling with the Devil. As their pews emptied they took courage from the numerous accounts of fake mediums who had been exposed by the press and they vented their righteous indignation on those fraudsters who had preyed on the bereaved and the gullible. But despite the damage done to its reputation, the new movement continued to spread at a phenomenal rate. Even Queen Victoria and Prince Albert declared themselves convinced after enjoying a table-turning (the manipulation of a table during a séance, attributed to spirits) session at one of their country retreats. While some treated a séance as nothing more than a fashionable new party game to amuse their dinner guests, and the scientific establishment dismissed the whole business on principle, there was also a sense that something significant had come to light. Perhaps science and religion no longer had all the answers.

## THE HAUNTING OF CHARLES DICKENS

The Victorians were very fond of ghost stories and the most popular authors of the period relished competing with one another to see who could make their readers' flesh creep the most. One of the era's best-loved storytellers was Charles Dickens, though surprisingly the author of *A Christmas Carol*, *Oliver Twist* and many supernatural short stories on ghosts was not a believer in the paranormal. In fact, Dickens was a hardened sceptic until he had a disquieting paranormal experience of his own.

In 1861, Dickens contributed a ghost story to the popular magazine *All The Year Round* which centred on an encounter between a portrait painter and a young lady in a railway carriage. During the journey, the story goes, the pale-looking lady inquired as to whether the artist could paint a portrait from memory to which he replied that he probably could. When asked the reason for her question she responded, 'Look at me again. You may have to take a likeness of me.' Shortly afterwards they parted and the painter travelled on to his destination. Two years later, an elderly gentleman by the name of Wylde called on the artist and asked if he would accept a commission to paint a portrait of his daughter from a description as she was not available to sit for the portrait in person for she had died some time earlier. Puzzled but intrigued the artist agreed and began to sketch a young lady in accordance with Mr Wylde's description. After several failed attempts to capture her likeness he was on the verge of giving up when in desperation he recalled the young woman whom he had met on the train and used her as his inspiration. 'Instantly, a bright look of recognition and pleasure lighted up the father's face,' Dickens wrote, 'and he exclaimed, "That is she!"' In the course of conversation, the artist asked when the young lady had died and was told it was two years previously on 13 September – the very date the painter had met the pale young woman on the train.

Such twists were almost clichés even in Victorian fiction, but what makes this particular story significant is that it was to have a resonance in real life. Shortly after publication, Dickens received an irate letter from a painter who claimed that the story was not fiction, but fact. It had been his own personal experience which he had written down with the intention of submitting it for publication, but had delayed and he was now convinced that Dickens had heard his story somehow and copied it – even down to the date chosen for the girl's death. The painter had told the story to his friends but had never mentioned the date until the time he wrote it all down. This is what particularly unnerved Dickens. He later wrote, 'Now my [original] story had *no date*; but seeing when I looked over the proofs the great importance of having a date, I wrote in, unconsciously, the exact date on the margin of the proof!'

## GHOST LIGHTS

Not all spirits appear in human form. Often entities will register on video film and photographs as moving lights. The following true story recorded by the Reverend Charles Jupp, warden of a Scottish orphanage, in 1878 is of great interest because it was seen by two witnesses both of whom found its presence reassuring.

> As near as I can tell I fell asleep about 11 o'clock, and slept soundly for some time. I suddenly awoke without any apparent reason, and felt an impulse to turn round, my face being turned towards the wall, from the children. Before turning, I looked up and saw a soft light in the room. The gas was burning low in the hall, and the dormitory door being open, I thought it was probable that the light came from the source. It was soon evident, however, that such was not the case. I turned round, and then a wonderful vision met my gaze. Over the second bed from mine, and on the same side of the room, there was floating

> a small cloud of light, forming a halo like the brightness of the moon on an ordinary moonlit night. I sat upright in bed looking at this strange appearance, took up my watch and found the hands pointing at five minutes to one. Everything was quiet, and all the children sleeping soundly. In the bed, over which the light seemed to float, slept the youngest of the . . . children mentioned above.
>
> I asked myself, 'Am I dreaming?' No! I was wide awake. I was seized with a strong impulse to rise and touch the substance, or whatever it might be (for it was about five feet high), and was getting up when something seemed to hold me back. I am certain I heard nothing, yet I *felt* and perfectly understood the words – 'No, lie down, it won't hurt you.' I *at once* did what I *felt* I was told to do. I fell asleep shortly afterwards and rose at half-past five, that being my usual time.
>
> At 6 . . . I began dressing the children beginning at the bed farthest from the one in which I slept. Presently I came to the bed over which I had seen the light hovering. I took the little boy out, placed him on my knee, and put on some of his clothes. The child had been talking with the others; suddenly he was silent. And then, looking me hard in the face with an extraordinary expression, he said, 'Oh Mr Jupp, my mother came to me last night. Did you see her?' For a moment I could not answer the child. I then thought it better to pass it off, and said, 'Come, we must make haste, or we shall be late for breakfast.'

The incident preyed on Jupp's mind and perhaps it was guilt at not having reassured the child that later compelled him to write an account of that night for the orphanage magazine. When the child read it his expression changed and looking up at the reverend he said, 'Mr Jupp, that is me.' Jupp answered, 'Yes, that is what we saw.' Satisfied that he had not dreamt it the child fell into deep thought, 'evidently with pleasant remembrances, for he smiled so sweetly to himself,' recalled Jupp, 'and seemed to forget I was present.'

# PHANTOMS IN PHOTOS

In the second half of the 19th century, the North American city of Boston was buzzing with talk of technological advances that promised to transform it into a modern metropolis to rival New York and Washington, DC. The First Transcontinental Railroad would soon link the Eastern Seaboard with California to unite a nation that was still in mourning after five years of civil war.

Meanwhile, inventions such as electricity and the telegraph promised a life of faster communication and greater comfort and convenience. Into this heady whirl of progress and expectation emerged the new science of photography, greeted as a modern miracle in an age still dependent on horse-drawn transport, gas street lighting and dirt roads.

Sadly, the remarkable inventions of the age gave scant comfort to grieving families for whom the recent conflict was still a lingering presence. Many could not accept that they would never see their fathers, sons and brothers again. While some people took solace in religion, others sought reassurance in the flourishing spiritualist movement that offered them the possibility of communicating with the dear departed, however briefly. It also, inevitably, exposed them to the risk of being fleeced by conmen and unscrupulous individuals posing as genuine mediums.

Boston photographer William Mumler did not set out to prey on the bereaved by promising to capture the spirit of their loved ones on film, but he saw how eagerly they queued at his studio to have their portraits taken and how willingly they handed over $10 for the privilege. Few complained that he charged five times more than his competitors, but then no one else offered their clients the possibility of a 'reunion' with their deceased loved ones that could be photographed for posterity.

In 1861, while developing a plate in his darkroom, Mumler, a former jewellery engraver, had chanced on what appeared to be a new phenomenon, 'spirit photography'. The photo he was working on was a self-portrait, but it had a blemish of some kind which, when printed and examined in daylight, was revealed to be the likeness of a young girl. Mumler showed it to a friend as a curiosity and joked that the mysterious figure was that of his dead cousin. To his astonishment, his friend assumed he was serious and urged him to send the photo to a leading spiritualist publication, the *Banner of Light*, which duly published it as irrefutable evidence that spirits could be seen by the new science. Photography was still a relative mystery to the general public, who assumed that the camera recorded only what it saw. Photographic phenomena, effects and tricks of the light were then unknown. Few people considered that the picture might be a fake or an accidental double exposure.

## A Booming Business

Whatever misgivings Mumler might have entertained at the thought of conning the public and profiting from their grief were cast aside when he saw the busy waiting room at his Washington Street studio in the days following the picture's publication. His wife Hannah, a clairvoyant, didn't need much persuading to aid him in the deception. She engaged the clients in small talk while they waited their turn and then passed on the information to her husband, so that he could make his performance behind the camera more convincing. He was the 'channel' for the spirits and his wife was the medium who drew them from the world beyond. But there was no guarantee at all that the dead would comply. Often clients would leave with only a conventional family portrait and the hope that the deceased would put in an appearance at a subsequent sitting – for another $10. In this way, the couple ensured themselves a regular and substantial income for a minimal outlay.

Mumler's rivals were not so naïve, however, and were incensed that he was turning their profession into a freak show. They had their suspicions about how he achieved his phantom effects, but proving them was another matter. The whole affair was complicated by the fact that fake phantom photography had become a fashionable business, with stereoscopic cards of 'ghosts' and 'devils' being offered for the amusement of the middle classes, who purchased them as a novelty item. In his autobiography, Mumler described how a competitor, James Black, wagered $50 that he could expose the phantom photographs as fakes. However, after examining the camera and watching Mumler develop the plates, Black admitted he had failed to find anything suspicious. Mumler claimed he had even converted the sceptic, who left the studio muttering, 'My God! Is it possible?' But we only have Mumler's version of events.

In 1863, Mumler invited Dr Child, a Philadelphia physician, to study his methods and put an end to the growing rumours that the phenomenon was nothing more than an effect achieved by double exposure, trick lenses, reflections or concealed accomplices dressed as 'apparitions'. The latter was a favourite trick of fraudsters, who capitalized on the fact that their sitters were required to remain absolutely still while the shutter remained open for up to a minute. This gave ample time for assistants to appear and disappear, leaving a ghostly impression on the plate.

## Closer Inspection

Dr Child accepted the challenge and visited the Boston studio with several friends who oversaw the entire process, from the preparation of the plates to the developing of the prints. They also examined the equipment and made a thorough search of the studio for compartments where an accomplice could be hidden. To eliminate the chance that the plates might be switched at some stage, Dr Child marked each of them with a diamond but still Mumler produced his phantom portraits, to the astonishment of the sceptics.

Yet the doubters would not be persuaded. That same year the physician, poet and essayist Oliver Wendell Holmes Snr. wrote a damning exposé of spirit photography in the influential magazine *The Atlantic Monthly*. He poured scorn on those who were duped into accepting such images as genuine as well as those who fabricated them for profit.

As a result of the article, Mumler's clients took a closer look at their precious 'evidence'. Several of them realized that there was something suspiciously familiar in the faint impressions, which bore a striking similarity to photographs of their loved ones taken while they were alive. Prominent spiritualists who had previously greeted the photographs with enthusiasm also began to question their authenticity, and were forced to examine their faith in the movement when told that several of the 'spirits' were very much alive and well and living in Boston! Mumler didn't protest his innocence, but quietly left town. In 1868 he set up business on Broadway. Evidently, news of his chicanery hadn't filtered through to New York, where he enjoyed a roaring trade, encouraged by a flair for shameless self-publicity. 'It is now some eight years since I commenced to take these remarkable pictures,' he boasted, 'and thousands... bear testimony to the truthful likeness of their spirit friends they have received through my mediumistic power.'

Mumler was prone to exaggeration, but it is estimated that he must have taken around 500 photographs by this time, which, at $10 a sitting, amounted to a considerable sum. But his satisfaction was short-lived – in March 1869 several members of the Photographic Section of the American Institute of the City of New York took their suspicions to the press and demanded an investigation into his activities.

## Brought to Court

A few weeks later, Joseph Tooker, an undercover police officer posing as a grieving client, paid for a portrait with a deceased relative. When Mumler failed to produce the goods, Tooker arrested him and threw him into the notorious city prison known as the 'Tombs'.

Incredibly, when Mumler emerged to stand trial on 21 April, he found the courtroom packed with spiritualists offering moral support to the man they felt had produced irrefutable evidence validating their beliefs. It was clear from the hostile and mocking tone adopted by the press that it was not only Mumler on trial, but the spiritualist movement itself. The *New York Times* poured scorn on the women who packed the public gallery and filled the court 'with a cold and clammy atmosphere... worn down [by] ethereal essences'. Other publications declared Mumler 'a stupendous fraud'.

But if the prosecution thought they had ample evidence to convict, they were mistaken. Tooker's testimony was soon overwhelmed by a series of defence witnesses who swore on oath that Mumler had provided them with proof of life after death. One of the most convincing was Charles Livermore, who identified the spectral image in a photograph as that of his late wife. He declared that several of his friends were also prepared to testify to the fact. 'I went there with my eyes open, as a sceptic,' he told the court. He had even tried to put Mumler to the test by arriving a day early for his sitting to foil any preparations the photographer might have been making to produce the desired effect. During the sitting he altered his pose in order to 'defeat any arrangement he might have made... I was on the lookout all the while'. For those unable to attend the trial, *Harper's Weekly* published two photographs of Livermore and his 'wife' in the 8 May edition and invited its readers to examine them and decide for themselves. Perhaps the most dramatic testimony was given by a former justice of the New York Supreme Court, Judge John Edmonds, who confessed that he communed with the dead during murder trials. He claimed that they provided him with details of how they had died and whether or not the accused had done the foul deed. Judge Edmonds was in no doubt that Mumler's photographs were genuine.

## A Hollow Victory

Sensing defeat, the prosecution called several photographic experts to the stand to explain how the effects might have been produced. One of them observed that the Livermore 'ghost' cast a shadow, which no ethereal phantom should do. Furthermore, the shadow was cast in the opposite direction to that of the living subject, indicating that there were two separate light sources and that two separate pictures had been taken at different times of the day. The conflicting shadows could not possibly have been cast at the same time.

To conclude, the prosecution called the celebrated carnival showman P.T. Barnum, who boasted that he knew a conman when he saw one. The accused had allegedly sold Barnum a collection of spirit photographs which the showman had put on display in his museum of curiosities. The merchandise had come with an incriminating letter in which Mumler had admitted faking the photographs – or so Barnum claimed, for he had lost the letter in a fire and was unable to produce it to prove his story.

On 3 May Mumler took the stand and asserted, 'I have never used any trick or device, or availed myself of any deception or fraud.' Following this, the defence summed up by implying that the case was nothing less than a witch hunt – Mumler was being persecuted for his 'faith', just as Galileo had been persecuted by the Catholic Church. Judge Dowling was not persuaded and declared he was convinced that Mumler had defrauded his clients – but as the prosecution had not proven how the deception had been achieved, he had no choice but to set the photographer free.

It was a hollow victory, however, for Mumler was now deep in debt and unable to pay his legal bills. He returned to Boston to live as a lodger with his mother-in-law and there carried on his work, defiantly claiming that he alone could capture the spirits of the deceased on camera. He died in 1884, reviled by the photographic profession which accused him of bringing the new science into disrepute, and after having destroyed his entire archive of negatives, presumably in an effort to remove the evidence of his deception.

## Photograph of a President

If Mumler was a fraud, he was also later seen as a significant figure in the history of photography. He is now credited with several innovations (which he patented), including Mumler's Process, which enabled photographs to be reproduced in publications with no loss of detail. In spite of his sullied reputation as a spirit photographer, his photographs are still of historical interest. His most famous photograph, taken in his cramped Boston studio in 1871, shows an elderly woman dressed in mourning. But the photo also shows her 'husband' standing behind her, his hands resting on her shoulders. The lady's name was Mary Todd Lincoln and the apparition was the late president, Abraham Lincoln. Mary had unmasked several fake mediums, but she had recently been to a séance where her dead husband had communed with her and she wanted to have her photograph taken in the hope that he might appear again. A staunch believer in spiritualism, she accepted the 'evidence' of the photograph without question, but to the trained eye it is clearly a fake.

## THE FACE IS LIKE THAT OF A DEAD PERSON

Around the time that Mumler was defending his battered reputation in a New York court, an English photographer was attracting attention across the Atlantic by claiming to produce similar phenomena. Unlike Mumler, Frederick Hudson had the backing of a respected medium, Mrs Guppy, whose ringing endorsement guaranteed him a steady stream of clients who would not look too closely at his pictures. But others were not so willing to suspend disbelief, among them professional photographer John Beattie, who persuaded Hudson to participate in a controlled experiment and to consent to the results being published in the *British Journal of Photography*.

Hudson's garden studio was a large converted greenhouse, which also served as his darkroom. After the camera equipment and plates were examined, Hudson seated himself with his profile to the camera while his daughter stood next to him, acting as medium. The first photograph showed nothing unusual, but for the second portrait the girl retreated to the background and this time a third seated figure appeared on the print.

'The figure is in a three-quarter position – in front of me, but altogether between me and the background,' Beattie later wrote. 'The figure is draped in black, with a white coloured plaid over the head, and is like both a brother and a nephew of mine. This last point I do not press because the face is like that of a dead person and under-lighted.'

A third photograph produced another apparition, 'a standing female figure, clothed in a black skirt, and having a white-coloured, thin linen drapery something like a shawl pattern, upon her shoulders, over which a mass of black hair loosely hung. The figure is in front of me and, as it were, partially between me and the camera.'

Beattie still had his doubts about the authenticity of the images, but he couldn't figure out how Hudson had achieved the results. However, there was one explanation he hadn't considered, perhaps because it was just too simple. Hudson had switched the plates. Such a trick must have aroused suspicion among critics within the spiritualist movement, because in September 1872 they began voicing their doubts in the pages of the *Spiritualist* magazine, accusing Hudson of double-printing two separate plates or preparing his plates in advance. They cited a photograph in which the pattern of a carpet could be seen superimposed over the fabric of a sitter's clothing, an anomaly that could only have occurred if the carpet had been on the first exposure with the fake spirit.

By this time, the pages of the 'yellow press' were full of sensational exposés of fraudulent mediums and their theatrical parlour tricks. The favourite manifestation was ectoplasm, a dense misty miasma said to indicate the presence of a ghostly spirit. To achieve this effect, a roll of cheesecloth would be teased out of the medium's mouth or dropped down from the ceiling on a string at the climax of the séance.

## GENUINE PHOTOGRAPHS

In the 1890s, just as spirit photography looked as though it had lost all credibility, support came from a most unexpected source. J. Traill Taylor, editor of the *British Journal of Photography*, published a series of articles in which he and his staff revealed how certain ghostly effects could be achieved, but they also suggested that some photographs may have been genuine after all. Using a stereoscopic camera to prove his theory, Taylor discovered that 'genuine' images remained two-dimensional and, he argued, they would not have done so had they been faked double exposures.

The following year, Alfred Wallace, co-creator of the theory of evolution, also came to the defence of spiritualism and spirit photography, arguing along the same lines as Taylor. Just because many photographs were obvious fakes, he wrote, it did not mean that they all were, and consequently photos of dubious veracity should be examined scientifically.

## ONE LAST LOOK ROUND

One example of a 'genuine' spirit photo deserving of serious study is commonly known as the 'Lord Combermere Photograph'. Taken in 1891 by amateur photographer Sybell Corbett in the library of Combermere Abbey, Cheshire, it appears to show the faint, glowing figure of a man seated in what Sybell swore had been an empty chair. The exposure was made during the course of an hour and Sybell, who was staying in the house at the time, went to great lengths to ensure no one entered the room while the picture was being taken. The servants would not have dared to sit in the chair, even if they had managed to sneak in. Besides, there was no question as to the chair's occupant; the family and servants identified the figure as Lord Combermere himself. The only problem was that his Lordship was being interred in the family vault at the same time as the picture was being taken. But perhaps the fact that the photograph was taken on the day of his funeral only adds to the validity of the image. What better time for a ghost to take one last look round his ancestral home?

## PHOTOGRAPHING THE INVISIBLE

In the first decade of the new century, many other inexplicable photographs were published in the mainstream press as well as in spiritualist periodicals – so many, in fact, that books began to appear on the subject. The first bestseller was *Photographing the Invisible* (1911) by James Coates, which made a compelling case for the camera as the new medium for preserving fleeting appearances of the recently deceased. The book was such a success that it was republished ten years later in a considerably expanded edition and is thought to have prompted a series of rigorously scientific experiments devised and monitored by American photographer Charles Cook.

In 1916, Cook put two 'spirit photographers', Edward Wyllie and Alex Martin, to the test, providing them with his own plates and insisting that the negatives be developed by a commercial studio to prevent deception. Cook was convinced that the images the two men produced were genuine and that their rare psychic faculties had helped to conduct the spirit's etheric energy on to the photographic plates. For this reason, he preferred to call the results 'psychic photography', a term that suggested the phenomenon was attributable to the mediumistic abilities of the photographer rather than the camera. His theory was supported by Columbia University's Professor James Hyslop, who endorsed the publication of Cook's study with an enthusiastic introduction that attracted interest from within the academic establishment.

Among the most notable studies was the one undertaken by the eminent British chemist Sir William Crookes of the Royal Society, himself a keen amateur photographer. Sir William spent several years examining all the evidence he could accrue and came to the conclusion that much of what he had seen supported the case for psychic phenomena and spirit photography. However, the more frequently he affirmed his beliefs, the greater the scorn he suffered from colleagues, who accused him of being a credulous eccentric who had lost sight of his scientific principles.

## A Confession

Matters were not helped by the activities of the Crewe Circle in the 1920s. William Hope, their de facto leader, made great show of offering prospective clients the opportunity to provide their own photographic plates; however, no one seemed suspicious when he demanded that they leave them in his studio overnight so that they could be 'magnetized' to make them more sensitive to etheric presences!

Hope was frequently accused of fraud and sleight of hand – primarily swapping plates during the handing out of hymn books – but he was never caught. However, he once admitted to Archbishop Thomas Colley, a fervent believer in the supernatural, that he had doctored his photographs. Hope claimed to be a medium and boasted that he could channel the spirit of the archbishop's late mother; but he mistakenly used the wrong image on the plate and confessed to the deception in an attempt to avoid prosecution. To his relief, the archbishop was more than charitable, declaring that the old woman in the photograph was indeed his mother. Colley even put a notice in the local paper, inviting those who remembered his mother to call at the rectory to identify her from a selection of photographs that included Hope's 'mistake'. Eighteen people duly confirmed that the unknown woman was the archbishop's mother, and the incident provided Hope with much-welcome publicity as well as an enthusiastic new patron.

After losing his son and brother in the Great War, the novelist Arthur Conan Doyle had become a convert to the spiritualist cause. He sprang to Hope's defence after the celebrated ghost-hunter, Harry Price, questioned the veracity of several of Hope's photographs. Price and Conan Doyle were friends, sharing a passion for the paranormal and maintaining an affectionate rivalry, but the heated dispute over Hope's claim to be a genuine medium blighted their relationship. Years later, it came to light that a member of Hope's circle had found a flash lamp and cut-out faces with which the 'medium' had produced his effects. Had this been known at the time, Doyle and Price may have remained friends and Hope would have been exposed.

## A Magician Among the Spirits

Another of Conan Doyle's fellow seekers was the celebrated escapologist and illusionist Harry Houdini. It is not generally known that Houdini began his career as a fake medium. However, he soon realized how dishonourable the practice was when he lost a close member of his family and yearned for genuine contact with the deceased. Ashamed of his own small part in the 'great deception', Houdini began a comprehensive investigation and in 1924 published his damning conclusions in a book called *A Magician Among the Spirits*. He had attended countless séances and considered none of them to be genuine; he went on to produce a rational explanation for every form of spectral manifestation he had witnessed, including table rapping, automatic writing and apports (the manifestation of physical objects). His enthusiastic debunking of the paranormal did not endear him to Conan Doyle and others who refused to have their unshakable faith questioned.

Compelling evidence against spirit photography was mounting and deception was becoming more difficult. The public were generally less gullible than they had been during the height of the spiritualist craze and the various tricks and crude effects that had been perpetrated upon them were now widely known and easier to identify.

## The Brown Lady and Others

Almost a century later, the photographs that survived scrutiny remain tantalizing glimpses of a new frontier of paranormal research. One such example was the 'Brown Lady of Raynham Hall'. This apparition is remarkable not only because it has defied rational explanation since the picture was taken in September 1936 by *Country Life* photographer Captain Hubert Provand, but also because his assistant, Indre Shira, actually saw the ghost descending the staircase. Shira had urged Provand to take the picture, which duly depicted what the assistant described ('a vapour form which gradually assumed the shape of a woman in a veil'). Provand admitted that he hadn't noticed anything at the time, which suggests that Shira was the more psychically sensitive of the two (assuming, of course, that the photograph is not a fake). Both men were considered reliable witnesses, not given to practical jokes. The ghost is thought to be Lady Dorothy Walpole, who died in 1726 of a broken neck caused by being pushed down the staircase by her husband after he learned of her affair with another man. She is known as 'the Brown Lady' because her spirit has been seen on several occasions wearing a brown brocade dress.

Between the wars, many supposed 'spirit photographs' were subjected to examination by experts at the leading photographic equipment manufacturer Kodak, who presumably knew a fake when they saw one. Even they failed to find evidence of natural phenomena or fraud in some of the photographs they were asked to assess. There was also the testimony of witnesses who appeared to have nothing to gain from deceiving the public and everything to lose if exposed. Three of the most famous phantom photographs of the post-war years were taken by men of the cloth. The first of these was a colour picture taken by the Reverend R.S. Blance in 1959 at Corroboree Rock in the Australian outback, 160 km (100 miles) from Alice Springs. The site was said to be the location of Native Australian rituals involving animal sacrifice.

The photograph shows a translucent woman emerging from the bush. Reverend Blance was not aware of anyone else in the area at the time.

The second photograph, taken in the 1960s by the Reverend K.F. Lord, captures a hooded figure on the steps of the altar at Newby Church in Yorkshire, England. Reverend Lord stated that he didn't see anything at the time and was only photographing the empty sanctuary for his album.

The third image, commonly known as 'the Greenwich Ghost', was snapped in 1966 by a Canadian cleric, the Reverend R.W. Hardy at Queen's House, Greenwich, London. It shows a shrouded figure ascending the Grand Tulip Staircase. All three photographs were scrutinized by experts who assumed them to be fakes, but who subsequently ruled out the possibility of a hoax, a reflection or flaws in the camera or on the film.

## The Phantom Passenger

A typical photograph that defied explanation was taken by Mrs Mabel Chimney in 1959. Mrs Chimney was visiting her mother's grave in an English churchyard when she decided to photograph it; she then took a separate photo of her husband who was waiting in the car. Although he was alone in the vehicle at the time, the print clearly shows the ghostly presence of an elderly woman in the back seat. The couple identified the mystery woman as Mabel's late mother and offered both the print and the negative to experts at a national newspaper, who declared themselves satisfied that neither had been tampered with.

However, one respected expert, Dr Eric John Dingwall (1890–1986), who devoted 60 years of his life to studying the paranormal as an author and chief researcher for the Society of Psychical Research, remained unconvinced. Dingwall was a firm believer in ghosts and other paranormal phenomena, but he had found fault or fakery in almost every spirit photograph he was asked to examine. When he could not discern any fault, he contended that there must be a rational explanation even if he couldn't provide one. Dingwall's suspicions cannot be easily dismissed, as he repeatedly cautioned against scepticism and was widely respected in psychic circles as a diligent observer and a man who prided himself on keeping accurate records.

In a private letter to parapsychologist Guy Playfair in 1976, Dingwall stated his views: 'We know practically nothing about the "real" nature of the material world in which we live... the more we peer into our surroundings the most indefinite becomes the boundary. The investigation of the relationship between matter and what you call spirit is only just beginning.... The scrapheap of science is high with discarded theories derived from insufficient experimentation.'

## REAL OR FAKE?

There are arguably more fake spirit photographs and phantom film clips now than at any time since the phenomenon came to light, because such images are so easy to create today. Almost every schoolchild knows how to use a computer to manipulate images and edit video. However, among the obvious hoaxes there are occasional images that defy rational explanation.

The much-published shot of the 'uninvited guest' at a holidaymaker's farewell party in 1988 is one such example. In this picture, a group of guests are seated round a table at the Hotel Vier Jahreszeiten in Maurach, Austria. To take the photo, a camera was set up on an adjacent table and the timer was primed, but when the shutter clicked the flash failed to trigger. A second shot was set up and this time the flash fired. When the prints came back from the laboratory the group discovered they had a new member – the head of a young woman can clearly be seen materializing at the edge of the table. Her head is noticeably larger than those of the other guests and she is slightly out of focus. This would suggest that her image comes from a previous undeveloped shot, making the photograph an accidental double exposure – yet neither the photographer nor anyone else at the party recognized the woman. The Royal Photographic Society and the photographic department at Leicester University subjected both the print and negative to rigorous tests and concluded that it was not a case of double exposure.

The 'Guildhall Monk' is another example. In January 1985, St

Mary's Guildhall was the setting for a formal dinner hosted by the Coventry Freemen's Guild. As the guests bowed their heads in prayer, a photograph was taken. When it was developed, the group of guests had been joined by a tall, hooded figure in what looked like a monk's habit. The mayor affirmed that no one had attended the dinner dressed in that fashion, and none of the other guests recalled seeing a person in such clothes. It is worth noting that the building dates from the 14th century and served as a prison for Mary, Queen of Scots.

## The Phantom Pilot and the Woman in White

The 'Phantom Pilot' is another case that appears to substantiate belief in ghosts. In 1987, Mrs Sayer and a group of friends were visiting the Fleet Air Arm Station at Yelverton in south-west England. Mrs Sayer was persuaded to sit in the cockpit of a helicopter and have her picture taken. She remembers it was a hot summer's day, yet she felt cold sitting in the co-pilot's seat. Of the number of snaps taken, only one came out and it showed a hazy figure in a white shirt sitting in the pilot's seat next to Mrs Sayer. The helicopter had seen action in the Falklands War, but it is not known whether or not the pilot had been killed.

The 'Woman in White' is another convincing example. On 10 August 1991, Mari Huff, a member of the Ghost Research Society, took a photograph at Bachelor's Grove Cemetery near Chicago. The cemetery was noted for occurrences such as strange lights, unearthly sounds and sightings of hooded figures, so the GRS brought cameras loaded with high-speed infrared black-and-white film that was acutely sensitive to low light sources. The GRS saw nothing extraordinary until Mari's film was developed. Her photo clearly shows a young woman dressed in white, sitting on a tombstone. She appears to be brooding and her dress is old-fashioned and semi-transparent. It looks like a 'classic' ghost photo of the kind that might adorn a book jacket, but Mari and her colleagues swear that this is what the camera 'saw' that day.

With the advent of digital photography and image manipulation software, one might think that spirit photography is an anachronism from a more innocent age. But photographs purporting to show glowing orbs, blurred shadowy figures and milky-white phantoms continue to appear in periodicals and on the internet. The fact that some of these images have been subjected to analysis by sophisticated software and declared 'genuine' (or at least 'un-tampered with') only intensifies our enduring fascination with paranormal phenomena. We all know how such effects are created and how easily we can be deceived, but it seems we still need to believe in the paranormal because we live in hope of a better life – for many of us, the life that begins after our present one ends.

## SIMULACRA

A final word of caution, before you are tempted to see ghostly faces and figures in your own family photographs. The human brain is wired to identify patterns so that we can recognize familiar faces and distinguish friend from foe. The problem is that we often 'see' faces where there are none. An example of this is the famous 'Face on Mars', which prompted wild speculation among purveyors of the 'ancient astronaut' theory that there was now irrefutable evidence of the remains of pyramid-like structures on the planet's surface. It was later revealed to be nothing more than a play of shadows. This is such a common phenomenon that scientists have given it a name, matrixing (or pareidolia), and the illusory objects it produces are known as simulacra.

One of the most macabre examples of a simulacrum is that of the 'Tennessee Electric Chair'. When the state penitentiary decided that 'Old Sparky' needed modifying, the job was given to local engineer Fred Leuchter who had it delivered to his basement workshop. The chair had been made of timber from the local gallows, so it had violently despatched more than its share of miscreants and no doubt some poor innocent souls too, making it a prime candidate for a haunting. Leuchter took several photographs before he began his work. In some of these there are luminous orbs, which could be reflections; but something that appears to be a human hand grips an armrest on the chair, although it has been suggested that this, too, is a reflection. One image in particular invites a second look – that of a face at the back of the chair. The strangest aspect is the size of the face, which is much smaller than a human head would be if a living person occupied the chair. Remember, in the Austrian party photograph described on page 70, the disembodied head of the 'uninvited guest' was notably larger than those of the other people seated round the table. If the Austrian image was genuine, then the Tennessee picture might be as well. But it is yet another anomaly that stretches our credulity to the limit.

## MOVING IMAGES

If just one of the numerous unexplained photographs is genuine, then it follows that we should be able to capture moving images of a phantom. While it is not unreasonable to assume that the majority of clips posted by private individuals on YouTube and other internet sites are crude hoaxes, the same cannot be said about those sourced from surveillance cameras in public places – particularly if that public place is reputed to be haunted.

In December 2003, security cameras at Hampton Court Palace, a London residence of the Tudor king, Henry VIII, recorded an unidentified male figure opening fire doors that the staff had been given strict instructions to keep shut. The man was robed and had an unnaturally white face; no features were discernible when the frames were frozen or enlarged. One of the palace security guards admitted that his co-workers had been spooked because the face 'didn't look human'. Naturally the press suspected it was a publicity prank, but a spokeswoman for Hampton Court Palace fended off the accusation by assuring journalists that staff were just as baffled as everyone else who had seen the footage. 'My first reaction was that someone was having a laugh, so I asked my colleagues to take a look. We spoke to our costumed guides, but they don't own a costume like that worn by the figure. It is actually quite unnerving.'

Ghost hunters were in no doubt that the cameras had caught a genuine manifestation. The palace is reputedly haunted by several spirits. Jane Seymour, Henry's third wife, died there in childbirth and Catherine Howard, Henry's fifth wife, was imprisoned there before her execution at the Tower of London. Their spirits have been seen on numerous occasions, as has that of Sibell Penn, nursemaid to Seymour's son, Edward. Sibell died in 1562 but was disinterred in 1829, after which a strange sound like that of a spinning wheel was heard and traced to the room she had used for spinning.

An image from the 'fire door' sequence was published to much fanfare in periodicals around the world, but not everyone was convinced. Debunkers make the point that the 'spirit' appears unusually solid and seems strangely familiar with the procedure of securing a modern fire door (the safety handle has to be pulled down and the left-hand door must be closed before the right-hand door)! This makes it more likely that one of the guides in period costume was playing a prank. However, to date no one has admitted responsibility for the Hampton Court 'haunting'.

## A Racing Cert

Across the Atlantic in California, a group of paranormal investigators recently recorded a man-sized shadow walking through the bar and exiting through a solid wall at the Del Mar racetrack, a noted haunt of Hollywood celebrities in the 1930s and 1940s. Stars such as Bing Crosby, Mickey Rooney, W. C. Fields and Lucille Ball lived the high life in a private dining club at the track, but the most domineering personality of the era was horse trainer Charlie Whittingham, whose framed photographs still adorn the walls. Numerous witnesses have heard his voice ordering his favourite drink, a martini, and answering their question 'Is anyone there?' with a hearty, disembodied laugh. But his most unnerving appearance was on a night in July 2010, when his shadow was recorded on the paranormal investigators' videotape. As his ghost passes through the wall there is a small flash of light, even though there is nothing but a hall beyond.

Employees have spoken of sensing a cold spot they can measure with their hands when they are feeling brave enough. Some have also seen a small glowing ball floating through the hallways, which then visits each of the guest bedrooms in turn as if searching for something or someone.

One or two people have even challenged the celebrity spirits to make their presence known and have been answered with a hoarse laugh or called by name, only to find that they are alone in the room.

## The School Spook

On 8 August 2008, surveillance cameras recorded what appeared to be the ghost of a child in Asheville High School, North Carolina, which was closed for the summer vacation. The apparition appears as a shadow on the right of the picture by the elevator, then takes form as it reaches the other side. Even the city schools' spokesman Charlie Glazener, who stated he wasn't a believer in ghosts, told local TV reporters that he didn't have an answer and was now 'one step closer to believing in what we don't normally see'. But one has to ask why a child – dead or otherwise – would choose to go to school when he or she didn't have to, and at 3 o'clock in the morning!

## Ghosts of Gettysburg

If you plan to film ghosts but don't live near a castle or haunted house, a battlefield is the next best thing and should be a site worth staking out. Gettysburg, the scene of one of the bloodiest encounters in the American Civil War, has had its share of sightings. In November 2001, a local family saw some lights moving among the trees and decided to investigate. Fortunately, they took a video camera and filmed what they saw. If you are a disbeliever, the short clip won't be enough to convince you, but if you do believe in ghosts, it could freak you out! After a couple of small lights are seen for a second or two, a number of white figures can be glimpsed among the trees in an area of sacred ground that is strictly off-limits to tourists.

## Open to Doubt

It's hard to raise much enthusiasm for a brief clip shot by After Dark Paranormal Investigations, an American organization who set up a camera in an unnamed cemetery and recorded an unusually frisky sprite gambolling in the top right of the frame. While it's possible that a young, prematurely deceased individual might have decided to return from the dead to dance among the tombstones, it's too fleeting an appearance and not sufficiently distinct to be convincing.

Kathy Henley, an employee at Puckett's Car Wrecking Service in Oklahoma City, is convinced that her workplace is haunted by a victim of a fatal crash. In surveillance footage, a white figure can be seen circling the lot as if searching for a car. The three vehicles it approaches were all impounded following fatal accidents and Kathy insists that no one could have climbed the security fence and entered the lot without triggering the alarm. But there is a fair chance that another employee was playing a prank on her, so this sighting will have to be filed as 'doubtful'.

If ghosts are insubstantial vaporous mists of residual energy, it would be possible for them to reflect sufficient light to leave an impression on film. However, there are so few credible examples that, while the evidence for belief in the existence of ghosts may be overwhelming, their appearances on film are woefully insufficient to support it.

## THE GHOST CLUB

It has been said that if two Englishmen found themselves marooned on a desert island, the first thing that they would do would be to form a club. In 1873, two eminent English academics did just that after finding themselves isolated on an island of doubt surrounded by a sea of certainty.

Professor Henry Sedgwick of Trinity College, Cambridge, had earlier resigned his fellowship because he no longer felt he could subscribe to the Thirty-Nine Articles of Faith central to the Church of England. He was later reinstated when the religious qualifications for the fellowship were rescinded, but his disillusionment was deep-rooted and he no longer felt able to accept what the rest of Christian society accepted in blind faith. Inevitably, his adoring students began to side with their mentor, among them Frederick Myers, the son of a clergyman.

One crisp winter's evening in 1869, Myers called on the professor and persuaded him to take a walk to discuss their reservations regarding religion. As they looked up at the stars Myers voiced his frustration with philosophy and idly asked if his companion had given any thought to the rise of spiritualism and if it might signify a breakthrough in man's understanding of the universe. Sedgwick was doubtful but a seed had been planted that was later to grow into the Society for Psychical Research (SPR), an informal collective of intellectuals and the restlessly inquisitive formed by Myers and his former mentor. Its stated aim was to investigate all forms of paranormal phenomena in a strictly scientific manner and settle the matter once and for all. Its strength was that its members included sceptics as well as believers, among them two future prime ministers – Arthur Balfour and William Gladstone – the poet Alfred Lord Tennyson, novelist Mark Twain, intellectual and critic John Ruskin and academic Charles Dodgson (better known as Lewis Carroll). The SPR investigated more than 700 paranormal incidents from telepathy to out-of-body experiences which they compiled in an exhaustive 2,000-page study published in several volumes as *Phantasms of the Living* in 1886.

During the four years of intense research prior to publication, Myers, who is credited with coining the term telepathy, attended several séances without success until, one evening, as he sat in a circle with the medium Charles Williams, a disembodied hand materialized in mid-air. Such phenomena had been faked by other psychics who had resorted to paying an assistant to appear in a darkened room dressed in black with only their hand exposed. Fearing another fake, Myers had grasped the phantom hand and felt it grow steadily smaller until it disappeared altogether like a deflating balloon, only there was nothing in his fist when he unclenched it. Myers concluded, 'Whatever else a "ghost" may be, it is probably the most complex phenomenon in nature . . . Instead of describing a "ghost" as a dead person permitted to communicating with the living let us define it as a manifestation of persistent personal energy.' It was Myers' belief that phantoms were not physical in the sense that they were solid, but occupied a physical space in a fourth dimension.

## A GHOSTLY INTRUDER

The following is typical of the type of ghost stories the society investigated. It is significant because it was one of the rare occasions when a ghost was heard to speak, and also was so solid as to cast a shadow. Its appearance was witnessed by two people and supported by their signed statements along with those of another couple to whom they had told their story shortly after it had happened.

A married couple, who chose to be identified in the report as Mr and Mrs P (but whose real identity and address are on file in the SPR archives), were in bed when Mrs P was startled to see a stranger standing at the foot of the bed. He was dressed in a naval officer's uniform. She woke her husband who demanded to know what the man was doing in their bedroom at night. The officer simply spoke the husband's name as if reproving him for being so readily offended and then turned about and walked through the facing wall.

Mrs P had assumed that it prefigured some disaster for her brother who was in the navy, but her husband recognized the intruder as his father who had died several years earlier. Shortly afterwards, Mr P fell ill and remained in a serious condition for several weeks. When he recovered he confessed to his wife that he had accumulated a considerable debt and was so desperate that he had been considering going into business with a disreputable character whom he now realized might have ruined him for certain. He had taken his father's appearance and remonstration as a warning and was now determined to resolve his financial difficulties by himself.

## CONCERN FROM BEYOND THE GRAVE

After the Great War, paranormal research was almost exclusively pursued by elderly academics and matronly mediums, but in February 1932 two investigators from the SPR arrived in the English village of Ramsbury, Wiltshire, to investigate a local haunting only to discover that the local vicar had beaten them to the story.

The grandchildren of chimney sweep Samuel Bull had complained that they could not sleep because they were aware of a presence outside their damp and dilapidated cottage. The case is noteworthy because the whole family witnessed the apparition on several occasions and instinctively reacted to it without prompting from the others.

Bull had died the previous summer but on several occasions his ghost appeared in full view of the children, their mother, Mary Edwards and Samuel's invalid wife, Jane, who lived with them. They saw him walking across the living room, up the stairs and through the closed door of the bedroom where he had died. At first they were all terrified, but they gradually became used to seeing the old man and were curiously reassured by his presence. He didn't look like a ghost and it was clear that he was aware of their presence. On two occasions he put his hand on Jane's head and spoke her name, but there was a sadness in his expression which the family assumed was his reaction to seeing them living in such squalid conditions. Shortly before the hauntings ceased Mrs Edwards received news that they were to be re-housed and thereafter the spectre of Samuel Bull appeared with a less troubled look on his face. When they moved he did not appear to them again.

## SUICIDE SIGHTING

The SPR were scrupulous in their methods and, in an effort to satisfy their most hostile critics who were within their own ranks, subjected every case to the degree of scrutiny usually reserved for the natural sciences. Several of their members were distinguished physicists and guarded their reputations as staunchly as the clergy protected the sanctity of the Church. They were not interested simply in collecting ghost stories in the manner that amateur historians collected folklore. They were in search of incontrovertible evidence and that meant securing the written testimony of as many witnesses as possible. The following case is a prime example of the kind of incident they were keen to include.

One pleasant summer evening, a mother and her son were sitting in the back garden of their suburban house in Clapham, south London, when the young man exclaimed with surprise, 'Look mother, there's Ellen!' Ellen was the elder of his two sisters and had been sent to

Brighton on the south coast by her parents to cool her heels after she had been forbidden to see an unsuitable suitor. The young lady was at the far end of the lawn walking toward the garden gate which led to the fields beyond. Fearing that her father might see her before she had a chance to explain her daughter's unexpected return, the mother asked her son to go after Ellen and bring her back to the house. 'I can't run after her,' he reminded her. He had sprained his ankle earlier that day. 'You'll have to send Mary.' So the mother called her younger daughter from the house and told her to run after Ellen and bring her back before her father saw her. They would send her back to Brighton in the morning without him knowing anything about it and so they would avoid an unpleasant scene.

Mary ran across the lawn and through the gate calling her sister's name, but Ellen did not respond. She continued to walk down a path across the fields leading away from the house, her black cloak billowing in the breeze. 'Ellen, where are you going?' asked Mary as she finally caught up with her sister. Then, as she grasped her sister's arm, she found her hand passing right through the apparently solid figure as through a mist. When she had collected herself, she walked back in a daze to where her mother and brother were waiting and told them what she had seen and that she feared the worst. The next day the family learnt that Ellen had thrown herself into the sea and drowned at the very hour that she had appeared to them in the garden.

## LAST WILL AND TESTAMENT

One of the most famous and convincing accounts of survival after death preserved in the SPR archives described an occurrence on the other side of the Atlantic in 1885. An American farmer, Michael Conley of Chicasaw County, died of natural causes at an old people's home and was stripped of his filthy work clothes at the Dubuque County morgue. When his daughter was informed of his death she fainted, but when she recovered consciousness she claimed that her father had appeared to her and told her to recover a roll of dollar bills he had sewn into the lining of his grey shirt. Remarkably, she was able to describe the clothes he had been wearing at the time of his death, even down to the fact that he had wrapped the money in a square of red cloth torn from one of her old dresses. No one believed her, attributing her 'delusion' to grief, but to calm her down they decided to humour her by fetching the clothes from Dubuque and allowing her to examine them. In the lining of the grey shirt, wrapped in a patch of red cloth, they found the money just as the daughter had said they would.

A similar incident was recorded 40 years later by the American branch of the SPR. In Davie County, North Carolina, James Chaffin, a farmer's son, dreamt that his dead father appeared at his bedside and urged the boy to look for his missing will in the pocket of the overcoat that he was wearing in the dream. When James awoke he was puzzled as the farm had been left to the elder of his three brothers, Marshall Chaffin, according to the terms of the one and only will that the family had been aware of. Besides, the old man had been dead for four years. Why had he appeared now when the matter had long been settled? His curiosity aroused, James visited his mother and asked about the coat. She told him that it had been given to his brother John. John dutifully handed it over and was witness to what happened next. James tore open the lining of the inside pocket and inside found a message in his father's handwriting. It said, 'Read the 27th chapter of Genesis in my daddy's old Bible.'

Returning to his mother's house James found the family Bible and exactly at the place indicated they found the missing will. It had been written after the one that had left the farm to Marshall and expressed the father's wish that the land be divided equally between his widow and the four boys. Initially, Marshall was inclined to contest it, but backed down when ten witnesses testified that it was in the old man's own handwriting.

When the case came to the attention of the SPR, they hired a lawyer to investigate it and he concluded that all the facts were correct. Old man Chaffin had chosen the 27th chapter of Genesis to make a point. It described how Jacob deceived his blind father Isaac into giving him what rightly belonged to his brother Esau. Unfortunately, the family

*'Read the 27th chapter of Genesis in my daddy's old Bible'*

were not habitual Bible readers and so the father was forced to make a belated appearance in order to ensure his last wish was respected.

## A DISPIRITING RESPONSE

*Phantasms of the Living* presented a formidable accumulation of similar cases to convince many hardened sceptics. Although the general public was deterred from reading it by the mass of witness testimony and dry scholarly discussions regarding the validity of the evidence, several devout sceptics were converted. Professor James Hyslop, who was disliked by his fellow SPR members for his entrenched cynicism, felt compelled to urge other sceptics to admit defeat.

> I regard the existence of discarnate spirits as scientifically proved and I no longer refer to the sceptic as having any right to speak on the subject. Any man who does not accept the existence of discarnate spirits and the proof of it is either ignorant or a moral coward.

Nevertheless, the scientific establishment was unimpressed. It was not that they did not accept the evidence, but rather that they lost interest in phenomena since apparitions and apports did not add to their understanding of the inner workings of nature. As the novelist Nathaniel Hawthorne observed after having compiled convincing evidence purporting to prove the existence of the paranormal:

> These soberly attested incredibilities are so numerous that I forget nine tenths of them . . . they are absolutely proved to be sober facts by evidence that would satisfy us of any other alleged realities: and yet I cannot force my mind to interest itself in them.

And this attitude has been the bane of believers ever since. Phenomena in themselves tell us nothing about the nature of the universe or human potential. No amount of table-turning, inexplicable rapping sounds or phantom materializations add to our understanding, only to the catalogue of anomalies. In the end a person either believes in ghosts or they do not. Those who were inclined to disbelieve may have been converted by the wealth of experiential evidence, but unless they had been disillusioned with their religion and felt fired up by spiritualism they might be inclined to say, 'All right, ghosts exist, but so what? What does it all mean?'

## TIME-DELAYED PROOF

The fact that *Phantasms of the Living* was not a bestseller did not dampen SPR members' enthusiasm, nor lessen their conviction that they were on the threshold of a new world and they were braced for a radical new understanding of the universe. The first study was only 'the foundation stone', as Myers liked to call it. A second study was hastily commissioned under the title *Census of Hallucinations* and attracted an astonishing 17,000 replies from individuals as far apart as Russia and Brazil. It appeared that the SPR had breached a dam. Paranormal experiences were more common than even the SPR had imagined, but

*'The mast on his vessel had fallen, splitting his skull on the very night she had seen her son standing in the doorway'*

many people had felt unable to admit to having had such experiences. Now the SPR and the spiritualists made it socially acceptable to talk about such things. Again, the most persuasive evidence was the cases confirmed by several witnesses. The following incident must rank as one of the most convincing cases ever recorded.

On the night of 3 January 1856, a New Jersey housewife, Mrs Anne Collye, awoke to see her son Joseph standing in the doorway of her bedroom in a dreadful state. He had severe head injuries which had been hastily wrapped in bandages and he was wearing a soiled white nightshirt. A moment later he vanished. Her family comforted Mrs Collye as best they could, reminding her that Joseph was 1,000 miles away in command of a Mississippi steamboat and that it must have been a nightmare brought on by worry. However, Mrs Collye protested that she had been wide awake. It wasn't until two weeks later that the family learned that Joseph had been killed in a collision with another boat. The mast on his vessel had fallen, splitting his skull on the very night she had seen her son standing in the doorway. When Joseph's brother viewed the body, he found it still wrapped in the soiled white nightshirt

Joseph had been wearing when called from his cabin in the middle of the night to attend to the disaster. Fortunately for the SPR, Mrs Collye had described her experience to her husband and four daughters the next morning, a full two weeks before news reached them of the tragedy.

## FRAUDS AND FAKES

Sadly, the society's efforts to bring such evidence to the attention of the scientific establishment were fatally undermined by several well-publicized scandals involving fake mediums. These occurred just prior to, and in the years immediately after, publication of *Census of Hallucinations* and consequently public ardour towards spiritualism was dampened and the sceptics had further cause to doubt. Several SPR members were duped by hoaxers who exploited their eagerness to believe, leaving the reputation of the society irreparably damaged by the turn of the century. The episode gave rise to the saying, 'for those who believe, no proof is necessary; for those who doubt, no proof is enough.'

Though their pride had been punctured SPR members continued to pursue their investigations independently, producing some of the most significant and influential studies of the period. Sir Oliver Lodge, twice president of the SPR, recorded his communications with his dead son Raymond in a bestselling book of the same name. Raymond had been killed at Ypres in August 1915 and Sir Oliver required incontestable evidence that his son's spirit survived his physical death. He received it in a remarkable way.

Sir Oliver's wife, Lady Lodge, was eventually persuaded to attend a séance presided over by a medium who did not know her by name and who was unaware of her situation. During the evening the medium, Mrs Leonard, declared that she had a message from a young man named Raymond who had recently passed over and that he had met several of his father's friends including a man named Myers. Frederick Myers had died in 1901 and *Phantasms of the Living* had been published posthumously.

'Raymond' reappeared at a second séance held by a male medium, Vout Peters, during which he referred to a recent photograph in which

*Sir Oliver Joseph Lodge (1851–1940) sought to bring together the transcendental world with the physical universe*

Raymond was shown with a group of friends holding a walking stick. Raymond's parents did not possess such a photograph so Sir Oliver took the opportunity to raise the subject with Mrs Leonard on a subsequent visit. He was told that it had been taken outdoors and showed a comrade leaning on Raymond for support. A few days later a photograph arrived in the post from the mother of one of Raymond's fellow officers. She had known nothing of the séances, but had sent the photo to Lady Lodge because she had just learnt of Raymond's death. She realized that it must have been the last photo taken of her son. It showed Raymond sitting in the front row with a walking stick by his side and another officer standing behind, leaning on his shoulders.

## SPECTRAL SOLDIERS

During the First World War, both the Germans and the Allies reported several sightings of spectral soldiers who intervened to save the lives of their comrades. The most famous was the legendary 'Angels of Mons', which may have been the creation of the English novelist Arthur Maachen. However, the following story is generally considered to be authentic. It appeared in the August 1919 issue of the popular *Pearson's Magazine* and was credited to Captain W.E. Newcome.

> It was in September, 1916, that the 2nd Suffolks left Loos to go up into the northern sector of Albert. I accompanied them, and whilst in the front line trenches of that sector I, with others, witnessed one of the most remarkable occurrences of the war.
>
> About the end of October, up to November 5th, we were actually holding that part of the line with very few troops. On November 1st the Germans made a very determined attack, doing their utmost to break through. I had occasion to go down to the reserve line, and during my absence the German attack began.
>
> I hurried back to my company with all speed, and arrived in time to give a helping hand in throwing the enemy back to his own line. He never gained a footing in our trenches. The assault was sharp and short, and we had settled down to watch and wait again for his next attack.
>
> We had not long to wait, for we soon saw Germans again coming over No Man's Land in massed waves; but before they reached our wire a white, spiritual figure of a soldier rose from a shell-hole, or out of the ground about one hundred yards on our left, just in front of our wire and between the first line of Germans and ourselves. The spectral figure then slowly walked along our front for a distance of about one thousand yards. Its outline suggested to my mind that of an old pre-war officer, for it appeared to be in a shell coat, with field-service cap on its head. It looked, first, across at the oncoming Germans, then turned its head away and commenced to walk slowly outside our wire along the sector that we were holding.
>
> Our SOS signal had been answered by our artillery. Shells and bullets were whistling across No Man's Land . . . but none

in any way impeded the spectre's progress. It steadily marched from the left of us till it got to the extreme right of the sector, then it turned its face right full on to us. It seemed to look up and down our trench, and as each Véry light [flare] rose it stood out more prominently. After a brief survey of us it turned sharply to the right and made a bee-line for the German trenches. The Germans scattered back . . . and no more was seen of them that night.

The Angels of Mons seemed to be the first thought of the men; then some said it looked like Lord Kitchener, and others said its face, when turned full on to us, was not unlike Lord Roberts. I know that it gave me personally a great shock, and for some time it was the talk of the company. Its appearance can be vouched for by sergeants and men of my section.

*'Our SOS signal had been answered by our artillery. Shells and bullets were whistling across No Man's Land . . . '*

Later in the same article, another officer, William M. Speight, describes seeing the phantom figure in his dug-out that night. The next evening Speight invited another officer to serve as a witness in the hope that the vision might make another appearance. The dead officer duly appeared, pointed to a spot on the floor of the dug-out, then vanished. Intrigued and somewhat superstitious, Speight ordered a hole to be dug at the spot. To the amazement of Speight and the whole company, the sappers unearthed a narrow tunnel that had been excavated by the Germans, primed with mines timed to explode 13 hours later. The timers and explosives were excavated safely and destroyed.

From the numerous accounts of spectral soldiers on file it would seem that fighting men take such sightings in their stride. No doubt frayed nerves, fatigue and the proximity of death play their part in lowering the threshold of awareness which protects ordinary people from glimpsing the world beyond. In his memoirs of the First World War, the English poet Robert Graves recalled a sighting which produced only mild curiosity, rather than fear, at the time.

> I saw a ghost at Bethune. He was a man called Private Challoner who had been at Lancaster with me and again in F Company at Wrexham. When he went out with a draft to join the First Battalion, he shook my hand and said: 'I'll meet you again in France, sir.' He was killed at Festubert in May and in June he passed by our C Company billet where we were just having a special dinner to celebrate our safe return from Cuinchy . . . Challoner looked in at the window, saluted and passed on. There was no mistaking him or the cap badge he was wearing. There was no Royal Welch battalion billeted within miles of Bethune at the time. I jumped up and looked out of the window, but saw nothing except a fag end smoking on the pavement. Ghosts were numerous in France at the time.

Years later Graves was asked what he thought ghosts might be and he elaborated in the same dispassionate manner.

> I think that one should accept ghosts very much as one accepts fire – a common but equally mysterious phenomenon. What is fire? It is not really an element, not a principle of motion, not a living creature – not even a disease, though a house can catch it from its neighbours. It is an event rather than a thing or a creature. Ghosts, similarly, seem to be events rather than things or creatures.

## A 'STRANGE MEETING'

One of the finest poets of the First World War, Wilfred Owen – who is perhaps best remembered for his atmospheric verse 'Strange Meeting' in which a German and a British soldier encounter each other in the underworld – was killed just one week before the Armistice was declared. On the day the guns finally fell silent, his brother Harold, a naval officer, was overwhelmed by a feeling of apprehension and was later 'visited' in his cabin by Wilfred's spirit. Harold's reaction to the presence of his brother contrasts with the fears of fictional characters who are confronted by unquiet spirits and for that reason his experience is strangely comforting. Harold was unaware of his brother's death at the time of their strange meeting.

> I had gone down to my cabin thinking to write some letters. I drew aside the door curtain and stepped inside and to my amazement I saw Wilfred sitting in my chair. I felt shock run through me with appalling force and with it I could feel the blood draining away from my face. I did not rush towards him but walked jerkily into the cabin – all my limbs stiff and slow to respond. I did not sit down but looking at him I spoke quietly: 'Wilfred, how did you get here?' He did not rise and I saw that he was involuntarily immobile, but his eyes which had never left mine were alive with the familiar look of trying to make me understand; when I spoke his whole face broke into his sweetest and endearing dark smile. I felt no fear – I

*The war poet Wilfred Owen (1893–1918), who was killed just a few days before Armistice Day*

had not when I first drew my door curtain and saw him there; only exquisite mental pleasure at thus beholding him. All I was conscious of was a sensation of enormous shock and profound astonishment that he should be here in my cabin. I spoke again, 'Wilfred dear, how can you be here, it is just not possible . . . ' But still he did not speak but only smiled his most gentle smile. This not speaking did not now as it had done at first seem strange or even unnatural; it was not only in some inexplicable way perfectly natural but radiated a quality which made his presence with me undeniably right and in no way out of the ordinary. I loved having him there: I could not and did not want to try to understand how he had got there. I was content to accept him, that he was here with me was sufficient. I could not question anything, the meeting in itself was complete and strangely perfect. He was in uniform and I remember thinking how out of place the khaki looked among the cabin furnishings. With this thought I must have turned my eyes away from him; when I looked back my cabin chair was empty . . .

I felt the blood run slowly back to my face and looseness into my limbs and with these an overpowering sense of emptiness and absolute loss . . . I wondered if I had been dreaming but looking down I saw that I was still standing. Suddenly I felt terribly tired and moving to my bunk I lay down; instantly I went into a deep and oblivious sleep. When I woke up I knew with absolute certainty that Wilfred was dead.

## THE CONVERSION OF CONAN DOYLE

Sir Arthur Conan Doyle, creator of the fictional detective Sherlock Holmes, became an enthusiastic advocate of spiritualism in the early days of the First World War. This was much to the dismay of his closest friends and most ardent admirers, among them King George V, Prime Minister Lloyd George and Winston Churchill. They were appalled that the man who had created the very embodiment of deductive reasoning

*Sir Arthur Conan Doyle (1859–1930), best known for his creation Sherlock Holmes, was a keen follower of the spiritualist movement*

should dabble with the specious world of spirits. They suspected it was due to his inability to cope with the death of his son Kingsley who had been killed in France, and his father, but Doyle's enthusiasm for the new fad had been awakened by a remarkable personal experience.

The author and his wife had been nursing a young lady, Lily Loder-Symonds, who was in poor health and spent much of her time practising automatic writing. Doyle was fascinated but had attributed the messages to the action of Lily's subconscious mind until one morning, in May 1915, she declared in some agitation that she had received a warning of impending disaster. 'It is terrible. Terrible. And will have a great influence on the war.' Later that day there came news that the transatlantic liner the *Lusitania* had been sunk by a German submarine with the loss of more than 1,000 lives, 128 of them American. It was the turning point of the war. The Americans were outraged and shortly after entered the war on the side of the Allies. Germany's fate was sealed.

Doyle began to take an active interest in 'spirit messages' after this and received what he considered to be incontrovertible proof of the soul's survival after death. It came in the form of a 'conversation' with his dead brother-in-law, Malcolm Leckie, who had been killed at Mons in April 1915. Doyle was stunned to witness Lily writing in Malcolm's unmistakable hand and struck up a dialogue during which he asked probing personal questions which only his brother-in-law could have known, relating to details of a private conversation which they had just before Malcolm returned to the front. Doyle had not even confided the gist of the conversation to his wife so Lily could not have learned about it from her hostess.

Doyle's interest in the paranormal intensified as he investigated the phenomenon and brought his conversion from agnostic to ardent believer to public attention. He became an active member of the Society for Psychical Research and attended many séances including one at which he heard the voice of his son and saw the revenants of his mother and nephew – an event witnessed by two independent observers. Galvanized by the experience, he embarked on a worldwide lecture tour to promote the cause to which he was now wholeheartedly committed. This was

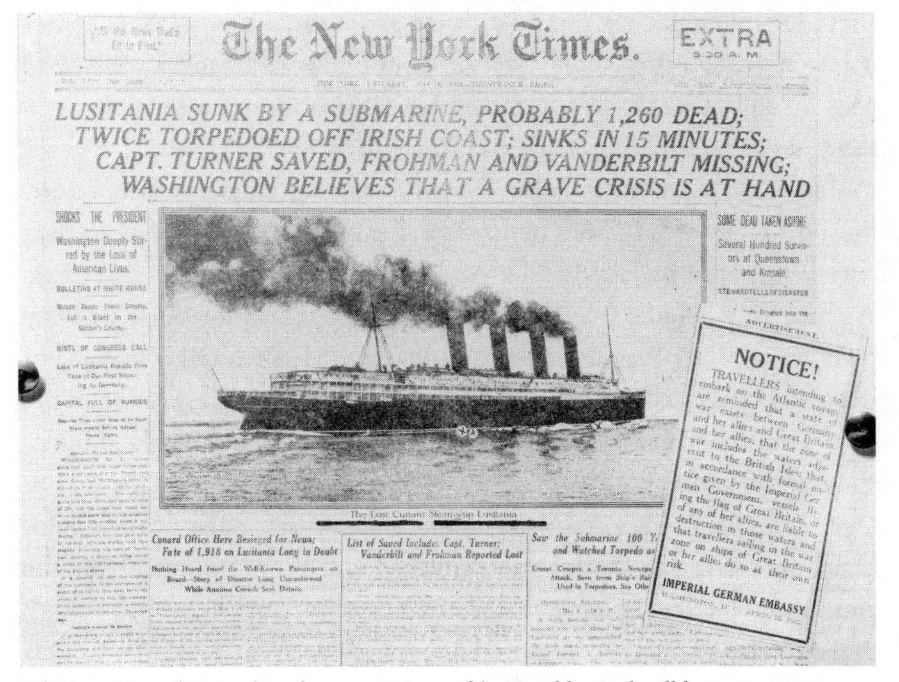
The New York Times. EXTRA 3.30 A. M.

LUSITANIA SUNK BY A SUBMARINE, PROBABLY 1,260 DEAD;
TWICE TORPEDOED OFF IRISH COAST; SINKS IN 15 MINUTES;
CAPT. TURNER SAVED, FROHMAN AND VANDERBILT MISSING;
WASHINGTON BELIEVES THAT A GRAVE CRISIS IS AT HAND

SHOCKS THE PRESIDENT

Washington Deeply Stirred by the Loss of American Lives.

BULLETINS AT WHITE HOUSE

HINTS OF CONGRESS CALL

CAPITAL FULL OF RUMORS

SOME DEAD TAKEN ASHORE

Several Hundred Survivors at Queenstown and Kinsale.

The Lost Cunard Steamship Lusitania

Cunard Office Here Besieged for News; Fate of 1,918 on Lusitania Long in Doubt

Nothing Heard from the Well-Known Passengers on Board—Story of Disaster Long Unconfirmed While Anxious Crowds Seek Details.

List of Saved Includes Capt. Turner; Vanderbilt and Frohman Reported Lost

Saw the Submarine 100 Y[ards] and Watched Torpedo as

Ernest Cowper, a Toronto Newspa[per man] ... Attack, Seen from Ship's Rai[l] ... Used in Torpedoes, Say Oth[ers]

NOTICE!

TRAVELLERS intending to embark on the Atlantic voyage are reminded that a state of war exists between Germany and her allies and Great Britain and her allies; that the zone of war includes the waters adjacent to the British Isles; that, in accordance with formal notice given by the Imperial German Government, vessels flying the flag of Great Britain, or of any of her allies, are liable to destruction in those waters and that travellers sailing in the war zone on ships of Great Britain or her allies do so at their own risk.

IMPERIAL GERMAN EMBASSY

WASHINGTON, D. C., APRIL 22, 1915.

*Lily's warning of impending disaster: 'It is terrible. Terrible. And will have a great influence on the war'*

against the advice of his more sceptical friends and much to the derision of his less sympathetic readers. His own spirit photographs were pored over by fellow enthusiasts but were dismissed out of hand by critics who saw him as a credulous old fool taken in by fraudulent mediums.

Doyle shared the belief at the core of the spiritualist creed that the soul is an etheric blueprint of the body and that this explained why discarnate spirits assumed human form. In *The Vital Message*, he wrote:

> The physical basis of all psychic belief, is that the soul is a complete duplicate of the body, resembling it in the smallest particular, although constructed of some far more tenuous material. In ordinary conditions these two bodies are intermingled so that the identity of the finer one is entirely obscured. At death, however, and under certain conditions in the course of life, the two can divide and be seen separately.

In 1926, he published *The History of Spiritualism*, the result of more than ten years' research into the subject. The book made a convincing case for the existence of psychic phenomena while acknowledging that there were many fake mediums who had no scruples about fleecing the unwary. During the latter years of his life, Doyle befriended the illusionist Harry Houdini who was incensed by the crude parlour tricks employed by fake mediums and he was intent on exposing them. He and Doyle made an odd but amiable partnership – each with his own agenda – as they attended séances around the country. Ironically, they eventually fell out over Doyle's insistence on crediting Houdini's miraculous escapes to the illusionist's unconscious paranormal abilities, a theory he expounded in *The Edge of the Unknown*.

Ultimately, Doyle's credibility took a fatal blow after it was revealed that the Cottingley fairy photographs which he had publicly and enthusiastically declared to be genuine were in fact fakes, but his faith in the afterlife remained unshakable until his death in 1930.

## THE PHANTOM FAYRE

In October 1916, Edith Olivier turned off the main road to Swindon in Wiltshire, in search of a public house in which she could spend the night. It was beginning to rain and she was in no hurry to reach her destination. As she peered through the darkness she saw ahead of her the imposing black monoliths which lined the road to the megalithic stone circle at Avebury. Despite the drizzle she was keen to see the site which at the time was rumoured to have been the scene of Bacchanalian rituals in pagan times.

She stopped the car at the end of a long dirt road and climbed a small mound to get a better view. From here she could see a cluster of cottages in the middle of the circle and what appeared to be a village fayre in progress. From the sound of the laughter and the applause which greeted the fire eaters, acrobats and jugglers, the villagers were clearly enjoying themselves, undaunted by the weather. But then she noticed something peculiar. The fiery torches they carried were undimmed by the rain and not a single man, woman or child wore a raincoat nor carried an

*The Avebury circle in Wiltshire is reputed to have been the site of Bacchanalian rituals in pagan times*

umbrella. It was as if they walked between the raindrops, indifferent to the drizzle which by now was becoming a steady downpour.

It was nine years before Edith visited the site again. On this occasion she was part of a guided tour and she took the first opportunity to ask the guide about the fayre. He confirmed that the villagers had held an annual fayre on the site, but the custom had stopped in 1850. It was then that Edith realized that the road approaching the mound she had stood upon was no longer there. No trace of it remained. The guide agreed that there had been a long dirt road leading to the site in former times, but it had vanished from all maps made after 1800.

## MASS MATERIALIZATIONS

While some apparitions appear to be those of earthbound spirits, this explanation cannot account for the many sightings of phantom armies or groups such as the revellers seen by Edith Olivier at Avebury. The conventional theory is that such souls are unaware that they are dead and so continue to relive the drama of their last hours as if trapped in a recurring dream. While this may be true of certain stubbornly persistent personalities, it seems unlikely that hundreds of individual souls would reconvene on the anniversary of their death to relive such an event. What would have compelled the country folk of Avebury, for example, to relive their night at the fayre if there was no tragedy that had entrapped them? It seems more likely that sightings involving a group are an echo across time which can be picked up by anyone possessing heightened perception. In short, the phantoms are not fighting their battles again, the witness is simply tuning into it in their mind and the stronger the emotional residue, the easier it is for one or more people to tune into it. If all phantom battles were genuine collective hauntings, most of Europe would echo to ghostly gunfire from dusk to dawn. Why, then, is one battlefield or village the setting for a spectral restaging and not another? Is it because the phantoms are mere ripples in the ether?

The best known example of a mass re-imagining is the phantom battle of Edgehill which was originally fought on 23 October 1642 between the Royalist Army of King Charles I and the Parliamentary Army commanded by Oliver Cromwell during the English Civil War. So violent was the clash that the ripples were seen and heard by the locals on consecutive weekends two months later.

Naturally, the king was perturbed when he heard rumours that his defeat was being replayed with the same ignominious result so he despatched three of his most loyal officers to see if there was any truth in the tales. They returned ashen-faced to report that not only had they witnessed the re-enactment but that they had recognized several of their friends who had been killed on that day, as well as the king's nephew Prince Rupert who had survived.

It is tempting to dismiss such tales as the stuff of a more superstitious age, but such phenomena continue to be reported in more modern times. Two English women, holidaying in Dieppe, swore that they heard the sounds of a modern battle just before dawn on the morning of 4 August 1951. The sound of Stuka dive bombers, artillery shells and even the distinctive sound of landing craft hitting the beach was so loud they thought the French army was carrying out a training exercise or perhaps someone was making a war movie. But when they threw open the shutters of their hotel room they saw only empty streets. It was then that they remembered the significance of the date. On the same day nine years previously, a disastrous commando raid cost the lives of almost 1,000 Canadian soldiers.

# CHAPTER THREE

# LIVING APPARITIONS

If we want to understand what a ghost is, we only need to look at living apparitions, which include out-of-body experiences, *doppelgängers*, crisis apparitions and other ethereal phenomena.

After devoting much of his life to paranormal research, Sir Oliver Lodge came to the conclusion that ghosts were not conscious entities but emotional energy recorded in matter. He wrote:

> Take, for example, a haunted house wherein one room is the scene of a ghostly representation of some long past tragedy . . . the original tragedy has been literally photographed on its material surroundings, nay even on the ether itself, by reason of the intensity of emotion felt by those who enacted it; and thenceforth in certain persons an hallucinatory effect is experienced corresponding to such an impression. It is this theory that is made to account for the feeling one has on entering certain rooms, that there is an alien presence therein . . .

## THE STONE TAPE THEORY

This theory was to become known as the 'stone tape' theory, and may account for those sightings in which ghosts replay events from the most traumatic moments in their lives, exhibiting no conscious awareness of any witnesses who may be present. According to the hypothesis this type of ghost is merely an echo. But it does not explain the many incidents where apparitions of the living appear in one location while their body resides elsewhere. Neither does it explain how a living apparition can appear carrying an object, unless they have charged that object with their personal energy at the moment they are projecting their etheric body to the second location.

The SPR recorded a typical example of this in which a lady saw her uncle appear in her home carrying a roll of paper. She naturally assumed that he had decided to pay her a visit, but her uncle looked anxious as he strode across the room and out through an open door. By the time she had followed him outside he was nowhere to be seen. Later that day she received a letter from her father informing her that her uncle was gravely ill. He had died at the very same moment he had appeared in her home. As she stood by her uncle's bed, she felt an urge to look under his pillow and there she found a roll of paper on which, she assumed, he had intended to write a new will favouring her or her father.

It seems that the connection between the uncle's spirit and his body were weakening in the final moments of his life and so he was able to project his essence or his thought form to his niece's home. However, there are also well-documented cases of people who were in the best of health when they projected their image many miles away. The most famous example is that of the French schoolteacher Emilie Sagee.

## IN TWO PLACES AT ONCE

Miss Sagee was a popular addition to the staff at the Neuwelcke finishing school for young ladies at Livonia (now Latvia) in 1845, but there was something unsettling about her which her pupils could not put into words. She was pretty, capable and conscientious, but at the same time distracted, as if her mind was elsewhere. The trouble was that it was not only her mind that was elsewhere. So was her *doppelgänger*, her spirit double.

For weeks there had been rumours that Miss Sagee had been seen in two parts of the school at the same time. Naturally, her colleagues scoffed at the very idea and dismissed it as schoolgirl gossip, but they were soon forced to face the fact that there was more to Emilie than met the eye. One of her pupils, Antoine von Wrangel, was unusually anxious the day she prepared for a high society party. Even so, her girlish excitement cannot account for what she thought she saw when she looked over her shoulder to admire herself in the mirror. There, attending to the hem of her dress, was not one but two Mademoiselle Sagees. Not surprisingly the poor girl fainted on the spot. It became no longer a matter of rumour when a class of 13 girls saw Miss Sagee's *doppelgänger* standing next to its more solid counterpart at the blackboard one day, mimicking the movements of the 'real' Emilie.

However, no one could blame the teacher – she had done nothing improper. By now the whole school was on edge and rife with wild unfounded stories as the girls embellished their experiences for the entertainment of their friends. Eventually, these stories reached the ears of the headmistress, but there were no grounds for a reprimand, never mind a dismissal. Emilie continued to be a conscientious member of staff. The next summer, matters came to a head.

The entire school was assembled one morning in a room overlooking the garden where Miss Sagee could be seen picking flowers. But when the supervising teacher left the room another Miss Sagee appeared in her chair as if from nowhere. Outside, the 'real' Emilie could still be clearly seen gathering flowers, although her movements appeared to be sluggish, as if her vitality had drained away. Two of the more inquisitive girls took the opportunity to step forward and gingerly touch the double in the chair. To one it felt like muslin, but not entirely solid. Another girl passed right through the apparition by walking between the table and the chair. The *doppelgänger* remained still and lifeless. Moments later it faded and the girls observed that the real Emilie became herself again, moving among the flower beds with some purpose.

The girls quizzed Miss Sagee at the first opportunity, but all she could remember was that when she had seen the teacher leave the room she had wished that she could have been there to supervise the class until their teacher returned. Evidently, her thoughts had preceded her.

Unfortunately for Miss Sagee and the school this incident was not the last. Thirty fee-paying pupils were removed by their concerned parents over the following 18 months after stories about the phenomenon became the prime subject of the girls' letters home. Reluctantly, the headmistress was finally forced to let Miss Sagee go. Emilie was saddened but not surprised. It was the 19th position she had been forced to leave in her 16-year career.

## THE ABSENT MP

Politicians are not usually considered to be imaginative individuals and so the British newspapers made the most of an incident in 1905 in which the living apparition of British MP Sir Frederick Carne Rasch appeared in the House of Commons at the same moment that his body lay in bed suffering from influenza. Sir Frederick had been so anxious to attend the debate that he had obviously willed himself to appear, but his concentration must have weakened because he vanished before the vote was taken. When he returned to Parliament a few days later MPs delighted in prodding him to see if he was really there in the flesh.

## PHANTOM FORERUNNERS

Bi-location may be uncommon, but it is not inconceivable that the mind might be capable of disassociation to such a degree that it enables the essence of a person to appear elsewhere. However, the phenomenon known as the 'phantom forerunner' is far more difficult to explain. The best known example is that of businessman Erkson Gorique, who visited Norway in July 1955 for the first time in his life. Or was it?

When Erkson checked into his hotel the clerk greeted him like a valued customer. 'It's good to have you back, Mr Gorique,' said the clerk. 'But I've never been here before,' Gorique replied. 'You must have mistaken me for someone else.' The clerk was certain he was not mistaken. 'But sir, don't you remember? Just a few months ago you dropped in to make a reservation and said you'd be along about this time in the summer. Your name is unusual. That's why I remembered it.' Erkson assured the clerk that this was his first visit to the country. The next day he went to introduce himself to his first potential client, a wholesaler named Olsen, and again he was greeted like a valued customer. 'Ah, Mr Gorique. I'm glad to see you again. Your last visit was much too short.' Erkson was confused and explained what had happened to him at the hotel. To his surprise, Olsen just smiled. 'This is not so unusual here in Norway,' he said. 'In fact, it happens so often we have a name for it. We call it the *vardoger*, or forerunner.'

The phantom forerunner is not exclusively a Norwegian phenomenon, but the country has such an uncommonly high occurrence of such incidents that it has given rise to the greeting, 'Is that you or your *vardoger*?'

In England such apparitions have traditionally been filed away as just another inexplicable ghost story. In 1882, Dr George Wyld reported an incident involving a close acquaintance, Miss Jackson. She had been distributing food to the poor in the neighbourhood on a bitterly cold day when she had a sudden urge to return home to warm herself by the kitchen stove. At that moment her two maids were sitting in the kitchen and observed the doorknob turning and the door open, revealing a very lifelike Miss Jackson. Startled at their employer's early return they jumped to their feet and watched as she walked to the stove, took off her green kid gloves and warmed her hands. She then vanished. The maids ran to Miss Jackson's mother and described what they had seen, but the old woman assured them that her daughter did not own a pair of green gloves, so they must have imagined it. Half an hour later the lady herself arrived, walked to the kitchen stove, removed her green kid gloves and warmed her hands.

## GETTING AHEAD OF THEMSELVES

Frederick Myers' *Phantasms of the Living* includes a case of a multiple forerunner, complete with a horse and carriage.

The Reverend W. Mountford of Boston was visiting a friend when he looked out of the dining room window and saw a carriage approaching the rear of the house. 'Your guests have arrived,' said Mountford, whereupon his host joined him at the window. Both men observed the carriage turn the corner as if it was going to the entrance. But no one rang the doorbell and the servants did not announce the arrival of their visitors. Instead, the host's niece entered looking rather flustered having walked all the way from her home, and informed Mountford and his host that her parents had just passed her without acknowledging her or offering her a lift. Ten minutes later the real carriage arrived with the host's brother and his wife. They denied all knowledge of having passed their daughter en route.

Such incidents are not, however, confined to the 19th century. As recently as 1980 an Austrian woman, Hilda Saxer, reported seeing a grey Audi belonging to her sister's fiancé, Johann Hofer, passing by at 11.30 pm as she left the restaurant where she worked. She waved and the driver, whom she saw clearly and recognized as Johann, smiled and waved back. As she watched the car disappear into the distance the incident struck her as odd because Johann had left the restaurant half an hour earlier.

An hour later Johann's father heard his son's car pull into the driveway and the characteristic sound of the engine as the young man manoeuvred into his parking space. But he did not hear Johann enter the house. The next morning the father was worried when his son did not join him for breakfast. The radio had reported a tunnel collapse on the route Johann had taken on his way home from the restaurant at 11.30 pm that same night. The father had heard the car in the drive and assumed his son must have left early that morning. It was only days later that rescuers found the wreckage of the car and its driver, crushed beneath tons of rubble.

## THOUGHT FORMS

Science is slowly and reluctantly beginning to acknowledge that the human mind has the power to project a self-image to another location or to separate spirit and body at will. But what is not generally known, even among the earlier pioneers of parapsychology, is the capacity of the human mind to create and sustain images, or thought forms, which can be empowered with a life of their own. Such forms are known as *tulpas* in the Tibetan esoteric tradition and Golem in the Jewish magical tradition where their creation is considered one of the advanced techniques which must be mastered by initiates before they can become adepts.

The only known record describing the creation of one of these man-made ghosts is the account written by the French mystic and adventurer Alexandra David-Neel (1868–1969) who became the first female lama and the only outsider to be initiated into the secret doctrine of Tibetan Buddhism.

> Besides having had the opportunities of seeing thought-forms, my habitual incredulity led me to make experiments for myself, and my efforts were attended with some success . . . I chose for my experiment a most insignificant character: a monk short and fat, of an innocent and jolly type.
>
> I shut myself in *tsams* (meditative seclusion) and proceeded to perform the prescribed concentration of thought and other rites. After a few months the phantom monk was formed. His form grew gradually 'fixed' and life-like. He became a kind of guest, living in my apartment. I then broke my seclusion and started for a tour, with my servants and tents.
>
> The monk included himself in the party. Though I lived in the open, riding on horseback for miles each day, the illusion persisted. I saw the fat *trapa* (novice monk), now and then it was not necessary for me to think of him to make him appear. The phantom performed various actions of the kind that are natural to travellers and that I had not commanded. For instance, he walked, stopped, looked around him. The illusion was mostly visual, but sometimes I felt as if a robe was lightly rubbing against me and once a hand seemed to touch my shoulder.
>
> The features which I had imagined when building my

phantom, gradually underwent a change. The fat, chubby-cheeked fellow grew leaner, his face assumed a vaguely mocking, sly malignant look. He became more troublesome and bold. In brief, he escaped my control.

Once, a herdsman who brought me a present of butter saw the tulpa in my tent and took it for a live lama. I ought to have let the phenomenon follow its course, but the presence of that unwanted companion began to prove trying to my nerves; it turned into a 'day-nightmare'. Moreover, I was . . . [going] to Lahsa . . . so I decided to dissolve the phantom. I succeeded, but only after six months of hard struggle. My mind-creature was tenacious of life.

## CRISIS APPARITIONS

Sailors have always been notoriously fond of a good ghost story, but the tale told by seaman Robert Bruce to the 19th-century paranormal researcher Robert Dale Owen is both singular and significant as it is one of the earliest recorded examples of a crisis apparition, a phenomenon which is more common than one might imagine.

In 1828, Bruce was the first mate aboard a cargo ship ploughing through the icy waters off the Canadian coast. During the voyage he entered the captain's cabin to find a stranger bent over a slate, writing intensely and in great haste. The figure appeared solid, but there was an other-worldly aspect to him and a grave expression on his face which unnerved Bruce.

When the stranger raised his head and looked at him, Bruce fled, fearing that the presence of the phantom foretold disaster for all on board. He found the skipper on deck and persuaded him to return to the cabin. 'I never was a believer in ghosts,' said Bruce as they made their way below deck, 'but if the truth must be told sir, I'd rather not face it alone.' But when they entered the cabin it was empty. However, they found the slate and on it were scrawled the words 'Steer to the nor'west.'

*'Within hours they came upon a stricken vessel that had been critically damaged by an iceberg'*

At first the skipper suspected that the crew were playing a practical joke, so he ordered them all to copy the message. After comparing their handwriting with the original he had to admit he could not identify the culprit. A search of the entire ship failed to find any stowaways, leaving the captain with an unusual dilemma: to ignore the message and risk having the lives of untold lost souls on his conscience, or change his course and risk being thought of as a superstitious old fool in the eyes of the crew. He chose to change course.

Fortunately, he had made the right decision. Within hours they came upon a stricken vessel that had been critically damaged by an iceberg. There were only minutes to save the passengers and crew before it sank beneath the waves. Bruce watched with grim satisfaction and relief as the survivors were brought aboard, but then he saw something which haunted him to his dying day. He came face to face with the stranger he had seen scrawling the message earlier that day in the captain's cabin.

After the man had recovered sufficiently to be questioned, Bruce and the captain asked him to copy the message on the slate. They compared the two sets of handwriting. There was no question about it – they were identical. Initially, the 'stranger' couldn't account for his early presence on the ship until he recalled a dream that he had had about the same time that Bruce had seen his 'ghost' in the captain's cabin. After falling asleep from exhaustion he had dreamt that he was aboard a ship that was coming to rescue him and his fellow survivors. He told the others of his dream to reassure them that help was on its way and he even described the rescue ship, all of which proved correct in every detail. The captain of the wrecked ship confirmed his story. 'He described her appearance and rig,' he told their rescuers, 'and to our utter astonishment, when your vessel hove in sight, she corresponded exactly to his description of her.'

## ESCAPING WORLDLY BONDS

One of the most revealing examples of an out-of-body experience was published in a respected medical journal, the *St Louis Medical and Surgical Journal*, in February 1890. It is also of great interest because the subject was a doctor who understood what was happening to him and was able to observe his own 'death' with clinical detachment.

Dr A.S. Wiltse of Kansas contracted typhoid fever in the summer of 1889. After saying his last goodbyes to his family, he lapsed into unconsciousness. But although his body exhibited no signs of life – neither pulse nor heartbeat – inside his own dead body, Dr Wiltse was fully conscious and observing the grieving around him with a curious detachment. It was as if he had reverted to pure consciousness, acutely alert but unemotional. 'I learned that the epidermis [skin] was the outside boundary of the ultimate tissues, so to speak, of the soul.' He then felt a gentle swaying and a separation which he compared to the snapping of tiny cords. In another moment he was looking out from his skull. 'As I emerged from the head I floated up and down . . . like a soap bubble . . . until I at last broke loose from the body and fell lightly to the floor, where I slowly rose and expanded into the full stature of a man.'

At this point he felt embarrassed to discover that there were two women in the room, but then he realized that he was not naked but clothed – merely by wishing to be so.

Here, perhaps, is a crucial clue as to why ghosts appear in the form that they do, often younger and in better health than when their physical shell expired. Dr Wiltse had left his body as a shapeless, colourless bubble of etheric energy, but as soon as he became aware of his surroundings he was able to assume a more acceptable form and projected his own self-image which would have been his ideal self. It was then that he passed straight through another man in the room before he realized what he was doing. He saw the funny side of the situation, which may have been partly due to the relief in finding himself very much alive in this new reality. He intuitively 'knew' that this was his natural state, his true self. His personality was the same after death as it had been in life, but he had left behind his fears and his sense of identity. He no longer identified with the body on the bed. He was no longer concerned with what happened to it. That was the part of him that felt pain, disappointment, regrets. This 'greater self' was beyond those petty, worldly concerns. If this was 'death', it was nothing more than slipping off a worn-out coat or walking through an open door into the world outside.

He was becoming accustomed to his new 'body' and was eager to explore. As he passed through the door he looked back and saw a thin elasticated web-like cord connecting him to the lifeless body on the bed, the etheric equivalent of the umbilical cord. So long as he remained attached by this cord he knew he could return to his body at will. He was not dead, as he had originally thought, but merely temporarily detached – a living ghost. He walked along a road idly wondering where the other 'dead' people might be and if this is all there was to being dead. Suddenly he lost consciousness and when he next became aware of where he was he found himself in an unfamiliar landscape over which hung a black cloud. Ahead he saw three enormous rocks which an inner voice informed him was the boundary to the 'eternal world'. At this point he intuitively knew that this was as far as he would be permitted to go on this occasion and with that realization he woke up – much to the surprise of his doctor. Dr Wiltse had been clinically dead for four hours, but had suffered no permanent brain damage or other ill effects, contrary to the laws of medical science. A religious man might call this a miracle, but in the years that followed it became increasingly evident that such out-of-body experiences have been shared by hundreds of thousands of people around the world and that they are neither miraculous nor supernatural. They are perfectly natural.

## A GHOST IN THE MIRROR

Vermont housewife Caroline Larsen considered herself an unremarkable person, preoccupied with social conventions, her standing in the community and her obligations as the dutiful middle-class wife of an amateur musician. But, one autumn evening in 1910, she discovered her true self as she went one step further than Dr Wiltse had done during a strikingly similar out-of-body experience.

As Mrs Larsen lay in bed listening to her husband and his friends practising a Beethoven string quartet she began to feel a creeping sense of foreboding. No matter how hard she tried to focus on the soothing strains of the music she was unable to relax and throw off her apprehension.

> The overpowering oppression deepened and soon numbness crept over me until every muscle became paralyzed . . . finally everything became a blank. The next thing I knew was that I, I myself, was standing on the floor beside my bed looking down attentively on my own physical body lying in it.

She observed that her room was unchanged. But after heading for the bathroom, she instinctively reached for the light switch and was surprised that she couldn't connect with it. It was then that she noticed that the room was illuminated by a softer light emanating from her own body.

> Looking in to the mirror I became aware for the first time of the astonishing transformation I had undergone. Instead of seeing a middle-aged woman, I beheld the figure of a girl

> about 18 years of age. I recognized the form and features of my girlhood. But I was now infinitely more beautiful. My face appeared as if it were chiselled out of the finest alabaster and it seemed transparent, as did my arms and hands when I raised them to touch my hair . . . But they were not entirely translucent for in the centre of the arms and hands and fingers there was a darker, more compact substance, as in x-ray photographs. My eyes, quite strong in the physical body, were piercingly keen now . . . my hair, no longer grey, was now, as in my youth, dark brown and it fell in waves over my shoulders and down my back. And, to my delight, I was dressed in the loveliest white shining garment imaginable – a sleeveless one-piece dress, cut low at the neck and reaching almost to the ankles.

She then had the idea to walk down the stairs and surprise her husband and his friends in her new youthful form.

> Turning away from the mirror I walked out into the hall, enjoying in anticipation the success of my plan, I stepped on gaily. I revelled in the feeling of bodily lightness . . . I moved with the freedom of thought.
>
> [But] just as I came to the little platform which divides the stairway into two flights I saw, standing before me, a woman spirit in shining clothes with arms outstretched and with forefinger pointing upwards . . . she spoke to me sternly, 'Where are you going? Go back to your body!' . . . I knew instinctively – that from this spirit's command and authority there was no appeal.

Returning to her room she found her body on the bed, just as 'still and lifeless' as she had left it.

> I viewed it with feelings of loathing and disappointment. I knew that I would soon have to enter it again, no matter how ugly it

> seemed to me or how much I shrank from it. In another instant I had again joined with my physical form. With a gasp and a start, I woke up in it.

The image she describes may sound like an aging person's fantasy, but the deceased often appear as their younger selves. In effect, they are so used to having a physical body that they cannot imagine themselves without one and so manifest as their ideal self-image.

## PROJECTING HIS OWN GHOST

Most of the hundreds of thousands of out-of-body experiences and near-death experiences that have been recorded involve the involuntary separation of the spirit from the body at a moment of crisis or physical danger or during an altered state of consciousness. But there are a surprising number of incidents in which the astral traveller (see page 118) has consciously projected their spirit double to another location.

Sylvan Joseph Muldoon, the son of a spiritualist in Clinton, Iowa, claimed to have acquired the ability to leave his body at will. He had enjoyed dozens of liberating out-of-body experiences since the age of 12, but it was not until ten years later, in 1925, that he had the confirmation that what he was experiencing was more than a lucid dream.

During this excursion he found himself propelled at incredible speed to an unfamiliar farmhouse somewhere in the same rural region where he lived. There he observed four people passing a pleasant evening, including an attractive young girl who was engaged in sewing a black dress. They seemed unaware of his presence so he wandered around the room noting the furnishings and ornaments until it occurred to him that he had no business being there. With that thought he returned to his body. It was more than a month later that Muldoon happened to see the same girl in town and asked her where she lived. She thought he was prying or being 'fresh' and told him to mind his own business, but when he described her home in astonishing detail and told her how he knew this, she confirmed everything that he had seen.

*'During this excursion he found himself propelled at incredible speed to an unfamiliar farmhouse somewhere in the same rural region where he lived'*

## INDUCING AN OUT-OF-BODY EXPERIENCE

If you wish to prove the existence of the etheric body for yourself, this exercise can be used to trigger an OBE. Although such experiences occur naturally and should never be forced, this safe and simple technique for the gradual separation of spirit and body has been practised by mystics through the centuries. However, it needs to be stressed that such techniques should never be attempted while under the influence of alcohol or drugs of any kind. Nor should they be attempted by anyone who has, or is currently suffering from, any form of psychological disturbance, abnormal grief or trauma. If in doubt you should seek medical advice before attempting any of these techniques.

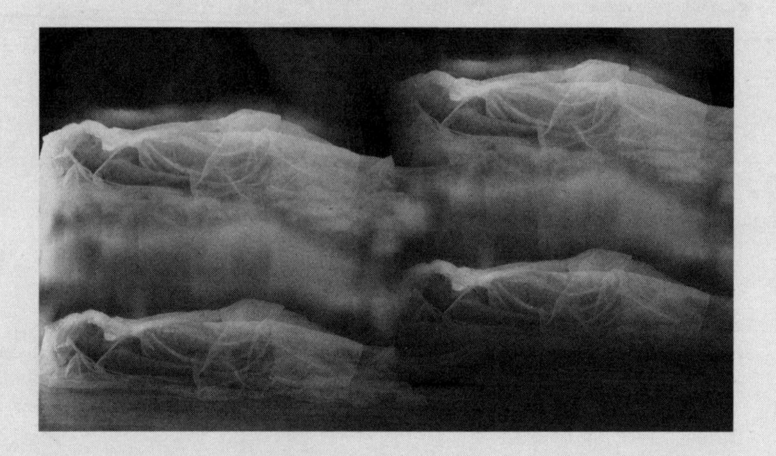

1. Lie on your back on the floor, an exercise mat or bed and ensure you support your neck with a small pillow or cushion. Your arms should be loose by your side and not crossed over on your chest or stomach. Your legs must be straight.

2. Establish a steady rhythm of breathing and, as you dissolve deeper into relaxation, repeat a phrase that relaxes

you and induces a sense of security, such as 'calm and centred' or 'I am perfect and at peace'.

3. After a few minutes you may sense a warming of the solar plexus centre beneath your navel. Visualize a soft pulsing light in your abdomen as this energy centre softens, loosening the silver umbilical cord of etheric energy which connects your spirit double to your physical shell. Feel it unwinding as you sink deeper and deeper into a detached state. As you do so you will begin to lose the sense of the weight and solidity of your body. You will become lighter with every breath.

4. Now visualize your breath forming a cushion of air under your back until you feel that you can float away like a cloud on the breeze. Feel yourself rising a few inches above your body and then being drawn back by the silver cord as you enjoy exercising control over your new-found ability. You are safe and in control at all times. You only have to wish to return to your body and you will do so in an instant.

5. Transfer your awareness to this 'real you' by visualizing the room from a new perspective as if you were standing and walking around. Then imagine yourself looking down on your physical body from the ceiling – you may find you have 'popped out' and are now free to explore. If not, visualize yourself exploring the room in your spirit body and your awareness will be transferred to it. Until you are comfortable being outside your body it would be advisable to stay within the confines of your own home, but as soon as you feel confident you can begin to explore the neighbourhood and beyond.

- Be patient and persistent. It may take several attempts to make the breakthrough. You will know that you are out of the body and not dreaming because you will experience a euphoria as you realize you have liberated the real you. If you want to obtain absolute proof of this you can try the following experiment. However, if you do so, make sure your partner will treat it seriously or you risk having your confidence undermined.

- Remember: You are under no obligation to try this exercise. Out-of-body experiences are natural phenomena and should never be forced. If you feel uncomfortable for any reason do not attempt this exercise or you risk instilling fear in your self which may inhibit your development.

## THE ASTRAL VISIT

To obtain a truly objective result in this experiment you will need the co-operation of a friend whom you can trust to take the exercise seriously. The object of the exercise is to obtain conclusive proof of your ability to visit them at will in your etheric body.

To do this ask your friend to put a book of their choice on a chair in their bedroom with the cover face up. They must not tell you what they are going to place there and they should not decide which book to use until shortly beforehand, otherwise it is possible that you will obtain the answer by telepathy instead. Decide on a specific time for the experiment so that your partner can note any changes that may occur in the atmosphere and can be alert at the allotted time.

Again, be patient. It may take several attempts to make the breakthrough.

## A MESSAGE FROM THE OTHER SIDE

Near-death experiences typically involve an individual leaving their body, passing through then returning to their body with a renewed appetite for life. But the experience of Dr Karl Novotny was different in one significant respect. He did not return. Instead he described the process of dying from the other side using the services of a medium. Such anecdotal evidence usually has the sceptics shrieking with derision, but the case of Dr Novotny is notable for several reasons.

Two days prior to his death in Easter 1965, Novotny's friend, Grete Schroeder, dreamt that he appeared before her to announce his death. Neither Schroeder nor Novotny were interested in psychic phenomena – in fact quite the reverse. Novotny was a pupil of the celebrated psychologist Arthur Adler and was inclined to explain every phenomenon in terms of the untapped powers of the unconscious. When Novotny died as 'he' had predicted, Grete felt compelled to consult a medium rather than risk becoming prey to doubts for the rest of her life. She evidently chose a reputable psychic because not only did the details of his death – as relayed by the medium – tally with the facts, she also transcribed what he told her in a script which Grete recognized as Novotny's own handwriting even though the medium had never met him. The description of his dying moments is uncannily similar to that related by thousands of other individuals from around the world who have had a near-death experience and it is worth quoting for comparison.

> I turned back to my companions and found myself looking down at my own body on the ground. My friends were in despair, calling for a doctor, and trying to get a car to take me home. But I was well and felt no pains. I couldn't understand what had happened. I bent down and felt the heart of the body lying on the ground. Yes – it had ceased to beat – I was dead. But I was still alive! I spoke to my friends, but they neither saw me nor answered me . . .
>
> And then there was my dog, who kept whining pitifully, unable to decide to which of me he should go, for he saw me in two places at once, standing up and lying down on the ground.
>
> When all the formalities were concluded and my body had been put in a coffin, I realized that I must be dead. But

> I wouldn't acknowledge the fact; for, like my teacher Arthur Adler, I did not believe in after-life.

Novotny then visited his friend Grete and found her sitting alone and immersed in grief, but again his attempts to communicate were fruitless. She did not seem aware of his presence and did not respond when he spoke to her.

> It was no use. I had to recognize the truth. When finally I did so I saw my dear mother coming to meet me with open arms, telling me that I had passed into the next world – not in words, of course, since these only belong to the earth. Even so, I couldn't credit her statement and thought I must be dreaming. This belief continued for a long time. I fought against the truth and was most unhappy . . .

## THE PSYCHOLOGIST AND THE SPIRIT

Dutch psychologist Elleke Van Kraalingen was a pragmatic, scientifically minded woman who prided herself on having a healthy scepticism towards the supernatural. The demands of her professional life meant that she was totally grounded in the here and now and had no desire to probe the secrets of life and death. That was until she witnessed the sudden and violent death of her fiancé, Hermod, in a hit and run accident. In her autobiography, *Love Beyond Death*, Elleke describes how she was awoken to the reality of the soul's survival after death as she knelt over his body and sensed a 'tearing apart' of the subtle bond between them, as it was severed. She then 'saw' his soul leave his body as a mist and sensed his presence standing behind her during her desperate efforts to revive him. While the emotional part of her was in turmoil, the intellectual aspect of her being calmly reassured her that he was well. After the ambulance had taken his body, Elleke walked back to their hotel, all the while sensing that Hermod was beside her holding her hand.

That evening he materialized in their room, sitting on the edge of her bed as solid as he had been 24 hours earlier. Having been trained to dismiss everything connected with the paranormal as irrational and the creation of a troubled mind, Elleke instinctively denied what she was seeing as a hallucination brought on by grief. She covered her eyes and affirmed that she was imagining it, but when she looked again he was still there, as large as life. It was at this point that she heard him speak inside her head in a quiet consoling tone that was quite distinct from her own thoughts. 'I'm still here,' he told her. 'There is no death, there is no time, there's only reality.'

He was not the only discarnate spirit in the room. Elleke sensed the presence of others that she felt were there to help his transition from this world to the next. When he and his companions had gone she wrote everything down so that she could analyze her thought processes at a later date when she was not so emotionally involved. She hoped this would help her discover the cause of her delusion. Even at this point Elleke was convinced that what she had seen was a projection of her own internal turmoil. Perhaps this was a replay of her memories of Hermod triggered automatically as a result of an emotional crisis, like a drowning person who sees their life replayed in their mind like a film.

But the next day Hermod reappeared again, as solid as he was when he was alive. Elleke was the only person who could see him, presumably because she perceived him with the eyes of the spirit – the inner eye or third eye of psychic sight. That day he remained with her as she sleepwalked through the traumatic process of identifying his body and dealing with the police. It was only after the funeral that she sensed him withdraw, leaving her to cope with life alone.

And then an extraordinary thing happened. Several days later, while Elleke was meditating in an attempt to calm and centre herself, he reappeared and drew her out of her body. In this state she was able to look down at her physical self sitting cross-legged on the floor and view the world with a detachment she could not have attained while in her body. She described this state as liberating and more vibrantly real than what she had previously considered to be reality. When they embraced she felt totally absorbed in the core of his being, not merely comforted or connected as she had done when they were in their physical bodies. She sensed that it was only when they were out of body that they could truly know each other. Soon she felt drained and snapped back into her physical shell – either the effort of remaining out of the body for a long period was too much for her, or perhaps he was unintentionally draining her of her life force in order to remain at this level.

Over the following months, Hermod materialized and took her on an astral tour of other realms or realities where discarnate beings communicated with them by thought alone. In these realms the dead created their own heaven and hell according to their expectations and beliefs. Those who could not accept their own death remained earthbound, reliving the most significant experiences of their lives as if in a recurring dream and visible to the living as ghosts.

## PSYCHOLOGY AND THE PARANORMAL

Mainstream science and orthodox religion are considered custodians of good sense by those who believe in the infallibility of science or the absolute truth of the Bible. But both fields have their share of individualists who are not as rigid in their thinking as one might suspect.

Carl Jung (1875–1961), the founding father of analytical psychology, was fiercely proud of his reputation as a pioneer of the new science, but in private he continually wrestled to reconcile psychology and the paranormal. He wrote:

> In the end the only events in my life worth telling are those when the imperishable world irrupted into this transitory one. That is why I speak chiefly of inner experiences, among which I include my dreams and visions. These form the prima materia of my scientific work. They were the fiery magma out of which the stone that had to be worked was crystallized.

Jung's maternal grandfather was the vicar of Kesswil, Switzerland, and was said to be blessed with 'second sight'. His family blithely

*Psychoanalyst Carl Jung (1875–1961) who, together with his teacher and mentor Sigmund Freud, and Alfred Adler, formed the basis of modern psychology and psychotherapy*

accepted that he conversed with the dead in defiance of Church edicts. As Jung wrote:

> My mother often told me how she had to sit behind him while he wrote his sermons because he could not bear [to have] ghosts pass behind him while he was studying. The presence of a living human being at his back frightened them away!

His own home life was equally unconventional. As a child Jung was constantly aware of the presence of spirits.

> From the door to my mother's room came a frightening influence. At night Mother was strange and mysterious. One night I saw coming from her door a faintly luminous indefinite figure whose head detached itself from the neck and floated along in front of it, in the air like a little moon.

In his youth Jung witnessed at first hand phenomena during séances held by his 15-year-old cousin, Helene Preiswerk, who had developed mediumistic powers. Helene channelled a number of dead relatives who spoke in their own distinctive voices and passed on personal details which the young 'Helly' could not have known about. Jung was particularly struck by the change in his cousin's manner when she went into a trance. She exhibited a maturity and breadth of knowledge that was at odds with her provincial frivolous nature. But although Jung was initially convinced that her abilities were genuine, he later felt obliged to find a rational explanation when writing up the case for his inaugural dissertation. It was a classic example of multiple personality, he concluded, brought on by hysteria and sexual repression. Although such a diagnosis might account for a good number of fraudulent mediums, Jung also knew that he risked being discredited as a serious man of science if he subscribed to the spiritualist creed. Privately, however, he remained a firm believer in the paranormal and was intolerant of those, like Freud, who scoffed at such things on principle.

> I wondered at the sureness with which they could assert that things like ghosts and table-turning were impossible and therefore fraudulent, and on the other hand, at the evidently anxious nature of their defensiveness. For myself I found such possibilities extremely interesting and attractive. They added another dimension to my life; the world gained depth and background.

In his autobiography, *Memories, Dreams, Reflections*, Jung describes his own paranormal experiences including the plague of poltergeist activity with which his home was besieged in the summer of 1916.

> The house was filled as if it was crammed full of spirits and the air was so thick it was scarcely possible to breathe . . . My eldest daughter saw a white figure pass through her room. My second daughter, independently . . . related that twice in the night her blanket had been snatched away . . .

Over three successive evenings he channelled a series of messages from discarnate spirits which formed the basis of *Seven Sermons To The Dead*, a series of Hermetic discourses on the nature of God, and Good and Evil in a contrived archaic style. It was only when he had completed this task that the spirits withdrew and the 'haunting' ceased. Jung dismissed the attendant poltergeist activity as 'exteriorization phenomena', meaning that he interpreted it as his own unconscious demanding his attention to the coming task.

> It has taken me virtually forty-five years to distil within the vessel of my scientific work the things I experienced and wrote down at that time . . . The years when I was pursuing my inner images were the most important in my life – in them everything essential was decided. It all began then; the later details are only supplements and clarifications of the material that burst

forth from the unconscious, and at first swamped me. It was the prima materia for a lifetime's work.

## THE HAUNTED COTTAGE

Despite a lifetime of witnessing paranormal phenomena at first hand, Jung still felt the need to hedge his bets. In 1919, he wrote a paper for the SPR entitled 'The Psychological Foundation of Belief in Spirits', in which he stated that such phenomena can be dismissed as projections of the unconscious mind. The following year the spirits had their revenge.

In 1920, Jung arrived in Britain on a lecture tour and stayed in a country cottage so that he could be alone. The rent was nominal, but either Jung did not suspect that this might be because the place was haunted, or he didn't attach any importance to it. On the first weekend he was disturbed by a rancid odour permeating the bedroom, although there was no obvious source of the smell. The following weekend, the smell returned accompanied by a rustling noise as if an animal was exploring the room, or perhaps a woman in a crinoline dress was brushing against the walls. On the third weekend, his work was interrupted by inexplicable rapping sounds. Again, there was no obvious source for these noises. On the fifth weekend, he was startled to wake up next to the ghost of an old woman, her face partly dissolved as if pressed into a pillow.

The locals subsequently confirmed that the cottage was inhabited by a malevolent spirit and that is why they refused to stay there after dusk. But Jung was not so easily disturbed. He invited the friend who had rented the cottage for him to spend the night, and the man was so terrified when he heard phantom footsteps that he abandoned his bed after just a few hours and spent the rest of the night sleeping in the garden with a shotgun by his side. Jung recollected, 'It gave me considerable satisfaction after my colleague had laughed so loudly at my fear of ghosts.'

His own attitude to such phenomena remained ambiguous despite his extraordinary experiences. He was clearly impressed with the 'performance' of respected medium Rudi Schneider (whose talents were detailed in Thomas Mann's essay 'An Experience With The Occult') although he could not bring himself to credit his cousin Helly with the same abilities. For all his insights into the human mind, Jung was forced to admit that he did not have an explanation for these phenomena. 'Either there are physical processes which cause psychic happenings, or there is a pre-existent psyche which organises matter.'

If he expected his mentor Sigmund Freud to resolve the question he was to be cruelly disappointed. In one particularly memorable episode, Jung and Freud were arguing about the existence of poltergeists when a loud report shook a nearby bookcase. Freud insisted it was merely the furniture settling, even though the weather was mild and could not have caused the wood to contract or expand. But Jung had felt heat building up in his solar plexus from his frustration at being treated like a wilful student of the great man and he was certain that he himself was the source of the kinetic activity. 'There will be another report in a moment,' he predicted and, sure enough, there was.

## OUT OF THIS WORLD

Paranormal phenomena and psychic experiences pursued Jung all through his life. Then, in April 1944, at the age of 68, he had an out-of-body experience that was to have a profound effect on his perception of the world and which turned his concept of reality on its head. The extracts below are from his autobiography, *Memories, Dreams, Reflections* (1961):

> It seemed to me that I was high up in space. Far below I saw the globe of the earth, bathed in a gloriously blue light. I saw the deep blue sea and the continents. Far below my feet lay Ceylon, and in the distance ahead of me the subcontinent of India. My field of vision did not include the whole earth, but its global shape was plainly distinguishable and its outlines shone with a silvery gleam through that wonderful blue light . . . I knew that I was on the point of departing from the earth.

> Later I discovered how high in space one would have to be to have so extensive a view – approximately a thousand miles! The sight of the earth from this height was the most glorious thing I had ever seen . . . I myself was floating in space.

At this point Jung felt that he was stripped down to the essence of his being.

> . . . everything I aimed at or wished for or thought, the whole phantasmagoria of earthly existence, fell away or was stripped from me – an extremely painful process. Nevertheless something remained; it was as if I now carried along with me everything I had ever experienced or done, everything that had happened around me . . . This experience gave me a feeling of extreme poverty, but at the same time of great fullness. There was no longer anything I wanted or desired. I existed in an objective form; I was what I had been and lived. At first the sense of annihilation predominated, of having been stripped or pillaged; but suddenly that became of no consequence. Everything seemed to be past.

While he was contemplating the significance of this greater reality he became aware of another presence, that of his doctor who appeared before Jung in his 'primal form'.

> . . . a mute exchange of thought took place between us. The doctor had been delegated by the earth to deliver a message to me, to tell me that there was a protest against my going away. I had no right to leave the earth and must return. The moment I heard that, the vision ceased.
>
> I was profoundly disappointed, for now it all seemed to have been for nothing. The painful process of defoliation had been in vain . . . Life and the whole world struck me as a prison, and it bothered me beyond measure that I should again be finding

> all that quite in order. I had been so glad to shed it all . . . I felt violent resistance to my doctor because he had brought me back to life. At the same time, I was worried about him. 'His life is in danger, for heaven's sake! He has appeared to me in his primal form! When anybody attains this form it means he is going to die, for already he belongs to the "greater company".' Suddenly the terrifying thought came to me that the doctor would have to die in my stead. I tried my best to talk to him about it, but he did not understand me. Then I became angry with him.
>
> In actual fact I was his last patient. On April 4, 1944 . . . I was allowed to sit up on the edge of my bed for the first time since the beginning of my illness, and on this same day the doctor took to his bed and did not leave it again. I heard that he was having intermittent attacks of fever. Soon afterward he died of septicemia . . .
>
> It was not a product of imagination. The visions and experiences were utterly real; there was nothing subjective about them; they all had a quality of absolute objectivity.

In *Synchronicity* (1952), Jung cites the case of a woman patient who left her body during childbirth and observed the medical procedures used to revive her which she described to her nurse after recovering consciousness. She was correct in every detail. The most astonishing part was her discovery that while in her astral body she possessed perceptions independent of her physical senses. At the same moment that she was watching the frantic efforts of the medical staff, she was also aware of a vivid pastoral landscape 'behind' her which she knew to be the 'other world'. By a conscious effort of will she remained focused on the doctors and nurses for fear that she might be tempted by the bliss of the other world to drift into it and not return.

## CRISIS OF FAITH

Eminent theological scholar Canon J.B. Phillips regarded himself as a conscientious servant of the Church of the England with an unshakable belief in the articles of his faith. These denied the existence of apparitions other than the Holy Ghost, yet Canon Phillips was convinced that he had had a visitation from C.S. Lewis, the recently deceased Christian philosopher and author of the *Narnia* novels, in late November 1963. He confided the details of his encounter in his journal.

> Let me say at once that I am incredulous by nature and as unsuperstitious as they come. I have never bothered about . . . any of the current superstitions which may occupy the human heart in the absence of faith . . . But the late C.S. Lewis, whom I did not know very well and had only seen in the flesh once, but with whom I had corresponded a fair amount, gave me an unusual experience. A few days after his death, while I was watching television, he 'appeared' sitting in a chair a few feet from me, and spoke a few words which were particularly relevant to the difficult circumstances through which I was passing. He was ruddier in complexion than ever, grinning all over his face, and, as the saying has it, positively glowing with health. The interesting thing to me was that I had not been thinking about him at all . . . A week later, this time when I was in bed reading before going to sleep, he appeared again, even more rosily radiant than before, and repeated to me the same message, which was very important to me at the time. I was a little puzzled by this and mentioned it to a certain saintly bishop who was then living in retirement in Dorset. His reply was, 'My dear J. this sort of thing is happening all the time.'

Canon Phillips' experience is noteworthy for several reasons, the first being that he was not a believer in spirits – in fact he was effectively under orders to deny their existence and had much to lose by admitting to what he had seen. Secondly, he saw the same apparition on two separate occasions which would seem to rule out the possibility that they were hypnagogic hallucinations (the hypnagogic state is that state between being awake and falling asleep), or waking dreams caused by fatigue or stress. Thirdly, Lewis' 'ghost' spoke and the advice he gave was relevant to Canon Phillips' situation. Furthermore, on the one occasion when Phillips had met Lewis during the latter's lifetime, Lewis was dressed in clerical robes and not the 'well-worn tweeds' in which he appeared after death and which was his customary mode of dress. It was only after Phillips had reported his encounter with the author's ghost

*C. S. Lewis (1898–1963) in his usual 'well-worn' tweeds*

that he learnt that Lewis dressed in tweeds. And, lastly, the bishop had evidently heard of such things in the course of his ministrations and took it all in his stride. If it was not a genuine encounter there is only one other explanation, that the apparition was a projection of Canon Phillips' subconscious which took the form of a friend he admired and whose advice he would heed. And that is no less remarkable a phenomenon.

## VOICES FROM BEYOND

In the 1920s, Thomas Edison, the prolific American inventor of the phonograph, the electric lamp, the microphone and the kinetoscope (a forerunner of the movie projector), to name but a few of his creations, admitted to working on a device for contacting the dead. He told *Scientific American* magazine that he believed it was perfectly possible 'to construct an apparatus which will be so delicate that if there are personalities in another existence or sphere who wish to get in touch with us in this existence or sphere, this apparatus will at least give them a better opportunity to express themselves than the tilting tables and raps and Ouija boards and mediums and the other crude methods now purported to be the only means of communication.' Unfortunately, Edison passed over before he could build the contraption, but it now seems that his dream may be closer to being realized than ever before.

The first serious hint that audible communication with the departed may be feasible occurred in June 1959 when Swedish ornithologist Friedrich Jurgenson replayed a recording of birdsong and heard a faint Norwegian voice discussing the habits of nocturnal birds. At first he thought it must be interference from a local broadcaster or amateur radio enthusiast, but there was no transmitter in the area. Intrigued, he decided to make test recordings at his home to determine whether or not the tape recorder was faulty, but when he listened to the recordings he caught something which chilled him to the marrow. There were voices on the tape that he had not heard when he was recording. They mentioned Jurgenson and his dog by name and correctly predicted an incoming phone call and the name of the caller.

*Thomas Edison (1847–1931) in 1928. In 1892, he received a patent for his invention of a two-way telegraph machine, going on to think of designs for a device to contact the dead*

In subsequent recording sessions, Jurgenson merely had to turn on the tape for an unspecified length of time and then play it back to hear a babble of faint voices talking among themselves, commenting on him and the other people whom he had invited to be present as witnesses.

As Jurgenson researched the subject he discovered that EVP (Electronic Voice Phenomena) were only one aspect of a wider range of phenomena known collectively as Instrumental Transcommunication (ITC) covering spirit communication through all manner of electronic equipment including radios, telephones, television sets and even computers. Although the more common forms of ITC are indistinct disembodied voices, there have been incidents where the face of the deceased has been seen and positively identified by their relatives breaking through a regular broadcast on a television screen.

## RECORDING EVP

If you want to experiment with EVP all you need is a digital recording device such as a mini-disc, DAT recorder or computer and an analogue radio. Cassette recorders are unsuitable as they produce excessive hiss at low volume and also mechanical noise which can cloak the signal. The radio needs to be tuned to a frequency between stations so that a background of white noise is audible for the voices to print through. You will have to be objective when analyzing what you have recorded as it is possible to interpret random interference, 'print-through' from previous recordings, digital 'artefacts' and signals bleeding from adjacent stations as being significant. The potential for misinterpretation is so strong that a medical term has been coined to describe it – auditory pareidolia. Consequently, it is necessary to remain detached and foster a healthy scepticism, otherwise you are at risk of reading something significant into what is really only random interference.

## THE POPE'S PARAPSYCHOLOGISTS

In 1952, two Italian Catholic priests, Father Ernetti and Father Gemelli, were playing back a tape recording they had made of Gregorian chants when they heard an inaudible whispering in the silence when the singing had stopped. At first they thought it might be radio interference or 'print through', the echo of an earlier recording which occurs when the tape has not been properly erased or the playback heads are misaligned. But when they turned up the volume Father Gemelli recognized the whispering as the voice of his father who had died many years earlier. It was calling Gemelli by his childhood nickname. 'Zucchini, it is clear, don't you know it is I?'

Contact with the dead is forbidden by the Catholic Church, but there was no denying what they had heard. So the priests dutifully asked for an audience with Pope Pius XII in Rome and put the problem before him. The Pope's verdict was later published in the Italian journal *Astra*.

> Dear Father Gemelli, you really need not worry about this. The existence of this voice is strictly a scientific fact and has nothing to do with spiritism. The recorder is totally objective. It receives and records only sound waves from wherever they come. This experiment may perhaps become the cornerstone

*Pope Pius XII at the age of 75, in 1951*

> for a building for scientific studies which will strengthen people's faith in a hereafter.

The nonchalant reply stunned the priests, but evidently such phenomena were not news to the Vatican. It later transpired that the Pope's cousin, the Rev Professor Dr Gebhard Frei, co-founder of the Jung Institute, was the president of the International Society for Catholic Parapsychologists and had collaborated with an early pioneer of EVP, Dr Konstantin Raudive, of Germany.

Before his death in October 1967, Frei had gone on record as a staunch advocate of investigating EVP. 'All that I have read and heard forces me to believe that the voices come from transcendental, individual entities. Whether it suits me or not, I have no right to doubt the reality of the voices.' Ironically, as if to validate his own life's work, just a month after his death, the voice of Dr Frei was caught on tape and identified by Professor Peter Hohenwarter of the University of Vienna.

Pope Paul VI, successor to Pope Pius XII, continued the good work, giving his blessing to researches carried out by Swedish film producer Friedrich Jurgenson, who confided to a British voice researcher in the 1960s, 'I have found a sympathetic ear for the Voice Phenomenon in the Vatican. I have won many wonderful friends among the leading figures in the Holy City. Today "the bridge" stands firmly on its foundations.' Presumably, 'the bridge' referred to the work which would reconcile the Church with what it insisted on calling spiritism.

It is believed that the Vatican even agreed to novice priests attending a course in parapsychology under the auspices of Father Andreas Resch. The Church's interest in these phenomena was hardly a secret although it was certainly not widely known. In 1970, the International Society of Catholic Parapsychologists convened in Austria and openly discussed such phenomena as EVP.

Perhaps the Church's most active involvement with such matters was the Pye Recording Studio sessions which took place in England in 1972, funded by the *Sunday Mirror*. The sessions were conducted by theologian Dr Peter Bander, a senior lecturer in Religious and Moral

*Dr Konstantin Raudive with apparatus for receiving messages from the dead*

Education at the Cambridge Institute of Education, who was initially hostile to the whole notion of communicating with the dead by any means. Prior to the experiment, Bander declared that it was 'not only far-fetched but outrageous' to even consider the possibility of recording spirit voices. He invited four senior members of the Catholic hierarchy to witness the proceedings in expectation that they would put the matter to rest once and for all. But during the recordings, which were held in a soundproof studio to eliminate the possibility of external interference, it was claimed that the participants heard the voice of a naval officer who had committed suicide two years earlier, a voice that had been recorded by Dr Raudive at an earlier session. The studio's chief engineer, Ken Attwood, conceded, 'I have done everything in my power to break the mystery of the voices without success; the same applies to other experts. I suppose we must learn to accept them.'

When the *Sunday Mirror* refused to publish Bander's conclusions, he published them himself the following year in a book entitled *Breakthrough*. Father Pistone, Superior of the Society of St Paul in England, gave Bander's experiment and his book what sounded like a positive endorsement.

> I do not see anything against the teaching of the Catholic Church in the Voices, they are something extra-ordinary but there is no reason to fear them, nor can I see any danger. The Church realizes that she cannot control the evolution of science. Here we are dealing with a scientific phenomenon; this is progress and the Church is progressive. I am happy to see that representatives of most Churches have adopted the same attitude as we have: we recognize that the subject of the Voice Phenomena stirs the imagination even of those who have always maintained that there could never be any proof or basis for discussion on the question of life after death. This book and the subsequent experiments raise serious doubts, even in the minds of atheists. This alone is a good reason for the Church supporting the experiments. A second reason may be

> found in the greater flexibility of the Church since Vatican II; we are willing to keep an open mind on all matters which do not contradict Christ's teaching.

Bander also managed to convert Archbishop H.E. Cardinale, Apostolic Nuncio to Belgium, who remarked, 'Naturally it is all very mysterious, but we know the voices are there for all to hear them'. The Right Reverend Monsignor, Professor C. Pfleger added, 'Facts have made us realize that between death and resurrection, there is another realm of post-mortal existence. Christian theology has little to say about this realm.'

Following the publicity surrounding the Pye sessions, the Vatican commissioned Swiss theologist Father Leo Schmid to embark on further research. Schmid went on to amass over 10,000 recordings which were transcribed and edited in his posthumously published book *When the Dead Speak* (1976). More recently, Vatican spokesman Father Gino Concetti told the papal newspaper *Osservatore Romano*:

> According to the modern catechism, God allows our dear departed persons who live in an ultra-terrestrial dimension, to send messages to guide us in certain difficult moments of our lives. The Church has decided not to forbid any more the dialogue with the deceased with the condition that these contacts are carried out with a serious religious and scientific purpose.

It would appear that the Church has made its peace with the dead.

# CHAPTER FOUR
# TALKING TO THE DEAD

The most convincing evidence of the soul's survival after death comes from psychic mediums who act as a channel between the living and the dead.

Most people have never seen a ghost, but that does not mean that ghosts do not exist. There is considerable experiential evidence that discarnate spirits do exist, but in an alternate reality to our own. This is a non-physical dimension of which we are not conscious because our perception of this greater reality is limited by our five physical senses.

## SCIENCE AND THE SPIRIT WORLD

We operate at the lowest frequency of existence on the densest level, the physical plane. Naturally, we tend to believe that what we perceive is real and that anything we cannot touch, taste, see, smell or hear does not exist. Our world appears solid but, as science has recently discovered, this is an illusion created by the comparatively low processing power of the human brain which cannot see the spaces that exist between matter at the subatomic level. It is comparable to looking at a photograph in a newspaper. We do not see the millions of dots that make up the image and the white spaces in between unless we look at it through a magnifying glass. Nevertheless, the dots are there. The same is true of moving images. Movie film is composed of hundreds of thousands of individual frames passing through a projector gate at the rate of 24 frames per second, giving the illusion of continuous movement. We do not see the individual frames, only fluid action. Although our apparently solid, physical world is an illusion, it is a reality to us while we remain within our physical bodies, but there is another world of finer matter operating at a higher frequency in the spaces in between our own.

Quantum physicists now theorize that subatomic particles, known as 'dark matter', combine to produce the illusion of solidity in the same way that tones and overtones combine to create identifiable sounds. In a similar way, ghosts may be a transitory image indicative of a real presence, or a vibration in the ether created by residual personal energy but having no more physical substance than a sound wave created by a musical note. And like a note this residual energy will pass away, echoing presumably into eternity but imperceptible to human beings. Consequently, we cannot afford to dismiss the existence of ghosts and other paranormal phenomena as unscientific and irrational simply because we are not aware of their presence. In fact, we can alter our perception to become aware of these other realities and we most often do so involuntarily when we are not so intensely focused on material matters.

## OUR SIXTH SENSE

We have all experienced an involuntary shift in consciousness such as when we intuitively 'know' that someone will phone us moments before they do so, or when we meet someone who we had been thinking about the day before. Carl Jung, the Swiss analytical psychologist, whose own mystical experiences and insights formed the basis of today's modern psychotherapy, coined the useful term 'synchronicity' for these seeming coincidences.

So strong is our need to believe that our physical world is the only reality that more significant experiences such as the lucid dream in which we sense ourselves floating or flying are rarely accepted for what they are (genuine out-of-body experiences) and what they reveal about our true nature. However, we all possess an innate sixth sense which is merely an acute sensitivity to the more subtle forces and presences around us and not something abnormal or supernatural.

There are some people who are not only aware that they possess this heightened sensitivity but who have developed it to a remarkable degree. We call them psychics and attribute all manner of paranormal powers to them such as precognition (foreseeing future events), psychometry (picking up impressions from personal objects) and remote viewing (projecting consciousness to another location). Those psychics who claim to be able to communicate with the dead are known as mediums and are either regarded as gifted by those who have received comfort and closure from having been given compelling evidence of their loved ones' survival after death, or as charlatans by those who remain sceptical.

When the dead try to communicate with us we tend to block them out, either because we fear that acknowledging their presence will disturb our sense of reality or because we need to be grounded in the material world. Many of us have been conditioned to dismiss their influence on our lives as coincidences or as figments of our imagination. However, if we continue to ignore their presence they may intensify their efforts, moving small objects around and contriving to arrange uncanny coincidences. To this end, mediums are able to facilitate a meeting of minds between this world and the next, until we are willing and able to do this for ourselves.

There are those who are sceptical of mediums on principle and they accuse their 'gullible' clients of unconsciously colluding with the medium and of being highly selective in what they choose to remember from a session. Sceptics frequently charge psychics with 'fishing' for information, but they disregard the many thousands of mediums who offer personal information that the client could not possibly have known – consciously or otherwise. Although, no doubt, it does occur, many mediums do not tease clues from their clients or trick them into revealing information, then take credit for having 'channelled' those facts from the dead. In fact, they explicitly instruct their clients not to tell them anything until after the session has finished so that they will not be unduly influenced. Also, many refuse to accept money for themselves, agreeing only to accept a modest donation for their chosen charity.

## CONVINCING EVIDENCE

Karin Page, founder of the Star of the East spiritual healing centre in Kent, England, had been seeing ghosts since the age of six, but it took a message from the 'other side' to finally convince her.

> One day my elderly mother-in-law promised me that she would come back after her death so that I would have proof of the survival of the soul. I didn't take it seriously at the time, but two months after her passing all the clocks in the house starting behaving strangely. They all showed a different time and a travelling alarm clock rolled off the shelf and crashed at my feet just as I was telling my daughter about how oddly they were all behaving. Another day the phone jumped off its holder on the wall and started swinging from side to side. Then the electric blanket and toaster switched themselves on. Each time I felt a chill in the air. It was Mary trying to tell me that she was with me.
>
> The final proof came when I went to a spiritualist meeting and was told by a medium, who I'd never met before, that my husband's mother was trying to communicate, that her name was Mary and that she had died of cancer, both of which were true. She just wanted to say thank you for all the time I had looked after her. Then the medium said that Mary sent her love to my husband, my son and his girlfriend and she named them all which left me speechless. The only thing I couldn't understand was when she said, 'I'm with Emma now', because I didn't know of an Emma in the family. Mary had never mentioned her. Afterwards I learnt that Emma had been Mary's

> sister who had died 11 years earlier. Since then I have smelt Mary's talcum powder on many occasions and I know then that she is watching over me.

## POSITIVE BENEFITS

English medium Jill Nash believes that the job of a psychic is to provide evidence of survival on the other side to give comfort to those left behind, not to impress clients with manifestations of ectoplasm and moving objects.

> Initially I talk to spirit in my mind and ask for their help. I feel their presence and can sense if they are male or female, but I never see them. I'm not communicating with the dead because nobody ever dies. They are the same personalities that they were in life. They are simply discarnate. I ask them to give me names and details that only the client will know which helps the client to relax and open up. Then I close my eyes and visualize drawing that person closer so that I am absorbed into their aura. When I make the connection I get excited. It's like having a present that you can't wait to open. At that point I usually feel a warmth and I might see a colour or a letter, or a combination of letters. If, for example I see them surrounded by blue I will know it is a communication issue and I'll ask them if they know of anyone whose name begins with the letter I've seen or a place beginning with that letter that has a significance for them. That's the starting point. It's an entirely intuitive, automatic process. It's like picking at a strand in a ball of wool. It unravels slowly. When spirit has something to add it impresses itself in my mind. I only receive what spirit wants me to have at that time. It wouldn't help me or the client to know all the answers. We would stop working things out for ourselves and would only put an effort into something that would guarantee to reward our efforts.

Unfortunately I couldn't tell my parents about my psychic experiences when I was young because they were very religious and were frightened of anything which challenged their faith. It made them uncomfortable. I used to sense a presence

*'I described the plant and the type of pot it was in and the fact that it was underneath the front window of their bungalow'*

occasionally and my mother would shut me up by shouting, 'I don't want to hear about dead people.' But I was never scared because I know nothing really dies. Energy can't die. It can only be transformed.

Jill sees a medium's role as helping the bereaved attain closure by facilitating a reunion with their loved ones.

On one particularly memorable occasion I opened the door expecting to see a little elderly lady and instead saw her and her late husband. He walked in behind her. She was, of course, unaware that he was with her but I could see him plain as day, although he was fainter than a living person, almost transparent and there was nothing to see below the knee. He was tall and slim and when she sat down he stood behind her with a satisfied grin on his face as if he was thinking, 'At last, now I can tell her what I have been trying to say to her for months.'

As soon as we were settled he communicated to me telepathically, mind to mind, that he wanted me to tell her about a rose. Of course I didn't know what he meant, I hadn't met this lady before. But she did. He had apparently been trying to create a new type of rose by grafting and it hadn't taken while he was alive but he wanted her to keep the plant alive because he knew it was going to work. I described the plant and the type of pot it was in and the fact that it was underneath the front window of their bungalow. Of course I had never seen their house but I could see it in my mind as he transferred his thoughts to mine.

He wanted her to know that he was alright and that he was with her if she wanted to say anything or share her feelings. He told me to tell her that he often stood behind her when she sat in her armchair in the evenings and that if she felt something like a cobweb brushing against her cheek or a gentle pat on the head that it was only him reassuring her that he was still around. And as soon as I said that, she admitted that she had felt these things and had wondered if it was him, although she couldn't trust her own feelings or believe that he was really there.

Jill's experiences have convinced her that the dead remain the same personalities they were on this side of life and recalls an incident with her father's ghost which revealed that he had not lost his mischievous sense of humour when he passed over.

I went to an open day at Stansted Hall which is popularly known as England's 'psychic school'. Some of the best mediums in the country were giving readings in various rooms and my friends and I began our 'tour' in the main hall which was filled to capacity with several hundred people. We were standing at the back when the medium said that he had to interrupt his demonstration because he was being literally nagged by a spirit who was insisting he be allowed to come through. It was an elderly man by the name of Percy who had passed over 20 years ago. The medium described Percy and his habits including his compulsive need to pat his hair and the fact that one of his fingers was missing. And it was my dad! He had lost a finger in a factory accident when he was a young man. He just wanted to tell me that he was fine and that I had been right about what I told him would be waiting for him on the other side.

But the funniest thing was that when I went on to watch a demonstration of direct voice mediumship in the next room my dad's spirit followed me and said 'hello' again through that medium. The medium actually spoke in his voice which I recognized immediately. And if that wasn't enough he did it again in the next room through another medium, so then I had to tell him to stop and give someone else a turn!

## BETTY SHINE

Some people are born with an acute psychic sensitivity or 'sixth sense' which enables them to see and communicate with discarnate spirits while others seem to develop this ability as the result of a traumatic event. Celebrity psychic Betty Shine, dubbed 'the World's number one healer' by the British popular press, was evidently blessed with more than her share of mediumistic gifts but was initially reluctant to develop them.

At the outbreak of the Second World War she was evacuated to the comparative safety of the English countryside with thousands of other children whose parents were desperate to save them from the dangers of the London Blitz. One night a stray bomb landed near the house in which she was staying, blowing in all the windows and sending a large shard of glass into the headboard just an inch above her head. The shock appears to have stimulated her psychic sensitivity because the following night Betty began to see 'misty people' passing through her bedroom door, across the room and through the opposite wall. Even though they seemed oblivious to her she found their presence oddly reassuring and accepted her extraordinary psychic experiences as entirely natural. At the time she thought that everyone shared the same clairvoyant gifts until a friend assured her that seeing dead people was unusual to say the least.

While the traditional view is that ghosts are discarnate spirits haunting our world, Betty had a more rational interpretation for the visitations – she believed she was looking into another dimension in which the discarnate spirits were going about their normal activities. That would explain why many ghosts appear unaware of the living – they are not intruding into our world but we are peering into theirs.

At first Betty was reluctant to pursue her calling as a medium and healer, but by the time she had reached adulthood the build-up of suppressed psychic energy was making her physically ill. When she finally opened up to the power within she was overwhelmed by self-generated phenomena such as moving objects and disturbances which are commonly associated with poltergeist activity. 'I was seeing spirit

*Thousands of children were evacuated from London during the Second World War. For Betty Shine, it was to prove a life-changing experience*

faces everywhere – on the walls, in the carpet, everywhere and I would hear voices too as if I was suddenly able to hear people talking in the next room, only they weren't in this world but the next.'

She claims to have seen spirits in airports, on buses, in pubs and all manner of public places, perhaps proving that our world and theirs are simply different facets of a greater, multi-dimensional reality and that there is no need to create a special atmosphere with candles and paranormal paraphernalia in order to communicate with our loved ones.

Most spirits are evidently content to co-exist with the living in a parallel plane, but according to Betty the dead can refuse to pass into their own world and instead linger in the presence of the living if they have 'unfinished business' to resolve.

On one occasion she sensed a dark entity overshadowing a female patient and heard its voice in her own head saying, 'I will never leave her, she's mine.' As soon as she began praying for protection, Betty saw a bright white light appear around the entity putting it into silhouette. It was a man and as he was pulled away by some unseen force into the light he screamed. At the same moment, the woman instinctively covered her ears, though she later told Betty that she hadn't actually heard anything. After the session the woman told Betty that she had once been married to a possessive, sadistic man who had pursued her for years after she had left him before finally suffering a fatal heart attack on her doorstep. After his death she remarried but still felt his suffocating overbearing presence and had become chronically depressed. A few weeks after the exorcism the woman returned to Betty's healing centre radiant and relieved, finally free of the black cloud she felt had been smothering her for years.

Betty's experiences have given her a unique insight into the true nature of ghosts – or spirits as she prefers to call them. It is her understanding that we are not purely physical beings but possess an energy counterpart which animates the body and which can be seen by psychics as an aura of vital energy which radiates from each living person. It may be this residual energy which lingers in the atmosphere after death and is mistaken for a ghost while our spirit moves on to the next world.

## THE PSYCHIC CLERIC

It is believed by some that everyone attends their own funeral in spirit, if only to see who has turned out to say goodbye. It is not uncommon for family members to see the deceased who often appear bemused at what they perceive as the fuss being made over their empty shell. Catholic sacristan Tina Hamilton often senses the presence of discarnate spirits during the funeral services at which she presides at St Thomas Church, Canterbury, England.

> I rarely see them, but I hear them and sense the force of their personality which has survived the death of the physical body. Sometimes I may even feel an arm around my shoulder. If it is a particularly strong presence they might try to communicate in which case I will hear them as another voice in my head. These are not my own thoughts. The tone of voice is quite distinct from my own. They tell me that they feel more alive than they did in life and will express frustration at not being able to be seen by their friends and family. Many express surprise at the number of people who have come to pay their respects while others seem amused at seeing a relative who didn't like them but who has reluctantly turned up out of a sense of duty. Curiously, it's usually their sense of humour that touches me most strongly. I suspect it stems from the relief of having been unburdened of their earthly responsibilities and fears and the sense that they are now free from the constraints of the physical body.
>
> I have been presiding over funeral services for more than 50 years and can truly say that I have never sensed a spirit that appeared disturbed, although I once conducted the funeral service for a teenage suicide who came through to say how sorry she was for having brought her parents so much pain. She asked me to tell them that it wasn't their fault. She had been suffering from depression and other problems which her family later confirmed to have contributed to her death.
>
> Unfortunately being 'open' or receptive means that I attract

lost souls like a moth to a flame. A psychic is like a lighthouse in a storm for those spirits who are disorientated after a fatal accident or sudden, unexpected death. Occasionally, when I am walking in the town I will hear someone calling my name and it is only when I turn round and find that there is no one there that I'll realize that it is a spirit. So I'll ask who it is in my mind and what they want with me. If I have a name it helps me to establish an empathy and later I can find out who it was that I was helping. If they were unprepared for death they may be confused and even anxious as they can see us but most people can't see or hear them. So I tell them to remain calm and go into the light which is the threshold to the next dimension and moments later I will sense the presence fade and a feeling of peace or relief overwhelming me. A typical incident was that involving a young man who had just been killed on the dual carriageway while travelling down from Scotland. He couldn't understand how he could be in the town as he couldn't remember the end of the journey. He kept reliving the accident like a bad dream and couldn't accept that he had not survived the crash which had killed him. He identified himself by name so I was able to verify later. But even he wasn't distressed, simply confused. My experience leads me to believe that the soul does not suffer even a violent death, but is simply separated from the physical body by the event.

## THE SOUL RESCUER

Exorcisms are rarely performed these days. The most common method of clearing a haunted house of earthbound spirits today is a technique known as 'soul rescuing'.

British psychic Pamela Redwood typifies the new breed of 'sensitives' who can sense spirits – malign or otherwise – and work quietly to rid homeowners of their uninvited guests, bringing both parties peace of mind. She explains:

What is sad is when someone cannot return to the light after their death because they are so attached to their life. I have cleared several houses where there have been disturbances or where the owner complains that they cannot live there because a certain room is cold even in the summer. They call me in and the first thing I pick up on is a thickness in the atmosphere as if it is charged with an invisible presence. Sometimes my spirit guides will give me different colours and I will see that soul taken up through the ray of colour by my guides into the light and then the atmosphere will clear as if the room has been aired. I used to take the spirit up through my own body as I thought that I had to act as a channel for its return to the light but now the guides do it for me. Which is just as well as it could be very exhausting to be a host to someone else's spirit even for a few minutes. I would feel as if I'd absorbed their essence into my own being but occasionally if they were reluctant to go I would still have them with me when I went home. My daughter is very psychic and she would see me hobbling down the garden path, bent double like an old hag with a spirit on my shoulder and calmly say to her dad, 'Mum's back and she's brought a ghost home.'

I don't feel any fear when I do soul rescuing otherwise I couldn't do it. I know my guides are assisting me and it is work that needs to be done. Unfortunately people are too eager to build anywhere these days and most of my work comes from people who have bought new houses built on the site of old burial grounds.

You have to treat earthbound spirits as if they were still alive as they are the same personalities that they were in life. I once had to persuade the spirit of a pipe-smoking stubborn old man to pass over by promising him that he would have all the tobacco he could smoke if he went over to the other side!

## JOHN EDWARD

The young American medium John Edward (whose hugely popular TV show *Crossing Over* has been syndicated around the world) is one of a new generation of 'celebrity psychics'. His affability and commonsense approach have dispelled the suffocating gloom of Victorian spiritualism that gave mediumship a bad name with its candlelit séances, Ouija boards and obsession with ectoplasm. His extraordinary experiences demonstrate that spirits are not an unsettling paranormal phenomena but simply discarnate individuals who initiate contact with the living because they wish to assure their grieving loved ones that they are fine and to encourage them to move on with their own lives. John's experiences offer more insights into the true nature of the spirit world than were ever revealed by the mediums of the spiritualism movement. This suggests that we might now be ready to accept the existence of a wider reality. Perhaps we are even being prepared by being drip-fed insights into the mysteries of the universe as an aid to our understanding, and evolution of our beliefs. John Edward was tested and his abilities verified under rigorous laboratory conditions by Gary Schwarz, Professor of Psychology at the University of Arizona.

The first hint that he possessed an unusual talent came at an early age when he casually commented on events in his family history. These were events which he shouldn't have known about as they had occurred before he was born, yet he assured his parents that he remembered being there at the time. By the age of five he had informed his teachers that he could see a radiance around them. It was only much later that he learnt that not everyone could see these coloured auras. The first flowering of his psychic

*Tarot cards from the Rider Waite tarot deck*

*John Edward, in a publicity shot for his show* Crossing Over with John Edward

gifts began with visions of his maternal grandfather who had died in 1962, seven years before John was born. He saw the old man sitting at the dinner table next to his grandmother who took John's announcement that the old man was present as a comfort, even though she couldn't see her husband herself. John soon graduated to premonitions that relatives would drop by unexpectedly – a talent his mother soon learned to take seriously and be grateful for.

John's particular ability for communicating with the departed developed in fits and starts during his adolescence. At first, the connection was tentative and difficult to decipher like receiving a weak signal from a distant radio station. There was considerable static obscuring the communications, but over time he learnt how to 'tune in' and filter out the interference. By the time he was 16, John was giving readings using tarot cards at psychic fairs, but then he began to receive messages for his clients in the form of intrusive thoughts which evidently did not originate in his own unconscious. To begin with they were simply names of dead people who were obviously attempting to communicate with his clients, but John felt uncomfortable being 'used' in this way. He resented the distraction as he was trying to concentrate on the cards. Predicting the future was fine as far as he was concerned, but talking to the dead spooked him. It also didn't sit well with his Catholic faith. Eventually, John began to trust these inner voices which became increasingly louder and more insistent. Subsequently, the names evolved into messages which he passed on to the delight of the living. The relief on the faces of anxious or grieving loved ones convinced him that what he was doing could not be a sin, but was instead a blessing.

Then one day, while he was still in his teens, he witnessed his first significant materialization. His aunt Anna had teased him into reading the tarot cards which she regarded as little more than a child's magic trick. But when John looked up from the cards he saw a woman standing behind his aunt. She was a stout lady in her sixties, wearing a black dress and a flower-shaped brooch and she appeared to have only one leg. John's description gave Aunt Anna a start. She immediately identified the mystery woman as her mother-in-law who had lost her leg through diabetes. Aunt Anna had never met her and neither had John because the old lady had died before he was born. But that was only the beginning. As John looked past his aunt, the old woman vanished and another figure appeared in her place. It was an impeccably dressed man in a pinstripe suit carrying a pocket watch. He was tall and slender with grey hair. This time Aunt Anna didn't recognize him from John's description so John opened up a dialogue with the man in his head. 'Show me something so that she will know who you are,' he said and was rewarded with a vision of the man lifting a large comb from his pocket and then pointing to a clock surrounded by flowers. The time on the clock read ten past two. The vision faded, leaving John and his aunt none the wiser.

One week later, John's Uncle Carmine died unexpectedly of a heart attack. Only it wasn't such a shock to John because he had seen his uncle dying before his eyes in a particularly vivid vision three months earlier. It was so strong in fact that John had insisted that his uncle see a doctor, but the physicians gave the old man a clean bill of health. Three months later at his uncle's wake, John stood before the coffin staring at a clock surrounded by roses. The time on the clock was ten minutes past two, the moment of his uncle's death. It was a family tradition to mark the time of death in this way. That same day John learnt the identity of the man with the comb. A cousin recognized the description as that of Uncle Carmine's father who had been a barber. From that moment, John's psychic sensitivity went into overdrive.

## Interpreting the Spirits

The number of readings he was asked to give put enormous demands on his time, but the most taxing aspect was the sheer intellectual effort he had to make in order to interpret the subtle signs the spirits were showing him. Often they would use obscure references because they couldn't communicate directly, but on one occasion John learnt that there was a danger in trying too hard. During a reading for a recently bereaved lady, her dead husband kept showing John a bell. The reading had been going well up to that point and she had been able to verify everything John had passed on to her. But he was puzzled by the bell. He asked if she or her husband had had any connection with Philadelphia or Ben Franklin.

Did they know of anyone called Ben or Franklin? It was only when John said that he kept seeing the image of a bell but couldn't think of another association for that image that the woman understood and became tearful. On the morning of his death her husband had given her a souvenir bell he had picked up on a business trip. 'If you ever need me, ring this and I'll be there,' he had said. Then he kissed his wife goodbye and went to work. He was killed in a car accident later that day. Sometimes a bell just means a bell.

As his fame spread, first by word of mouth and then through his TV show, John found his appointments diary filled to overflowing and the spirits crowding in, jostling for his attention in their eagerness to have their messages passed on to their loved ones. They would pull him to one side of the room and home him in on a particular member of the audience, then tease him with tantalizing clues. The atmosphere was good-natured, although often emotional, as friends and family members recognized a pet name or a half-forgotten incident which the spirit recalled to validate the evidence of their survival. Occasionally, the experience was dramatic. A victim of a car accident came through to give her version of events, offering unknown evidence implicating another vehicle's involvement which was subsequently verified by the police. And several murder victims described the guilty party which the family recognized as fitting the description of a suspect the police had had under observation but could not arrest for lack of evidence.

More often, though, spirits speak of mundane matters which sceptics argue is proof that mediumship is a dangerous delusion. If it was a genuine communication from the afterlife, they argue, then surely the spirit would have something profound to say about life after death. Instead, they usually talk of routine family matters. John Edward contends that such minor personal details are more important for the grieving family as what they really need is proof that they are talking to their loved ones.

# LIVING WITH THE DEAD

Ghosts are everywhere these days. They haunt the internet, and there's a paranormal reality television show on almost every channel. But if you want to get up close and personal with the spirit world there's only one way you can be certain you are communing with the dead – and that is by consulting a medium. It's the medium's job to encourage the dead to share their secrets. Mediums also act as interpreters of verbal and visual messages from beyond the grave. So how do mediums discover their abilities and develop the talent to tune into the spirit world at will? How do they overcome their own fear of communing with the dead and, most important of all, how can they tell that what they see and hear is real and not a figment of their imagination?

## BECOMING A MEDIUM

June Mayfield (real name withheld by request) is a professional medium. She gives regular readings at psychic fairs and at a complementary health centre near her home in London, England. This is her account of how she became a medium.

> I'd always been interested in the paranormal, but it wasn't until I experienced a number of life-changing events that had been accurately predicted by another psychic that I seriously considered exploring the possibility that I might have some degree of psychic sensitivity that could be of practical help to people.
>
> I was very fortunate in having a psychic friend who was very experienced and who was willing to teach me. So I felt confident to open up and to allow whatever impressions came through, knowing that he was there holding my hand, so to speak. He was also the most grounded and calm

person I knew, so I felt safe, which is very important when you first begin to trust your intuition and invite whoever might be 'out there' to communicate with you. He taught me the importance of closing down and protecting myself so that I am in control at all times and not in danger of being overwhelmed, because once you open up and are receptive to the more subtle impressions in the ether, you can attract anyone from the other side who wants to communicate with their loved ones. It's a bit like being a beacon in the darkness. You have to link in with one spirit and not be distracted or tempted to help them all.

## Finding Spirit Guides

Once June had been taught to attune herself to the unseen presences who wished to communicate with her or her clients, she needed to establish a connection with her own spirit guides. This would enable her to ask for their advice whenever her friend wasn't present, or when she needed re-energizing or healing after a particularly exhausting session.

Clients come with all their anxieties and some with debilitating ailments which can drain the medium of vital energy, so I often need to replenish the life force after a few readings.

My guides come in various forms, some human, some animal, but I don't analyze why they take those forms or whether they are projections of an inner aspect of my personality or an external spirit. It's not important to me what they are, but how effective they can be in assisting me to help the people who come to me for guidance, or to rid them of something that has attached themselves and is draining them of the life force. The client won't be aware of what it is that is causing their chronic symptoms such as headaches, or leaving them feeling depressed and weak, but I can often see it. And when they leave they will often say how much better and more positive they feel, or that they feel as if they have been relieved of a burden they'd been carrying.

The quality of the energy associated with these leechlike entities is quite different to the energy that surrounds a spirit which accompanies a client to a reading because it wants to communicate something of importance or to simply reassure the client that there is no need to grieve or worry about the future. Some of those that attach themselves to the living aren't necessarily bad. They might have died suddenly and not be aware that they are dead, or be confused and living in a dream-like state in which they cling to someone they knew in life who has a strong life force. But these lost, earthbound souls need to be made aware of what happened to them and where they are and to accept that they need to move on.

## Working with a Guide

To connect with her guide, June visualizes a specific scene that she must enter, such as a walled garden or a winding staircase which she descends step by step; with each step, she sinks deeper until eventually she reaches a trance-like state. Visualizing the familiar scene helps to establish a connection with the guide, which will appear as if on cue to answer her questions or to reveal the reason behind something that has been of concern.

There was a time when I was convinced that a certain problem was going to have a disastrous outcome and everyone I had spoken to about this had told me this situation could only end with the person concerned going to prison. And yet my guide assured me that this person would be given another chance and that I shouldn't worry. He wasn't a family member or a friend, but I was still very worried for him and I couldn't imagine how he would escape a jail sentence under the circumstances, but my guide was proven right and I haven't doubted him since.

I believe that the more you trust your guides and also the impressions that you receive from a person that you are asked to do a reading for, the stronger those impressions will become and the more accurate will be your reading.

During readings, words will pop into my head faster than I could have thought of them, and after I have passed the message on or made a particular observation, I won't know why I said that, so that tells me it's not a product of my imagination. Often I'll pick up an energy around the client just before they arrive and the quality of that energy will give me a sense of what they have come to consult me about. I feel a different energy if they have come about a relationship than I do if they are considering a new job or pursuing an ambition which they aren't sure will be successful.

## Giving a Reading

Readings are not always dramatic and life-changing, but they can be important in convincing non-believers that psychics can see more than the average person. In one reading for an elderly man, June described his two daughters and their personalities in considerable detail and examined how they were coping with various events and changes in their lives.

Another example was when a young woman in a very troubled state came to her for a reading.

As always, I asked the client not to tell me anything, but simply to answer 'yes' or 'no' to any questions I might ask. I immediately had the impression that she had been jilted by a man who had left her for someone else and taken her money. I then got one word, 'leverage', and that was all she needed to hear. She had something on this man, something that if she told the police would certainly lead to him going to prison for a long time and though she didn't want to use it against him, the

> threat of revealing it was the only thing that would force him to return the money. So the spirits were telling her to use what she knew to recover what was rightfully hers – and she did so.

Mediums often feel a vibrant energy around a client that they can 'read', or they describe a sensation similar to having a bucket of water thrown over them. These sensations tell the medium that whatever the client is talking about will have a very positive outcome. But if, for example, June is listening to the client describe a relationship and she doesn't get a sense of a dynamic energy surrounding the client, then she knows that the relationship isn't working. Often she will feel a coldness at the back of her neck, when the spirits are standing behind her, or a light touch of fingers in her hair. It is always a reassuring sensation – it is never unsettling.

## The Astral Plane

June has a friend who regularly leaves his body at will to explore the astral plane – the non-physical world where the soul is said to reside after death while awaiting rebirth. He tells her that the people he has encountered there are just the same as they were when they were alive. Many are repeating their routine lives in this dream world because they cannot imagine doing anything more or breaking free of their addictions and attachments. Death does not necessarily give them insight, so communicating with these discarnate souls will not necessarily be positive or increase our understanding. Those more advanced souls who have managed to discard their attachment to people and possessions will either have chosen to reincarnate to continue their development, or will have passed on to a higher level beyond human contact.

> I wouldn't go to a haunted house for fun, knowing what I know. You wouldn't go into the jungle and poke around with a big stick to see if anything will come out and bite you, would you? And you don't wander into dangerous neighbourhoods after dark armed with a torch and a camera if you've got any sense.

> I don't see any point in going exploring unless you know what you are looking for and what you'll do when you find it. Ghosts are just people without physical form and we all know that there are people you wouldn't want to mix with when they're alive, so why seek them out after they've died?
>
> If there is anyone who wants to communicate with me from the other side I can wait for them to come to me. There is so much danger in dabbling in something you don't and can't ever really understand. It's not that there is a serious risk of being possessed, but rather of picking up attachments and of the psychological damage that might occur if you think you're possessed.
>
> That is the real danger that none of these ghost-hunters even consider. I left a Wicca group years ago because they were conjuring up all sorts of nature spirits and the people involved in the group were powerful personalities who knew what they were doing. But what guarantee was there that the spirits would do as they were told when they got here? There is no such thing as a tame and submissive spirit. If it has got a mind of its own, how do you know it won't turn on you? And if you can't see it and can't touch it then you can't contain it or put it back in the bottle!

June insists she doesn't see any value in the paranormal reality shows which seem to be everywhere at the moment. As she says, how can these ghost-hunters seriously expect to establish communication with the dead, let alone encourage a materialization, if they clamber all over a supposed 'hot spot' with tons of equipment and when they can't stand still and be quiet for more than five minutes!

> I recently visited Chartwell, the 500-year-old house that once belonged to Winston Churchill, and as soon as I entered I felt shivers from the residual energy in the room. But once the rest of the touring party came in behind me it dissipated. That's

why these shows can't hope to capture anything significant. Communing with spirits is a matter of tuning in and being acutely sensitive to 'echoes' in the atmosphere and residual energy in personal possessions. It's not a psychic safari!

I try not to be too sceptical, nor too trusting either. There is so much nonsense written and talked about ghosts and the spirit world by people who have no personal experience and little understanding of the paranormal. The unknown is part of our world and it operates according to natural laws. The supernatural is an extension of our world, not a world of superhuman powers and demons.

## BACK FROM THE DEAD

Some of the best evidence of the soul's survival after death has been obtained from mediums, acutely sensitive or psychic individuals who claim to be able to contact the dead. In rare cases they have been able to produce physical manifestations of the deceased which investigators were able to question at length and even to touch, confirming that their presence was not a hoax, nor the product of hypnotic suggestion.

> I cannot but think that it would be a great step if mankind could familiarise themselves with the idea that they are spirits incorporated for a time in the flesh; but that the dissolution of the connection between soul and body, though it changes the external condition of the former, leaves its moral state unaltered. What a man has made himself he will be; his state is the result of his past life, and his heaven or hell is in himself.
>
> Catherine Crowe, *The Night Side of Nature*, 1848

Psychics were once seen by the general public as eccentric and highly unstable individuals and many were exposed as charlatans who cynically exploited the bereaved for monetary gain, but fortunately the recent success of films such as *The Sixth Sense* and the TV series *Medium* have popularized the idea that ordinary people can communicate with the dead to bring comfort and closure to the grief-stricken and that ghosts are a natural and not a supernatural phenomenon.

Many of today's celebrity psychics such as Britain's Derek Acorah, Colin Fry and Tony Stockwell and American TV mediums John Edward and James Van Praagh saw their first apparitions when they were very young, when their connection to the spirit world was at its strongest. It was only when others insisted such things were figments of their imaginations that they learned to fear the appearance of ghosts and to deny the evidence of their own eyes to avoid their parents' displeasure and the jeers of other children.

It takes a rare and acute sensitivity to sense the presence of discarnate personalities and a willingness to openly acknowledge their existence in order to communicate with them. Few people choose to develop this innate ability and to accept the responsibility that goes with their 'gift' because it opens a whole 'Pandora's Box' of problems, from being accused of imagining things to being pestered by the dead who are desperate to reassure their loved ones that they have not ceased to exist but are merely living in a parallel dimension.

## MIRABELLI'S SÉANCES

In the early years of spiritualism, just prior to and following the First World War, several serious investigations by eminent scientists were hampered by the crude deceptions perpetrated by fraudulent mediums preying on the gullible and the grief-stricken. But not all could be so readily dismissed as fakes. There were some whose demonstrations appear to offer incontrovertible proof of ghosts. The most remarkable medium of this period was without doubt the young Brazilian Carlos Mirabelli, who first attracted public attention in 1919 when he was chosen as the subject of an intense and exhaustive investigation by the Cesare Lombroso Academy of Psychical Studies. During their tests Mirabelli agreed to conduct a series of 392 séances in broad daylight or in well-lit rooms. At one particularly memorable session he brought through the disembodied spirit of a little girl which assumed physical

*Carlos Mirabelli (left, in trance) with Dr Carlos de Castro (right) in the 1920s. Between them is a 'materialization' of dead poet Giuseppe Parini*

form in full view of the assembled witnesses. One of these, a Dr de Souza, rose slowly to his feet and in a voice quivering with emotion addressed the apparition which was dressed in a funeral shroud. He addressed it by name, certain that it was his little daughter who had recently died from influenza. Unable to contain himself, the doctor rushed at the ghost and embraced it. He was seen to converse with it for a full 30 minutes before it melted back into the ether. Afterwards he testified that it had talked of matters that only his dead daughter could have known.

At another sitting the spirit of a bishop who had lost his life at sea materialized for more than 20 minutes during which a physician examined it and noted the rumblings of its stomach and the saliva in its mouth.

Fortunately, someone had the presence of mind to bring a camera to one of the subsequent sessions during which Mirabelli conjured a robed figure who was sufficiently solid to cast a shadow and leave his image for all time on film. But such feats were sadly ignored by the public whose fascination for phenomena and need to believe had been cruelly exploited by a number of well-publicized scandals involving fraudulent mediums.

## MESSAGE FROM THE OTHER SIDE

Although all too many mediums pass on seemingly mundane messages from the dear departed which don't add a jot to our knowledge of the great beyond, there are others who appear to be able to help in very practical ways.

More recently English housewife Brenda Richardson was still mourning her recently deceased husband Charles when she was invited to a spiritualist church by a friend who thought it might offer her a crumb of comfort. Spiritualist meetings always feature a 'platform' medium who takes to the stage after the service to convey messages from the dead to their loved ones in the congregation.

Brenda was not a believer but her interest was aroused when the medium taking the meeting told her that she had a message from Charles who was standing next to her at that very moment. He wanted his widow to know that a painting he had bought and hung in their dining room had not been bought on a whim, as he had told her at the time, but as an investment and now was the time to sell it. It would solve her financial worries. Brenda had not told anyone of her money problems and she hadn't given a thought to the painting which didn't appear to be in any way remarkable. But the medium was insistent. The painting was valuable. The artist's name was W.H. Davies and his signature was to be found in the bottom right-hand corner of the canvas. Rushing home, Brenda didn't wait to take her shoes and coat off but burst into the living room and almost pulled the picture off the wall.

There in the bottom right-hand corner, as the medium had told her, was the artist's signature 'W.H. Davies' – a comparatively obscure but highly respected 19th-century English artist. The painting was subsequently put up for auction and realized a sum that solved Brenda's money troubles at a stroke.

## TALKING TO THE DEAD

Most of us would consider it extraordinary if we saw a ghost once in our lives, but there are people who see them every day. In fact, they sometimes have difficulty distinguishing the living from the dead.

These psychically gifted individuals are commonly called clairvoyants (meaning 'clear-sighted'), but many prefer to be called 'sensitives' for fear of being associated with fairground fortune tellers and the kind of eccentric old ladies who gave mediumship a bad reputation in the dark days of spiritualism and séances. Today's mediums are more likely to be ageing hippies offering spiritual guidance at new age fairs or young celebrity psychics with their own TV shows who give readings live on air in front of an enthralled studio audience.

Like many of his contemporaries, American TV psychic James Van Praagh was extremely reluctant to answer his 'calling', but was persuaded to put his gift to good use when the ghosts of several murdered children appealed to him to catch their killer.

The first victim had attempted to make contact when James was still a child, but he had been terrified by the appearance of the boy at his window at night and had prayed for the persistent phantom to leave him alone. His fear was aggravated by his parents' anger with what they thought was their son's morbid imagination. James later learnt that his mother's aversion to such stories stemmed from her own psychic experiences and the abilities which she had chosen to suppress because it conflicted with her strict Catholic upbringing. Unfortunately, she sent her son to a Catholic school where his 'gifts' brought him even more trouble.

*Medium and psychic James Van Praagh – 'only certain people are sensitive enough to act as mediums'*

One day he 'saw' a young girl in the playground carrying a pair of ice skates. James had the impression that she wanted to tell her brother that he was not to blame himself for her death which had occurred when she had fallen through the ice, but when James tried to tell his classmate that his dead sister had a message for him the boy flew into a rage and complained to the head of the school who branded James a fantasist and a liar. Things got worse later that same day when James warned his teacher that her son was going to be hit by a car but survive with a broken leg. That night she came to James' home to tell him that his prediction had come true, but she warned him that such 'gifts' were bestowed by the Devil.

## Meeting 'Eddie'

But the Devil couldn't have sent him the next vision. During a school outing to a local nature reserve, James met a boy in the forest who was the same age as himself and who was holding a pet turtle as if it was his only friend. The boy said that his name was Eddie, and James felt a bond with him which he put down to the fact that they were both outsiders.

But there was something about him that was not quite right. Eddie had an unfashionable haircut and wore hand-me-down clothes that a kid might have had in the 1940s or 1950s. He also had an air of melancholy about him which James attributed to the fact that he was wearing a leg brace that must have prevented him from playing with other children. When James started walking back to his group he turned to say goodbye but Eddie was gone. Soon after, the knocking at James' bedroom window began again, only this time the terrified child could see the face of the person who demanded to be let in. It was Eddie. As soon as he put the light on the vision vanished and James realized that Eddie was a ghost.

As a result, James prayed even harder to be spared the visits from the spirits and the visions eventually ceased.

## I See Dead People

It was only in middle age that the memories James had so long repressed came back to the surface. By this time he had his own manufacturing business and was looking for someone to design and maintain a website. The lady who answered his advertisement happened to be a psychic who during casual conversation made accurate predictions concerning family matters she couldn't have known by conventional methods. She even described a dream that James had had since the age of six in which he was an adult sitting at his mother's hospital bed when the spirit of his grandmother entered to claim her daughter for the other world.

James was naturally intrigued, but he didn't want anything to do with mediums for fear of awakening his own unwanted talents. 'I've had my fill of the supernatural,' he told her.

Nevertheless, she persisted and managed to persuade him to join her at a psychic demonstration presided over by a local medium she trusted. During the meeting the medium claimed to see James surrounded by dead people desperate to communicate with their loved ones through him. 'You can shut the door to the spirit world if you want to,' he told James, 'but they used to talk to you and they want to talk to you again. They tell me that you have dreamt again of your grandmother. It is the same dream you had when you were six years old. You are in the hospital and your grandmother comes to collect your mother who is dying.'

Dismissing it all as a cruel trick in which his new employee and the medium must have been complicit, James excused himself and left the meeting vowing never to be duped again. But he wasn't to be allowed to squander his gift so easily.

One day he 'saw' his recently deceased mother wandering aimlessly through the aisles at the local supermarket as if searching for something or someone. Before he could follow her a young black boy dropped a pack of eggs at his feet and walked off without a word. As James bent down to clean up the mess he noticed that the name on the packet was 'Mother Hen Nurseries'. It didn't mean anything to him at the time, but it was to prove a vital clue in the mystery of the missing children.

## Empty Nest

A second enigmatic clue came some time later when James opened his mailbox to find a bird's nest filled with seven blue eggs. Thinking the neighbourhood children were playing a prank he put it aside and thought no more of it. But that same night the black boy he had seen in the supermarket appeared in his living room holding the nest. But this time it was empty and the boy's hands were bound with rope.

James was clearly being asked to rescue an earthbound spirit, but when he asked the boy what he wanted, the child could say nothing. 'Tell me what you want of me,' James repeated, frustrated and somewhat frightened. This time the boy opened his mouth to speak and a stream of soil poured on to the carpet. These visions he was seeing with his inner eye, the so-called 'third eye' of psychic perception.

Suffering from headaches and with his business in serious trouble because of changing economic conditions, James consulted a counsellor, but his sessions provided little comfort. At one particularly memorable session he 'saw' a middle-aged woman burst into the counsellor's office in a highly agitated state and begin ransacking his desk. James couldn't understand why the counsellor failed to react and then he realized it was because he couldn't hear or see her. She was dead. A moment later he understood the significance of what he was seeing. She was the counsellor's late wife and this was a replay of the last moments of her life. James watched helpless as she discovered a bottle of tablets and swallowed the lot, dying right before his eyes. He described what he was seeing, but was cut short by the counsellor who recognized his late wife from the description and refused to hear as much as another word from his 'delusional' patient.

## The Old Man

Being psychic does not mean that you are immune from life's trials. Certainly James has had more than his share. Following his mother's death and the loss of his business he had to leave his home and find a more modest house. Some would say that it is these factors and the resulting stress which produced the 'visions', but they cannot explain what happened next.

During a visit to the local police station to report a break-in, he saw the spirit of a troubled old man vainly trying to communicate with his widow who had come in to find out how the police investigation into her husband's death was progressing. Reluctant though he was to intervene and acutely aware that he was likely to be accused of being insane, James felt obliged to pass on the old man's message.

Her son was predictably suspicious of a stranger who claimed to see dead people and over-protective towards his mother, but she was eager to have a last word with her beloved husband if there was any chance that this visitation was true. She had been distraught when he had failed to return home just days before and James was able to break the news that he did not die of a heart attack as the police assumed, but had been mugged when he took a shortcut home. A young man had stolen the watch that her husband had been so proud of together with his wedding ring.

While mention of the watch and ring could be credited to good guesswork, it didn't account for James' knowledge of the place where the old man's body had been found nor the fact that he knew that the old man's ghost had knocked their wedding photo from the shelf while she was dusting that morning.

Although the son managed to have James evicted from the station for harassment, his mother was not so easily put off. She called on James later that day, having found his address from the form he had been filling out at the station about the break-in, and she asked for more information.

Restoring contact with the old man, James was able to give her specific personal details including the number of the hotel room in which they spent their honeymoon. Then James' heightened sense of empathy helped him relive the agony of the old man's last moments – the fear he felt when confronted with the mugger and the pain of his fatal heart attack brought about by the struggle.

From this James was able to give the widow a detailed description of the mugger and the house he shared with his parents. Better still, he told her that the young man was known to the police. In fact, he was a police informant and his first name was Ronnie. James revealed that Ronnie had hidden her husband's watch and ring together with other stolen items in a cigar box under the steps leading to the front porch.

Naturally the police were sceptical and questioned James before deciding whether or not to act on his information. But he was able to convince the female detective assigned to the case that his insights were genuine by telling her precisely where she could find the reading glasses that she had mislaid that morning. The tip proved accurate: Ronnie was arrested and the stolen items were recovered.

## Psychometric Insight

But not every message James brought from the beyond was appreciated. When he felt compelled to pass on a message from the detective's dead sister who had died in a car crash years before, she didn't want to hear it and was angry that he had intruded on her private grief. She was clearly uncomfortable with the idea that the dead can haunt the living, but she could not afford to ignore the clues he brought to her regarding Eddie and the other dead children which now began to accumulate thick and fast.

By this time James was working in a bookshop. One day he happened to be wrapping a copy of Edgar Allan Poe's *Collected Tales* when it fell open at an illustration for *The Premature Burial*. Instinctively James realized why the black boy had appeared to him mute and bound. He had been buried alive. Desperate for more details that he could bring to the police, he consulted a Ouija board and asked to be given the name of the boy who had repeatedly appeared holding the bird's nest. Obligingly the board spelt out the name Dennis Branston. The following day James was driving home when Dennis suddenly appeared in front of him, forcing him to brake suddenly. The next moment the boy was sitting beside him with the nest cupped in his lap. 'What are you trying to tell me?' asked James more in frustration than in fright. It was then that he noticed where he was – in Bird's Nest Lane. Surely, it couldn't be a coincidence. This had to be Dennis' way of telling James where he had died.

Continuing along the road without his guide James came to Mother Hen Nurseries, the same name that had appeared on the box of eggs Dennis had dropped at his feet in the supermarket. He must be on the right road. Minutes later he pulled into Turtleback Park – the nature reserve where he had met Eddie all those years earlier.

Leaving the car, James wandered through the woods, all the while appealing to the spirits of Eddie and Dennis to make themselves known to him and tell him how he could help bring them peace. He was answered in a way that would send lesser psychics running for cover. One by one the restless spirits of seven dead boys rose from the ground – Eddie, Dennis and five others who had been buried with them.

When the police arrived at the scene they unearthed the bodies of all seven children, their hands bound at the wrists just as James had seen them – all except one. The body of Eddie Katz was recovered, the leg brace still intact – proof if needed that James' insights were genuine. But Eddie's hands were not bound and the autopsy revealed that he had died from a single gunshot wound. Forensic tests showed that he had died many years before the others – 30 years earlier in fact, which coincided with the date of his disappearance in May 1963.

A cold case is the hardest to crack and a case this cold yielded up no forensic evidence of any use at all. When James learnt of this he offered to try to get what impressions he could of the killer from Eddie's leg brace, a technique known as psychometry. Psychics believe that inanimate objects can retain residual personal energy and that it is possible to tune in to the 'memories' stored in an object simply by holding it. Personal possessions such as watches and rings are potentially the most promising

*James consulted a Ouija board and asked for the name of the boy who had repeatedly appeared holding the bird's nest*

material, but any object associated with a strong emotion – such as a murder weapon – can reveal vital information if the psychic is acutely sensitive. With little else to go on the police reluctantly agreed to let James attempt his experiment. To their amazement it yielded the crucial clues they were looking for.

By simply holding the brace James instantly connected with the strongest emotions Eddie had experienced – the moment of his death. For a few vital seconds, James looked out through Eddie's eyes. He was alone in the forest at Turtleback Reserve in the very spot where James had first seen him as a boy all those years ago. Two hunters were stalking deer less than a hundred yards away. One was Lester Petrocelli and the other was his brother Richard. They heard a movement in the undergrowth and believing that they had their prey in their sights Richard shouted to Lester to fire. He hit Eddie in the head and the boy died instantly. When they found the body they panicked and buried it, promising each other never to speak to anyone of what they had done.

On questioning Mrs Katz the police discovered that someone had been sending her flowers every Christmas with a card in his name and that is why she had assumed that her son was still alive. The man had protected his anonymity by paying the florist in cash sent in the mail, but after three decades he must have felt he was in the clear because that Christmas he turned up in person. Asked if she could give the police a description, the florist assured them she wouldn't need to as he was a familiar face in town. He was the man the Revenue Service used every year on billboards and leaflets in their advertising campaign to remind people to file their income tax returns. His name was Lester Petrocelli.

Ghosts aren't satisfied with haunting a location if they have revenge on their mind. Through our dreams and by influencing our thoughts they can conspire to arrange a meeting that might seem like an uncanny coincidence to the unsuspecting pawns in their play. It can surely be no coincidence that just days later James saw Lester Petrocelli in a local restaurant with the spirit of his recently deceased brother Richard standing behind him urging James to convey a vital message from beyond the grave.

*They heard a movement in the undergrowth and Richard shouted to Lester to fire*

'Excuse me,' James interrupted as politely as he could. 'I don't know how to tell you this so I'm just going to say it. Your brother is standing behind you and he says you are not to blame yourself for the death of the boy even though you pulled the trigger. It was an accident.'

'Go away, go away. I don't want to hear this,' Lester protested, becoming more agitated by the minute. His face reddened and before his dinner companions could intervene Lester gripped his chest in pain and fell to the floor, the victim of a heart attack. At the hospital he was revived but given only days to live. With that knowledge and the belief that his dead brother had been urging him to confess before it was too late, he told the story of that fatal shooting to the police who had gathered at his bedside.

## Killing for Company

James had been vindicated again. But this was not the end of the story – not yet. The detectives were extremely puzzled as to why the sixth grave was dug outside the circle formed by the others. Then it occurred to them – this one marked the beginning of a second circle. The killer was still out there and on the prowl for new victims. Eddie had been accidentally shot by Lester Petrocelli, but someone was kidnapping boys of roughly the same age and burying them alive at the spot where Eddie had died. Could it be that the killer did not have the heart for cold-blooded murder, but was insane – perhaps driven by grief to kill to keep Eddie company?

While the police were actively considering this possibility, James begged the dead boys to appear before him one last time and reveal the name of the killer.

As their spirits gathered in the darkness James sank into a light trance reliving the last abduction – a victim who was still alive and being held in a locked basement until his abductor was ready to bury him by Eddie's side. Now convinced that James' insights could be acted upon, the lead detective ordered her team back to the nature reserve to save the new boy from certain death, but there was nothing to be seen. While the police officers made snide remarks at the detective's expense James realized his mistake. The killer would not bury the latest victim at Turtleback Reserve as the bodies had all been removed for burial elsewhere. The boy would be buried alive at the cemetery where Eddie was now interred.

Racing through the night, the police reached the cemetery just as a car sped past them through the gate. James jumped out and rushed to the freshly dug grave while the detective turned her car around to give chase. With only seconds to spare James clawed at the ground and rescued the terrified child; at the same moment the detective pulled up outside a house not far away and followed the driver inside. With her gun drawn she moved through the house but the driver was nowhere to be found. Then she noticed the door to the basement. Cautiously she pushed it ajar and descended the steps to a green door – the very same door James saw in his last vision of the abducted boy. There, on her knees scrubbing the cell where her last victim had been held was Molly Katz, mother of Eddie, oblivious to the presence of the policewoman, muttering in her madness how much trouble the little boy had been to keep and to feed.

## Forgiveness

During her interrogation it transpired that Molly Katz had learnt of her son's death from Richard Petrocelli, who had confessed to covering up the crime as part of his penance on the insistence of his priest. In the madness of her grief she had abducted boys in the belief that they would keep her Eddie company and had no sense of the suffering she had caused them or their families. As the police watched through the one-way mirror of the interrogation room James approached Molly and asked the boys to appear one last time and forgive her, freeing themselves in the process.

# CHAPTER FIVE

# THE UNINVITED POSSESSION

Before the advent of online auction houses such as eBay, amateur treasure-hunters had to scour out-of-the-way antique shops or sift through cobwebbed attics and basements full of other people's junk in the hope of unearthing a priceless painting or a valuable ornament that the current owner would hopefully part with for a small sum.

But now every bargain-hunter sees themself as an amateur antiques expert and every seller prices their bric-a-brac as if they were family heirlooms.

Some shrewd sellers have even come up with a novel method of getting an edge on their competitors in the potentially lucrative online auctions. They claim that their item, be it a doll, a painting or even a games console, is haunted. Many are clearly trying it on, or have their tongues firmly in their cheeks, but to read some of the descriptions and the earnestness with which the seller states their case one has to wonder.

Are the attics and basements of the US and Europe being emptied of genuine possessed possessions? And if so, does the legal term *caveat emptor* (let the buyer beware) now assume a new meaning?

Arguably the most fascinating and unsettling items on offer are the battered dolls and eerie paintings which must surely give even the most sceptical buyer cause to pause and wonder.

## PORTRAIT OF A KILLER?

In 2003 a Florida couple listed a macabre oil painting for sale on eBay entitled 'Stricken Life' which was said to have been the work of a wife murderer who later committed suicide. It was a portrait of an anguished-looking young man smartly dressed in shirt and tie with blood splatter to one side of the canvas and the spookiest part of the matter, say the owners, is that a second face can be seen in the blood and it's screaming!

On the reverse was attached an equally unsettling self-penned poem:

> SCRAPING THE SIDES, RUNNING THEN SLOWING TO A CRAWL-REAJUSTING (sic) THE PACE NUMEROUS TIMES REAPING AND SOWING THIS ROTTEN CROP. TRAFFIC SIGNS LEADING ME TO THE MESSIA (sic) OF RED LIGHTS. STRUCK BY A NOTION TO BURY THE LIVING AND SAVE THE DEAD. . .

Knowing that many would laugh into their laptops at such a loopy story the buyers added a lengthy description, explaining how the painting came to be in their possession and assuring potential bidders that they would provide a complete provenance with the work, 'including signed and NOTORIZED depositions by my wife and I, a local publication's account of the night of the murder-suicide, a copy of the release we had to sign before we could purchase the house, ALL pertinent names and information, as well as anything else we can come up with that pertains to this subject.'

They claim that it was one of the items left behind by the former owner of their new home, which they had purchased at a greatly reduced price because it was rumoured to be haunted. He was the son of a Cuban national who had lived in the house since the mid-1970s. The only other facts that they knew about him, or that they were prepared to divulge online, was that his name was Harold, he had been born in 1949 and he killed his bedridden wife with a shotgun after he had been diagnosed with brain cancer and would not be able to look after her. The sellers take up the story:

> Our initial thought was to get rid of the painting, but our teenage son thought it was 'cool'. So on the wall it went, along with an interesting story for our friends. Then the strange sounds in the night started. Always in the night, when it was the darkest. My wife and I were in the master bedroom. It was after midnight, and it was our third night in the new house. I had just dozed off when BOOOM!!! the explosive sound of a shotgun blast jerked me awake. SERIOUSLY. My heart about to explode out of my chest, I sat up in bed. My wife still slept. After securing the house, I came back to bed, thinking it was a dream. Several hours later I was awakened again by the most ungodly howling I had ever heard.

This was their dog. When the husband went to see what was troubling it he found the dog howling at the painting. Disturbed and unable to sleep, he took the painting down and locked it in a closet. Then a couple of nights later his wife woke screaming. She said she had seen a woman in a wheelchair at the end of the bed. But there was no sign of her when the husband finally rubbed the sleep out of his eyes. Then the electrical problems began.

Every bulb in a chandelier in their living room burst, the TV would turn itself on and a woman's voice could be heard calling from the master bedroom.

It was then that they decided to list the portrait on eBay, the only picture 'Harold' is thought to have painted. The whereabouts of the painting are not known and the successful bidder's name has never been disclosed, but the former owners should be getting a good night's sleep from now on.

## The Haunted Painting

Haunted paintings have been the subject of several traditional Victorian ghost stories in which the main protagonist becomes transfixed by a picture which appears to have a life of its own. Whenever the owner returns to admire his purchase he is convinced that the figures have moved. Such stories have become a cliché, so when buyers saw a painting advertised as haunted on online auction house eBay in February 2000, many must have thought it was a joke. But the anonymous owners, a couple from California, had the last laugh when it sold for over a thousand dollars. The question that remains unanswered though, is whether this was a genuine paranormal artefact, or merely a clever sales pitch. The picture depicted two children and, although there was very little remarkable in the subject or the manner in which it was painted, the seller claimed in their sales pitch that it possessed a distinctly singular quality.

> When we received this painting we thought it was really good art. A 'picker' had found it abandoned behind an old brewery. At the time we wondered a little why a seemingly fine painting would be discarded like that (today we don't!).
>
> One morning our 4-year-old daughter claimed that the children in the picture were fighting and coming into the room at night. Now, I don't believe in UFOs or in Elvis being alive, but my husband was alarmed. To my amusement he set up a motion-triggered camera for the night.
>
> After three nights there were pictures. After seeing the boy seemingly exiting the painting under threat we decided that the painting had to go.

The only clue to the origin of the mysterious picture, which is thought to date from the mid-1960s to the mid-1970s, are the words *The Hands That Resist Him* inscribed in pencil across the back.

The Hands That Resist Him, *a disquieting title for an unsettling painting*

The sellers felt it necessary to add a disclaimer, either to indemnify themselves against possible future litigation in the event of supernatural phenomena or perhaps to make it more appealing.

> By bidding on this painting you agree to release the owners of all liability in relation to the sale or any events happening after the sale that might be contributed to this painting. This painting may or may not possess supernatural powers that could impact (on you) or change your life. However, by bidding, you agree to exclusively bid on the value of the artwork with disregard to the last two photos featured in this auction, and hold the owners harmless [sic] in regard to them and their impact, expressed or implied.

This was sufficient to encourage a flurry of inquiries which seems to have set the sellers on the defensive. Their response was:

> To deter questions in this direction, there are no ghosts in this world, no supernatural powers, this is just a painting and most of these things have an explanation, in this case probably a fluke light effect.
>
> I encourage you to bid on the artwork and consider the last two photographs as pure entertainment and please do not take them into consideration.

But several potential purchasers reported that the power of the painting extended to their own computers after viewing it online.

'Seven emails reported strange or irregular events taking place when viewing this image,' the seller reported after the sale had closed, 'and I will relay two suggestions made by the senders. First, not to use this image as the background on [your] screen and second, not to display this image around juveniles or children.'

So who paid more than a thousand dollars for an otherwise

unremarkable painting? Who else but a shrewd art dealer who knew a good investment when he saw one.

There is a postscript to this story. Following the sale the BBC became interested and managed to track down its artist, Bill Stoneham.

He explained how he came to create such an unsettling picture.

> When I painted *The Hands That Resist Him* in 1972 I lived in an old stage-coach station deep in the woods of the Matilija surrounded by 600-year-old oak trees and a stream filled with ancient fossils. I used a family album photo of myself at age five in front of our Chicago, Illinois apartment. The hands are the 'other' lives. The glass door, the thin veil between waking and dreaming. The girl-doll is my imagined companion, the ally or guide of Joseph Campbell's *Hero's Journey*. Some of what I paint resonates in other people, opening their inner door, or basement.

## GHOST IN A BOTTLE

Without doubt the most unusual spooked item to be listed online has to be the 'ghost in a bottle' auctioned on eBay in December 2004 which a national newspaper claimed had aroused the interest of an agent representing the singer Michael Jackson. Whether Jackson put in the winning bid is not known as the buyer's identity was never revealed.

The bottle was the property of retired mill worker John McMenamin from Spamount, County Tyrone, Northern Ireland, who discovered it cemented into a bricked-up window of their reputedly haunted mill house, but held on to it for 25 years before deciding to cash in.

It was described as being at least a hundred years old and said to contain the imprisoned spirit of a ruthless landlord who had committed suicide after getting a young girl pregnant and then abandoning her to her fate. Angry locals then hounded him to his death. Apparently a local priest had failed to exorcize the ghost from the house, but had managed to force it into the bottle, presumably by promising the disembodied drunkard that stronger spirits awaited him in the bottom of the bottle.

Incredibly, the story caught the imagination of a Northern Irish radio presenter who tracked down and interviewed McMenamin's sister, Marie Maguire, who told the listeners that the bottle contains black dust and is sealed with a page of the Bible. She revealed that when her family moved into the house they knew it was haunted – indeed, that was why the previous occupants left. Maguire went on to describe childhood experiences, including 'waking up, screaming that somebody was looking at me in bed'. Her brother had reported something coming up the bed 'like a cat's paws'. She concluded by saying that the family wanted the purchaser to treat this 'genuine Irish ghost in a bottle with respect'.

## VOODOO DOLLS

There are now so many 'haunted dolls' for sale on eBay that they have their own listings category. Some dealers specialize in these novelties and curiosities which vary from battered, blank-eyed babies that would send any kiddie screaming to its mummy, to sweet old lady dolls designed to serve as surrogate grannies. Some sellers claim that they created their dolls to capture the spirit of a loved one or a friendly ghost which they now offer as house guests for those in need of companionship or protection. But even the cutest come with a warning that they are not to be given to children or people of a nervous and imaginative disposition. The following is typical of those on offer.

> Granny is extremely active and looking for a new home.
>
> My grandmother always collected dolls, and as a child I never knew why I wasn't allowed playing with her 'special' dolls, until they were given to me after her passing two years ago.

According to this seller her dolls become animated after dark, talking and laughing with each other, which the new owners might find unsettling if they are not prepared for it. She claims to have captured the secret life of the dolls on infrared video and EVP recordings (ethereal sounds beyond the range of the human ear). The pride of her collection contains the spirit of a 92-year-old widow named 'Granny' for whom she provides a biography. The old lady was said to be a kindly 'wise woman' who kept a garden to raise vegetables to feed the needy and herbs to cure ailments until she was cruelly murdered by an intruder.

After her death the seller's grandmother and an aunt who was a medium made the doll in the old lady's image right down to the moles on her face and a miniature copy of her wedding ring. Her clothes too were copied from those she had worn on the last day of her life. Revealingly, no mention is made of the method by which the spirit was summoned and bound in the doll's body, but we do get a list of 'Granny's' likes and dislikes and of her nocturnal activities.

> I hear Granny at night rocking back and forth in her rocking chair, I have found her moved in different positions, sometimes it looks like she is trying to stand, but can't get up by herself. I have seen her as a full-bodied apparition. She looks through my kitchen cabinets, moving dishes around and moving things in one place to another. . . I have heard her humming and whistling, she starts about 1:00 am and can go for hours sometimes.
>
> I have found Granny in different rooms from which I put her, and moved from one place to another. Sometimes the look on her face turns from a smile to a frown. I have tried to do EVPs on Granny, but it seems to mess up the tape in the recorder. I don't think she cares too much for modern conveniences. Granny is a LOVING lady, who wants a family to look after. She loves children and animals. She needs a good home, where she can stay and be needed and loved, for the wonderful woman she is.
>
> If you feel a strong connection or bond to Granny then please bid, you could be the one destined to watch over her. Let her help you and watch over you as well. Please Remember:
>
> Do not let anyone touch Granny until she is used to you and her new home!

The seller shrewdly adds a warning intended for those who might demand their money back if the dolls don't perform on command.

> My dolls are not 'evil'. Some have more attitude than others, they have their own unique personality because they were all living, breathing individuals at one time or another.

It is evident from the buyers' responses that they entered into the spirit (sic) of the sale and treat the dolls as nothing more than new age novelties. One buyer wrote of a doll she had bought called Teena:

> It turns out she is quite a little talker. . . she calls us mom and dad. It's really cute. . . We found out there is another spirit in our home that she does not like. She gave us his name and everything. We thought there might have been another one there but we didn't know for sure. . . she's going to help us try to get rid of him. . . and oh, she scares the dog a lot.

Others wrote to tell of doors which locked by themselves, computer breakdowns, lights switching on and off and of fleeting sightings of the spirit leaving its host!

## THE DIBBUK BOX

The whole subject of 'haunted' possessions invites a healthy dose of scepticism, but it is worth noting that one item has attracted so much attention that it has become the subject of a website devoted to uncovering its mysterious origins.

In September 2001 it is claimed that among the items included in a house clearance sale in Portland, Oregon was a box containing an evil spirit known in Jewish mythology as a 'Dibbuk'. The former owner was said to be an elderly Jewish immigrant who had been the sole surviving member of her family to be liberated from a Nazi concentration camp in Poland. With no reason or desire to remain in her own country after the war she emigrated to America with her only remaining possessions

*The box could have had perfectly innocent origins, but it seemed to cause serious problems wherever it ended up*

– a small trunk, a sewing case and the Dibbuk box.

It was her granddaughter who had organized the sale and who related the story of the cabinet to a prospective buyer. She confided that the old lady had kept it locked and out of the reach of curious children. When asked what it contained she would spit three times through her fingers and mumble something about a 'Dibbuk' and 'keselim'; the granddaughter was unfamiliar with both words.

Her dying wish was that the box should be buried with her, but orthodox Jewish tradition forbade that, so it was included in the sale.

It was listed as an antique wooden wine cabinet, although one of its subsequent owners has speculated that it was too small to contain wine bottles and glasses would not fit in the rack. However, it may have had a perfectly innocent origin as a liquor cabinet in which could be stored a decanter, shot glasses and tumblers. Or it may have been a container for sacred religious scrolls such as would be needed by a persecuted people who could not worship openly at a synagogue. Inside were two pennies dated 1928 and 1925, two locks of hair bound with string (one fair and one dark), a small statuette engraved with the Hebrew word SHALOM (peace), one dried rosebud, a golden wine cup and a black cast-iron candlestick holder with octopus legs.

The buyer stored it in the basement of his furniture store where he intended to refurbish it as soon as he found some free time. But before he could do so, he became uncomfortable in its presence and decided to sell it on. Apparently, all nine bulbs in the basement had burst and ten fluorescent strip lights, each four feet long, had blown simultaneously. His female assistant had been reduced to a gibbering wreck by 'something' that she had seen and which had locked her in while he had been away. She refused to return to work.

Two weeks later he examined the box more closely prior to working on it and discovered an inscription on the back which he later learned was a Jewish prayer of consecration and protection.

When he presented his mother with the refurbished cabinet as a birthday present she seemed pleased, but within minutes he claims she suffered a stroke which left her partially paralysed. The only means she had of communicating was to write shakily and the message she scrawled was anything but reassuring: 'H-A-T-E-G-I-F-T'.

It was sold this time through eBay to a young man who began to suffer recurring nightmares of being attacked by an old hag. When he gave it to his sister and brother-in-law they returned it complaining of having a strikingly similar dream. The young man in turn sold it to a middle-aged couple who left it on his doorstep soon after without asking for their money back.

Bad luck seemed to plague him from that day on. The lease on his store was terminated without explanation and all the fish in his aquarium died for no apparent reason. While researching the legend of the Dibbuk he fell asleep at his computer and awoke to feel something breathing down his neck. He then watched incredulously as a hulking shadow lurched down the hall.

That did it. The box was back online and bought by a college student in Missouri who was made aware of its unhealthy reputation, but who bought it none the less. Within days he was keeping a journal detailing the uncanny events.

> *Sunday, 31 August 2003* Over the last week some interesting, though possibly coincidental, items of note have come up. Firstly, I share a house with six other people; we have been taking turns sleeping with the box in each of our rooms.
>
> Two people are now complaining of burning eyes, one is listless and depleted of energy, and another became spontaneously sick. [In retrospect I would say it was allergies.]
>
> A few days after these ongoing annoyances started, the air outside our house was filled with small bugs for several hours (a Friday). [Weird summer stuff?] Last night (Saturday) we discovered that the box, now located in the back corner of the house, had come mostly open, though it had been shut and it seems unlikely that anyone could or would have touched it.
>
> *Wednesday, 10 September 2003* Though it seems impossible to prove that the box is a direct cause of misfortune, we have definitely seen a tidal wave of bad luck. Strange odors now permeate the house, the dumpster out back overflows with trash and decay, one roommate suddenly got bronchitis, and I broke a finger. Several mice have died in the engine of one car, and more electronic devices seem to be dying every day: xbox, toaster, t.v., and watches.

Within months he had re-listed it for sale adding:

> I don't really want to talk about anything between September and January, so I'll just say that I'm selling the box now for a couple of reasons:
>
> Around October 6th, I started feeling bad, with trouble sleeping. This problem has persisted through today.
>
> I live alone now, and as of late I have noticed I have been

replacing a lot of burnt-out lightbulbs, and getting many unusual car repairs (transmission fluid was burned out of the reservoir). I've started seeing things, sort of like large vertical dark blurs in my peripheral vision. I smell something like juniper bushes or stingy ammonia in my garage often, and I have no idea what from.

Most disturbingly, last Tuesday (1-27-2004), my hair began to fall out. Today (Friday) it's about half gone. I'm in my early twenties, and I just got a clean blood test back from the doctor's. Maybe it's stress-related, I don't know.

Anyhow, for personal reasons I very strongly do not want this box anymore. I hope there's someone on eBay that will take this thing off of my hands. [I would just throw it away in the woods or something, but I know there has been some interest in it in the past.]

## The History of the Box

The previous owner hadn't simply destroyed it either for fear that by doing so he would free the evil within or because he sensed there was something to be gained from passing it on.

In February 2004 the box was acquired for $280 by its present owner who made great efforts to learn its history. This is what he claims to have discovered:

The box had been used in séances by the Jewish lady who had emigrated from Poland.

In November 1938 she and her friends had come to the realization that their harmless parlour game had succeeded in establishing contact with a malevolent entity which desired entry for itself and other evil spirits into our world.

It would not let the group rest until they had acceded to its demands, so they planned to invoke it one last time and trap it in the box by means of certain spells and incantations.

The artefacts such as the braids of hair and the pennies were part of the charms that would bind it in the box. But the ritual did not go according to plan and although the entity was eventually subdued it managed to reap destruction on a scale unprecedented until that time. 10 November 1938 was the night the Nazis unleashed *Kristallnacht* (the night of broken glass) when their thugs burnt synagogues throughout Germany and smashed the windows of Jewish-owned shops and businesses.

The whole episode has echoes of *Raiders of the Lost Ark* and *The Spear of Destiny* with a touch of H.P. Lovecraft thrown in and it is highly suspicious that the silver-plated wine cup it contains was made by the Leonard Company whose factory was in Oregon, the town in which the Dibbuk box was purchased.

*The box may have been connected with a Jewish lady who emigrated from Poland around the time of* Kristallnacht *(the night of broken glass)*

The real significance of these haunted items is the speed with which such stories are replacing traditional ghost stories and urban legends for a new generation.

## GHOST IN THE MACHINE

But who can safely scoff and say that the next time their computer crashes while they are online it isn't because they have inadvertently downloaded a cyber spook? Be very careful the next time you curse your computer – you may be invoking an evil spirit!

We have all damned our computers when they freeze up or crash losing valuable data, but we don't seriously believe that our PCs are possessed. But there are frustrated users who would swear on a stack of Bibles that their hard drive is haunted.

Down south in God's own country, Savannah, Georgia, the Reverend Jim Peasboro regularly takes to his pulpit to preach against that spawn of Satan, the World Wide Web. He warns of how computers have 'opened yet another door through which Lucifer and his minions can enter and corrupt men's souls'.

Peasboro contends that PCs have enough storage capacity to house evil spirits, and that members of his congregation have come into contact with a 'dark force' when they have used their computers.

He tells of how happily married men have been drawn to pornographic websites and 'forced to witness unspeakable abominations'.

Some might argue that it is not Satan who forces these men to explore their dark side but human nature, and that Satan is merely a convenient excuse for them to absolve themselves of the responsibility for their actions.

But it's not only men apparently who have been tempted off the straight and narrow, from the path of righteousness. According to the minister, even God-fearing Christian women felt compelled to visit online chat rooms which have turned them from desperate housewives into foul-mouthed, fornicating sinners.

The minister tells of how one woman wept as she confessed to a feeling of being 'taken over' when online. In this particular case the crusading preacher took it upon himself to fight the good fight.

He visited the woman's house, where the computer 'talked to and openly mocked' him. It even typed by itself, calling Peasboro a 'weakling' and told him that 'your God is a damn liar'.

Then without being instructed it spewed out pages of doggerel, an experience that most of us will be familiar with. But the minister is adamant this was not a simple malfunction. He claimed to have had an expert in dead languages examine the text. The expert asserted it to be a 'stream of obscenities written in a 2,800-year-old Mesopotamian dialect'!

Reverend Peasboro is also confident that many school shootings like the tragedy at Columbine were perpetrated by computer buffs, having 'no doubt that computer demons exerted an influence on them'.

So what is to be done about this invasion? Is exorcism the only answer? According to the Reverend Peasboro there is a less drastic solution.

'Technicians can replace the hard drive and reinstall the software,' he says with confidence, 'getting rid of the wicked spirit permanently.'

Amen to that.

## PHANTOM PHONE CALLS

If it is true that ghosts are merely the discarnate spirits of the living and that they possess the same personality that they had in life, then it is to be expected that the recently deceased would try to communicate with us using the telephone or even email rather than by table-rapping and ectoplasmic manifestations favoured by Victorian spooks.

Julia K's 5-year-old son had shown no interest in the family phone until one day when he stopped playing to answer it. Only it wasn't ringing. At least his mother couldn't hear anything. The child picked up the receiver and entered into a lively conversation, then paused to pass the receiver to his mother who was in the kitchen preparing dinner.

'Who is it?' she asked him, wondering if it could have rung while she was too distracted to hear it.

'Grandmom,' he answered.

'What does she want?'

'She wants to talk to you. She wants to say goodbye.'

His mother took the phone, and anxiously put it to her ear, but she heard nothing. She was relieved and uneasy at the same time. Her mother had died five years earlier and she had never talked about the old lady to her son because she felt he was too young to understand about death. He had not even mentioned her name until that moment.

There was no mistaking the voice on the other end of the line which woke 'Michelle' one Sunday morning. It was her father who she describes as having a great bear of a voice like the actor James Earl Jones who lent his voice to Darth Vader in the *Star Wars* films. She was recovering from surgery at the time and he began by asking how she was feeling. He also inquired whether she had heard of the death of two people they knew, but she hadn't. At least, not yet. Before he hung up he assured her that life would improve for her and told her that she was not to allow the illness to sap her strength or her spirits. 'When I hung up the phone, it was as if I stepped from another level back into this one,' she later wrote. The call had occurred on 13 September – the second anniversary of his death.

## COLD CALLING

The following incident sounds like an urban legend, but Terrie, the young lady who reported it to about.com, insists she experienced this herself while working as a temp for an American telemarketing firm.

Telemarketing calls are commonly made by a computer so the salespeople don't have to dial, but if and when the call is answered they have a scripted sales pitch taped to the desk which they are trained to run through before the caller has a chance to hang up. On this particular occasion an elderly man answered and listened patiently while Terrie went through her prepared speech. When she had finished he asked her how much it was going to cost because he and his wife were on social security and had to be careful what they spent.

But as soon as Terrie started to explain she was interrupted by an old woman who called out 'Hello?' Terrie explained that she was talking to Mr Smith to which the woman replied, 'Miss, I'm sorry, Mr Smith has been gone for three years now. He passed away.'

Unperturbed, Terrie asked, 'Is there someone else there I could have been talking to?' to which the old lady replied, 'No, honey. I'm here by myself. Can I help you with something?'

Terrie must have looked as white as a sheet when she hung up because the following day her supervisor pulled the call logs and dialled the number in case an intruder had answered the phone. But the old woman assured the supervisor that she was alone in the house and she was well.

In fact, it took some time before she was convinced that the salespeople weren't pulling her leg about the old man.

## PHANTOM FORERUNNERS

Not all spooky phone calls come from the spirit world. An American visitor to the about.com website, who gave her name only as Barbara, described a phone conversation that made her wonder if she had received a call from the 'twilight zone'.

She was awoken at 4.20 one morning by a call from her brother. He was ringing at that unnatural hour because he was bursting with good news and wanted her to be the first to know he had just got married. The call lasted about five minutes and was overheard by Barbara's husband who had also been woken by it. A week or so later Barbara met her brother and his new bride at their mother's house and during the conversation she mentioned the phone call. Her brother looked shocked. He insisted he hadn't called her and then asked her what he was supposed to have said. When she finished both the brother and mother confirmed that those were almost the exact words that had passed between them when he had rung the mother at exactly 4.20 am.

Phantom forerunners, which precede the real person on a journey, are a well-documented phenomenon, but phantom forerunner phone calls are a rarity. The following was posted on about.com by a lady wishing to be known only as Cian B.

Cian was driving home from work one Tuesday night with her mother when she casually asked how her father was coping with his Tuesday evening computer course. Cian had talked to him on the phone earlier that day when he had called to say he was having trouble with the second assignment (out of three!) because his computer had malfunctioned. Later that night her father asked her how she knew about his problem and she reminded him they had discussed it on the phone just a few hours earlier. He denied it. She must have been mistaken. What he couldn't understand was how his daughter knew about this before he had left for that evening's class. Even he couldn't have known in advance that he was going to be given three assignments as he had missed the previous week's lesson.

# POLTERGEISTS

The word poltergeist derives from the German name for a 'noisy ghost', but there is compelling evidence to suggest that in many cases the 'victims' are unconsciously practising a form of psychokinesis, in which an excess of unchannelled mental energy is discharged into the atmosphere affecting electrical equipment and even moving small objects.

That, of course, leaves a number of incidents for which there can be little doubt that a malevolent entity was responsible for the often violent assaults and other disturbing phenomena.

> I think a Person who is thus terrified with the Imagination of Ghosts and Spectres much more reasonable, than one who contrary to the Reports of all Historians sacred and profane, ancient and modern, and to the Traditions of all Nations, thinks the Appearance of Spirits fabulous and groundless.
>
> Joseph Addison, *The Spectator*, 1711

## THE ROSENHEIM CASE

In one of the most remarkable incidents of poltergeist activity on record the disturbances were attributed to an 18-year-old girl whose neurotic disposition is thought to have triggered what amounted to a psychic temper tantrum.

In November 1967 Sigmund Adam, a Munich solicitor, was becoming concerned about a number of electrical faults in his office which were threatening to disrupt his business. He was having to buy new fluorescent strip lights every few days when they should have lasted months and the electric meter had registered inexplicable surges of current which also added to his bill.

The electricians he called in were baffled. During tests their voltmeters registered 3 volts when connected to a 1.5 volt battery which indicated that there was another source of power leaking into the atmosphere. Such a thing was simply impossible. On Adam's insistence the lighting company installed a generator in case the fault was in the power lines and they advised Adam to use bulbs in place of the strip lights. But the power surges continued and the bulbs blew with monotonous regularity. The generator was replaced, but the problems persisted. Then other phenomena began to occur. The next telephone bill that Adam received listed dozens of calls every day to the speaking clock. None of the staff admitted to making the calls and besides, the speaking clock was being dialled up to six times a minute which was

*Munich solicitor Sigmund Adam was becoming concerned about the number of electrical faults in his office*

impossible as it took at least 17 seconds to dial the number and be put through. Before Adam could figure that one out, the office was besieged by more 'conventional' poltergeist activity. On several occasions a heavy filing cabinet moved of its own accord and pictures spun on the wall as if turned by unseen hands.

Rumours of the disturbances attracted the attention of the national newspapers and as a result of the publicity Professor Hans Bender of the Institute of Paranormal Research at Freiburg offered to investigate. Bender soon discovered that the disturbances only occurred when clerk Ann-Marie Schaberl was present. He also learnt that the ceiling lights were seen to swing whenever she walked underneath them. But the most remarkable aspect of the case concerned the calls to the speaking clock. Under questioning, Ann-Marie admitted that she had watched the clock obsessively as she was so bored with the work she had been given. It was Bender's contention that she was unconsciously generating psychokinetic energy to an abnormal degree due to her frustration and, as if to prove his theory, the activity abruptly ceased when she left the office to undergo a series of tests at the institute.

Bender concluded that Ann-Marie's intense, neurotic personality had manifested in certain paranormal phenomena and he wondered if it meant that she might possess other psychic abilities which could be scrutinized under laboratory conditions. In the initial tests she showed no signs of such talents, but after the professor raised the subject of a traumatic illness she had suffered for a whole year her scores increased dramatically.

When she returned to Adam's office the activity resumed, forcing him to dispense with her services. Similar disturbances occurred at her next two jobs with apparently tragic consequences. Ann-Marie was blamed for a colleague's death by the other members of staff, although there was no evidence to support their suspicions and she was forced to move on. Things deteriorated further when her fiancé broke off their engagement, complaining that every time he took her bowling the electronic scoring system would malfunction. It was only after she met and married another man and settled down to raise a family that the phenomena ceased and Ann-Marie was left in peace.

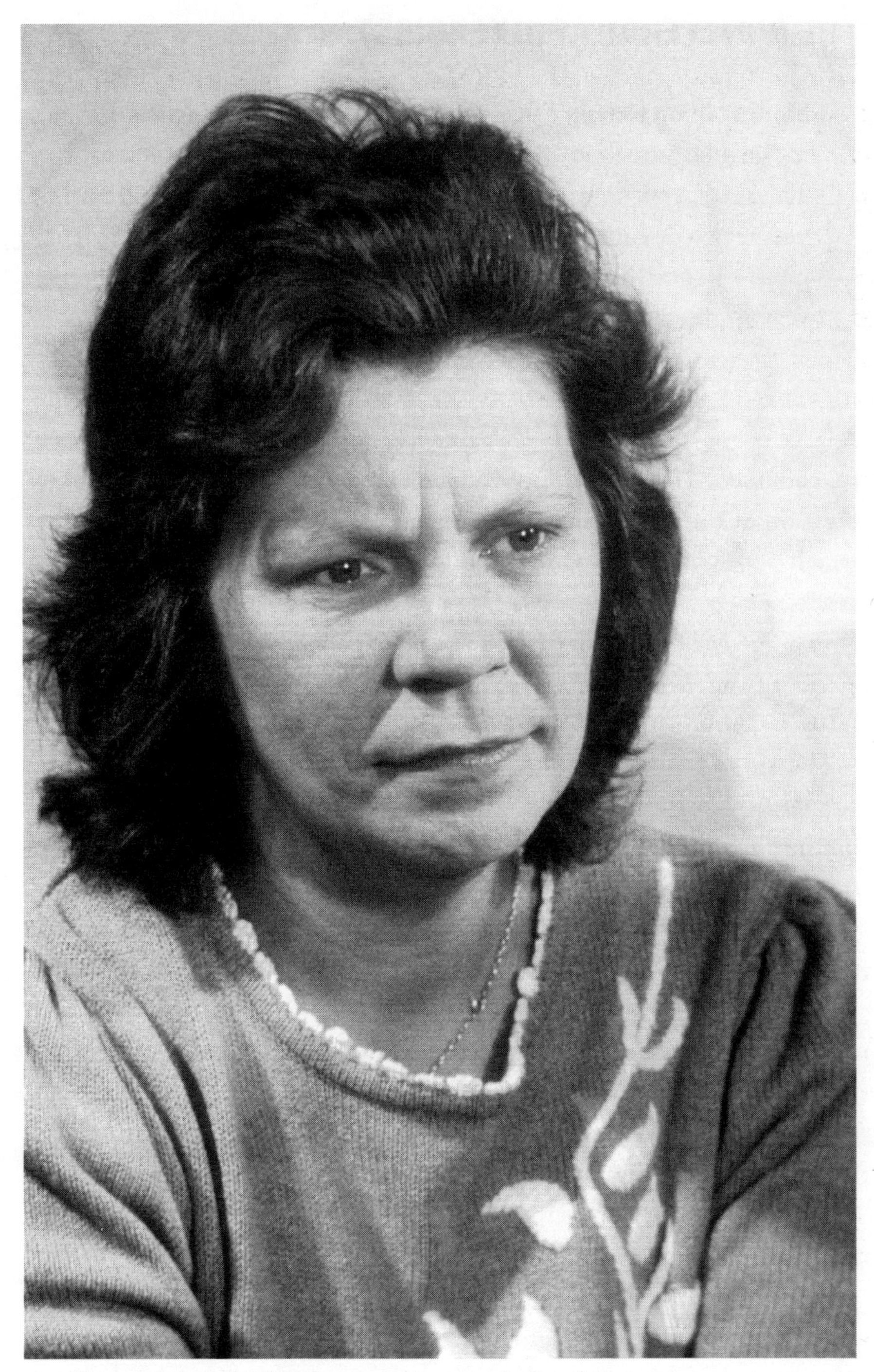

*Ann-Marie Schaberl: the disturbances only occurred when she was present*

## THE PONTEFRACT POLTERGEIST

> Stones fall on to your kitchen floor, as if they had come through the ceiling. Somebody, or something, starts banging on the wall. Things disappear, and reappear somewhere else. Before long, you realize it can't be an earthquake, or Concorde, or mice. It must be something else – something entirely inexplicable and very frightening indeed.
>
> Guy Lyon Playfair, *This House is Haunted*, 1980

A large proportion of poltergeist activity may be attributable to surges of psychokinetic energy and in rare incidents, possibly to the unconscious creation of thought forms, but there are several well-documented cases which appear to offer compelling proof of the presence of malevolent spirits.

In 1966 the Pritchards of Pontefract, Yorkshire were a typical middle-class British family. Mr Pritchard had a good, steady job which allowed his wife Jean to stay at home to look after their two children, 14-year-old Diane and 5-year-old Philip. But their safe suburban life was soon to be violently disrupted. It began innocuously enough with pools of water on the kitchen floor. What puzzled the Pritchards was the fact that there were no splash marks. But as both the children furiously denied having played a prank there was nothing for them to do but mop up and shrug their shoulders. They weren't aware at the time that the unexplained appearance of water on walls and floors is a characteristic feature of a poltergeist attack. But they were soon to get a crash course on the subject of the paranormal.

When more pools appeared the water board inspectors were called in but they could find no trace of a leak. The following days saw more minor phenomena, but before they could be investigated seriously they ceased and the Pritchards went back to normal. They had two years of normality before the phenomena returned, this time centring on Diane.

Loud reports accompanied the smashing of crockery and other ornaments. So loud were these noises that neighbours would gather outside the house and wonder if the normally placid couple were having an all-out domestic spat.

Yorkshire people pride themselves on their down-to-earth, commonsense attitude to whatever unpleasant surprises life throws at them, but even the tightly knit community to which the Pritchards belonged was beginning to talk of poltergeists. The children told their friends that Diane had been dragged out of bed by unseen hands and the parents confided to the neighbours that she had been pinned to the floor on several occasions by falling furniture which took both of them to lift off her.

Curiously, despite the damage it caused, all this activity never actually hurt anyone. Even Diane emerged uninjured from the attacks. Only at the end did the spirit turn nasty, dragging Diane up the stairs in full view of her father, mother and brother who tackled the unseen entity, forcing it to loosen its grip on her throat. But in case anyone thought this was the girl's attempt to get attention she was able to show them a set of angry red fingermarks on her neck. And Diane's mother confirmed her story, adding that she had seen large footprints at the bottom of the stairs that day and that the carpet had been soaking wet.

The poltergeist was evidently not content with being a nuisance. Soon after the attack on Diane it decided to scare the family to death by manifesting in the form of a hooded monk. Mr and Mrs Pritchard described seeing a spectral figure in the night framed in an open doorway and several independent witnesses saw shadowy glimpses of what appeared to be a hooded figure in black elsewhere in the house. On one occasion a neighbour claimed to have felt a distinctive presence behind her and when she turned around found herself confronting a tall hooded monk whose face was hidden by a cowl. An instant later it disappeared. The final sighting occurred one evening when Mr and Mrs Pritchard saw a tall silhouette darken the frosted glass of the dining room door. When they looked inside the room they saw a shadowy shape sink slowly into the floor. It was the last incident in the baffling Pontefract case.

Subsequent research has unearthed the fact that the Pritchard house had been built on the site of a gallows where a Cluniac monk

*When she turned she found herself confronting a tall hooded monk whose face was hidden by a cowl*

had been hanged for rape during the reign of Henry VIII.

In 1980 the writer Colin Wilson, an expert on the paranormal and an avowed sceptic on the subject of spirits, visited the Pritchard family and interviewed other witnesses including their neighbours.

Their testimonies, together with tape recordings of the violent banging noise and contemporary news reports, finally convinced Wilson that this was a genuine case of poltergeist activity by 'an independent entity'. He later wrote, 'The evidence points clearly in that direction and it would be simple dishonesty not to admit it.'

## THE PYROMANIAC POLTERGEIST

> The general character of the phenomena is nearly always the same, and it appears incredible that such coincidental happenings could possibly have taken place in all ages and in all parts of the world, had there not been some genuine manifestations behind these reports.
>
> H. Carrington,
> *The Story of the Poltergeist Down the Centuries*, 1953

The standard explanation for all poltergeist activity is that it is caused by displaced energy emitting from an emotionally volatile member of the household, usually an adolescent in the midst of puberty. But this cannot account for the life-threatening disturbances that plagued the Gallo family of Orland Hills, Chicago in the spring and summer of 1988.

It was Dina, one of the couple's two teenage daughters, who first became aware that there might be a phantom firebug in their home when she noticed a shower of sparks from an electrical outlet which quickly set a pair of curtains ablaze. She managed to smother the fire before it could take hold and then she called the fire department, but they failed to find a fault. The only clue Dina could offer was the fact that she had heard a strange popping sound seconds before the sparks appeared. The firemen could do little but sympathize with the family and compliment the girl on her alertness, but they were soon to realize that it had not been a freak accident. Something was seriously wrong in the Gallo residence.

Dina was not present at the second and more serious fire which began in an empty room and which inexplicably extinguished itself before the family could race to the scene, leaving scorched drapes, a blackened carpet and the room full of smoke. The next mysterious blaze began in an unoccupied upstairs room and consumed a desk and yet another set of curtains. This time the fire department were called in and undertook a thorough investigation. But again, they could find no logical explanation for the fire. Furthermore, there was an aspect to the blaze that even they could not explain. Why, they wondered, had several objects near to the source of the flames escaped scorching while the desk had not? By now they were seriously concerned for the welfare of the family who were becoming increasingly uneasy. In an effort to reassure them and get to the bottom of the mystery the fire department called in electrical engineers to check out the wiring and the outside cables in the belief that there might have been a periodic build-up of current. But nothing unusual could be found. It all seemed in order, except for the fact that even after the power had been cut off and all appliances had been pulled out, several sockets started to emit choking smoke.

It was clear that the entire wiring set-up would have to be ripped out and replaced. It was a costly and disruptive cure, but even this did not solve the problem. Now the new sockets emitted sparks. It was at this point that several members of the investigation team began to talk of seeing a white fog of sulphurous fumes which gave them throbbing headaches. But when they brought in sophisticated equipment to measure the levels of carbon monoxide and other poisonous fumes the meters failed to register gas of any kind.

Then on 7 April the sulphurous cloud appeared again, this time in plain sight of several family members who witnessed a long blue flame shooting out of one outlet and scorch marks appearing around others. The climax of this particular display was the spontaneous incineration of a mattress which was later inspected by experts who estimated that the heat which consumed it must have been in excess of 1,500 degrees Fahrenheit (816 degrees Celsius).

The Gallos were desperate and so too was their insurance company which had paid out on every claim and now faced the possibility that the next claim might be more than they could afford. Reluctantly they agreed to pay for the demolition of the house and the building of a new home from scratch.

Inevitably the story was picked up by the local media who repeated rumours that fire investigators had consulted psychics and that they had confirmed that the house had been built on the site of three unknown graves. There was also speculation centring on the Gallos' daughter Dina who, it was said, was always in close proximity to the fires, as it was a known fact that most poltergeist activity happened around adolescent girls and abruptly ceased when they grew out of puberty. It is true that in this case the phenomenon did die down after Dina grew out of her teens, but surely even the most emotional teen could not cause the appearance of two-feet-high flames and thick miasmas of sulphurous fog, not to mention intense conflagrations in excess of 1,500 degrees Fahrenheit. Insurance investigators are not renowned for their gullibility or their generosity, so it is safe to assume that they made a thorough study of the phenomenon and concluded that there was a genuine claim to settle.

## THE BOY WHO SAW GHOSTS

> Poltergeist phenomena are generally supposed by the sceptical to be the work of artful and mischievous children. . . But in many cases which seem to have been carefully observed and reported the physical effects are of a nature quite incompatible with child agency. A child may produce strange noises or throw an occasional stone, but the movement of heavy furniture, or the flinging of missiles which enter a room from outside when the child is in the room and actually under observation cannot be explained in that way.
>
> Herbert Thurston, *Ghosts and Poltergeists*

Most of us enjoy being frightened by tales of hauntings, possessions and poltergeists in the safety of a cinema, or while curled up in an armchair reading novels by authors such as Dean Koontz and Stephen King. But what is it like to experience these horrors for real? If the claims of Connecticut housewife and mother Denice Jones are to be believed any family can be caught up in these living nightmares.

Having survived an unrelenting assault by malevolent and spiteful spirits single-handed for several years, she was determined to set up a non-profit-making support group for families plagued by poltergeists and other terrifying phenomena, L.I.F.E. (Living In Fear Ends), which she says has helped numerous people in a similar situation.

Denice also documented her ordeal in a bestselling book, *The Other Side – The True Story Of The Boy Who Sees Ghosts* (New Horizon Press, 2000), in the hope that it would exorcize the fear and frustration her family had endured.

*The Other Side* reads like a classic case of poltergeist activity, but it appears that the focus of the phenomenon was not the family home but Denice's son Michael, who was five years old when the problems began.

'There were many incidents before we moved to that house,' she explains. 'My son was always afraid of the dark. But he was young and I assumed it was the normal scared of the dark syndrome.'

It appears that Michael had a troubled birth and it was touch and go whether he would survive. During those crucial first weeks of his life he was declared technically dead on more than one occasion. Denice thinks that he crossed over and returned so many times that when he came back he 'left a door open' to the next world.

## Family History

> Our family was not new to strange experiences. Both my parents have seen the dead in their homes, and my childhood home was haunted. My mother would have premonitions.
>
> For instance, one day while my parents were in bed, my mother woke up in a panic and told my dad to get dressed as his mother was coming because his dad had just had a heart attack.

My father told her to go to bed as she must be dreaming. So she started yelling at him and during this the knock came at the door and it was my grandmother with the news that his dad had suffered a heart attack.

My father sees spirits sometimes, but not all the time like Mike, though once he saw a woman's face at the side of his bed. He pinched himself to prove he wasn't dreaming and when he knew he was awake, he asked her not to hurt his family. She then disappeared. Shaken, he went downstairs to check out the house only to see the cabinets and refrigerator doors open and slam shut by themselves.

Perhaps it's not surprising that I was a fearful child and found it difficult to go to sleep at night for fear that there might be something in the dark. I frequently had the sense of being watched. In some sense I feel now I was being ready as a child for what was to come as an adult with my son. I know that sounds strange. But I do think that. I never knew, however, how serious it would become for my son and family.

I also had a few experiences later in life that shook me.

One time while driving I 'saw' myself hit a deer. I thought I was going crazy. I kept hearing a voice urging me to 'turn around' and I had flashes of this deer in my headlight, but I disregarded it as a hallucination brought on by stress or fatigue. I fought this for two miles. Then suddenly it happened just as I had foreseen it. I hit that deer. It was strange, if I had only listened to myself it would not have happened, but at the time I couldn't accept the possibility that this might be a genuine premonition.

Another time while I was washing dishes something came over me and I started screaming at my husband to get Kenny, my oldest son, as he was hurt. Kenny was outside playing at the time and nothing had happened. But just as my husband came back inside to reassure me Kenny let out a terrible scream. He had been throwing a pole around and it had landed on his foot. He was in agony and had to be rushed to hospital. This sort of thing happens very rarely, but when it does it freaks me out.

## Early Signs

Denice is convinced that her younger son Michael inherited this 'gift' as a direct result of his early brushes with death.

As soon as Michael was able to talk he would look at things that no one else could see. He'd ask who was upstairs talking when there was no one up there. I would brush them away I guess, hoping it would go away. When I remarried I didn't want to alarm my new husband, Bruce, so whenever Michael woke up screaming in the night I would tell him that Michael was afraid of the dark. It was partly true – he was scared of the dark, but he had good reason to be!

Bruce had two daughters and when one of them asked if she could move in with us we decided we had to move out of our small apartment and find a four-bedroom family house.

We couldn't believe it when we found what seemed to be the perfect place and for half the going rate. We thought we'd won the lottery.

I didn't have any bad feelings at all. I thought it was nice. The upstairs hall was a bit creepy as it was so long and it felt like it did not stop, but the house seemed ideal and came just at the right time. The other thing we all noticed was the number of rosaries in the rooms. There seemed to be one in almost every room which was odd. At first I thought it was a nice touch, like a blessing on the house, but later I suspected they might have been put there to protect the previous owners from something or maybe they were left by the previous owners to protect the new owners – us.

## The Old Man

The first indication that Bruce and Denice had that something was seriously wrong in the new house occurred one idyllic autumn afternoon shortly after they had moved in. Denice was working in the garden when she heard a piercing scream. Rushing up to Michael's room, she saw him cowering in the corner muttering something about an old man who had appeared from nowhere and touched him on the shoulder.

> I didn't think it might be a ghost at that time. It was around 4 pm, and ghosts only come out at night, or so I thought. Now I know they come at all hours. All I could think was who else might be in the house. I grabbed my son's metal toy truck and ran around the upstairs, my heart pumping, thinking I am going to have to beat someone with a metal truck! When I failed to find anyone in the house and seeing how scared my son still was, I held him and we talked about the man as calmly as we could under the circumstances. Michael said he was crayon-coloured white. And he said that the man had tried to touch his shoulder. Of course, there was no man in the house. I didn't know what to do. I was Catholic and my boys went to catechism. I believed in the other side, growing up in a haunted home and having parents who were different, but just because you believe in such things it doesn't mean you automatically attribute such incidents to apparitions. Who would want to believe that they're sharing their home with the spirits of dead people?
>
> That night I took my kids to my parents' home because I wanted to talk to my mom. While we were talking we heard a cry from the other room. Michael had seen a sculpture my father had made of his father and Michael had recognized the face as being that of the man who had appeared in his room.
>
> My father assured Mike that his great grandfather would never hurt him and that he was not to be afraid of him. Great grandfather was an angel who would look after him. This made

Michael feel a bit better, but I was very uneasy with the whole idea. Mike was seeing my dead grandfather. I did pray to my grandfather when Michael was born to look over him as I was close to my grandpa. And I gave Michael my grandfather's middle name so maybe Grandpa was watching. But now maybe he was watching over Mike because he needed protection.

## Talking to the Angels

It was nice that Mike was okay with this, except a few days later I heard Mike upstairs talking so I went upstairs and he was on his knees on the floor, looking up and chatting away. When I asked him who he was talking to he said they were his guardian angels. After that I took Mike to every doctor I could find from psychiatrists to neurologists, even eye doctors and so on. But none of them could find anything physically wrong so they suggested I consult a psychic.

He was being hit, scratched and choked in front of us, but by what or whom we couldn't tell. I didn't know what to do. But I knew it was important to record everything. I just wanted answers and I was desperate for help.

Sometimes Michael would lapse into a comatose-like state and had to be taken to hospital. He would appear to be asleep, but afterwards he could recall what we had been saying while we were watching him. The hospital called in the priest one time when they couldn't wake him. The priest prayed over Mike and he woke up. I was sure it was a spiritual condition, but you just never know as a parent and I was not sure what I wanted. Sometimes I would think a pill could cure him as if it was an illness. But no pill would or could cure Mike.

The whole experience alarmed me – Mike screaming every night because there was a woman in his room, or a man; someone on the stairs, a little boy running around, a man with a bandana standing in his doorway, his bed jumping up and down, him being scratched and blood coming from it as I sat next to him. He choked every time I put holy water or a cross on him while in those paralyzed states. But it wasn't just Mike who was the target of the phenomena. Our hair was being pulled by unseen entities, something would tug at our feet, objects were moving on their own in the house, things were disappearing never to be found, electrical outlets blew up when Mike walked past them and a black smoke or fog would hang over them.

What made my sceptical husband a true believer was when he and I were on the couch downstairs in the living room watching TV and we heard a banging on the ceiling and the kids screaming upstairs. We raced up to see Bruce's daughter and Mike's older brother Kenny standing in the doorway of Mike's room in a state of real fear watching Mike's bunk bed banging up and down on its own while Mike was hanging on to it for dear life. Bruce grabbed Mike and we all ran downstairs. We all slept together that night and we could hear things being smashed in Mike's room. When we got up Bruce opened Mike's door and all his toys were on the floor, many of them smashed to pieces. At that moment I knew we couldn't run. We had to fight. We all felt so alone and in our own little world. But that is what finally convinced my husband that we were dealing with something supernatural.

## Unseen Attackers

Denice says that the hardest part was not knowing what they were dealing with as they couldn't see who was hurting Michael. Their only defence at the time was to pray for him.

It was pretty scary when he was being choked as he would gasp for air and you could see his throat go in. I actually recorded this on tape because I knew people would find it hard to believe otherwise. And there was the time my mother was dragged out

> of bed by her feet by an unseen entity while trying to protect my son who was staying with her at the time. The ghost had followed him to her home miles away. It was then that I realized that it wasn't our house that was haunted, but rather that Michael was the focus of some malevolent beings.
>
> Another time, Michael was staying with my parents when something attacked him and my father stepped in and called on it to attack him instead. He regretted that. The next moment it leapt on him and pinned him to the floor. My dad had the impression it was a big beast like a lion. He was paralysed by the energy emanating out of this thing for a few minutes until it let him go. He was badly shaken and told me that he didn't know how Michael was able to survive such terrifying experiences.

The Jones family were evidently not the only people to be taunted by the entities in their home. On an occasion when Denice's sister and her children came to stay with them, Denice's young niece ran screaming from the bathroom. Something had turned the water full on in the hand basin and was laughing at her. The children and their mother refused to stay in the house a moment longer.

Then the growling began. It was an ominous, threatening sound which couldn't be traced to any specific spot. That's what made it so unnerving.

As the attacks on Michael intensified, leaving him in a paralysed state for anything between two and six hours, Denice was forced to take him out of school and educate him at home. Life for the whole family was becoming intolerable. The other children wouldn't go to the bathroom alone or take a shower without a parent being present. Whenever they wanted to fetch a drink or snack they would go in pairs. Even Denice was afraid to stay in the house alone when the children were at school and Bruce was at work.

She would sit in her car in the parking lot until it was time to collect the kids, or she would busy herself with chores around town.

## Inviting the Investigators

Eventually they turned to a team of paranormal investigators for help. The investigators captured EVP (electronic voice phenomena) and what Denice refers to as 'abnormalities' in several photographs that they took, but she felt they were more interested in using her story to promote themselves and notes wryly that they got themselves a speeding ticket on the way to a TV station. Eventually their relationship degenerated to the point where the Joneses brought in their lawyers to argue their claim over the rights to the material that had been collected and the potentially lucrative story which the investigators wanted to see in print. But Denice was grateful to them for bringing in the local Catholic bishop, who performed the first of several exorcisms which appeared to have reduced the severity of the attacks that Michael was suffering from at the time.

> Watching my son being hit, scratched and choked by unseen entities was as painful as watching a human hurting him, but with the added trauma of not knowing what it was or being able to pull them off. I had to fight back and the only way I knew how was through my faith.

## The Exorcist

> Initially I went to my church for help as I had put my kids through catechism there, but they refused to listen to me. I begged them to bless my home, but they told me they do not do that anymore. I felt like I had been slapped in the face. I was angry and upset. So, I wrote to the archdiocese, but received no answer. Then I called them and they told me it would be months before I heard from someone. I begged them to help. I told them it was urgent, that my son was being hurt and we cannot wait any longer. I told them I had medical reports and video evidence, but they were totally unsympathetic and I never heard from them again. Then I was told about a bishop

in Monroe. He asked for all the evidence we had and said he would help my son. But I would have to wait another three days after he had studied all the papers and video as he said Michael would need the exorcism in Latin and he would need to fast for three days to be in a state of grace for that to be effective. When we met I felt so sorry for him. The poor man was thin enough and looked like he could do with a decent meal.

He conducted the exorcism in an empty church. Michael sat at the front and was very quiet. He complained of feeling sick and the bishop gave him holy water to drink. He kept looking off to one side as if he could see something there. Later he told me that he had seen a shadowy figure laughing at him. I was very emotional during the ceremony although I didn't understand what was being said. It was all in Latin. There were no histrionics. No demonic voices or special effects like in the movies. It was very dignified and moving. I felt a great sense of love wash over me, but at one point I felt a cold breeze in my face and I caught the smell of roses. Afterwards Michael told me that he had felt the same chill and had also smelt the flowers and that he now felt that everything looked brighter than it had before.

When it was over the bishop said it may take more than one session and that I could call him at any time. He refused to take any money – even a donation. This sense of relief and of a weight being lifted from us only lasted a short time, then it all just went crazy again. Sensitive souls attract spirits and you can't pick and choose what comes in. Mike's psychic gifts made him a torch in the darkness.

## Every Home Has Its Spirits

Eventually the family were forced out of the house by the relentless poltergeist activity, but that didn't solve the matter.

Every home has its own spirits. Luckily those in the next house were not as mean as those in the first place, but nevertheless it was hard. We moved many times to flee the memories of what had occurred in those houses. But it wasn't until Mike was 16 that he came to the realization that he needed to live with them and even learn from them.

By this time we understood that it was Michael's sensitivity and abilities that attracted things to him, or awakened what was already there. A few weeks after we moved into our present home, Mike told me that there was an old lady with long gray hair bending over the counter by the microwave. He described the mother-in-law of the previous owner who I had seen in a photograph they'd left behind. This time Mike was not afraid. The spirits do not scare him anymore and because he has lost a lot of his fear, the negative entities have not been attracted to him and the number of worrying incidents has been dramatically reduced.

## Going Public

I concluded my interview with Denice by asking what prompted her to write the book and whether she regretted making her experiences public.

I had a lot of publicity before the book was published as the result of the investigators who wanted to make themselves famous from our story. I was on national TV shows such as *Primetime Live*, *Unsolved Mysteries* and so on. The next day I opened my door to see news cameras parked in my front yard so I slammed the door and within minutes the investigators were at my house asking why I wasn't co-operating.

They told me that the press was saying my son's exorcism was not sanctioned by the Roman Catholic Church. I had the bishop do it because I wouldn't wait for months as the Church wanted me to. They urged me to defend the bishop which I did. I refused to let anyone say what the bishop did was wrong. He helped my son when the Church refused to do so. And this is why I went to the media. But once the story was out, it was relentless. The intrusion into our lives just wouldn't stop.

The movie *The Sixth Sense* came out many months after I did the TV shows and newspaper interviews and I was told on many occasions by the journalists that they thought the film had been based on my son's experiences. It was such a similar story. When Michael saw that film he couldn't sit through it to the end though. It was too close to what he had been through. It was suggested that I do something about it through my attorneys, but I didn't publicize our story to make money. I did it to make people aware that they are not alone in this. Other families have shared our experiences and suffered as we have done simply because they have a son or daughter who is sensitive to the other side.

I did not enjoy the media attention. Some were nice, but others were aggressive, intrusive, cynical and mean. I received a lot of support from families of different faiths and I still receive letters of support in the mail from people. I try to answer all of them personally.

I don't mind sceptics at all. It is hard for anyone who has not been through a haunting to believe in such things and to fully understand what it is like.

There are many people who wish to see ghosts and experience all sorts of paranormal and psychic phenomena. What I'd say to them is, 'be careful what you wish for'. As far as the sceptics are concerned, if they went through a quarter of what we had experienced they would no longer be sceptics and I wouldn't wish that on anyone. So if they are still sceptical after reading our story, it only means they had not experienced the power of the paranormal. Isn't that a wonderful life? I wish I could say the same!

## THE PHANTOM PAINTER

Not all cases of possession are unpleasant or distressing. In 1905 Frederick Thompson, an undistinguished amateur English artist, began to paint remarkable pictures in the style of the celebrated Robert Swain Gifford who had recently died. The two artists had met briefly, but Thompson was not familiar with Gifford's work [see 'Trees and Meadow', below]. It was only when he visited an exhibition of Gifford's work that he saw the similarity between his new creations and that of the dead artist.

While studying one of Gifford's pictures Thompson heard a voice in his head urging him to continue his work. 'You see what I have done. Can you not take up and finish my work?' It was the same voice Thompson had been hearing for the past 18 months which had suggested the subjects he was to paint. Thompson feared he was going out of his mind, but the paintings were far more accomplished than he had previously been able to create and he was even able to sell some of them. In time these came to the attention of an art critic who remarked

on the fact that several of Thompson's works were uncannily similar to sketches Gifford had left unfinished at the time of his death. In time Gifford's influence waned, but Thompson retained his new-found skills and gradually gained the respect of the art world.

# EXORCISTS

If ghosts are either residual personal energy echoing in the ether or discarnate earthbound spirits and poltergeist phenomena can be attributable mainly to involuntary bursts of telekinetic energy, is there any compelling evidence for belief in the existence of evil spirits? Or are the cases of demonic possession a symptom of ingrained superstition and the misdiagnosis of serious personality disorders?

## DEMONS AND DEVILS

The date 11 December 1937 was as infamous as any in the history of warfare for it was the date of the atrocious massacre at Nanking. Hundreds of thousands of innocent Chinese civilians were butchered by invading Japanese troops who were running amok in the wake of the bombing that had razed the sprawling city of wooden buildings to the ground. It was a scene of hell on earth, but in the midst of the carnage and chaos the gates of the underworld were gaping wide for a real demon, a cannibalistic serial killer who had been tracked down to his hideout in a disused grain store. The police had surrounded the building and were determined to see justice done even though his murders seemed almost inconsequential compared to the mass slaughter taking place on the other side of the city.

But this was no ordinary criminal case. The police had been summoned to the scene by Father Michael Strong, the local parish priest who had sent word for them to delay the arrest while he conducted an exorcism. It was Father Michael's unshakable belief that the fugitive, Thomas Wu, had murdered and eaten his victims while possessed by a demon and he was going to drive it out if the authorities and the

*The infamous massacre of Nanking which took place in 1937, but it was not just the Japanese who were slaying citizens*

Japanese bombardment would give him just ten minutes to confront the real perpetrator of those atrocious crimes face to face.

When the police captain arrived on the scene he found Father Michael standing over the cowering naked figure of Thomas Wu, who brandished a knife in one hand. He was in a severely agitated state and looked like a cornered animal who might spring out of his lair at any moment. As the captain's eyes adjusted to the lamplight he caught a glimpse of a sight that must have haunted him to his dying day. Arranged around the walls on wide wooden shelves were the decaying corpses of dozens of Wu's victims. What kind of man could have perpetrated these atrocities? But it was not a man. It was a demon and he was about to reveal his true face, or faces, for the astonished onlookers.

'YOU!' screamed Wu in a voice both the captain and the priest did not recognize even though they had known him since he had been a boy. 'YOU want to know MY name!'

At this outburst Father Michael staggered backwards as if the force of the words had dealt him a body blow. Father Michael's exhortations in the name of Jesus had no effect on the grinning, slavering man who seemed to summon up inhuman reserves of strength to draw himself up to his full height and bellow like some wounded beast. 'Get out of here. Get the hell out of here, you filthy old eunuch!'

It took all of Father Michael's faith to remain upright and, his voice shaking with emotion, continue to demand that the unclean spirit depart.

Wu roared a string of expletives at the beleaguered priest which were suddenly cut short when the roof timbers caught alight. It must have been a stray incendiary, or perhaps it was the Devil's way of robbing the priest of his prey. The next instant the police captain had grabbed Father Michael and was pulling him from the burning building.

From just a few feet away they watched the flames consume the wooden grain store together with their quarry and the mutilated bodies of his victims. But Thomas Wu did not go quietly and neither did the spirit which possessed him. A face appeared at the window, a hideous, contorted face which Father Michael later described as having 'the thumbprint of Cain' upon it. From within they heard a hideous mocking laugh and then they witnessed a shocking sight. Wu's features dissolved and in its place a succession of faces appeared as if the demon's former hosts were being released in Wu's death agony. They were the half-remembered faces of Father Michael's nightmares. Others he thought he had seen in old churches. Some were male, some female. They were of every race and nationality, but they shared one characteristic. They were all evil. Then the window went black and the wooden structure collapsed in a sheet of flame and smoke. It was too much for the ageing priest. He clutched at his chest in agony and collapsed. But he lived to tell the tale.

Such a scene might sound like a script from a horror movie, but this event is said to be as true as the massacre of Nanking and not untypical of the confrontations experienced by real exorcists who claim to be fighting the good fight to this day.

(Source: *The Diaries of Father Strong* as reproduced in *Hostage to the Devil* by Father Malachi Martin)

## THE EXORCIST

Author Peter Blatty based his bestselling novel *The Exorcist* (which became the basis for the controversial film of the same name) on a real case of alleged demonic possession which had occurred in a suburb of Washington DC in the first four months of 1949. According to a report in the *Washington Post* that year, a 14-year-old boy by the name of Robbie Mannheim had exhibited classic symptoms of possession, specifically spontaneous body wounds, involuntary bouts of abusive language and a distinct change of personality after trying to communicate with the spirit world using a Ouija board. Doctors who examined Robbie could find no medical reason for his behaviour, or for the physical cuts. The best explanation they could offer was that he was suffering some form of mental breakdown because he could not accept the recent death of a favourite aunt. According to their theories his persistent denial might have produced a number of psychological disorders ranging from automatism (involuntary physical actions), obsessive-compulsive disorder (irrational fears or paranoia and possession) and even Gilles de la Tourette's syndrome (which produces physical and verbal tics, along with foul language). But such rational explanations did not satisfy the family, who brought in a Catholic priest in the belief that their son was possessed by a demon. How else could they explain the scratches on his chest which spelt out the words HELL and SPITE, or the fact that he taunted them in Latin – a language he had never studied?

While the boy writhed in his hospital bed the priest began the Roman Ritual of exorcism, but the struggle was cut short when the boy lashed out with a loosened bedspring, causing a deep gash down the priest's right arm that required more than a hundred stitches. Undaunted, another priest took his place and for 24 successive nights the two priests – Father Walter Halloran and Father William Bowdern – prayed at the boy's bedside. On the final night, Robbie opened his eyes and said calmly, 'He's gone.'

The Catholic Church has distanced itself in recent years from the practice of exorcism and no longer endorses it, while a 1972 Church of England report condemned the practice as 'extremely dubious'. In a notorious British murder case in 1974 in which a mentally unstable individual, Michael Taylor, killed his wife after being subjected to an all-night exorcism his lawyer criticized the group who had agreed to exorcize him by saying that they had fed 'neuroses to a neurotic'.

But despite such criticisms there are those who still believe that good and evil are constantly at war for the possession of our souls. Father Halloran, who took part in the Robbie Mannheim case, recalled a conversation he had with Father Bowdern at the time in which the latter observed, 'They will never say whether it was, or it wasn't [a genuine case], but you and I know it. We were there.'

## THE REAL EXORCIST

I do not fear Satan half so much as I fear those who fear him.
St Teresa of Avila

During his 16 years on the front line fighting crime in the South Bronx, New York City cop Ralph Sarchie has seen the darkest side of human nature, but he claims that tackling murderers, drug addicts and armed robbers is easy compared to the fiends he faces off duty. When Sergeant Sarchie hangs up his gun at the end of his shift he arms himself with what he believes to be the only effective defence against the forces of evil – a vial of holy water and a crucifix, for Sarchie is a real-life exorcist – and the Devil had better watch his step when this guy is on his tail. 'As devout Catholics we take Jesus' biblical injunction to "cast out demons in my name" literally,' he says with obvious pride.

### Exorcists at Work

Sarchie's colleagues at the 46th Precinct used to tease him unmercifully, but this latter day 'night stalker' has had the last laugh. His most dramatic 'cases' are now the basis of a bestseller, *Beware of the Night*,

*St Teresa of Avila: courage in the face of the Devil*

which reads like a hardboiled crime novel, but with demons cast in the role of the bad guys. The book has earned him a reputation as a courageous latter-day crusader among America's Christian right who believe the Devil is behind every evil act on earth, but it has brought condemnation from those who fear that in blaming society's ills on a mythical villain we are absolving ourselves of the responsibility for our own actions and risk being dragged back to the Dark Ages.

Sarchie's critics point out that while there is compelling anecdotal and photographic evidence for the existence of ghosts, no one outside a lunatic asylum has claimed to have seen the Devil since the Middle Ages. They cite the fact that publication of the book also contradicts Sarchie's own edict prohibiting anyone from discussing such experiences because to acknowledge the existence of a demon is to empower it, to which he replies that the public needs to be warned about the growing threat from the Devil and his disciples. He quotes Father James LeBar, one of four exorcists currently serving the Archdiocese of New York, who has stated that exorcisms increased from none in 1990 to 'over 300 hundred' by the turn of the millennium. Each year there are said to be between 800 and 1,300 authorized exorcisms around the world.

In an interview for the Christian network Enigma Radio in October

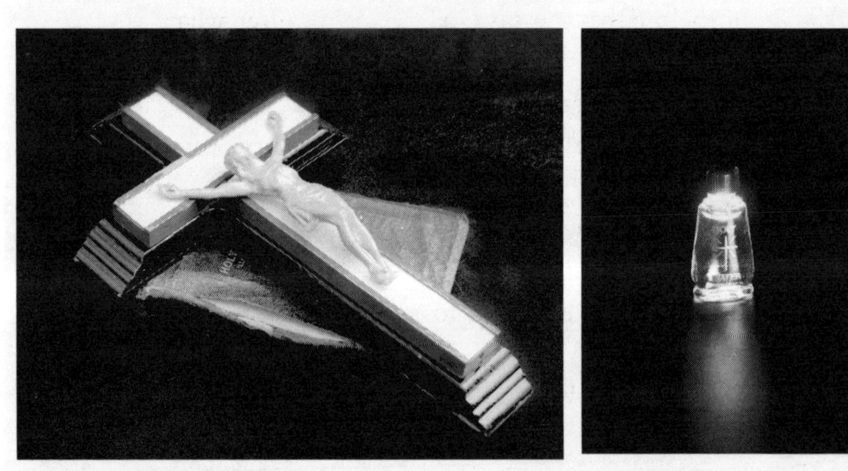

*Vital weapons against the forces of evil: a vial of holy water and a crucifix*

2005 he offered his theory as to why demonic possessions are on the increase. He believes that more people are 'dabbling in the occult' than ever before which makes them a target for roaming malevolent entities. The only defence, he says, is a strong religious faith and a diet of daily prayer. According to Sarchie, who describes himself as a devoutly religious man, the battle lines were drawn after the September 11 attacks and we are now entering the so-called 'end time' prophesied in the Bible when it will not be enough to sit on the fence and watch the apocalyptic struggle from the sidelines.

## Policemen of the Spiritual World

Sarchie claims to have assisted at more than 20 exorcisms where he acted as 'the muscle', restraining the possessed person while a Catholic priest performed the rite. But with his mentor Father Martin recently deceased, he is finding it increasingly difficult to persuade a member of the clergy to agree to perform an exorcism, a situation he sees as symptomatic of Satan's influence in the priesthood! Priests, he reasons, are the 'policemen of the spiritual world' and he points out that even Jesus performed exorcisms. He argues that Satan has got his hand in everything 'from politics to religion' and yet 'many priests and even bishops of the Catholic Church don't believe in the Devil'. Protestant clergy are no help either, he says, as they only offer what they call 'a deliverance' which involves praying to God to intervene in cases of poltergeist infestation or possession. Only Catholic priests are authorized to confront evil in person, so to speak, so Sarchie now offers to take on the heavies himself.

He denies the accusation that he is a self-righteous 'religious fanatic' and admits he is 'anything but holy', but he is deadly serious about his one-man mission which he refers to as 'the Work', to distinguish his calling from his career.

And he sincerely believes that his experience in interrogating killers and rapists has prepared him for the 'real struggle' with an adversary who is more sly and seductive than any conman he has ever confronted.

## Stages of Possession

It is Sarchie's understanding that the aim of the demonic is to create 'self-doubt and emotional turmoil which eats away at their prey's willpower paving the way for possession'.

The first stage of possession, he says, is obsession, which involves the individual brooding on irrational fears, indulging in aberrant behaviour, indulging in a morbid preoccupation with violent crime, or dabbling in the occult such as experimenting with Ouija boards.

> There ought to be a law against these evil, occult toys. I can hear some of you out there saying, 'Hey, I used a Ouija board and nothing happened.' Consider yourself lucky, then. It's like playing Russian roulette. When you put the gun to your head, if you don't hear a loud noise, you made it. Same thing with the board: The more times you pull the trigger, the more likely that on the next shot your entire world will go black.

Such obsessions, he says, aim to destroy a person's spirituality from the inside.

In Sarchie's supernatural scheme of things the second stage, 'oppression', will see the entity assault the senses with hideous animal shrieks, loud noises and other inexplicable phenomena, all of which are intended to unnerve them and break down their resistance like a city under siege. These attacks tend to occur at around 3 am when their victims are at their lowest ebb, the same time that most suicides take place.

> Not only do satanic powers often do things in threes, to show contempt for the Holy Trinity, but their terrorist strikes frequently occur at 3 am. This is another insult to God, whose Son Jesus Christ died on the cross at 3 pm. The demonic will do the opposite of anything holy, so they like to attack at exactly the opposite hour – with supernatural phenomena you might call miracles in reverse.

The third and final stage is full physical possession when the victim becomes subject to the greater will of the demon. The victim will appear normal until the entity is challenged to reveal its true nature during the exorcism, and then Sarchie says he can see 'it', meaning evil, in their eyes.

## Purification Through Fasting

In preparation for the rite an exorcist must fast for three days to purify himself, which means that he will not be in the best condition for what is often a long and exhausting struggle. Aside from the mental and emotional strain, he invariably has to subdue the possessed person who may have acquired exceptional physical strength, which also happens to be a phenomenon in cases of certain mental disorders.

One rite took two gruelling hours to cast out the 'unclean spirit' and left the muscular cop shaking and exhausted as if he'd been 'working out in the gym'. Such experiences do not appear to have dampened Sarchie's enthusiasm for the work or to have dented his conviction that 'God doesn't let people take on more than they can handle', which he offers as the only explanation for the fact that in a previous attack it had taken five people to hold the victim down, but miraculously he was able to do it alone on this occasion.

According to Sarchie demonic entities 'can level a house in a second. The amount of power even the lowest demon has is stunning', but they are subject to the limitations imposed on them by God who 'uses them to test us'.

So how do we combat this unseen threat?

> Direct confrontation is the only way. Otherwise it's just human Will against the demonic and we know where that can lead . . . I try to take myself out, so I say, 'You are commanded in the name of Jesus Christ' and not 'I command you'. We don't have the power over the demonic. It's all in God. We're being attacked all the time, but spiritually aware people know who is attacking them and are able to defend themselves despite their fear.

This self-appointed saviour clearly considers himself one of the 'spiritually aware' and believes he is able to distinguish between a ghost and one of Satan's soldiers.

Ghosts, he says, are the spirits of the deceased while demons were once angelic beings who have lost their supernatural graces, but not their powers. They range from violent brutes which grunt and growl like the beasts of the earth to those which attack using their intellect. It is Sarchie's assertion that a demon can't masquerade as a friendly spirit for long and must eventually reveal its true nature. At this point the victim will be too weak to help themselves so only an exorcist can compel the entity to depart. Sarchie's strategy is to bind it, meaning that he commands it not to interfere in a manner which sounds suspiciously like that practised by medieval magicians. Evidently the line between magic and religious ritual is a very fine one indeed.

'I don't want to see manifestations or phenomena,' he says. 'I don't want to smell things that will make me vomit and see things thrown around. Once I got a whiff as I was tying them down and vomited. I had fasted for three days before so I was dry heaving. Very unpleasant.'

He then breaks contact with the subject of the cleansing so as not to be drawn into a dialogue. From this point on he assumes that anything issuing from the mouth of the victim comes from the demon and so ignores any 'pitiful pleas for help'.

He also refuses to look into the eyes of the host for fear of being distracted from his task, claiming that the demon will interpret his gaze as a challenge. This may be a good tactic if the attack is genuine, but if the victim is suffering from any form of psychological disorder, ignoring their distress and avoiding eye contact while berating them for being possessed by an unclean spirit might be counterproductive to say the least.

## Demons and Stockholm Syndrome

Often the host will see the exorcist as a threat rather than as a rescuer – someone who is intending to cause them psychological and physical pain – and will vigorously resist all efforts to drive the demon from their body. It is Sarchie's belief that the parasitic nature of the entity can even create a psychological state similar to Stockholm Syndrome in which kidnap victims identify with their abductors, meaning that the victim may resent his interference. Of course, if the individual was suffering a psychological rather than a psychic disorder then their resentment and resistance will be more than justified.

A typical case will begin with a frantic phone call from a desperate spouse or family member claiming that their beloved husband, wife or child has undergone a drastic personality change. But Sarchie says he can only intervene when invited to do so by the person suffering from the alleged possession and obviously no demon worth the name is going to allow their host to do that, unless they're spoiling for a fight. However, permission isn't required if their home is the scene of what he calls an 'infestation', meaning that the possessed person has become the focus of demonic (i.e., poltergeist) activity and is likely to cause harm to himself or to other members of the family.

## The Halloween Exorcism

Of the 20 cases of alleged demonic possession that Sarchie has had to deal with he considers the most harrowing to be the one he faced on Halloween night in 1991. It began when his late partner, Joe Forrester, a polygraph examiner in the legal aid department, received a phone call from a Catholic priest in wealthy Westchester County, north of New York City. Joe, whose balding head framed with brown hair led to him being mistaken for a Benedictine monk, was no soft touch when it came to the supernatural. A former Vietnam veteran, he boasted what Sarchie called a 'built-in bullshit meter', meaning that he knew when he was being conned.

But Sarchie claims that this incident had all the hallmarks of a genuine case of demonic possession. A young suburban housewife and mother, Gabby Villanova, had been pestered by a sorrowful-sounding spirit by the name of Virginia who claimed to have been murdered on her wedding night and was seeking to be reunited with her family. Her fiancé had been falsely accused of the murder and had taken his own life while awaiting trial. When pressed by Gabby to name the guilty party the grieving spirit is said to have wailed, 'Must not say!' Evidently its strategy was to draw its intended victim in by spinning a tale of unrequited love as histrionic as a Victorian melodrama in the hope of eliciting sympathy.

Having ensured Gabby's attention, 'Virginia' then manifested in broad daylight while Gabby was alone in the basement. This is what she told her rescuer after the 'spirit' had been exorcized and she had recovered her composure:

> My attention was drawn to a large mirror we have hanging there. And in it I saw Virginia. Again she said, 'Parents, help.' Then she told me she had been in a finishing school abroad and had followed her parents here. In quaint old-fashioned speech she said, 'What manner of place is this?' On looking around the room and at me she asked, 'What manner of dress is this?' I answered, 'This is how we dress in the 1990s,' but she insisted that the year was 1901. I felt no fear of her, and we had a lengthy conversation.

The next time it literally took possession of Gabby against her will.

> I felt her presence and said, 'If you wish to speak do not enter me. I will relate whatever you say.' She paid no attention and immediately entered me. When she came into me her voice was stuttery and she kept saying, 'Parents, help.'

Sarchie notes that 'a demon has no respect for human pleas, requests or even orders for it to depart unless the command is made in the name of Jesus Christ'.

At the time Gabby was sharing her home with a middle-aged woman by the name of Ruth and Ruth's 25-year-old son Carl, who had become engaged to Gabby's daughter. Ruth was said to have 'witnessed' telepathic conversations between Gabby and 'Virginia', whose emotional outbursts were becoming more hysterical. Ruth, of course, only heard Gabby's side of the conversation. Nevertheless, she too was allegedly taken in by the heartbreaking story and wept at the sad and sorry tale.

In this particular case Sarchie considered the entity to be far more persuasive and subtle than any professional con artist that he had encountered in his career with the NYPD.

Sarchie says that Gabby's suspicions should have been aroused by the numerous coincidences between her own life and strikingly similar episodes in the spirit's life story.

But she allowed her maternal instincts to be exploited.

## Possession or Schizophrenia?

Sarchie's staunch Catholicism has clearly coloured his perception of definitions of good and evil, but he is adamant that he can differentiate between neurosis and a genuine case of possession.

According to Sarchie, the trouble with diagnosing a genuine case of possession is that demonic behaviour is virtually indistinguishable from many common mental and emotional disorders, so self-appointed exorcists must make their own on-the-spot psychological evaluations, which many are not qualified to do, or they must rely on 'secular psychiatrists' who don't believe in demons or the Devil.

This leaves the burden of proof with the exorcist, and his only criteria for deciding if a case is genuine or not appears to be the subject's aversion to religious artefacts, fits of foul language and an understandable reluctance to be physically restrained and subjected to being sprayed with holy water and hours of intensive prayer. It's a highly subjective diagnosis of behaviour which mental health professionals would say is far more likely to have a psychological rather than a supernatural explanation, specifically a condition known as undifferentiated schizophrenia. The symptoms of this particularly distressing disorder could all too easily be 'mistaken' for those associated with possession by someone with no medical knowledge as it includes periods of lucidity and the ineffective nature of drugs which are normally effective against schizophrenia.

In one case he investigated, an 8-year-old girl displayed no signs of aggression, but spoke in fluent Latin which Sarchie says he found deeply distressing, yet 'speaking in tongues' is considered to be a miraculous phenomenon by many in the Church.

### 'The Devil Won't Let You Go'

When asked what advice he would give to would-be exorcists he answers bluntly that his advice is not to do it unless you can see people suffering and still want to help them. 'It's not something that you can do for a short time then move on as the Devil won't let you go and if he can't get you he'll get at you through a loved one.'

However, if someone is determined to fight the good fight they should pray for guidance to ensure that the impulse comes from God and not from personal ambition. It shouldn't be simply to witness phenomena or 'to see someone's head spin round'.

His parting advice reminds us of one of the reassurances which crime show presenters on TV impart to their viewers at the end of each show.

## THE VENNUM CASE

Possession has decidedly negative connotations, but there have been incidents in which the uninvited spirit proved to have a benign purpose. In the summer of 1877, Mary Lurancy Vennum, a 13-year-old girl from Watseka, Illinois, suffered a series of convulsions, falling into a trance-like state for hours at a time. All efforts to awaken her failed.

While she was in this state she spoke of seeing angels and a brother and sister who had died some years earlier. Shortly after this, Lurancy was subdued by a succession of dominant personalities who spoke through her, including a crotchety old woman called Katrina Hogan. The family finally resigned themselves to having their daughter committed to an asylum, but then a neighbouring family named Roff intervened. They persuaded Lurancy's parents to consult a doctor from Wisconsin who had treated their own daughter, also with the name of Mary, in the months before she died. Mary Roff had suffered similar 'fits' in which she demonstrated clairvoyant abilities such as being able to read through

*'The next morning "Mary" calmly announced her intention of going "home" . . .'*

a blindfold. These episodes had been witnessed by several eminent and respectable citizens of Watseka who were prepared to swear to what they had seen.

When Dr Stevens visited the Vennum house on 1 February 1878, Katrina Hogan was in control. At first she was cold and aloof, gazing abstractedly into space and ordering Dr Stevens to leave her be whenever he attempted to come near. But his persistence paid off and by and by Dr Stevens was able to draw out 'Katrina's' personal history. Soon another personality appeared, a young man named Willie Canning whose hold on Lurancy was erratic and offered little of value that the doctor could verify. With the parents' permission Dr Stevens tried hypnosis and Lurancy reasserted herself but remained in a trance. She spoke of having been possessed by evil spirits, but that may have been her interpretation conditioned by her strict religious upbringing. Then events took an even more interesting turn.

Lurancy announced that she could see other spirits around her, one of whom was Mary Roff. Lurancy did not know Mary Roff, who had died when Lurancy was just a year old, nor had she visited the Roff home up to that point.

Mrs Roff was present when her 'Mary' came through, speaking through Lurancy, but there is no suggestion that Lurancy was faking to impress or ingratiate herself with the dead girl's mother. The next morning 'Mary' calmly announced her intention to go 'home' by which she meant the Roff household. This naturally created some embarrassment for Mr and Mrs Vennum who were reluctant to have their daughter 'adopted' by a neighbour, but in her present state of mind it could have been argued that Lurancy was no longer their daughter. On 11 February, after much soul searching the Vennums agreed to let their daughter have her way.

En route they passed the Roffs' old house where their daughter had died and 'Mary' insisted on being taken there, but she was eventually persuaded that it was no longer the family home. When she arrived at the new house she expressed delight at seeing her old piano and appeared to recognize the relatives who greeted her. Of course, none of this proves anything. Lurancy could have been shamming in order to secure attention. There was little risk in claiming to recognize the Roffs' previous home as in those days everyone knew their neighbours and the history of the town. As for the piano, it was a fair assumption that it would have been in the family for some years and presumably had occupied pride of place in the previous house.

But even the most cynical witnesses were astonished to hear 'Mary' greet her old Sunday School teacher using her maiden name which Lurancy could not have known. Intrigued, the family subjected 'Mary' to a barrage of probing personal questions relating to seemingly insignificant incidents in her childhood which even the most imaginative impostor could not have faked. She satisfied them on all counts. She even remembered details of a family holiday and could name the spot where her pet dog had died. Most remarkably of all, she recalled the exact words written many years earlier by a medium during a séance who claimed to be channelling Mary's spirit communications.

Over the following weeks she recognized personal items that she had owned which Mr and Mrs Roff left unobtrusively in the hope of them being identified, but 'Mary' did more than acknowledge them. She would snatch them up in delight and offer some minor detail related to the item that her parents could verify. Clearly this was something more than a remarkable performance. It was a phenomenon, a rare example of benign possession which was similar in many ways to recorded cases of reincarnation, except that Mary Roff died when Lurancy was a small child. It could not be explained as a multiple personality disorder since 'Mary Roff' evidently had intimate personal knowledge of the Roff family and her previous life.

On her arrival at the Roff house 'Mary' had predicted that she would be using Lurancy for three weeks after which she would return to the spirit world and allow Lurancy to continue with her life. She kept her word. On the morning of 21 May, 'Mary Roff' vacated the body of her host and Lurancy returned to her parents. She later married and lived a normal happy life, but from time to time Mr and Mrs Roff would pay a visit at which time their daughter would make an appearance to reassure them that all was well. In gratitude for being allowed to say goodbye to her family, the benign spirit even intervened during the birth of Lurancy's first child, putting her into a trance to alleviate the pain of childbirth.

## SOUL MUSIC

Not all cases of possession are as inconvenient for their host as the Mary Lurancy Vennum case, or as unpleasant as that portrayed in *The Exorcist*. The following is a case in point.

On New Year's Day 1970, the musicologist Sir Donald Tovey gave his expert opinion on the authenticity of certain compositions by Beethoven and Liszt which had reputedly been 'channelled' through London medium Mrs Rosemary Brown. He then took the opportunity to share his insights into why the world was now ready to receive these gifts from heaven.

> To understand himself fully [Man] should become aware of the fact that he does not consist merely of a temporary form which is doomed to age and die. He has an immortal soul which is housed in an immortal body and endowed with a mind that is independent of a physical brain. In communication through music and conversation, an organized group of musicians who have departed from your world are attempting to establish a precept for humanity; i.e. that physical death is a transition from one state of consciousness to another wherein one retains one's individuality. The realization of this fact should assist man to a greater insight into his own nature and potential superterrestrial activities.

This was profound and revealing stuff. The only problem was that Sir Donald Tovey had been dead for some years when he gave this 'lecture' through the auspices of Mrs Brown. Sceptics might say that it was extremely convenient that Mrs Brown was able to channel both the great composers and a respected music critic to verify their work, but there was no disputing the fact that the music was of a very high quality and that its complexity was way beyond Mrs Brown's humble talents. By all accounts she was a pianist of moderate ability and her knowledge of music was rudimentary at best. Yet for the last five years she had been taking dictation from Liszt, Beethoven, Chopin, Schubert, Brahms and Debussy at a speed she could barely keep up with and, according to a number of influential musicologists, in their distinctive style.

There was one problem, however, and this appears to be the key to the whole mystery. The music was 'first class' according to one critic, but it was not music of genius. If the great composers were active again on the other side, why then did they not produce masterworks rather than highly proficient imitations which any serious music student could conceivably have created to impress their professor? And why choose Mrs Brown? Admittedly she was a practising medium, but surely they would have attempted to commune with a serious musician who would have done their new compositions justice and with whom they would have had a greater empathy.

Although this appears to be a clear case of possession, there is a distinct possibility that it might be an example of split personality disorder, albeit a highly productive one. Word association tests carried out by researcher Whately Carrington in 1935 with the mediums Osborne Leonard and Eileen Garrett suggest that the 'controls' which mediums claim are the mediators between themselves and the spirits might actually be their own sub-personalities and that these sink back into the unconscious when the dominant personality reclaims control (when the medium wakes from their trance). In comparing their responses to key words Carrington discovered that the controls were mirror images of the mediums – a characteristic of multiple personalities. This would account for the mediums' inability to remember what they had channelled and also for the mysterious appearance of their phenomenal latent talents. At the same time it might also explain why the music was technically impressive, but not of the quality that such men of genius would be expected to produce if they had been given a chance to continue working from the 'other side'.

*In the same way as Mrs Brown channelled long-gone composers, artists claim to have been so inspired. The top picture is by F Thompson which was later found to resemble a painting by the dead artist R S Gifford (bottom picture), who was supposed to have 'drawn through' Thompson (see also page 221)*

This theory does not explain incidents of genuine mediumship in which the medium has communicated personal information that he or she could not have had access to, unconsciously or otherwise, and which was subsequently verified as correct by the bereaved. But it could be significant that subjects have exhibited telepathic abilities under hypnosis, such as sharing physical sensations with the hypnotist, which might suggest that when the left side of the brain (the objective or ordinary mind) is put to sleep, the right side of the brain (also known as the subjective or subliminal mind) might then be receptive to spirit communications.

## THE ARTIST WITHIN

Automatic art, or automatism to give it its clinical name, is not a recent phenomenon. In the 1930s, the American psychiatrist Dr Anita Muhl experimented with the technique to see if she could connect with her mentally ill patients. Against all the laws of logic and the expectations of her medical colleagues, many of Dr Muhl's patients produced impressive prose, paintings, sketches and musical compositions with their passive hand (the one they did not normally use to write with), with both hands simultaneously, occasionally writing and drawing upside down or even backwards. A number of patients were even able to draw 'blind', without looking at the paper. All of this was done fluidly, at great speed and without error. Dr Muhl believed that these latent talents originated in the unconscious, but there are those on the fringes of the scientific community who suspect that there might be spirits or a past-life personality at work. What other explanation, they say, can account for the feats of former antiques dealer John Tuckey who can complete epic Dickensian novels in a distinctive 19th-century copperplate script in a matter of weeks? Or what about the remarkable achievements of the Brazilian automatic artist Luiz Gasparetto who can produce two paintings in the style of different great masters simultaneously, one working upright and the other created upside down? Often Gasparetto will take less than a minute to produce a sketch worthy of Cézanne or Manet – and he doesn't even use brushes. He will employ his fingers and even his toes to create a one-minute masterpiece.

There is another theory to account for such accomplishments and this is that each of us contains more than one personality which are normally controlled by the dominant persona that has, effectively, taken the driving seat.

## THE THREE CLARAS

When psychiatrist Morton Prince placed patient Clara Fowler under hypnosis he unwittingly freed two contrasting personalities, each unaware of the other. Clara had been morose, subdued and suffered from depression while her two alter egos could not have been more different. One was considerably more mature and self-assured while the second, which identified herself as 'Sally', was a lively and mischievous little girl who would 'possess' Clara at inconvenient moments. Without warning 'Sally' would take over for hours at a time and when Clara regained control she would find herself in another part of town, bewildered as to how she got there. At the height of her influence, 'Sally' moved to another town, secured a job as a waitress for two weeks and then vacated her host who consequently had to talk her way out of a job she hadn't applied for and find her own way back home.

Spiritualists might interpret these experiences as evidence of possession, while a psychiatrist would regard them as sub-personalities, but if they are merely aspects of our unconscious why then do they create a separate personal history for themselves, speak in another voice and exhibit talents which the dominant personality does not possess? Could it be that they are, in fact, transitory memories and talents from that person's former lives which have been reawakened?

## The Question of Reincarnation

A belief in ghosts does not necessarily lead to an acceptance of reincarnation – the idea that we all experience a series of lives in order to achieve enlightenment or self-realization – but the cyclic nature of life as reflected in the changing seasons and the principle of evolution suggests that it is not only logical but highly desirable that we need more than one life in order to fulfil our full potential. While the evidence for reincarnation may be seen to be as compelling as that for the existence of spirits, it was not until the late 1960s when the Beatles popularly introduced the West to meditation and mind-expanding drugs that this spiritual world view entered Western consciousness, although it had been a core belief of the Celts and the ancient Greeks.

In post-war Britain the concept of reincarnation was considered to be an alien idea peculiar to the exotic Eastern philosophies of Hinduism, Shintoism and Buddhism. So when, in 1962, a Catholic father announced that his daughters were living proof of the existence of reincarnation it was seen as a challenge to the authority of the Church which had declared the concept heretical.

John Pollock had lost his first two daughters, Joanna, 11, and

Jacqueline, 6, in May 1957 when a driver lost control of her car and careered into the children near their home in Hexham, Northumberland. Pollock assumed that God had taken his girls to punish him for believing in reincarnation, but a year later, when his wife learnt that she was pregnant, Pollock became convinced that the souls of the two girls would be reborn in order to demonstrate that the Church was wrong to deny the natural process of death and rebirth. When his wife's gynaecologist informed the couple that they were to expect a single child Pollock assured him he was wrong – there would be twins, both girls. On 4 October 1958, he was proved correct.

The twins were monozygotic (meaning they developed from a single egg) yet the second twin, Jennifer, was born with a thin white line on her forehead in the same place that her dead sister Jacqueline had sustained a wound while falling from her bicycle. Her parents were also puzzled by the appearance of a distinctive birth mark on her left hip, identical to the one that Jacqueline had.

The girls grew up in Whitley Bay, but when they were three and a half their father took them back to Hexham and was astonished to

*'. . . when they were three and a half their father took them back to Hexham and was astonished to hear the girls point out places they had never seen in this life . . .'*

hear the girls point out places they had never seen in this life and talk about where they had played, even though they had left the town before they could walk. They knew when they were approaching their school although it was out of sight, and they recognized their old home as they passed it although their father had said nothing.

Six months later, they were given Joanna and Jacqueline's toy box. They identified all their dead sisters' dolls by name. They were also observed playing a game that their mother, Florence Pollock, found disturbing. Jennifer lay on the floor with her head in Gillian's lap, play-acting that she was dying and her sister would say, 'The blood's coming out of your eyes. That's where the car hit you.' Neither parent had discussed the accident with the children. On another occasion their mother heard them screaming in the street. When she came out she saw them clutching each other and looking terrified in the direction of a stationary car with its motor running. The girls were crying, 'The car! It's coming at us!'

The possibility that they might be the reincarnation of their elder, deceased sisters brought no comfort to their mother who could not reconcile the evidence of her own eyes with the Church's edict that belief in reincarnation was a mortal sin. For this reason she made an excellent impartial witness. To Florence Pollock's relief, however, the incident with the car marked the end of the affair. At the age of five the girls abruptly ceased to seem conscious of the connection with their former lives and developed into normal, healthy children.

This is consistent with a belief that at the age of five all children lose their link with the other world. At this point, to borrow an expression from the esoteric tradition, 'the veil comes down'. Children cease to play with imaginary friends and become grounded in the 'real' world. And perhaps something of the magic of childhood and worldly innocence dies with it.

# CHAPTER SIX

# HAUNTED HOUSES

Ghosts do not only haunt crumbling castles, but have been sighted in the homes of celebrities, hotels, aircraft, restaurants and even a Toys "R" Us store.

If any site deserves its formidable reputation for spectral sightings it is the Tower of London, whose weathered stones are soaked in the blood of countless executed martyrs and traitors. It is said that the walls still echo with the screams of those who were tortured there during the most violent chapters of English history and with the muffled sobbing of those innocents who were put to death for displeasing the monarchy. It is a place of pain where the unquiet souls of those who were imprisoned relive their suffering seemingly for eternity with no prospect of finding peace.

## THE BLOODY TOWER

Its long and bloody history began almost 1,000 years ago in 1078 when William the Conqueror built the White Tower in a strategically significant location on the River Thames. Over the next 500 years, the 18-acre site was developed into a formidable fortress within which a succession of kings exercised their divine right over the lives and deaths

*The White Tower was the first structure to be built on the site of the Tower of London and has a long history of hauntings*

of their subjects; former friends, wives and enemies alike. By the dawn of the 17th century, English royalty had moved to more palatial quarters and the Tower became a soldier's garrison and prison. On the morning of their execution, condemned prisoners were ceremoniously paraded past jeering crowds to the scaffold erected on nearby Tower Hill where they would be beheaded, or hung, drawn and quartered, and then their bodies would be brought back for burial within the walls of the Tower. These processions of sombre figures have been seen in modern times by sentries who were able to describe accurately the uniforms worn by the burial party.

Among the Tower's most illustrious residents were the young princes Edward and Richard who were declared illegitimate and imprisoned in the so-called Bloody Tower by their ambitious uncle the Duke of Gloucester. It is believed by some that he ordered their murder so that he could be crowned King Richard III. The princes have been sighted several times walking hand in hand through the chilly corridors after dusk, possibly in search of their murderous uncle. Their alleged murderer has not been seen skulking around the scene of his hideous crimes which may suggest that his conscience was clear. Given the murdered princes' sense of injustice or revenge, ghosts appear to be an emotional residue rather than a conscious presence.

This is borne out by the nature of the other ghosts which haunt the Tower – they are all victims, not the perpetrators, of the many crimes which took place there. Edward IV, father to the murdered princes, ordered the death of his Lancastrian rival Henry VI on 21 May 1471 at the end of the War of the Roses, but it is not Edward who haunts the oratory in the Wakefield Tower where the killing took place, but Henry who has been seen seated outside the oratory praying that his soul might find peace.

The second wife of Henry VIII is said to still walk in the Tower Chapel where she made her peace with her God before she was despatched to his heavenly kingdom in 1536. She is reported to have been seen leading a spectral procession through the chapel both with and without her head.

*Lady Margaret Pole, found guilty of treason, refused to kneel for the executioner and was hacked to pieces in a bloody chase around Tower Green*

One of the most gruesome episodes in the Tower's history was the botched execution of Margaret Pole, Countess of Salisbury. Margaret was 70 years old when she was condemned to death in 1541 by Henry VIII, even though she posed no threat to his dynasty. Standing resolutely regal on the scaffold, she refused to submit to the hooded executioner who waited for her to rest her head on the block, but instead she commanded him to sever her head from her neck where she stood. When he refused she fled, forcing him to pursue her around Tower Green swinging the axe like a serial killer in a modern splatter movie. Within minutes the hideous spectacle was at an end; the last female Plantagenet had been hacked to pieces. If you find that too gruesome to be true, you only have to ask permission to remain in the Tower after dark on 27 May, the anniversary of her execution, to see the scene re-enacted by the principal players themselves as Margaret's ghost tries once again to outrun her executioner.

Other apparitions are less active. The headless ghost of James Crofts Scott, the illegitimate son of King Charles II, for example, is said to do little more than walk the battlements connecting the Bell and Beauchamp Towers dressed in cavalier attire. Apparently, James was not satisfied with being made Duke of Monmouth as compensation for losing the crown to his uncle, James II, in 1685, and chose to assert his claim by force of arms. His rebellion was short-lived and he paid for his disloyalty by forfeiting his head.

Arguably the most tragic figure to haunt the site of her untimely death is Lady Jane Grey who was a pawn in the Duke of Northumberland's stratagem to usurp the English crown from the rightful heir, Mary Tudor. Lady Jane, who was only 15, ruled for less than two weeks before she was arrested and condemned to death together with her young husband and his father in February 1554. Her grieving ghost has been sighted by reliable witnesses on several occasions. In 1957, two sentries swore they witnessed the apparition of the young queen form from a ball of light on the roof of the Salt Tower while others have reported seeing the spirit of the Duke sobbing at the window of the Beauchamp Tower as he had done on the morning of his execution.

One would imagine that a spell in the Tower would be sufficient to bring even the most rebellious subjects to their senses, but Sir Walter Raleigh incurred the monarch's displeasure more than once. In 1592, Queen Elizabeth I ordered him to be thrown into the Tower, but upon his release he continued to bait the queen in the belief that he was too popular to be executed. After Elizabeth's death, James I lost patience with Raleigh's preening and boasting and had him convicted on a trumped up charge of treason. He was eventually freed in 1616 on condition that he journeyed to the New World in search of gold to fill the royal coffers, but he ignored the king's express orders not to plunder from England's Spanish allies and was beheaded on his return. His ghost still walks the battlements near what were once his apartments in the Bloody Tower.

Not all of the Tower's non-corporeal residents have returned because they cannot rest or because they desire revenge. The ghost of Henry Percy, 9th Earl of Northumberland, has been sighted strolling amiably on the roof of the Martin Tower where he enjoyed walks during his enforced incarceration which began in 1605. Percy, who had been implicated in the Gunpowder Plot, was one of the few prisoners to have been allowed to keep his head and he whiled away the days debating the latest advances in science and other subjects with other educated nobles until his release 16 years later. Percy owed his release to his willingness to pay a fine of £30,000. Since he is clearly reluctant to leave the Tower centuries after his death, perhaps he feels he hasn't had his money's worth.

## THE GHOSTS OF GLAMIS

If the typical collection of 'true' ghost stories is to be believed, every castle in the British Isles has its own resident ghost. Whether there is any truth in that or not, Glamis Castle in Scotland certainly has more than its share.

Glamis is the oldest inhabited castle north of the border and is renowned for being both the setting for the tragedy of *Macbeth* and also the ancestral home of the late Queen Mother, Elizabeth Bowes-Lyon. It also has an unenviable reputation as the most haunted castle in

*The forbidding exterior of Glamis Castle*

the world. Not all the ghosts are tortured souls. In the Queen Mother's sitting room the ghost of a cheeky black servant boy has been sighted playing hide and seek. There is no doubt that the legends of Glamis provide more gruesome thrills than an old-fashioned Gothic thriller. However, fact and fiction are so creatively intertwined that it is now impossible to know which is which.

Several visitors and guests have been distressed by the apparition of a pale and frightened young girl who has been seen pleading in mute terror at a barred window. Legend has it that she was imprisoned after having had her tongue cut out to keep her from betraying a family secret – but what that secret might be remains a mystery. In the 1920s, a workman was said to have accidentally uncovered a hidden tunnel and to have been driven to the edge of insanity by what he found there. Allegedly, the family bought his silence by paying for his passage to another country. There are also tales of a hideously deformed heir who was locked in the attic and an ancient family curse of which the 15th Earl is reputed to have said: 'If you could only guess the nature of the secret, you would go down on your knees and thank God that it was not yours.'

The family's troubles are believed to date from 1537 when the widow of the 6th Lord Glamis was accused of witchcraft and burned at the stake. From that day to this her ghost has been seen on the anniversary of her death on the roof of the clock tower, bathed in a smouldering red glow. Several of the castle's 90 rooms have a dark and bloody history. King Malcolm II of Scotland was murdered in one of them and the floor was boarded because the bloodstains could not be scrubbed clean. It is thought that this may have been the inspiration for the murder of King Duncan, Thane of Glamis, in Shakespeare's play *Macbeth*.

During the years of inter-clan warfare, the castle acquired an entire chamber of vengeful spirits when men from the Ogilvy clan were given refuge from their enemies in the dungeon, but were then betrayed by their host who walled them up alive. When the wall was torn down a century later, it is said that their skeletons were found in positions which suggested that they had been gnawing on their own flesh. The Scottish novelist Sir Walter Scott, who considered himself a hardy adventurer, braved a night there in 1793 and lived to regret it: 'I must own, that when I heard door after door shut, after my conductor had retired, I began to consider myself as too far from the living, and somewhat too near the dead.'

In his classic survey of supernatural stories, *The Ghost Book* (1936), Lord Halifax recounts the unnerving experience of a Mrs Monro who was the guest of the new owners Lord and Lady Strathmore in November 1869, a story later verified by Lady Strathmore herself.

> In the middle of the night, Mrs Monro awoke with a sensation as though someone was bending over her; indeed, I have heard that she felt a beard brush her face. The night-light having gone out, she called her husband to get up and find the matches. In the pale glimmer of the winter moon she saw a figure pass into the dressing room. Creeping to the end of the bed she felt for and found the matchbox and struck a light, calling out loudly, 'Cam, Cam I've found the matches.'

To her surprise she saw that he had not moved from her side. Very sleepily he grumbled, 'What are you bothering about?'

At that moment they heard a shriek of terror from the child in the dressing room. Rushing in, they found him in great alarm, declaring that he had seen a giant. They took him into their own room, and while they were quieting him off to sleep they heard a fearful crash as if a heavy piece of furniture had fallen.

At that moment the big clock had struck four.

Nothing more happened, and the next morning Mr Monro extracted a reluctant promise from his wife to say nothing about her fright, as the subject was known to be distasteful to their host. However, when breakfast was half over, [another guest] Fanny Trevanion came down, yawning and rubbing her eyes and complaining of a disturbed night. She always slept with a night-light and had her little dog with her on her bed. The dog, she said, had awakened her by howling. The night-light had gone out, and while she and her husband were hunting for matches they heard a tremendous crash, followed by the clock striking four. They were so frightened they could not sleep again.

Of course, this was too much for Mrs Monro, who burst out with her story. No explanation was offered and the three couples agreed on the following night to watch in their respective rooms. Nothing was seen, but they all heard the same loud crash and rushed out on to the landing. As they stood there with scared faces the clock again struck four. That was all; and the noise was not heard again.

## PURSUED BY DREAMS

So far this follows the customary ghost story tradition, but then it becomes even more intriguing. On the night of 28 September, Lord Halifax was staying at Tullyallan Castle, a modern comfortable home with no hint of a ghost when he dreamt that he was back at Glamis, which had once been his late brother-in-law's home. It was a fearful dream in which he was pursued by a huge man with a long beard. In a desperate effort to keep the ghost at bay – for in his dream Lord Halifax knew the man was dead – he offered him broken chains which a maid had found hidden in the hollow space below the grate in his room. His story continues:

*Lord Halifax (1881–1959), ambassador to the US 1941–46, and witness to a ghost*

> 'You have lifted a great weight off me,' sighed the ghost. 'Those irons have been weighing me down ever since ...'
>
> 'Ever since when?' asked his Lordship.
>
> 'Ever since 1486,' replied the ghost.

The next moment Halifax awoke.

In itself the dream would not be significant, but on the very same night the daughter of Lord Castletown was staying at Glamis unaware of the ghosts who were said to haunt several of its rooms. According to Lord Halifax:

> During the night she awoke with the feeling that someone was in the room and sitting up in bed she saw, seated in front of the fire, a huge old man with a long flowing beard. He turned his head and gazed fixedly at her and then she saw that although his beard rose and fell as he breathed the face was that of a dead man . . . after a few minutes he faded away and she went to sleep again.

Some years later, Lord Halifax had the chance to relate his dream to Lady Strathmore who remarked on the uncanny 'coincidence' and she gave a start when he mentioned the year of the ghost's death. Apparently Glamis' most infamous ghost, Earl Beardie, was murdered in 1486.

## THIRTEEN GUESTS

The Winchester Mansion in San Jose, California is unique among haunted houses. It was built by ghosts. Haunted houses are usually host to the restless spirits of their previous occupants, but in the case of the Winchester Mystery House, as it is known locally, its ghosts were not only invited to make themselves at home, they even directed the owner as to how they wanted the house built.

In 1884, Mrs Winchester was grieving for the loss of both her son and her husband who had made his fortune manufacturing the famous

Winchester repeating rifle – 'The gun that won the West'. In her grief Mrs Winchester became convinced that the restless spirits of those killed by her husband's weapons would torment her unless she devoted the rest of her life to extending the mansion according to their wishes so that they could while away eternity in comfort.

Every evening she presided over a spooky supper at a long dining table laid for 13, herself and 12 invisible guests. The servants indulged her eccentricities as they were allowed to partake of the leftovers. After dinner the widow conducted a private séance to hear the spirits' latest plans which she would interpret for the workmen the next morning. Either the spirits had a sense of mischievous humour or else Mrs Winchester may have been deliberately trying to disorientate her guests. The house features a number of staircases leading up to the ceiling and doors which open on to a brick wall or a sheer drop. In one particular room there is a single entrance but three exits on the facing wall, one of which leads to an 8 ft drop into the kitchen on the floor below and another into a windowless room. The door to this room has no handle on the other side, perhaps to entrap a curious ghost or because Mrs Winchester believed it wouldn't need a doorknob as a ghost could supposedly float through the door!

The ghosts seem to have had an obsession with the number 13. They demanded that every new staircase should have 13 steps and new rooms must have 13 windows. The chandeliers should boast 13 bulbs and the same number of coat hooks should be available in case they needed to hang up their spectral raincoats. There were even 13 fan lights in the greenhouse in case the spirits fancied a spell of hot house horticulture.

By the time Mrs Winchester passed away on 5 September 1922 at the age of 82, she had devoted the last 38 years of her life to extending the mansion which by then had grown to 160 rooms.

In the 1990s, a pair of paranormal investigators stayed overnight in the house and were aroused by music from a ghostly organ which, on examination, proved to be disconnected. Moments later they were unnerved by a violent disturbance as the house was shaken to its foundations. In the morning they asked the tour guides if any damage had been caused by the earthquake and were dumbfounded to learn that no tremors had been reported in the area, although in 1906 the destructive San Francisco earthquake had struck at the very same time and severely damaged part of the house.

Not surprisingly, perhaps, the mansion has become a popular tourist attraction, and in case any visitor sneers at the idea of a house being built for ghosts the guides are ready to assure them that at least three spirits walk the house – a young female servant, a carpenter who had died at the site and the indomitable Mrs Winchester, whom staff have seen in Victorian dress, sitting at a table. When they asked their colleagues why they needed someone dressed up as Mrs Winchester they were told that no one was employed to dress up and play the part.

## BORLEY RECTORY

During the 1930s and 1940s, Borley Rectory acquired a sinister reputation as 'The Most Haunted House in England'. This unimposing vicarage near Sudbury, Essex, was built in 1863 on the site of a Benedictine monastery which had a dark and unholy history. It was said that a Borley monk had seduced a local nun and the pair had planned to elope. They were caught and the monk was executed and the nun was walled up alive in the cellar.

The first incumbent of the new rectory was the Reverend Bull who built a summerhouse overlooking a path known as the Nun's Walk. From there he sometimes observed the materializations of the weeping woman as she wandered the gardens searching for her murdered lover. Bull often invited guests to join him on his ghost watch but few stayed long enough to share his vigil. Once they had caught the nun peering in through their ground floor bedroom window they made their excuses and cut their visit short. Bull's four daughters and his son Harry resigned themselves to regular sightings of the forlorn spirit drifting across the lawn in broad daylight, but when it was joined by a spectral coach and horses galloping up the drive, the surviving Bull children decided to move on. Their father had died in the Blue Room in 1892 and his son Harry in the same room in 1927.

At the end of the 1920s, the Reverend Eric Smith and his wife took up residence, shrugging off stories of phantom carriages and sobbing nuns. They had barely had time to unpack their belongings before a burst of poltergeist activity encouraged them to sell up and move out. However, during their two-year tenure they took the unusual step of calling in the man who was to ensure Borley a place in paranormal history – ghost hunter extraordinaire Harry Price.

Price was a notorious self-publicist and one-time music hall conjurer who had hoped to make a name for himself by exposing fake mediums and debunking the whole spiritualist movement as mere charlatanism. The more he saw at first hand, however, the more convinced he became that some of it was genuine. Eventually, he came to the conclusion that he was more likely to fulfil his ambition of getting into Debrett's (a directory of the rich and famous) if he could find proof of life after death than if he merely unmasked a few fraudulent mediums.

At the invitation of the Reverend Smith, and later with the encouragement of the next tenants Mr and Mrs Foyster, Price recorded

*Bones were found in the cellar of the rectory and, in an effort to quieten the ghost, given a decent burial in Liston churchyard in 1945, attended by the Rev. A.C. Henning, two local residents and Harry Price*

incidents involving phantom footsteps, flying objects and even physical attacks: on one notable occasion Mrs Foyster was even turned out of bed by an invisible assailant. She was also the subject of unintelligible messages scrawled on the walls. Her husband had the house exorcized but the spirits persisted. The servants' bells rang of their own accord and music could be heard coming from the chapel even though no one was in the building. The Foysters admitted defeat and left the spooks in peace. Subsequent owners fared little better. Eventually, the house burned down in a mysterious fire in 1939 as predicted by a spirit 11 months earlier during a séance conducted on the site by Price. Witnesses stated that they saw phantoms moving among the flames and the face of a nun staring from a window.

## THE GHOST-HUNTER'S BOOK

Price published his findings in 1940 under the title *The Most Haunted House in England*, boasting that it presented 'the best authenticated case of haunting in the annals of psychical research'. The book was an instant bestseller providing as it did some escapism in the first anxious months of the Second World War and quickly established a non-fiction genre of its own – the haunted house mystery. Its success generated a slew of similar books by self-proclaimed experts and sufficient interest in Price to spawn several (highly critical) biographies. Price revelled in his new-found fame, but it was short-lived. He died in 1948 having spent the last 40 years of his life providing what he believed to be irrefutable evidence of the paranormal. But he was not allowed to rest in peace. In the decade after his death there were spiteful personal attacks on his reputation by rival ghost hunters alleging that Price had faked certain phenomena. Mrs Smith wrote to the *Church Times* denying that she and her husband had claimed that the rectory was haunted, although it is thought that she may have done this to ingratiate herself with the Church authorities who had been embarrassed by the whole affair. An investigation by the SPR, conducted by members who were openly hostile to Harry Price, concluded that he had manipulated certain facts to substantiate his claims and that other incidents probably had a 'natural explanation'.

Price's reputation was seriously undermined, but the fact remains that the Reverend Bull and his family had said that they had seen spirits before Price arrived on the scene. (Miss Ethel Bull had reported seeing a phantom figure at the end of her bed and of sensing another sitting on the end of the bed on more than one occasion.) Also Mrs Foyster appears to have provoked an outbreak of genuine poltergeist activity. Price himself suspected that she augmented it with some phenomena of her own creation, perhaps because she craved attention, or at least so as not to disappoint his expectations.

Either way, questions remain. If Price had faked phenomena, why did he rent the rectory for a year after Mrs Foyster moved out, only to admit that there was nothing anomalous to report? He would have had more than enough time and opportunity to stage something truly astounding to substantiate his claims. The inactivity during that period suggests that the spirits might have been attracted by the presence of the Reverend Bull and Mrs Foyster, who perhaps possessed mediumistic abilities.

A subsequent investigation by the SPR under R. J. Hastings unearthed previously unpublished letters from the Reverend Smith and his wife to Price, written in 1929, in which Smith states emphatically that 'Borley is undoubtedly haunted'. This discovery forced the SPR to revise its earlier findings. Price had been vindicated. Whatever shortcuts Price may have taken to enhance his reputation as Britain's foremost ghost hunter, it cannot be denied that there was something out of the ordinary occurring at Borley.

A footnote to the Borley investigation was added in the 1950s by the novelist Dennis Wheatley, author of *The Devil Rides Out* and dozens of occult thrillers:

> Kenneth Allsop, the book reviewer of the *Daily Mail*, told me that when Borley was in the news he was sent down to do an article on it, and with him he took a photographer. Borley was then being 'debunked' so that had to be the tone of the article.

> But when the photographer developed his photos the figure of a nun could be quite clearly seen on one of them. He took it to Allsop, who took it to his editor, but the editor said, 'No, I just daren't print it.'

A curious postscript to the Borley saga occurred on 28 August 1977 when ley line expert Stephen Jenkins visited the area with a view to seeing if there was anything to the theory that the 'curious manifestations' might be linked to a spider's web of ley line alignments.

> The time was precisely 12.52 pm and we were driving south-west along the minor road which marks the north end of the hall ground, when on the road in front in the act of turning left into a hedge (I mean our left across the path of the car), instantaneously appeared four men in black – I thought them hooded and cloaked – carrying a black, old fashioned coffin, ornately trimmed with silver. The impression made on both of us was one of absolute physical presence, of complete material reality. Thelma and I at once agreed to make separate notes without comparing impressions. We did so and the descriptions tallied exactly, except that she noted the near left bearer turned his face towards her. I did not see this as I was abruptly braking at the time. What I had seen as a hood, she described as a soft tall hat with a kind of scarf falling to the left shoulder, thrown across the cloak body to the right. The face was that of a skull.
>
> The next day we returned to the spot at precisely the same time and took a picture. It is a Kodak colour slide. In the hedge near the gap where the 'funeral party' vanished (there's a path there leading to Belchamp Walter churchyard) is a short figure apparently cloaked, his face lowered with a skull-like dome to the head . . . I hazard a guess that the dress of the coffin bearer is that of the late 14th century. There seems to be no local legend of a phantom funeral.

## WEIRD NIGHT IN A HAUNTED HOUSE

While Harry Price was accused of having falsified some of the 'evidence' and having made fraudulent claims in order to boost his reputation as Britain's foremost ghost hunter, the following article from the *Daily Mirror* of 14 June 1929 suggests that Harry's first visit to Borley was lively enough without the need for artificial aids or exaggeration:

WEIRD NIGHT IN 'HAUNTED' HOUSE

*from our Special Correspondent*

There can no longer be any doubt that Borley Rectory, near here, is the scene of some remarkable incidents. Last night Mr Harry Price, Director of the National Laboratory For Psychical Research, his secretary Miss Lucy Kaye, the Reverend G.F. Smith, Rector of Borley, Mrs Smith and myself were witnesses to a series of remarkable happenings. All these things occurred without the assistance of a medium or any kind of apparatus. And Mr Price, who is a research expert only and not a spiritualist, expressed himself puzzled and astonished at the results. To give the phenomena a thorough test however, he is arranging for a séance to be held in the rectory with the aid of a prominent London medium.

The first remarkable happening was the dark figure that I saw in the garden. We were standing in the Summer House at dusk watching the lawn when I saw the 'apparition' which so many claim to have seen, but owing to the deep shadows it was impossible for one to discern any definite shape or attire. But something certainly moved along the path on the other side of the lawn and although I quickly ran across to investigate it had vanished when I reached the spot.

Then as we strolled towards the rectory discussing the figure there came a terrific crash and a pane of glass from the roof of a porch hurtled to the ground. We ran inside and upstairs to inspect the room immediately over the porch but found nobody. A few seconds later we were descending the stairs, Miss Kaye leading, and Mr Price behind me when something flew past my head, hit an iron stove in the hall and shattered. With our flash lamps we inspected the broken pieces and found them to be sections of a red vase which, with its companion, had been standing on the mantelpiece of what is known as the Blue Room which we had just searched. Mr Price was the only person behind me and he could not have thrown the vase at such an angle as to pass my head and hit the stove below.

We sat on the stairs in darkness for a few minutes and just as I turned to Mr Price to ask him whether we had waited long enough something hit my hand. This turned out to be a common moth ball and had apparently dropped from the same place as the vase. I laughed at the idea of a spirit throwing moth balls about, but Mr Price said that such methods of attracting attention were not unfamiliar to investigators.

Finally came the most astonishing event of the night. From one o'clock till nearly four this morning all of us, including the rector and his wife, actually questioned the spirit or whoever it was and received at times the most emphatic answers. A cake of soap on the washstand was lifted and thrown heavily onto a china jug standing on the floor with such force that the soap was deeply marked. All of us were at the other side of the room when this happened. Our questions which we asked out loud were answered by raps apparently made on the back of a mirror in the room and it must be remembered though that no medium or spiritualist was present.

## THE WHITE HOUSE

When the tour guides in Washington DC talk of the White House being haunted by the ghosts of former US presidents they are not speaking metaphorically, neither are they being melodramatic. It is known that Eleanor Roosevelt held séances in the White House during the Second

World War and she claimed to be in contact with the spirit of Abraham Lincoln. During the Roosevelt residency their guest Queen Wilhelmina of the Netherlands was awoken in the night by a knock on her bedroom door. Thinking that it might be Eleanor Roosevelt she got out of bed, put on her nightgown and opened the door. There, framed in the doorway and looking as large as life, was the ghost of Abe Lincoln. Queen Wilhelmina's reaction is not recorded.

Winston Churchill was a frequent visitor to the White House during the Second World War and he often indulged in a hot bath, together with a cigar and a glass of whisky. One evening he climbed out of the bath and went into the adjoining bedroom to look for a towel when he noticed a man standing by the fireplace. It was Abraham Lincoln. Unperturbed, Churchill apologized for his state of undress: 'Good evening, Mr President. You seem to have me at a disadvantage.' Lincoln is said to have smiled and tactfully withdrawn.

The wife of President Calvin Coolidge entertained guests to the White House with her recollections of the day she entered the Oval Office and saw Lincoln looking out across the Potomac with his hands clasped behind his back – a habit he acquired during the Civil War. Lincoln himself was a firm believer in the afterlife and enthusiastically participated in séances during his tenure in office prior to his assassination in 1865. He confided to his wife that he had a premonition of his own death. He dreamt that he was walking through the White House when he heard the sound of weeping coming from the East Room. When he entered he saw an open coffin surrounded by mourners and guarded by a detachment of Union soldiers. He asked one of the guards who it was who lay in the coffin, to be told, 'The President. He was killed by an assassin.' Lincoln then approached the coffin and saw his own corpse.

President Harry Truman often complained that he was prevented from working by Lincoln's ghost who would repeatedly knock on his door when he was attempting to draft an important speech. Truman wasn't known for his sense of humour and no one would have thought of playing practical jokes during his tenure in the Oval Office so it is assumed he was in earnest.

In the 1960s, Jacqueline Kennedy admitted that she had sensed Lincoln's presence on more than one occasion and 'took great comfort in it'. It is thought that Lincoln's ghost might be drawn to the White House because his son Willie died there and it is reported that the son has himself been seen wandering the corridors in search of his father.

## ALCATRAZ

Long before Alcatraz Island in San Francisco Bay was converted into a prison to house America's most notorious criminals, the Native Americans warned the US army not to build a fortress on 'the Rock' as it was the dwelling place of evil spirits. Needless to say, their warnings were ignored. When the fortress was converted into a military prison in 1912, several soldiers were said to have been driven insane by mysterious noises in the night, by cold spots which turned their breath to mist even on warm summer evenings and by the sight of two burning red eyes which appeared in the cells on the lower level.

By 1934, the spirits had company when the Rock re-opened for business to house the most notorious gangsters of the Prohibition era including 'Scarface' Al Capone and Machine Gun Kelly. But even the most hardened inmates feared being thrown into 'the hole', the windowless cells of D Block where the red-eyed demon was said to be waiting to consume lost souls.

On one memorable night during the 1940s a prisoner was hurled screaming into solitary in 14D and continued yelling until early the next morning. When the guards finally opened his cell, they found him dead with distinctive marks around his throat. An autopsy was conducted and the official cause of death was determined to be 'non self-inflicted strangulation'. The story gets more extraordinary when, according to the sworn statement of an eyewitness, the prisoners were lined up for roll-call the next morning and the number didn't tally. There was one extra prisoner in the line. So a guard walked along the line looking at each face to see if one of the inmates was playing a trick on him. He came face to face with the dead man who had been strangled in the night and who promptly vanished before his eyes. The

*'. . . Native Americans warned the US army not to build a fortress on "the Rock" as it was the dwelling place of evil spirits'*

*'Other parts of the prison are host to the unquiet spirits of the five suicides and eight murders which took place before the prison was closed in 1963'*

guard later related this story to others and swore on the lives of his children that it was true.

Despite the warden's boast that the prison was escape-proof, several inmates tried to break out and died in the attempt. Their ghosts are said to haunt the hospital block where their bodies were taken. Other parts of the prison are host to the unquiet spirits of the five suicides and eight murders which took place before the prison was closed in 1963.

Since the Rock opened to tourists, visitors have claimed to have seen cell doors closing by themselves and to have heard the sound of sobbing, moaning and phantom footsteps, the screams of prisoners being beaten as well as the delirious cries of those made ill or driven insane by their confinement. Others have spoken of seeing phantom soldiers and prisoners pass along the corridors and out through solid walls, and many have complained of being watched even though the corridors and cells were empty.

Those brave enough to try out one of the bunks for size have found themselves pinned down by a weight on their chest as the previous occupant made his presence known and showed his resentment at having his privacy invaded. In the lower cells, 12 and 14 in particular, even the least sensitive tourists have admitted to picking up feelings of despair, panic and pain, and they have excused themselves to catch a breath of fresh air. Whenever a thermometer has been placed in cell 14D it has consistently measured between 20–30 degrees colder than the other cells in that block.

And what of the Rock's most notorious inmate, 'Scarface' Capone? Well, Capone may have been a 'big shot' on the outside but in the 'big house' he was apparently a model prisoner who sat quietly on his bunk in cell B206 learning to play the banjo. It is said that if you sit quietly in that cell you can hear the ghostly strains of Capone whiling away eternity playing popular tunes of the Roaring 20s.

## THE EDGAR ALLAN POE HOUSE

The spirit of Edgar Allan Poe, author of *The Fall of the House of Usher* and other tales of terror, haunts both American fiction and the house

*'. . . there did stand the enshrouded figure of the lady Madeline . . . there was blood upon her white robes, and the evidence of some bitter struggle upon every portion of her emaciated frame. For a moment she remained trembling and reeling to and fro upon the threshold, then with a low moaning cry, fell heavily inward upon . . . her brother, and in her violent and now final death agonies, bore him to the floor a corpse . . . '*
*From* Fall of the House of Usher *by Edgar Allan Poe*

in Baltimore where he lived as a young man in the 1830s. The narrow two-and-a-half-storey brick house at 203 North Amity Street in an impoverished area is said to be so spooky that even local gangs are scared to break in. When the police arrived to investigate a reported burglary in 1968 they saw a phantom light in the ground floor window floating up to reappear on the second floor and then in the attic, but when they entered the property there was no one to be seen.

Even in daylight the house is unsettling. An eerie portrait of Poe's wife, painted as she lay in her coffin, hangs in one room, her melancholic gaze following visitors around the room. Local residents have also reported seeing a shadowy figure working at a desk at a second floor window, although Poe, whose morbid obsession with premature burial led to his incarceration in an asylum, worked in the attic.

The curator has recorded many incidents of poltergeist activity and this appears to originate in the bedroom that belonged to Poe's grandmother. Here, doors and windows have opened and closed by themselves, visitors have been tapped on the shoulder and disembodied voices have been heard. Psychic investigators have also reported seeing a stout, grey-haired old woman dressed in clothing of the period gliding through the rooms.

In a twist of which the master of the macabre might have been perversely proud, local parents still use the spectre of the horror writer to terrify their children into doing what they are told. Poe has become the bogeyman of Baltimore.

## TOYS "Я" US

It is a common misconception that ghosts only inhabit crumbling castles and mouldering mansions. The modern Toys "R" Us superstore in Sunnyvale, California occupies a substantial plot on what had been a ranch and an apple orchard back in the 19th century. It is assumed that the poltergeist activity that has been witnessed there is connected with the previous owner John Murphy who, it appears, disliked children, as well as the commercial development of his former home.

Each morning, employees arrive to find stock scattered across the floor and items placed on the wrong shelves. Turnover in staff increased when sensitive staff members heard a voice calling their name and were then touched by invisible hands. The fragrant scent of fresh flowers has unsettled several employees, but it was the unwanted attentions of a phantom who assaulted female staff in the ladies' washroom which brought the matter to the attention of the local press and ghost buffs around the globe in 1978.

As a result, local journalist Antoinette May and psychic Sylvia Brown camped out in the store overnight with a photographer and a number of ghost catchers. Once the staff had left for the night and the lights were dimmed, Sylvia began to sense a male presence approaching the group. In her mind's eye she 'saw' a tall, thin man striding down the aisle towards her with his hands in his pockets. In her head she heard him speak with a Swedish accent, identifying himself as Johnny Johnson and warning her that she would get wet if she stayed where she was. It later emerged that a well had existed on that spot. Sylvia established such a strong connection with Johnson that she was able to draw out his life history.

*'Each morning, employees arrive to find stock scattered across the floor and items placed on the wrong shelves'*

He had come to California in the mid-1800s from Pennsylvania where he had worked as a preacher before succumbing to an inflammation of the brain which affected his behaviour. This appears to account for his antics in the aisles and the ladies' washroom, as well as the nickname 'Crazy Johnny', given to him by locals at the time.

Johnny lived out his later years working as a ranch hand for John Murphy, pining for a woman named Elizabeth Tafee who broke his heart when she left him to marry a lawyer. Johnny was 80 when he died from loss of blood after an accident with an axe while chopping wood.

Infra-red photographs taken for Arthur Myers' book on the haunting, *The Ghostly Register*, appear to show the figure of a man in the aisles of the store. Surprisingly, the publicity surrounding the haunting hasn't put off the customers, and it has allayed the fears of the employees who are no longer upset by the disturbances – they now know it's only 'Crazy Johnny'.

# HAUNTED HOMES

If you think that ghosts are only to be found in places that were built a long time ago, think again. Today's spectral squatters are more likely to take up residence in a suburban semi where they can make a real nuisance of themselves. And if it's your home that's haunted, don't blame your uninvited guests – they may just have taken exception to your chosen colour scheme or even your taste in music. So prepare to consult a Ouija board the next time you're considering a makeover.

> For who can wonder that man should feel a vague belief in tales of disembodied spirits wandering through those places which they once dearly affected, when he himself, scarcely less separated from his old world than they, is for ever lingering upon past emotions and bygone times, and hovering, the ghost of his former self, about the places and people that warmed his heart of old?
>
> Charles Dickens, *Master Humphrey's Clock*

## IN EVERY HOME A HEARTACHE

> . . . if our ancestors attached too much importance to these ill-understood arcana of the night side of nature, we have attached too little.
>
> Catherine Crowe, *The Night Side of Nature*, 1848

The days when ghosts swept through cobwebbed corridors rattling rusty chains are long gone. Today's restless spirits are more likely to karaoke with MTV if they don't get the respect and recognition they believe they deserve. At least that's the message delivered by the late Professor Broersma, who died just before Christmas 1987 in the house he built at 2115 Martingale Drive in a suburb of Oklahoma. A house which he later returned to haunt until the new owners wised up to what he wanted.

The professor evidently found it difficult to communicate at first if the experiences of the new owners were anything to go by. In fact there were several new residents of the house in quick succession, each driven out by inexplicable noises and occurrences until, in 1994, newlyweds Jon and Agi Lurtz moved in. Jon and Agi were not put off by tales of a restless spirit or the fact that one previous owner had reportedly fled leaving all his earthly possessions behind. The house was all that they had dreamed of and they were not going to be evicted by anyone, living or dead.

The professor's campaign of intimidation began with regular radio broadcasts in the middle of the night – and it was loud, very loud. Try as they might, the couple couldn't locate the source of the signal.

Their own radio was unplugged. What's more, it was not a station they recognized. It was broadcasting old news from years gone by. It was like living through an episode of *The Twilight Zone*.

Eventually, they came to the conclusion that the sound was coming from beneath the floorboards. But when they lifted them, there was no radio to be found.

Having failed to dislodge the couple the ghost tried a new tactic. He took possession of the hi-fi and began blasting out heavy metal music at ear-bleeding volumes. His favourite band apparently was the German technogrunge group Rammstein, whose aural assault of overdriven guitars threatened to bring down plaster from the ceiling. Jon and Agi would frequently return from a shopping trip to find the hi-fi going at full blast, but the equipment had always been switched off before they had left the house.

But the professor had reckoned without Agi, a practical and determined young woman who had lived in haunted houses before and learnt how to assert her rights when confronted with spectral squatters.

One night in 1998 she awoke to see the figure of a man standing at the foot of her bed and, assuming it to be the professor, she demanded to know what he wanted. In a foreign accent he replied that all he wanted was an obituary as he had never had one. And with that he faded away.

All things considered, it didn't seem an unreasonable request and so later that day Agi began to research into the professor's past.

She discovered that his grievances were well founded. His death had not been reported in the local paper and no acknowledgement of his considerable achievements had been made. During the Second

*Aural overdrive: the ghost's favourite music came from German technogrunge group Rammstein*

World War the Dutch-born academic had served with distinction in the resistance movement at considerable risk to himself after which he moved to America. There he contributed to the development of advanced sensor technology for NASA (National Aeronautics and Space Administration).

All of these accomplishments were listed in Agi's glowing obituary which she wrote for the local paper. They were also included in the eulogy she read aloud at a belated memorial service that she arranged to commemorate his life. It was all the brooding spirit wanted, for immediately afterwards the disturbances ceased.

Some people prefer to keep their achievements to themselves, but clearly the professor felt that he was overdue some recognition before he could rest in peace.

'I guess he felt that he deserved that,' Agi told the paper. 'He needed that before he could go on.'

## HOUSE BY THE CEMETERY

In Stephen Spielberg's horror movie *Poltergeist*, a suburban family find themselves in the midst of a storm of paranormal activity which has been stirred up by restless spirits furious at the developers who desecrated their graves. Of course, such things don't happen in real life – or do they?

In 1983 Ben and Jean Williams learnt that such terrifying experiences can and do happen to ordinary people if they are unlucky enough to buy a home built on the site of a former burial ground.

When the couple first moved into their dream home they were delighted both with the house and the location. The new development at Newport, Texas was within commuting distance of Houston and boasted immaculate landscaped gardens and highly desirable upmarket homes. But there was a catch. Their garden seemed to attract an unusual number of poisonous snakes. But this was not all. Lights would switch themselves on and off, the garage door repeatedly malfunctioned and the atmosphere felt unusually oppressive. No matter how often they told themselves that they were now living the life they had always dreamed of, they could not shake off a sense of foreboding or the feeling that something, or someone, was watching them.

Whenever something inexplicable occurred, they came up with a rational explanation. The lights and garage door could be due to faulty wiring, the snakes to some natural phenomenon that would be unearthed one day and their paranoia to the stress of moving.

But there was no explanation for the series of large rectangular holes which seemed to form a pattern in their lawn. As soon as they filled them in, the soil would drain out of them, leaving the same grave-shaped impressions. It was the talk of the neighbourhood. Their unspoken suspicions finally surfaced when contractors began excavating the backyard of the home belonging to their neighbours Sam and Judith Haney and unearthed a pair of rotting coffins containing the corpses of a man and a woman. Nobody slept soundly on the Newport development that night.

The following day, their curiosity aroused, the Newport neighbours banded together to make not-so-discreet inquiries into the history of the site and discovered that it had once been the last resting place of poor black citizens of that region, many of them former slaves.

They even managed to locate a retired black gravedigger who was able to identify the disinterred remains as those of Bettie and Charlie Thomas who had died during the Depression. Out of genuine respect for the deceased, the Haneys insisted that the bodies be reburied in the garden and given a decent Christian funeral service. But that did not appear to have appeased the dead couple, or to pacify the 60 or so former occupants of Newport's Black Hope Cemetery. Over the following days the Haneys were subjected to a barrage of poltergeist activity: a clock spat sparks, phantom footsteps marched up and down the empty rooms after dark and a pair of Judith's shoes disappeared only to turn up on Bettie's freshly dug grave. That was it for the Haneys. They instigated legal action against the developer and won the case, but it was overturned on appeal, so they took the only course of action left open to them. They packed up and moved out, leaving a perfectly good house to the ghosts.

Meanwhile, Ben and Jean Williams were seriously considering selling up and moving out, but rumours of the weird goings-on had spread through the real estate community and no one was interested in having the house on their books. Then one night Ben returned home late to see a figure standing at the end of his bed while his wife slept. It was the last straw. They decided that if they were to succeed where their neighbours had failed in suing the developer they would have to provide physical proof. So, in the belief that other bodies were buried in their back garden, they decided to unearth these themselves. Jean began digging one afternoon but found the task too tiring so she gave the spade to her 30-year-old daughter, Tina. After only a short while Tina complained of breathlessness and chest pains, then collapsed. She died two days later. The Williams family moved out shortly afterwards and settled in Montana.

## THE SPECTRAL SQUATTER

There's only one thing worse than living with a ghost and that's living with a ghost with attitude. Housewife Frances Freeborn found this out to her cost when she moved into her new home in Bakersfield, California in November 1981.

Apparently, the previous owner, Meg Lyons, had departed the property and this earthly life in a hurry, leaving not only her furniture behind but also her clothes which were still hanging in the wardrobe. Frances wasted no time in disposing of everything in preparation for redecorating, but Ms Lyons' spirit was evidently not ready to depart in peace.

The first sign that something was not quite right came with a series of loud noises in the kitchen which Frances attributed to faulty plumbing. But the local handyman could find nothing wrong with the pipes or the heating system. As soon as he had packed up his tools the banging resumed. Frances shrugged it off as one of those things that can't be explained, but in the following days she started to doubt her own sanity when the kitchen cupboards opened by themselves and the lights that she had switched off turned themselves back on again whenever she went out.

Although she was not by nature a nervous woman she began to feel decidedly uneasy as the weeks went by. Instead of enjoying putting her own personal touches to the house she began to get the distinct impression that someone else was looking over her shoulder and that they disapproved of the changes she was making. A framed antique photograph that she tried to hang was repeatedly taken down undamaged and left propped up against the skirting while Frances was occupied elsewhere. This occurred no fewer than five times, leaving an increasingly uneasy Frances in no doubt that she would have to find another spot for the photo. Not long afterwards the late Ms Lyons' son-in-law came to call and was not surprised to learn of the moving picture. His mother-in-law had hung a similar photo in that very spot and was clearly not happy with its replacement.

Frances stuck it out through the New Year but come spring even the blossoming trees and flowers in the garden couldn't raise her spirits. She made one last determined effort to cheer up the old place and impose her personality upon it. She spent a small fortune at the local DIY store and returned home to smarten up the master bedroom. But the very next morning during breakfast while she looked through colour charts the windows and doors flew open, then slammed closed again as if unseen hands were showing her the nearest exit. Frances took the hint. Still dressed in her nightgown, she snatched up her barking dog and headed for the front door. But something was blocking her retreat.

'There was a zone of pressure, a mass out in the hall,' she later said, 'as if something ominous and ugly was concentrated there. I realized I had to get out of the house or I would die.'

With an enormous effort she screamed at the top of her voice and braced herself against the malevolent mass as if tearing through a downpour. A moment later she was out the door, sprinting down the path to her car. She never looked back.

## A LEGAL MATTER

In a similar case, the new owners of a large Victorian-style house in upstate New York took the seller to court in an attempt to recover their deposit on the grounds that they hadn't been informed that the house was haunted. The previous owner, Helen Ackley, responded by saying that the house's reputation for ghostly goings-on was common knowledge. She had, in fact, published several accounts of her experiences, as a result of which her home had been included in a walking tour of supernatural sites. But she had been less candid with potential purchasers, if the buyers Jeffrey and Patrice Stambovsky were to be believed. 'We were victims of ectoplasmic fraud,' the irate Jeffrey complained to reporters covering the case. The press relished the story, but the New York Appellate Court considered the matter seriously and ruled that, even if the ghostly guests did not actually exist, it was sufficient that some future buyer might believe in them and be dissuaded from purchasing the house as a result. Judge Justice Rubin summed up the decision by saying:

> Applying the strict rule of *caveat emptor* (buyer beware) to a contract involving a house possessed by poltergeists conjures up visions of a psychic or medium routinely accompanying the structural engineers and Terminix man on an inspection on every home subject to a contract of sale.
>
> In the interest of avoiding such untenable consequences, the notion that a haunting is a condition which can and should be ascertained upon reasonable inspection of the premises is a hobgoblin, which should be exorcized from the body of legal precedent and quietly laid to rest.

## PHANTOM PHOTOS

Little Lisa Swift hated piano lessons. It wasn't that she had no patience for practising. It was the accompanist she objected to – a 7,000-year-old Native American who played a discordant and distinctly haunting tune on his wooden flute whenever she sat down to play. And then there were the shadows which seemed to follow her from room to room accompanied by the sweet scent of burning wood. But none of these unsettling scents or sounds bothered her mother, California housewife Rita Swift, until much later. In the summer of 1969 Rita was too preoccupied with her new hobby, taking photographs of the family home and the pet cat. There was nothing remarkable about the camera she was using back then. It was an old Kodak Brownie Hawkeye and the film was standard black and white stock. So maybe it was something in the quality of the light in the backyard that September, or maybe there was a fault in the film or the camera because there was no rational explanation for the images which appeared on the last three frames when the negative was developed 30 years later.

Of course, it might have been the delay in processing the film which created the ghostly apparitions. Fogging is a common fault in amateur photography caused by light leaking into the camera casing and these milky white streaks have been mistaken for ghosts in the past. But the prints Rita Swift collected from the photo shop in 1999 were pin sharp and the strangers she had unknowingly photographed all those years ago were certainly not her neighbours.

The first shot showed three Native Americans in traditional costume dancing in a line. The other two captured a tribe in ceremonial dress grouped around a row of bodies prepared for ritual cremation.

*If the Swift home had been built on a Native American burial ground it would explain many things*

The thought occurred to Rita that someone at the photo store must have been playing a prank, but the other images on the roll were all of her own family. It couldn't have been tampered with by anyone in the family as she had locked the camera with the film still inside it in a trunk in September 1969 and no one had touched it until she found it by accident 30 years later.

When she plucked up the courage to show the photos to Native Americans living nearby they refused to look at them more closely, for fear of intruding on a sacred ceremony.

If the Swift home had been built on a Native American burial ground it would explain the ghostly flute and the smell of burning wood, but without physical evidence cynics would say that it was all down to the imagination and that one can see anything in a blurry or faded photograph if one wants to.

But that does not explain the charred bones unearthed in the Swifts' backyard in 1962, five years before the spooky photos were taken. Fortunately, someone had the presence of mind to send them to the California State College at Long Beach for analysis.

The experts there identified them as the partially cremated remains of a Native American female dating back approximately 7,000 years. It's a pity the Swifts didn't develop the photos earlier. If they had, maybe they wouldn't have built an extension on the site or placed the piano where the cremation took place. Little Lisa Swift might have been a more accomplished pianist if they had.

## THE FACE IN THE WINDOW

> Everything that relates, whether closely or more distantly, to psychic phenomena and to the action of psychic forces in general, should be studied just like any other science. There is nothing miraculous or supernatural in them, nothing that should engender or keep alive superstition.
>
> Alexandra David-Neel, *Magic and Mystery in Tibet*, 1932

Even in the days before digital photography photographs were comparatively easy to fake. Convincing apparitions could be created both deliberately and accidentally through double exposure and tricks of the light such as lens flare. But by the 1990s no self-respecting news editor would be taken in by such primitive tricks, so when *Indianapolis Star* photographer Mike Fender printed what appeared to be a genuine spook shot he thought long and hard about whether he should submit it and risk losing his job or destroy it.

On the morning of 29 April 1997 Fender had been assigned to record the removal of a historic 19th-century, Gothic Revival-style farmhouse from a hilltop just outside town to a choice location where it could be preserved by the Historic Landmarks Foundation. It was a delicate operation for the hauliers who had to manhandle the fragile 24-room home without dismantling it, but it should have been a routine assignment for Fender. Being a methodical and conscientious employee, he took several shots from every conceivable angle. Then as he stood in front of the trailer on which the house had been secured for its short journey, he noticed what he thought was a little girl in a blue dress standing at an upstairs window looking apprehensively at the scene below. But that couldn't be. The house was empty. It must have been the light playing on the curtains.

The next day the story appeared alongside the photo. Fender had had a deadline to meet and he had taken the chance that no one would notice the tiny figure in the window. But he was wrong.

'We got hundreds of calls,' he was later to say. 'Things like this usually fade after a day or two, but this went on and on and on.'

Everyone, it seemed, had a theory. It was the restless spirit of a little girl who had fallen to her death from the balcony; she had been a murder victim or she had been awoken from her eternal rest by the disturbance to her former home. But research by the Historic Landmarks Foundation had failed to unearth any records that would support any of these theories and the numerous inquiries which followed.

Fender, anxious to disassociate himself from anything 'kookie', subjected the picture to digital analysis. He scanned it into his computer and enlarged it in the expectation that the illusion would dissolve.

But to his puzzlement it remained clearly an image of a little girl in a blue dress. Only there was one element of the picture that no one had noticed until it was enlarged. The little girl had no face.

## THE FACE IN THE FLAMES

One of the most startling and controversial phantoms on film is that captured by an English amateur photographer, Tony O'Rahilly, during a blaze at Wem Town Hall, Shropshire in November 1995. O'Rahilly hadn't noticed anything unusual at the time, but when he developed the film there was no mistaking the image of a young girl standing in an open doorway on the fire escape. Two professional photographers (Tony Adams of the *Shropshire Star* and an expert from the *Daily Express*) examined both the print and the negative after which they declared themselves satisfied that it was not a hoax. The latter concluded that a hoaxer would have made a better job of it.

It was then passed to the former president of the Royal Photographic Society, Dr Vernon Harrison, then a member of the Association for the Scientific Study of Anomalous Phenomena (ASSAP) who stated that he was confident the photograph was genuine. However, Dr Harrison was puzzled by the fact that the head of the girl appeared to be above the railings of the fire escape while her body, if that's what it was, seemed to be behind them. Also a belt around her waist looked as if it extended in a line across and beyond her body instead of being wrapped around her. The image hadn't been faked, Dr Harrison concluded, but it was possible that the image was an illusion created by falling debris and tricks of the light. Subsequent examination of the fire service video of the blaze revealed a blackened roof beam where the girl's 'belt' had been, but it did not account for the unmistakable image of her 'face'.

The BBC (British Broadcasting Corporation) was next in line to examine the photo and submitted it to the experts of the National Photographic Museum as part of an investigation for their *Out Of This World* programme. The boffins at the museum pointed out several horizontal lines across the girl's face which they concluded

*The head of the girl appeared to be above the railings, while her body seemed to be behind them*

indicated that it had been computer generated, but Phil Walton of the ASSAP responded that 'it seemed the BBC had already made up their mind that the photograph was a hoax. . . I've a suspicion that the scan lines were incurred during the process they had used to produce the enlargement.'

Looking closely at the photograph, it is hard to imagine that the image could have been created by smoke and falling debris snapped at just the right moment when it happened to form a clearly discernible face.

## SPOOKS AT PSYCHIC SCHOOL

Burning embers do not, however, explain away the luminous swirls of vapour which have appeared on numerous photos taken by various visitors over the years to Stansted Hall, centre of the National Spiritualist Union. Perhaps it's not surprising that Stansted should be such a hive of paranormal activity as the hall is the venue for Britain's 'psychic school', where experienced psychics offer training courses and practical demonstrations of mediumship. But the ghostly manifestations might not be phantoms of former pupils, but are more likely to be the accumulation of residual personal energy generated by the fledgling mediums who attend the lectures and courses.

## CANDID CAMERA

Of course, it would be more convincing if such images were caught on video and that is exactly what occurred early on an October morning in 1991 in a nightclub in Lancashire, northern England. At 4.32 am the burglar alarm at the club was triggered by the appearance of a phantom figure which was evidently sufficiently solid to be picked up by its sensors.

When the manager arrived he ordered the night staff to search the building, but no signs of a break-in were found and all the employees could account for their whereabouts at the time. Baffled as to what might have activated the alarm, the manager ordered the surveillance tapes to be played. There for all to see was a ghostly figure moving soundlessly through the corridor and then passing through a solid locked door to the cash office. No explanation has been offered to explain the phenomenon.

## THE SPIRIT OF ROOM 422

> There are many ways of opening the doors of perception. Not all of them enable you to control what comes through the open doors, or to get them shut again.
>
> Guy Lion Playfair, *The Indefinite Boundary*, 1976

When best-selling horror author Stephen King wrote *The Shining*, about a haunted hotel which exerts an evil influence on its occupants, he may have taken inspiration from a real-life hostelry – the Holiday Inn, Grand Island in Buffalo, New York. Although this impressive establishment doesn't boast the remote mountainous setting of its fictional counterpart, it promises guests an equally memorable stay.

Many have commented on hearing what sounds like a child running along the empty halls and girlish giggling echoing in room 422. Staff have reported hearing a child calling their names and have had their duties interrupted by mischievous antics so often that they have come to refer to it affectionately as Tanya.

Locals say that she is the ghost of a child who burned to death in a fire in the house that occupied the site on which the hotel was built, but if that is true, she does not appear to be a troubled spirit. Apparently Tanya enjoys doing the same things all little girls like doing at her age, including bouncing on newly made beds and hiding cleaning products from the chambermaids. But in case anyone should suggest that it's just a clever marketing gimmick to drum up business for those who enjoy a good scare, staff are quick to point out that Tanya has been caught on camera, in the form of ghost lights which can be seen floating eerily down the corridors.

Curiously, this is one restless spirit that people don't seem to fear. In fact, they actually welcome it. Many a guest has been known to voice their disappointment if they arrive to find that room 422 is occupied, a problem some avoid by booking months in advance.

## HAUNTED HOTELS

The palatial, palm-lined Renaissance Vinoy Hotel in St Petersburg, Florida was built in the 'Roaring Twenties' for film stars, playboys and sporting celebrities, but now it seems it is home to some uninvited and rather unruly guests. In an interview for *Haunted Baseball* relief pitcher Scott Williamson of Tampa Bay's local team, the Devil Rays, told author Dan Gordon of the night he agreed to play host to a visiting team staying at the Vinoy in June 2003.

After climbing into bed and turning out the lights Williamson glanced through the parted curtains and thought he saw a faint luminous glow near the pool. At the sight of this a tingling sensation electrified his entire body as if someone was watching him. It unnerved him, but he tried to shrug it off and get some sleep. Rolling over on to his front, he suddenly felt pressure as if someone was pushing down on him which gave him trouble breathing.

With an effort he turned over on to his back, but it still felt as if someone was sitting on him. When he opened his eyes he saw a shadowy figure standing by the window. It was a man dressed in a long coat that seemed to belong to the 1930s or 1940s. Then it was gone.

Williamson was so distressed that he immediately phoned his wife who worked in a nearby hospital and asked her if there was any medical reason that might explain the pressure on his chest. He was relieved to hear that there was unlikely to be anything physically wrong as he had no other symptoms, but the feeling of unease wouldn't leave him.

The next day, after a restless night's sleep he asked a friend to research the history of the hotel and find out if there was a basis for the phantom

*Does a shadowy figure haunt the Renaissance Vinoy Hotel which was built during the 'Roaring Twenties' in St Petersburg, Florida?*

presence. Indeed, there was. The previous owner of the property, who had lived in the house before it had been converted into a hotel, had died there after a fire. His name, incredibly, was also Williamson.

It wasn't the last sighting of the shadowy stranger at the Vinoy.

The very next day, at 5 am, pitcher Frank Velasquez of the Pittsburgh Pirates awoke to see a transparent figure standing by the desk at the window. Velasquez later described him as being a sandy-haired and blue-eyed man wearing a long-sleeved white shirt and khaki-coloured trousers. Both his manner of dress and his haircut gave the pitcher the distinct impression that the visitor came from a previous age.

To make sure he was not dreaming Velasquez closed his eyes for a moment then opened them again. Sure enough, the man was still standing there. But being travel-weary, Velasquez just turned over and went back to sleep. It was only later that he learned of Williamson's story which he felt confirmed his own experience.

'The fact that it lined up with someone's story that I never knew anything about just kind of helps me know that it was real.'

But apparently that wasn't the only sighting of the 'old gentleman' that night. The team's assistant was standing in the hall trying to fiddle his room key into the lock when a man in a tailored suit passed soundlessly by, looking like an extra from a Humphrey Bogart movie. Unable to open the door, the assistant turned to ask the old man for help but the corridor was empty.

When these stories began to circulate among the players several elected to move out while others chose to commute from their home to the ballpark and back every day rather than have to sleep overnight in the hotel. The wife of one player fled with her children in the middle of the night when the taps in their bathroom repeatedly turned themselves on and there were numerous stories of flickering lights, slamming doors, clothes that mysteriously moved from the wardrobe to the bed and electrical cables which inexplicably pulled themselves out of the wall sockets and wrapped themselves around appliances.

But without doubt the most unsettling story was that told by Devil Rays pitcher Jon Switzer and his wife, who were awoken one night in their room on the fifth floor by the sound of scratching coming from the wall behind the headboard. They assumed it was a rat, but after a few moments it stopped and they went back to sleep. A quarter of an hour later it began again, but this time it was so loud that the Switzers leapt out of bed and turned on the lights.

To their horror and utter astonishment, they saw what appeared to be the painting above their bed come to life. It was a simple garden scene depicting a Victorian lady holding a basket with her right hand and her left resting on her chin. But now her left hand was scratching desperately at the glass as if trying to get out! Switzer and his wife exited the room faster than you could say 'Scooby Doo'.

## PHANTOM PITCHERS

Sportsmen are notoriously superstitious and baseball players are known to be more superstitious than most. They covet lucky bats, gloves that caught a curved ball and even shoes in which they made a winning home run. Many have their own pre-game rituals that help to calm their nerves which can involve putting on their equipment in a particular order and refusing to change worn-out shirts in case they interrupt a winning streak, while some even invoke the name of the great stars of the sport who have departed to play in the great stadium in the sky. It's a game steeped in tradition and its own mythology, so it is no surprise that the players have more than their share of ghost stories.

Ask any player to name the most haunted ballpark and they will all name Wrigley Field, home of the Chicago Cubs, where the ashes of Charlie Grimm, the Cubs manager during the 1930s, are said to have been scattered. His ghost has been seen by several security guards patrolling the stadium after dark and he is blamed for the unnerving phone calls to the dugout when the building is empty. Whenever a guard summons the nerve to pick up the receiver all he hears is an eerie silence, but they say that Charlie is on the other end giving orders from the bullpen where he used to direct the game. The bullpen phone is a direct line so there is no way that anyone could be calling from outside the stadium and the security guards are too spooked to play tricks of that sort on each other.

*Several Dodger Stadium employees have seen the image of a shrieking woman in white plunging over a cliff*

Wrigley is positively crawling with spirits of players and fans who couldn't let death come between them and their beloved game. Some fans have even had their own ashes scattered secretly at the ground which might account for the countless balls which disappear into the ivy. At one point, the owners of the ground brought in paranormal researchers to investigate the numerous sightings, but frustratingly their findings were never published.

Dan Gordon, co-author of *Haunted Baseball*, is a mine of lurid tales of hauntings, curses and legends about the game. He told interviewer Jeff Belanger of ghostvillage.com of the strangest legend he unearthed while researching the book.

> Dodger Stadium rests on the land of a former Mexican American community Chavez Ravine (and on the site of the former Hebrew Benevolent Society Cemetery, the first Jewish cemetery in LA – behind what is now parking lot 40-41) that was cleared to make room for the ballpark. The stadium rests on the levelled-off crest of a hill overlooking the city and according to urban

legend, a couple on their honeymoon taking in a breathtaking view of downtown LA from the hillside (at what is now the southern edge of the stadium parking lot) plummeted from the ravine to their deaths. The story went that the man fell first and upon discovering this, his wife leapt off the ridge. A story handed down from some of the old-time Dodger employees is that every now and then one could see an image of a shrieking woman dressed in white plunging over the cliff.

A souvenir vendor shared a story with us about his encounter with a 'fog-like object' that reminded him of *la llorona* stories he'd heard from co-workers. [Author's note: *La llorona* is a popular Mexican legend concerning a mother who drowns her own children and is cursed to roam the earth searching for them.] He was working late into the night counting inventory on the top deck behind the left field seats when he suddenly peered out on to the field and saw the white hazy formation originate at the Dodgers' bullpen and make its way across the field. He would witness the same occurrence happen quite a few times during his 20 years working with the team. He told us, 'One time, I actually brought a laser pointer that I used as part of my selling tools in my stand, and I pointed it at it to see what the hell it was, and it didn't disappear. It pretty much hovered around the field.'

He also reported hearing a child following him one evening when he was working on the mezzanine level. We heard reports of phantom footsteps from a lot of stadium workers (particularly the late-night security guards). One security guard told us an eerie story about how he and his fellow officers hear a woman in high heels walking the top deck.

That's just the tip of the iceberg of stories we discovered about the stadium. We recorded several from merchandise workers who work in the stadium's underground vaults that house historical memorabilia and lead into tunnels that travel deeper into the hill. Add to this the Hopi Legends of the domed headquarters of one of the three lost cities of 'Lizard People' alleged to exist further below the stadium and there's a whole lot of behind-the-scenes baseball strangeness in the City of Angels.

## BAD MOJO IN A BUNGALOW – THE SAN PEDRO HAUNTING

> When I see ghosts they look perfectly real and solid – like a living human being. They are not misty; I can't see through them; they don't wear sheets or bloody mummy bandages. They don't have their heads tucked under their arms. They just look like ordinary people, in living color, and sometimes it is hard to tell who is a ghost.
>
> Chris Woodyard, *Haunted Ohio*

So many amateur ghost hunters strike out after staking out a promising site for nights on end with nothing to show for their patience but a shot or two of fogged film or a mysterious streak of light which could be caused by lens flare. Barry Conrad and his friends were considerably luckier – if being assaulted by a malevolent entity is what you're after. They bagged the biggest game of the spirit world when they investigated an alleged haunting in a quiet suburb of San Pedro, California and managed to capture much of it on video.

Weldon is a quiet respectable neighbourhood and populated with rows of modest bungalows built at the turn of the previous century (1905). The last place one would expect to find a spook to rival that of *The Amityville Horror*. Fortunately for ghost aficionados, Conrad, an experienced TV cameraman, was on hand to record what went on in one particular house during the summer of 1989.

Barry has since produced a video of the investigation and appeared on internet radio show *Paranormal Café* to talk about his nerve-shredding experiences.

> I was determined to record the phenomena on film to avoid being accused of inventing yet another ghostly 'one that got away'. But the manifestations began even before I had a chance to unpack my gear. The first time we were in the house I felt pressure as if I was several fathoms underwater. But I really didn't expect to see anything so soon, so I suggested to a professional photographer friend who was with me that he take some photos of the attic where the owner of the house had said she had once seen a disembodied head. There isn't a ladder to the crawl space so my friend had to stand on a milk churn and poke his head through the trap door. After taking a few shots he came down and said that he felt someone had been watching him, but that it must just have been because he had heard all the spooky stories about the house. He was laughing it off, but I encouraged him to go back up and take some more shots, this time over his shoulder where he had sensed this presence. He thought it was a waste of time but did it to humour me and a moment later we heard him cry out. He bolted down the stairs and was shaking. All the colour had drained out of his hands. When he had calmed down he told us that just as he was about to squeeze off his third shot something or someone had jerked the camera out of his hands! He'd fled without it and was too frightened to go back and get it. I wouldn't have believed him if I hadn't seen the effect it had had on him. He was a wreck. That's when I knew we were really on to something.

While Jeff was catching his breath Barry went out to the car to get his video recording equipment which included powerful lights and a power supply. When he and Jeff cautiously approached the attic the camera was running, but as soon as Barry poked his head through the opening to film inside the crawl space the fully charged battery was drained of all power and the camera shut off. But the light was working and illuminated the whole loft space. There they could see that the floor was loosely boarded which would have made a noise if any hoaxer had been hiding up there and that there was no hiding place for anyone to avoid the glare of their lights. More perplexing was the discovery that the lens had been removed from the camera and left where Jeff thought he had sensed the presence, but the body of the camera had been placed in an open wooden crate on the other side of the loft! As Jeff struggled with shaking hands to screw the lens back on his camera Barry became aware of a 'foul odour' pervading the attic which he later compared to the stench of a rotting corpse.

It was time to get out.

As Barry clambered down out of the attic he saw the light on his camera turn green which meant that power had been restored. Looking up at Jeff he saw his friend's face contorted in terror. But he clearly couldn't speak.

Once they were safely back on the landing Jeff blurted out that he had been too terrified to talk. He had felt a long bony hand pressing into his back. As the friends stood bewildered and trying vainly to take in all that they had experienced they heard the unmistakable sound of footsteps in the empty space above them. According to Barry it sounded like a giant rat scampering across the floorboards. Fortunately, both the sound and the investigator's genuinely horrified reactions were captured on camera.

It took some time before Jeff got his nerve back and agreed to take another peek through the trap door. When he did so he saw what he described as a 'black mass' moving from side to side in the half-light. That proved to be the last straw for Jeff who refused to stay in the house a moment longer. It took all of Barry's persuasive powers to keep him alongside while he recorded an impromptu interview with the owner of the house, Jacqui Hernandez. But that was cut short when all the lights went out.

That night, at Barry's apartment, Jeff awoke screaming that someone was standing over him and couldn't be consoled. 'It was pretty frightening,' Barry recalled with characteristic understatement. It was to be another month before he had plucked up enough courage to go back to the house for a second look and only then because Jacqui had phoned him in the middle of the night in a highly agitated state and asking for his help. Her exact words were, 'all hell is breaking loose'. Apparently that night she had been in the kitchen when the refrigerator door opened by itself and the cap flew off a bottle of Pepsi, showering her with drink. She pushed the door closed, but it had opened again. That was when she claimed to have been attacked by an unseen entity which had pinned her to the floor. It took every ounce of her strength and her fear for the safety of her children to break free.

Forty-five minutes later, Barry pulled up in front of the bungalow in time to see Jacqui standing on the front lawn with her baby daughter cradled in one arm and her young son clinging tightly to the other hand.

'She thought we were coming to rescue her,' Barry remembers. 'But we burst out of that van with our cameras and lights like a bunch of ghostbusters.'

On this occasion Barry had brought reinforcements. Barry and Jeff had stopped off to pick up their friend Gary on the way as he was 'a born sceptic' with a serious interest in the scientific aspect of the paranormal and a person they could count on to look for a rational explanation before he would even consider the possibility of the supernatural.

Inside the house it was suspiciously quiet. But that was soon to change. Gary was keen to explore the attic having heard about his friends' earlier encounter and managed to persuade Jeff to accompany him. Barry remained behind in the laundry room underneath the trap door nursing his $15,000 video camera which he was determined to protect after having seen what had happened to Jeff's 35 mm. No sooner had the intrepid pair entered the loft than Barry saw a 'reddish orb' shoot down from the opening and vanish into the wall behind him. Thinking it might have been a flare from a flash he called to the others, but they assured him they hadn't taken any shots. It was then Barry's turn to get that sense that something was watching him from the open door of the bathroom to his right. Then there was the unmistakable sound of a loud groan from the attic and the noise of a struggle. Barry recorded these sounds which are followed by an eerie pause while he calls out to his friends. But they don't respond. After anxious moments they emerge pale and trembling into the light of the laundry room. Jeff is rubbing his throat which is marked with deep red weals. In the darkness something had grabbed on to his feet and wrapped a washing line around his neck, then strung him up to a nail in the rafters. If Gary hadn't lifted him up and unwound the cord he would have been the first-ever victim of a spectral lynching. In fact, Jeff very nearly didn't make it. While Gary was trying to lift his friend up by the waist to get some slack and loosen the cord, the entity was pulling at Jeff's legs to tighten the noose. At the last moment Gary bent the nail with his bare hands so the cord would come loose. Jeff had blacked out when the noose tightened, but he came to when the cord was loosened and it was then that he had felt something pulling on his legs. Incredible as it must sound, the evidence was there on film for all to see in the shape of the angry red welts around Jeff's neck.

'This had started out as spooky fun and games,' Barry remembers, 'but then we realized that it was a seriously dangerous business.'

No one could remember seeing the cord in the loft. On their initial inspection it had been empty apart from the fruit crate and some bric-a-brac. If there had been a cord it was certainly not attached to the nail. What was even more puzzling was the fact that it had been wound around Jeff's neck several times and secured to the nail by a bowline – a seaman's knot. Weldon is a coastal town and it's conceivable that the house had once been owned by a seafaring man. Jacqueline and her children moved out of the house and away from the area after that, but it wasn't quite the end of the haunting. Her friend, Susan Kastenedaz, called in Barry and his ghostbusters to check out her home which had been built next to a cemetery. It was also a turn-of-the-century home and had been designed by its first owner John Damon. While Barry was taking exterior shots of the house a side gate flew open by itself, but nothing could be seen with the naked eye. Later when Barry and Susan viewed the footage they could clearly see a light exiting the front door of the house and making a trail across the garden to the gate. As Barry pointed out, there are no fireflies in southern California and the front of the house was in deep shade when the film was shot. When he tracked the trail through the gate it led into the cemetery and disappeared into the ground over the grave of the late John Damon.

## DIARY OF A HAUNTING

Starr and Jessi Chaney, a mother and daughter team of 'certified ghost-hunters' in Nicholasville, Kentucky, kept a journal of their experiences in their haunted home beginning in the summer of 2005. These brief extracts, reproduced below, give some idea of what it is like to live with both the fear and fascination of spontaneous paranormal phenomena.

> Well, you can just imagine how excited we were to be buying our first home! We closed the loan on the Thursday before Memorial Day. While we were there with the lady who we were buying the house from, she told us that her first husband had passed away in the house several years before. She told us what a loving man he was, so we didn't really think much of it. We figured if he was still hanging around, he'd be following her to her new home with her new husband. We moved in that weekend, and with all the commotion going on with people in and out we didn't notice his presence for several days.
>
> My first experience with George was in our master bathroom. I walked past the open door, and saw a man standing in the bathroom. It took me a moment to realize that my husband wasn't home, so I quickly backtracked. . . only to find, of course, that the figure was gone. My daughters have seen him several times in there as well. He isn't scary, it's just the initial shock that gets ya.
>
> It didn't take long to realize we had another guest in our home, this one a young man. Research hasn't shown any other

deaths in our house, so we aren't sure who he is exactly. We can tell you that he likes a good laugh, no doubt. He likes to imitate our voices, so we come running thinking that another family member is calling us. I can't tell you how many times I've heard 'Mom!' come from the front hallway (where my daughters' bedrooms are), only to go in there and find them asleep or just watching TV and staring at me with a puzzled look at my hurried entrance. Then there are the times when Jessi and Nicki have stuck their head into my office and said, 'What?' Clueless, I say, 'What, what? I didn't say anything.' Never a dull moment!

We aren't quite sure which one of them it is who likes to open the kitchen cabinets though. For nearly a year I went nuts, chastising Jessi and Nicki for leaving them open all the time . . . then one day I was home alone and went into the kitchen to get a drink. Of course, all the cabinet doors were open, so I mumbled under my breath, got my glass and closed them all. After getting my drink, I returned to the office. About an hour later I went into the kitchen to make myself something for lunch, and found all the cabinet doors open again! So, I made a mental note to apologize to my daughters when they got home, fixed my lunch, and left the room.

The most jolting experience I've had was late one night in 2004. I was working on the computer, updating my candle website, and it was close to 3 am. It had been a hectic week, and this was the only time I had to get this task done. My husband had long since given up on me coming to bed, and had fallen asleep. I was intent on getting finished, so I barely noticed anything going on around me. . . until I felt a hand on my shoulder. I instantly assumed it was my husband coming to remind me of what time it was, so I quickly said, 'I know it's late, honey, but I really need to get this finished. I'll be to bed in just a b. . .' And that is when I looked over my shoulder and saw no one. At that very time there was a voice from the same area, definitely male; I heard one syllable and then it faded away. I immediately brought out my recorder and began asking questions, but the moment had passed. My visitor no longer had anything to say. . . but boy did he get my heart pumping!

We have gotten some photos with orbs, but nothing extraordinary like a mist or ectoplasm. And even though our fellas love to talk, apparently they don't care for being taped because they have never given us an EVP [electronic voice phenomena]. Not that we'll quit trying, of course!

*Saturday, June 25, 2005* – Nicki had to have her tonsils removed the prior Thursday, so she was in the master bedroom with me and we were watching TV. I had just muted the television, and Nicki was writing me a note (because she still had a hard time speaking). From my office, right next to our bedroom, came the sound of someone knocking on the door (my office door, which I keep closed). We both looked at each other, because it was a definite knock, just like someone knocking on your front door. I got up to see if someone was there, though I couldn't imagine who since we were alone in the house. . . of course, there was no one.

*Wednesday, June 29, 2005* – Another incidence of voice mimicry. Nicki came into my office from the den wanting to know what I wanted; I hadn't said anything. We were alone in the house.

*Monday, August 1, 2005* – My birthday! Nicki and I were alone in the house and we heard a clatter from my office. When we went to check it out, 4 of my pillar moulds were on the floor. They had previously been in a box on my shelf. I guess they were saying Happy Birthday, LOL.

*Sunday, August 14, 2005* – Our whole family was in the den, and we had our 2 dogs (Malachai and Belle) inside with us because it was raining. We were talking back and forth when we all heard a loud voice come from the front of the room that said, 'Puppy!' It didn't sound like a male, so we may have another spirit here now.

*Monday, September 5, 2005* – We had guests over for the Holiday for a cookout. Shortly after sitting down at the table to eat, we all heard a creaking noise coming from the other side of the kitchen. When we turned to look, one of the cabinet doors was slowly swinging open all on its own.

*Thursday, October 6, 2005* – Another incidence of voice mimicry. Ed swears he heard me calling out for him while he was in the den. I was in my office working on my computer and hadn't said anything.

*Thursday, October 13, 2005* – We went out for dinner and upon arriving back home I found several of my incense bundles placed on my desk. . . they were previously on a shelf on the other side of the room.

*Tuesday, October 31, 2005* – I was alone in the house during the day, working on getting ready for the evening's festivities, when I saw a man walk into our master bathroom. It startled me, to say the least, but I figured Ed must have gotten home early. When I went to the bathroom to check it out, no one was there.

*Sunday, November 27, 2005* – Jessi, Nicki and I were sitting on the bed in the master bedroom watching a movie when something thumped the bed hard enough to make it shudder. The bed is a queen size waterbed, the floor is carpeted, and underneath the bedroom is solid block concrete.

*Thursday, January 12, 2006* – Another incidence of voice mimicry. I clearly heard Jessi's voice from our master bathroom, asking me to come in there. When I went in I found the room empty. I found Jessi in her bedroom on the other side of the house.

*Wednesday, March 22, 2006* – While I was alone in the house, I walked into the kitchen to round up some lunch and found all the cabinet doors open. They were closed when I had gone in earlier for breakfast.

*Wednesday, May 17, 2006* – Nicki's birthday. We noticed the strong scent of Old Spice in the house. . . there isn't even a bottle of the stuff IN our house. My Dad used to wear it on special occasions, so I'm sure he was telling his granddaughter Happy Birthday.

*June through November 2006* – The activity in the house has really picked up, there is something on nearly a daily basis. Most involve objects being moved from where they were left, our kitchen cabinets being opened and closed, and actual sightings of people in the house. We have seen, several times, someone walk past the 'window' that is above the sink in the kitchen and looks into the den (due to a home extension, the window was removed and there is just a finished open area there now). We hear our cabinets being opened and closed as if someone is looking for something, but upon inspection no one is there.

*August 14, 2007* – Our ghosts were fairly inactive the first half of the year, we had even begun to think they were no longer around. . . they sure proved us wrong! Jessi, Nicki and I were all in the master bedroom having a girls' night, watching movies and eating popcorn while piled up on the bed, when we heard the back door open. That was followed immediately by footsteps of someone crossing the den and entering the kitchen, and the sound of cabinet doors being opened. We figured Ed had gotten home early, but when Nicki checked it out no one was in the house but us.

*September 13, 2007* – Today, just as we were setting up for the radio show, Jessi saw what she thought was Ed walking into our bedroom. She said, 'Is Dad home tonight?' to which I replied he wasn't. When we checked the bedroom, of course, we found it empty.

*October 1, 2007* – Things have really started hopping again! For the past week, on a daily basis we have encountered the bathroom and closet doors near the master bedroom opening on their own. We close them, and yank to make sure they are closed. Jessi and I actually happened to be looking down the hall from the master bedroom when the bathroom door opened on the first day it began happening, there was no one or no animal around it. All the other times it has happened we have heard the doors click, as if the handle was being turned, and then hear them open.

Most people would have sold up and moved out when confronted by such inexplicable incidents, but Starr, her husband Ed and their two daughters Jessi and Nicki were fascinated by the phenomenon. They founded an organization called PsyTech to investigate alleged hauntings and offered to organize ghost tours of spooky sites in their native state.

Business boomed and the family were so overwhelmed by the response from wannabe ghost hunters that they decided to offer one-day intensive certificated courses to train people in how to conduct a paranormal investigation.

CHAPTER SIX

# DEAD FAMOUS

We are, one and all, so pitifully afraid of the light.

Henrik Ibsen, *Ghosts*

## LENNON'S GHOST

Rock star Liam Gallagher of Britpop band Oasis is reported to be living in fear of a ghost which haunts his luxury London home.

In a British newspaper interview, a friend of the band confided that Liam now has difficulty sleeping because he believes he is being haunted by the phantom of former Beatle John Lennon, who was murdered in 1980. 'He lies awake listening with the lights on. He sometimes wakes up and feels as though he is being watched by someone from another walk of life.'

One would imagine that Liam would welcome the chance to chat with his musical hero, but it seems he fears he is being pursued by the restless spirit. 'I was in Manchester at a mate's house,' Liam confided to a friend after he first encountered Lennon's ghost during an out-of-body experience. 'I turned round and there I was, lying on the bed, and I sort of fell back into my body. There was a presence there and it was him, Lennon.'

Cynics might say that such experiences are often induced by an over-indulgence in alcohol and non-prescription pharmaceuticals, while music critics would no doubt claim that Lennon has come back to claim his share of the royalties for all the tunes the Gallagher brothers ripped off the old Beatles albums.

## IN SEARCH OF SINATRA AND OTHER CELEBRITY SPIRITS

Shows with a supernatural theme have become a ratings winner on the small screen in recent years, but sadly for the producers ghosts have proven to be camera-shy, while other paranormal phenomena seldom appear on

*Rock star Liam Gallagher believes he is being haunted by John Lennon*

cue. No matter how talented the programmes' resident psychics might be, they can't guarantee the thrills that viewers demand or even the proof that the scientists and parapsychologists are hoping for.

Take the case of professional psychic Chris Fleming.

Chris is co-presenter of the British TV series *Dead Famous*, the latest in a long line of paranormal reality shows which investigate alleged hauntings and share their findings with viewers in the safety of their living rooms.

Accompanying Chris on his televised tour is presenter Gail Porter, a self-confessed sceptic in all matters supernatural, who plays Scully to his Mulder. In reality, their investigations offer little more than a few words with the dead celeb's former acquaintances and the staff who now work at the sites of their former haunts. Then it's lights off for a vigil in a darkened room with a video camera and a lot of night-vision shots of the pair looking spooked and talking in awe of 'energy imprints'.

Their first subject was 'ol' Blue Eyes' himself, Frank Sinatra. As they set off on their trip to Las Vegas, Gail contemplated which side of Sinatra would be uncovered – the charming showman or the hard, abrasive friend of the Mob? This was clearly not going to be a serious investigation, but yet another entertainment special with a paranormal theme.

On day one they met with Tony Oppedisano, a 'personal friend' of Sinatra, who shared his impressions of the singer which amounted to little more than saying that he was a 'very complex man'. It seems that Frank was a believer in reincarnation which was bad news for 'Mulder and Scully' as it meant that he wouldn't be hanging around his old haunts if he had been reborn. But Tony was certain Frank was watching over him and that his larger-than-life personality guaranteed he would be hanging around the Golden Nugget, the casino and hotel that had been his second home. There, on the fifth floor where Sinatra had his suite, Chris felt 'strong energy', but couldn't identify the source.

In the luxury suite he dimmed the lights and lit a candle while asking Sinatra to bless them with his presence. Speaking into the camera in the darkness like a resident of the *Big Brother* house he was reduced to generalities such as 'something just went on' which must have angered ol' Blue Eyes as it was apparently answered by the sound of fingernails scraping on the window, although we couldn't hear it. Or maybe it was just the producer clawing to get out.

## Stranger in the Night

On day two, after Chris had shared his 'experiences' in Sinatra's suite the previous night, the pair set off for the Polo Lounge, an exclusive saloon on the banks of Lake Tahoe. En route they stopped in at the Thunderbird Lodge, a playboys' hideaway in the mountains boasting a secret room where Frank played cards with his cronies and allegedly met with the underworld figures who were said to have 'guided' his career. But in spite of all the talk of his larger-than-life personality Frank again failed to put in an appearance, although in the boathouse 'something' drained the batteries in Chris' camera and pushed him as he explored the former owner's bedroom. One has to wonder why a personality as imposing as Sinatra would miss the opportunity of a lifetime to make a comeback on camera.

It almost makes you question your belief in ghosts, or ghost hunters.

Day three saw our intrepid duo and the camera crew at Calneva, Frank's former residence on the California/Nevada border. It had been built on a sacred Native American tribal ground which might account for the phenomena which have spooked its staff over the years.

During a guided tour Chris and Gail learnt that the staff consider certain areas of the hotel off limits and they saw for themselves the damage to the large picture window in the lounge which mysteriously cracks when no one is looking.

As for the TV which turns itself on in one of the guest cabins, the pair had to take the tour guide's word for that, but there was no doubt in Chris' mind that there was a 'strong imprint' in that particular cabin. Mind you, that was after he had been told this was where Marilyn Monroe had suffered an overdose.

If only the programme's producer or the tour guide had thought to test Chris' abilities by taking him to a cabin where nothing untoward had happened and seeing if he had come up with the same impression after being told that story.

That night, obviously aware that they hadn't come up with anything to justify their travel expenses, or the viewers' patience, Chris took part in a séance in Frank's Celebrity Showroom, a private theatre where Sinatra and his buddies entertained their friends.

Casing the joint before the big event all Chris could come up with was another of his vague, groan-inducing observations, specifically, 'There's definitely some type of energy up there.'

As parapsychologist and impartial observer Janice Oberding remarked, 'It's very easy to convince yourself that you're feeling something when you get a group like this together,' meaning people who are believers to begin with and who have gathered in expectation of hearing 'something'.

If that's what they wanted, Chris didn't disappoint them. He mumbled that he was feeling 'really cold' and went into a trance during which he claimed he could not only sense Frank's spirit, but could see him 'at the end of a long tunnel'. He also claimed to have been taken over by the spirit of Sammy Davis, Jr, but said nothing in Sammy's voice nor did he imitate his mannerisms, at least not in the clip we were shown.

Then as the performance's climax he channelled the spirit of a Native American, but when asked to 'communicate' by another member of the circle all he could do was produce some incoherent chanting, although once again we can only judge by what was broadcast.

Whether Chris is a genuine psychic is not the question. He may well be the real deal, although he offers no compelling evidence to support this in the programme and too often he seems to bolt at the first sign of a spook. Why invite a clairvoyant to a supposedly haunted location if he is going to leave at the first sign of paranormal activity?

It wasn't as if anything had actually manifested or had thrown objects around. All we have is Chris claiming he has felt 'something' and that he isn't hanging around to find out what it is! Little old ladies who practise mediumship at spiritualist churches up and down the country show more backbone than this guy.

The *Dead Famous* team offer nothing substantial to support the belief in life after death other than their vague feelings of being scared of the dark. It's all so inconsequential that if it had been a one-to-one reading with a medium we would feel entitled to our money back.

It may have seemed a whizz of an idea in the network executives' meeting, but 'investigations' of this kind give ghosthunting a bad name.

Quite frankly, it's embarrassing to watch. If you want to see a serious demonstration of spirit communication, you only have to tune in to see the American celebrity psychics John Edward and James Van Praagh in action before a studio audience, or the compelling English 'street psychic' Tony Stockwell and his colleague Colin Fry. All of these presenters offer 'cold' spontaneous and uncannily accurate readings of complete strangers, the details of which are invariably confirmed by their astonished subjects.

The best that can be said for *Dead Famous* is that they haven't made any kind of convincing case for the existence of spooks and spirits – only for the public's seemingly insatiable appetite for celebrities and the supernatural.

## PARANORMAL INVESTIGATIONS INC – INTERVIEW WITH LOYD AUERBACH

Loyd Auerbach is director of the Office of Paranormal Investigations and the author of several seminal studies of the subject including *A Paranormal Casebook: Ghost Hunting in the New Millennium*, (Atriad Press, 2005), *Ghost Hunting: How to Investigate the Paranormal* (Ronin Publishing, 2004) and *ESP, Hauntings and Poltergeists* (Warner Books, 1986) which was named the 'Sacred Text' on ghosts by *Newsweek* magazine. Professor Auerbach has also taught parapsychology and related topics for several years in New York and San Francisco and holds an MS in Parapsychology from JFK University (1981), and so he is well qualified to carry out thorough and professional investigations.

*What exactly is the Office of Paranormal Investigations and what are its aims and achievements to date?*

The Office of Paranormal Investigations (OPI) is dedicated to the scientific investigation and understanding of spontaneous occurrences of psi phenomena.

Founded in 1989 by Loyd Auerbach, MS and Christopher Chacon, OPI was essentially an outgrowth of some of the function of the then recently defunct Graduate Parapsychology Program of John F. Kennedy University in northern California. At the founding, and since then, OPI as a group has consisted of parapsychological investigators, researchers and other consultants as well as psychic practitioners, who are interested

*Loyd Auerbach has been called a 'real-life ghostbuster'*

in exploring experiences and situations that people might consider psychic, paranormal, extrasensory, spiritual, or related to these. OPI's primary areas of investigation involve sightings of apparitions (ghosts), unusual happenings in homes or offices or other locations that people have felt are haunted, and poltergeist situations, where there are reported unusual physical effects or movement of objects. In addition, OPI is interested in other forms of psi, such as 'extrasensory perception' and 'extended perception' (including precognition, clairvoyance and telepathy), psychokinesis (mind over matter), psychic healing, reincarnation, near-death experiences, out-of-body experiences, trance channelling and mediumship, and other psychic experiences and practices.

OPI staff investigate the problems reported, first looking for any and all normal explanations before assuming a paranormal one, then they offer recommendations and service with respect to dealing with the phenomena or experiences. While it is effectively impossible to prove the existence of psychic phenomena in these situations given the current state of science and technology, OPI investigators have been successful in assisting people to understand such experiences and, when appropriate, in eliminating the phenomena. OPI does provide a thorough investigation in such cases and an understanding of what is most likely happening, but NO ONE CAN GUARANTEE the removal of such phenomena.

In reality the main contribution OPI makes is in providing educated, credible and ethical help to people who have what they believe are paranormal problems. Besides investigations into specific phenomena and locations, OPI provides consulting services for the media, scientific researchers, business people who wish to consult psychics, attorneys involved in cases with a supernatural element or who may be consulting psychics for jury selection and law enforcement personnel who might be considering calling in a psychic to assist in a difficult case.

*How do you reconcile your role as a serious investigator of paranormal phenomena with your professional activities as a psychic entertainer and can you explain what the latter involves?*

I first started in magic as a result of a course on magic, 'mentalism and psychic fraud' taught as part of the graduate parapsychology program at John F. Kennedy University when I was a student.

Once in the field of parapsychology I was further encouraged by new colleagues to learn more and get real performing experience and to hone my own expertise in magic and mentalism since this was so often held over the heads of researchers (that they had none).

Through the 1980s and early 1990s, I increased my knowledge of mentalism and psychic entertainment – performing effects in the mind-reading, prediction, and mind over matter vein. It was clear that I got much more out of this form of entertainment than regular magic, and an even better understanding of how people perceive things as paranormal or psychic.

*Does your knowledge of cold reading and the allied arts help you to expose fraudulent mediums and identify fake ghost stories?*

Knowledge of cold reading frankly does not help with investigations, nor with identifying 'fake' ghost stories. It can certainly help with assessing a purported psychic or medium.

Broader knowledge of the magical arts and mentalism/psychic entertainment absolutely has helped me. But where it's helped is mainly in understanding how people misperceive, misunderstand and mislabel ordinary (though sometimes rare) events as paranormal ones.

In other words, a greater understanding of the psychology of deception and misperception.

In addition, it's also given me an appreciation for there being multiple possible explanations for any reported event – each of which needs to be checked out before coming to a conclusion. There are many ways to saw a lady in half, find a selected card, or even levitate something.

Yes, no question that the knowledge – and more so the performing background – allows me to identify fraud. But as far as detecting fake ghost stories – and here I'm assuming you mean deliberate lying in the telling of a ghost story to me – it's my knowledge of parapsychology that helps the most.

*What do you consider has been your most fascinating investigation as far as a haunting or poltergeist activity is concerned and what has it revealed about the nature of the phenomenon?*

To me, the most fascinating single investigation was an apparition case (which is distinguished from a haunting or poltergeist) involving a family all occasionally seeing the former owner of the home they bought. Their son apparently had much more experience, as he reported having daily conversations with the ghost.

The investigation allowed me an opportunity to sit down with a 'ghost' – the boy, only 12, playing translator with the ghost and providing specific details of her life and family (later verified) and then allowing me to interview the 'ghost' about her experience of dying, her experience as a ghost and getting some idea as to why she thought ghosts had clothing on, could be seen at different ages, could or could not move objects, and so on.

That case, and others since then, certainly have convinced me that in some instances people do stick around after death as free-floating consciousness capable of interaction. But more than that, it's clear that we don't alter personality after death – basically ghosts are people, too.

*Can you please talk about your investigation of the haunting of the USS* Hornet *(a haunted WWII-era aircraft carrier in Alameda, CA)?*

The USS *Hornet* is a WWII vintage aircraft carrier with a distinguished history. It was decommissioned in the early 1970s. In 1995, it was brought to a pier at the newly closed Alameda Air Naval Station, where volunteers for a newly formed foundation began repairs and clean-up in order to open it as a museum in 1998. Shortly after the clean-up began, volunteers began seeing apparitions of sailors and officers. Footsteps and voices have been heard when no one else was aboard. Mysterious officers and enlisted men have been sighted (only to have them disappear fairly quickly). Sensations of temperature changes, wind in enclosed spaces and feelings that someone else is present – or touching – have been experienced.

In 1999, we began our investigations at the request of psychic Stache Margaret Murray, who'd already been working with several of the many witnesses to the phenomena on the *Hornet*. With occasional visits over the next few years, we've spoken to dozens of witnesses who have experienced the activity, and have identified more than 25 locations on the ship we might consider 'hot spots', for having multiple reported experiences. I've had my own experiences aboard the *Hornet* as well.

One of the more unusual facets of the case of the USS *Hornet* is that there are several instances of more than one person (in one case, five) having the exact same sighting of a sailor or officer at the same time, and in a few instances the witnesses have seen up to three apparitions at the same time. From descriptions alone, it would appear that there are several dozen apparitions of sailors and officers aboard the ship. It's fairly certain these are the ghosts of people who did NOT die aboard the *Hornet*, as the ship has a low death incidence throughout its working history. Not to mention that workers maintaining the ship when it sat in the shipyards for over 20 years swear it was not haunted at that time (and then proceeded to describe other ships that were haunted in the same shipyard).

We believe, as do most of the on-board witnesses, that these are the spirits of men who did serve aboard the ship, but died in retirement or civilian life after the ship was decommissioned.

The living folks aboard have stated their belief that the ghosts are there to help the ship continue on as a museum, a piece of living history.

We've videotaped interviews with many of the witnesses, and have produced a short documentary, *The Haunting of the USS* Hornet, *v.1*, which is still available through my website. We are currently editing all the footage into a more in-depth documentary.

The USS *Hornet* Aircraft Carrier Museum is open to the public in Alameda, CA. The ghost stories continue to come in, though our investigations there are infrequent due to a variety of issues.

*Can you tell us something about your work with psychic Annette Martin as far as it relates to ghosts and hauntings?*

Annette Martin is an accomplished psychic, with decades of professional experience doing readings for people, as well as working with police in missing persons and homicide cases and participating in research on psychic diagnoses of people's illnesses (with a medical doctor). In addition, she has mediumistic abilities, and I have worked with her in numerous investigations since the early 1990s.

She has demonstrated the ability to communicate with apparitions, and to act as a sort of counsellor to them. In the case of hauntings, she's able to sort out the historical imprint, providing us with information we can verify (not always, as the records are often not complete enough to tell us either way).

Unlike many psychics, she understands the need to eliminate normal explanations first – she even helps with this process.

She is more than willing to have her perceptions questioned in order to see if they fit the situation, or are incomplete, or if they might be off somehow.

In one case, apparent poltergeist activity (object movement) was observed only after an apparition had been seen. The family assumed the activity was caused by the apparition.

However, based on the family's description of both, and the reactions of the family members to the apparition experience, it seemed something more was happening.

Martin perceived the entity almost immediately, and laughed at his (the apparition's) denial of responsibility for the PK activity. After communicating with the discarnate entity, and discussing it with me, we concluded that the appearance of the apparition (a stranger) to the family was the source of the stress that set off the spontaneous psychokinetic activity.

Martin reported that both she and the entity sensed which of the family members the agent was. The activity was halted by utilizing this information in our discussion with the family, as we would with any poltergeist case. This was followed by communication with the apparition to determine his identity and to 'help him move on' as Martin put it.

The case that best exemplifies Annette Martin's abilities is the Moss Beach Distillery restaurant, south of San Francisco. This is a well-known case with a ghost, commonly called the 'Blue Lady', who has been haunting the place since her death in the early 1930s.

While I've worked with several psychics at the distillery, I've worked there with Martin most frequently, and feel she's made a great connection with the apparition we've come to know as 'Cayte'.

Each time I've visited with Martin with the intention to communicate with Cayte, we've gotten interesting information through Martin, sometimes about the history of the restaurant and town, sometimes about the Blue Lady's life, and often about the ghost's perspective on her decades-long existence in her current state. Some has been verified (where we can, the historical information), and other information is similar to what witnesses and other psychic practitioners have described as coming from the ghost.

In addition, Martin's been persuasive with Cayte to get her to co-operate with us. We've been able to use our equipment to detect SOMEthing whenever Annette is in communication with the Blue Lady.

*In February 2005 you launched a new basic Certificate Program in Parapsychological Studies supported by the HCH Institute in Lafayette, CA. Can you describe the contents of the program, the type of students you are hoping to attract and what they will be able to bring to an investigation following their studies?*

For those who do want to conduct field investigations after their studies, what they walk away with is a full understanding of how the phenomena of apparitions, hauntings and poltergeists as well as the experiences of people encountering them fit into the broader context of psi phenomena and research. Such things do not exist in a vacuum, and it is unfortunate that the vast majority of ghost hunters do not comprehend the connection between psi abilities (ESP and PK) and ghosts, hauntings or poltergeists. I've seen some state that psychokinesis does not exist (meaning, among the living) and turn around and describe a situation with moving objects caused by (the mind of) a ghost.

The Certificate Program in Parapsychological Studies is a 60-hour course series providing an overview to the field of parapsychology and the main areas of research and investigation: ESP, PsychoKinesis (Mind Matter Interactions), and Survival of Bodily Death.

Information on the program and course descriptions can be found at www.hypnotherapytraining.com/parapsych.cfm

*You are very interested and concerned with media portrayals of the phenomena and the science of parapsychology and have acted as a consultant to various television producers and writers, most notably with shows for the History Channel, A&E and the UK's LivingTV. What is your impression of the media's attitude to the paranormal? They appear to be cynical on principle.*

It's not that they're cynical and treat it with disdain, but that so many are ignorant of what the paranormal encompasses, who the real experts are (they so often do not check) and how the phenomena and experiences actually manifest themselves – which is quite different from the general perception that it's weird, scary, and so on, thanks to both religion and fiction (literature, film and television).

The subject is given short shrift for several reasons, some all happening at the same time. Ramp-up time for a series or show may not allow for real research on the part of the writers/producers/production assistants. The budget is generally too low to get the experts involved with more than a phone call – and there's a shortage of experts who know both the subject and television.

While the reality shows can provide some real information, the show itself may often be sensationalistic in order to get at the vast general public that would otherwise only have a passing interest. Fear sells better than education, unfortunately, and most programming is produced for commercial television – meaning the networks who buy the shows are concerned also about sponsors and what sells.

Yes, the networks muck about – mainly in the actual ordering of the show, and their stated expectations. This is hardly limited to shows about the paranormal. It happens in the movie industry all the time (the executives changing the story/plot/characters because of their own expectations of what the public will 'buy').

Often the production people have no real opinion either way as to whether the phenomena are real. Some of the production people are clearly sceptical, but are producing what the networks ask for anyway. The thing to remember is that this is SHOW BUSINESS.

As to whether the media has 'assumed the role once taken by the scientific community', the media has certainly not taken over assessment of psychic phenomena in any sort of way like science has. However, the viewing public seems to accept the often skewed (and sometimes downright wrong) portrayals of the paranormal because the show is labelled as 'reality' or a 'documentary'.

# CHAPTER SEVEN

# HIGHWAYS TO HELL

Long tedious journeys can be hell – particularly if they take a detour through the 'Twilight Zone' where phantom hitch-hikers wait by the side of the road to catch a lift from unwary drivers. Most tales of phantom passengers are no more than urban legends, but those described in the following pages have a ring of authenticity. But if these tales are true they beg the question – if the dead can walk through solid walls why do some choose to thumb a ride?

## ROUTE 666

As every God-fearing Bible reader and horror movie addict knows, '666' is the number of the beast – the Anti-Christ – who is prophesied to arise at the end of days for the final apocalyptic battle between good and evil. So what possessed an American highway official to name the western branch of the Chicago to Los Angeles highway US 666 is anyone's guess. Clearly he wasn't superstitious, or maybe it didn't occur to him that he might be invoking dark and destructive forces on what was to become known as the 'Devil's Highway'.

The name was well deserved for few stretches of road could boast such a catalogue of eerie encounters. These ranged from phantom hitch-hikers to blazing trucks that would bear down behind a lone driver at high speed, forcing him to put the pedal to the floor or risk being incinerated or driven off the road. There were also tales of savage dogs which would give chase, clawing and biting at tyres until the driver could outrun them. But wild dogs wouldn't attack a speeding car so these too would be attributed to supernatural beasts. It's possible that drivers were confusing these hounds from hell with a particular breed of shape-shifter known in the south-west as skinwalkers who were believed to assume the form of a man or animal then vanish the moment they had forced a driver to swerve into the oncoming traffic. There were numerous stories of gaunt, cadaverous figures materializing on the back seats of vehicles

*Blazing trucks would bear down behind a lone driver at high speed*

and scaring the living daylights out of unsuspecting drivers who caught a glimpse of their phantom passengers in their rear-view mirrors. More than a few drivers have stumbled from the wreckage ranting about the stranger on the back seat only for the cops to blame it on drink, drugs or fatigue. Some crash site investigators have even attributed the unusually high incidence of accidents on the route during the 1970s to a form of mass hysteria created by public interest in all things demonic during the decade which spawned a host of diabolical movies including *The Exorcist*, *The Omen* and not forgetting the possessed truck of Steven Spielberg's *Duel*.

Of course, maybe it really was hell and not Hollywood which was casting its shadow over this godforsaken highway. By 1991 the road's reputation was so bad that parts of it were practically deserted. Drivers would make tortuously long detours rather than risk falling prey to the many apparitions that were said to haunt it, though many were simply put off by the prospect of breaking down in the Arizona desert or driving over the edge of the twisting mountain passes. It didn't help that souvenir hunters were repeatedly stealing the road signs, leaving tourists scratching their heads as to which turning to take. Highway officials were also receiving complaints from truck stops and filling stations, complaining that trade was practically non-existent and demanding a name change. It was probably this commercial consideration rather than any talk of a curse that finally persuaded the Joint Board of Interstate Highways to redesignate it US 491. Since then the number of inexplicable incidents has decreased dramatically, but even today only the most trusting drivers will pull over for hitch-hikers and even these make sure they stay wide awake and alert at all times.

## THE DEAD ZONE

If you're planning to visit Florida in the near future, take a tip from the locals and avoid travelling on Interstate 4 just north of Orlando, especially the 400-metre stretch south of the St John's River Bridge. It's not the daily gridlock that could ruin your vacation, but something intangible and unnerving which is said to account for the uncommonly high accident rate at that spot. Mobile phones and car radios are plagued with static, or even worse, they pick up disturbing, ethereal voices which led to the locals naming this spot the 'Dead Zone'.

There is a sound historical basis for the name; back in 1885 the last surviving members of a devout Roman Catholic community known as St Joseph's Colony died of yellow fever, and were unceremoniously disposed of by other settlers in a field that served as the cemetery. Contrary to their dying wish they were denied the benefit of a Christian burial as there was no priest to officiate at the ceremony. The farmer who worked that land avoided the graves and was spared any supernatural activity, but when the construction workers arrived to build the highway in 1960 they didn't bother to disinter and rebury the bodies. They simply levelled the plot and began to concrete it over. And that's when the troubles began.

While the surface was being laid, Hurricane Donna cut a swathe through Florida, causing unprecedented destruction which set the project back several months. Witnesses claim that the epicentre of the storm appeared to be plum centre in the 'Field of the Dead' where the graves had been. Since then there have been sightings of so-called 'ghost lights' at night which tired drivers have swerved to avoid, mistaking them for approaching headlights and then there are the ominous dark clouds which appear in bright daylight and whisk across the lanes causing speeding drivers to slam on the brakes afraid that they might be ploughing into a flock of birds or a stray animal. No one knows how many accidents have been caused by these manifestations and we are never likely to know how many fatalities can be attributed to them as those who can tell us have joined the unquiet spirits in the Dead Zone.

## THE HAUNTED HIGHWAY

Another stretch of highway to avoid is the Pine Barrens section of the Garden State Parkway which appears to offer a comparatively quiet back road out of New Jersey. Many unsuspecting motorists have lived to regret taking this scenic route through the fog-wreathed New Jersey Pine Lands – especially those who chose to drive at night. Phantom hitch-hikers are a staple ingredient of urban legend, but the 'Parkway Phantom' is no myth. He's the real deal.

The New Jersey state police have been forced to file several reports by terrified drivers who claim to have swerved to avoid a tall thin man in shabby clothes who has been seen running on to the northbound lanes near exit 82 waving his arms frantically as if trying to flag down the

*Many motorists have lived to regret taking the scenic route through the fog-wreathed New Jersey Pine Lands*

speeding cars. A number of accidents have been blamed on his sudden appearance in the middle of a road which is otherwise straight and safe. Sightings of a stranded motorist answering the same description have been recorded elsewhere along the route. This lean figure, dressed in an old-fashioned long coat, is frequently seen standing beside a wrecked car at the side of the road attempting to wave down passing traffic. But whenever someone pulls over to offer help they find both the driver and the vehicle have disappeared.

## PHANTOM HITCH-HIKERS

Phantom hitch-hikers are a common urban legend in places as far apart as Malaysia, Hawaii and Russia. Most are dismissed out of hand as mere folk tales, but there are some which are worth closer investigation.

In the 1950s an American couple and their friend were driving to a dance when they stopped to offer a lift to a young blonde girl who was standing at the side of the road. It was a cold evening but she was wearing only a thin white dress and after climbing into the back of the car she commented on how warm it was. She told them her name was Rose White and during the course of conversation accepted their invitation to join them at the dance.

The evening was a success, but both men noted that their new friend was cold to the touch when they took turns dancing with her. Afterwards they dropped her off at the spot by the roadside where they had met and subsequently arranged to meet again the next day at an address she gave them.

But when they arrived there the following day they were shocked to find themselves outside a convent. When they told their story to one of the nuns she produced a photo of Rose which they all immediately identified as the girl they had given the lift to. Then the nun took them outside to the cemetery and showed them Rose's grave. She explained that they were not the first people to come looking for Rose White. Every 15 years, on the anniversary of her death, she would appear at the roadside in the hope of finding the company she longed for from the cold solitude of the grave.

A similar story is told in France of two married couples who picked up a young female hitch-hiker en route to Montpellier in 1981. The girl sat between the two women on the back seat and said nothing for the entire length of the journey. Then suddenly she screamed, causing the driver to brake. But there was nothing in the road. Then the two wives screamed and the men looked back to see the girl had gone – vanished into thin air.

Such stories, corroborated by several witnesses, appear to be genuine incidents of paranormal activity, but there is a more mundane explanation offered for those incidents in which a lone driver gives a lift to a hitch-hiker who promptly disappears without saying so much as 'goodbye'. Doctors have a term for this form of hallucination. They call it hypoxia and claim it is caused by a lack of oxygen to the brain often incurred during long car journeys, specifically when the driver has been smoking. It would seem to explain one of the most famous cases of a phantom hitch-hiker, that experienced by South African army corporal Dawie van Jaarsveld.

In 1978 Jaarsveld was riding his motorbike to meet his girlfriend in Uniondale, Cape Province when he saw a dark-haired young girl waiting by the side of the road. She accepted his offer of a lift into town and put on the spare helmet he kept for passengers. A few miles further on he pulled over because the bike was behaving oddly, only to discover that his passenger had gone. But the thing which unnerved him was seeing that the spare helmet was still strapped to the bike. Had he imagined the whole episode, or was it possible that the experience had occurred, but in some other reality? Crazy though it might sound, the latter seems more likely as Jaarsveld was later able to positively identify the girl from a photograph which he would not have done had he imagined the whole incident. She was 22-year-old Maria Roux who had been killed in a car crash in April 1968 on the same stretch of road.

## THE BLONDE OF BLUEBELL HILL

Pranksters, drunk drivers and attention-seekers are frequently found to have been the source of many phantom hitch-hiker stories, but those who have reported running over a young female ghost at the notorious accident black spot Bluebell Hill in the English county of Kent appear to have been in deadly earnest.

In 1972 a driver by the unusual name of Mr Goodenough went to the local police to report knocking down a young girl whose body he had covered with a blanket. But when the police arrived at the scene the body was gone.

There was no sign of blood, only the blanket and the skid marks where the 'accident' was said to have happened. Twenty years later the same thing happened again. A driver by the name of Mr Sharpe rushed into the local police station to report killing a young girl who had run out in front of his car before he had time to brake. Again, when the police drove out to the scene there was no body to be found. Curiously, both drivers had described the same girl – a young blonde wearing a white dress.

# CHAPTER EIGHT

# SPOOKY SITES

## CITY OF THE DEAD

Every city in the world has its share of ghosts, but surely none is more deserving of its reputation as the capital of the uncanny than Edinburgh. With its narrow, twisting alleyways, cobbled streets and ancient, imposing buildings, the Old Town resembles the set of a Hammer horror movie. All it needs is a shroud of creeping fog and one can imagine its more unsavoury inhabitants stalking the streets again.

Other cities have their serial killers and criminals, but Edinburgh can boast a whole rogues' gallery, enough to fill the chamber of horrors in Madame Tussauds several times over.

Long before Hannibal Lecter put cannibalistic killers on the menu Edinburgh was home to real-life people-eater Sawney Bean. Then there were the bodysnatchers Burke and Hare, cross-eyed lady killer Dr Neil Cream and criminal mastermind Deacon Brodie, the inspiration for Robert Louis Stevenson's *Dr Jekyll and Mr Hyde*. In fact several of Edinburgh's larger-than-life personalities served as the models for immortal literary figures, including Sherlock Holmes and his nemesis

Professor Moriarty. Conan Doyle studied medicine at Edinburgh University and based the master detective on his own teacher and mentor Dr Joseph Bell. Charles Dickens made only a brief sojourn to the city, but he returned with the seed for what is arguably the most famous ghost story ever written, *A Christmas Carol*. And let's not forget that his spiritual descendant, J.K. Rowling, conjured up her

*The chapel at Roslin is central to the plot of* The Da Vinci Code

finest creation, the boy wizard Harry Potter, in a café overlooking Greyfriars Graveyard.

But if it's 'real' history you're wanting, then your first stop must be the oldest haunted site in Edinburgh which lies just outside the city. As everyone who has read *The Da Vinci Code*, or seen the movie based on Dan Brown's bestseller, will know, the 15th-century chapel at Roslin is the centre of an alleged conspiracy concerning the true fate of Jesus of Nazareth and his supposed descendants, proof of which is said to be hidden in sealed vaults underneath the chapel. The hype surrounding the book has attracted thousands of tourists from around the world who might not have been so keen to linger had they known that the chapel is haunted by an order of Augustine monks known as the Black Canons. Judith Fiskin, a former archivist and curator at Roslin, claims to have seen a ghostly monk during her tenure in the 1980s and to have shared the experience with several reliable witnesses. But the brothers are not the only spirits wandering around. The site is also said to be haunted by the restless spirit of a mason's apprentice, reputedly killed by his master for having outshone his mentor by carving what is known as the Apprentice Pillar.

Animal spirits are also to be seen when conditions are favourable. According to local legend the spirit of a murdered hound can be seen and heard prowling the grounds of nearby Roslin Castle. The Mauthe Dog, as it is known, was cruelly put to death beside its English master during the Battle of Roslin in 1303 at which the Scots routed an English army of more than 30,000. Bad losers, the sassenachs.

There is even a local 'white lady' identified as Lady Bothwell who was evicted from her ancestral home by the heartless Regent Moray in the late 16th century. Presumably, she returns to search in vain for her tormentor and tear his merciless heart from his body.

## ARTHUR'S SEAT

Wife-murderer Nicol Muschat was hanged here in 1720. It is also the site of the burial place of the city's plague victims. Nearby Salisbury Crags was at one time the preferred jumping spot for suicides. Many others met their deaths at this precarious peak by accident and no doubt, foul play played its part in the premature demise of many more.

In 1836, some children made a curious find while playing at Arthur's Seat – 17 miniature coffins, each with a doll inside. Could it have been a memorial to unknown murder victims? Or part of a satanic ritual?

## BARONY STREET

A local coven known as the 'Witches Howff' were burned alive in a house in this street in the 17th century, just 13 of an estimated 300 women burned for practising the 'old religion' in Edinburgh at the time.

## PICARDY PLACE, TOP OF LEITH WALK

The birthplace of Sir Arthur Conan Doyle and formerly the site of public executions.

## NO. 5 HAZELDEAN TERRACE

In 1957 Edinburgh was able to boast two active poltergeists, both of which attracted national headlines. By all accounts the Rothesay Place poltergeist put on a fair show of strength, but came a poor second to the Hazeldean mischief-maker, which frequently threw a wooden chopping board and other kitchen utensils and crockery at the startled inhabitants. Being made of stronger stuff than their sassenach cousins down south, the residents of Hazeldean Terrace braved out the assault and eventually the activity died down.

## EDINBURGH PLAYHOUSE, GREENSIDE PLACE

Like all old theatres, the Playhouse claims to have a disembodied employee doing the rounds after dark, in this case an elderly man in a grey coat whom the staff refer to affectionately as 'Albert'. He is believed to have been either a stagehand who perished in an accident or a nightwatchman who topped himself.

Alternatively, he may have been just another victim of Edinburgh's rough justice, as Greenside Place was once the site of the public scaffold.

### ROYAL LYCEUM THEATRE, LOTHIAN ROAD

The actress Ellen Terry is said to haunt the stage on which she made her theatrical debut in 1856.

### GILLESPIE CRESCENT, BRUNTSFIELD

On this site once stood a celebrated haunted house known as The Wrychtishousis. In the 18th century it was the scene for regular visits by a headless woman who was believed to be the wife of James Clerk, who died leaving her and her baby to the tender mercies of his homicidal brother. With James out of the way, the brother murdered her in order to inherit the house, but he brought too short a trunk and had to cut her head off to get her body inside it. Then he hid the box in the cellar. Just another gruesome old legend? Nope. Her headless corpse and that of her child were unearthed by workmen when the house was being demolished, together with the killer's written confession.

### BALCARRES STREET, MORNINGSIDE

The Green Lady of Balcarres Street is said to be the restless spirit of Elizabeth Pittendale, wife of the 18th-century landowner Sir Thomas Elphinstone. He reputedly caught her in a compromising position with his son by a former marriage and stabbed her to death before committing suicide, leaving his son to inherit his estate.

### GILMERTON GRANGE

A similar melodrama occurred in the 14th century where this farmhouse bearing the same name now stands. Landowner Sir John Herring had forbidden his daughter Margaret from meeting her lover on this spot, but she defied him. In a fit of pique Sir John set the building ablaze with his daughter inside. Evidently, she still hasn't forgiven him, for her spirit has walked that spot for around 700 years.

### EDINBURGH FESTIVAL THEATRE, NICOLSON STREET

This is the former site of the Empire Palace Theatre, where illusionist Sigmund Neuberger (aka 'the Great Lafayette') was burned to death in 1911 after a fire broke out during his act. Nine stagehands and Neuberger's stage double also perished in the blaze.

### THE CORN EXCHANGE, BALTIC STREET

More grisly goings-on here, the site of several child murders in the 19th century. The killer was a former publican who hanged himself before his neighbours could lynch him. It is said that his victims can be heard crying in the night. Producers of the American TV series *Understanding the Paranormal* claimed to have caught the culprit on film.

### THE DOVECOT, DOVECOT ROAD, CORSTORPHINE

The White Lady of Corstorphine haunts this spot and can be seen brandishing a sword, the very same one with which she skewered her drunken lover. She was beheaded in 1679 after an unsuccessful escape attempt.

### CRAIGCROOK CASTLE, CORSTORPHINE HILL

All castles boast a resident ghost and Craigcrook is no exception. Its most famous owner, the author and Lord Advocate Lord Francis Jeffrey, drew his last breath here in 1850. His presence is said to be the cause of cold spots, phantom footsteps and a doorbell that rings of its own accord.

### CAROLINE PARK HOUSE (AKA ROYSTON HOUSE), GRANTON

The deceased wife of a former owner, Sir James Mackenzie has been seen to glide soundlessly through a wall at midnight and pass into the main entrance before reappearing in the east courtyard to the incessant ringing of an old bell. Locals know her as 'The Green Lady'.

### BORTHWICK CASTLE, GOREBRIDGE

The castle is now a hotel, and its Red Room is haunted by a young girl thought to be the spiteful spirit of Anne Grant, a peasant's daughter, said to be responsible for slamming doors on gentlemen's fingers. Local legend has it that she had been deflowered by her employer, Lord

Borthwick, who murdered her to ensure his secret was safe. Exorcisms have failed to dislodge her.

### CRICHTON CASTLE, MIDLOTHIAN

This imposing fortification is haunted by a figure on horseback who rides through the castle wall. It is thought to be Sir William Crichton, Chancellor of Scotland in the 15th century. It was he who organized the 'Black Dinner' in 1440 at Edinburgh Castle, to which the Earl of Douglas and his brother, both of whom were children, were invited. This was to dine with the boy king James II. Since they were contenders to the throne they were murdered when they arrived.

### DALHOUSIE CASTLE, LASSWADE

The 'Grey Lady' walks the clammy corridors of this formidable fortress. She is believed to be the mistress of one of the lairds, whose jealous wife contrived to lure her to the castle where she was imprisoned and starved to death.

### MOUNT LOTHIAN QUARRY, PENICUIK

Edinburgh has its own phantom horseman, but this one is no mere urban legend. It has its origins in historical fact. In the late 19th century a young labourer took his master's horse without permission to pay a call on his lover. At the quarry, he came upon a man pinned under his overturned cart, but instead of riding for help he rode on, presumably because he was desperate to avoid discovery. The injured man subsequently died, but not before he was able to tell his friends of the incident and describe the man who failed to help him. Vowing revenge, the friends are said to have tracked down and hung the young man who now rides past the spot driven, so to speak, by a guilty conscience.

## THE UNDERGROUND CITY

The focus of many of the city's supernatural encounters is the area around Edinburgh Castle known as the underground city. It's not actually a city, more of a labyrinth of tunnels and cavernous chambers carved out of the crag and tail on which the castle and Royal Mile were built. The ground beneath this long sloping street is composed of soft sandstone and the top of it towered so high above the rest of the city that it could be excavated from the side. When overcrowding in the city was at its height in the early years of the 18th century, the poor carved out their own living quarters from the rock to shelter from the worst of the Scottish weather and the authorities let them be as it eased pressure on the workhouses. Needless to say, many perished in the intolerable conditions from hunger, cold, disease and periodic cave-ins. Their spirits are thought to account for the moaning and wailing heard by the shopkeepers brave enough to venture down into their basement stock rooms after dark.

The world beneath the streets was expanded considerably at the end of the 18th century when the influx of migrant Irish workers put the city under greater strain. But Scottish engineers came up with an ingenious solution. They constructed a network of bridges to connect the central ridge to the surrounding hills and then built houses and shops around them to obscure the structures. The vaults under these viaducts were intended as cellars and storehouses for local traders, but when it was discovered that they were not waterproof the merchants moved out and the migrants moved in. Their existence was almost forgotten until social reformers evicted them some years later and crowded them into the tenements which became ghettos for the underprivileged.

In 1845 reformer Dr George Bell, M.D. visited Blackfriars Wynd, next to the South Bridge in an effort to publicize the living conditions of the beggars and hawkers who lived there.

> In a vault or cave under a large tenement, reside an old man, his invalid wife, and his two daughters, one of whom has a natural child and the other of whom is paralytic. The man has an air of respectability about him, but the family has no visible means of living. There were three beds in the vault; and on investigating the matter, (we) found that the said vault is a lodging house, and is often tenanted to repletion. This man is the type of class who

> live by subletting their miserable and dark abodes to as many as can be crammed into them. In another vault in the wynd we found a very fat Irishwoman, a widow, a pauper, and the mother of six children. By her own confession she occasionally takes in a lodger – in reality, however, she accommodates two or three all the year round.

It is here in creepy places such as Mary King's Close, the South Bridge Vaults and the Black Mausoleum in Greyfriars Graveyard that the most recent and disturbing sightings have taken place.

## HAUNTED HOT SPOTS

Arguably the most notorious haunted spot in the city is Mary King's Close, named after the daughter of a prosperous local merchant. The legends associated with this location are lurid and legion and centre on the victims of the plague of 1645 who were imprisoned by the city elders. Their jailers then locked the gates at both ends of the close for fear that the contagion might spread. This rather draconian measure saved the city from the scourge of the sickness, but none of the residents of Mary King's Close survived. Their decomposing corpses were later hacked up and the remains buried in an area known as The Meadows. No one would live in the close after that, or even go near it after dark for fear that the spirits of the dead would reach through the gates and drag them inside.

Its reputation as a haunting 'hot spot' remains undimmed to this day. As recently as 1992 a documentary film crew arrived with a Japanese psychic named Aiko Gibo. On entering one of the houses she claimed to be able to see an apparition in one corner of a room where several psychics had mentioned sensing a cold spot some months before. Gibo described this 'spirit' as a 10-year-old girl wearing a dirty white dress and boots. When asked for its name, Gibo was given the answer 'Annie'. Gibo and Annie communicated telepathically as Annie asked why her mother had abandoned her and where her favourite doll could be. When Gibo returned with a new doll Annie seemed comforted and more communicative. All of this could be put down to the imagination of the medium were it not for the fact that a short while later a female visitor to the site who had known nothing of the broadcast screamed when she entered the room, claiming to have seen a little girl in the

*Mary King's Close: shadowy residents include 'The Worried Man' and a lady who appears at the end of the close and then vanishes*

corner whose face was disfigured by sores. Research has unearthed the fact that a woman by the name of Jean Mackenzie and her little girl were forcibly quarantined in the house during the plague. It was not established whether the little girl's name was Annie, but it seems likely as it was a common name at that time. After the documentary was broadcast the number of visitors to the site increased dramatically, many of them leaving dolls for the little ghost to play with.

Other shadowy residents of the close include 'The Worried Man', who walks back and forth as if brooding on some dark deed he is planning, or perhaps he is simply searching for something. At other times a woman in black appears for a moment at the end of the close and then just as mysteriously vanishes, as does a young boy at the same location. A male figure, presumably a storekeeper, has been seen suspended in mid-air beneath the 'plague room' window at the spot where a staircase had once been and a middle-aged woman has been known to put in an appearance at the top of the steps leading into the street. If anyone is brave enough to venture inside the derelict houses they are sure to hear sufficient scratching, whispering and boisterous phantom carousing to convince them that some of the former residents are extremely reluctant to leave, despite its grim reputation.

## THE HAUNTED VAULT

Among the many tales told of uncanny encounters in the South Bridge Vaults, the case of Marion Duffy and her 6-year-old daughter Claire must rank as one of the most chilling.

Marion had serious doubts about joining a guided tour with such a young child in tow, but Claire had reassured her mother that she wouldn't be afraid. Even when the party entered the claustrophobic chamber deep underground the little girl lost none of her eagerness to explore. She joined in the nervous giggles and squeezed her mother's hand reassuringly as she might have done if they were going on a fairground ghost train. It was only when the guide turned off her torch to heighten the spooky atmosphere that Marion regretted letting her daughter talk her into taking the tour.

'Don't worry Claire,' she said. 'It's all just for show.' A small hand responded with a gentle squeeze. Then the grip became tighter. Evidently Claire was afraid. Very afraid. The grip tightened still further until Marion realized that she couldn't pull herself free. It was becoming painful. Instinctively she pulled hard and kicked, not caring in that moment if Claire was hurt as the pain was unbearable. But it couldn't be Claire. No child would be capable of such a vice-like grip. She kicked harder and in doing so lost her balance. She collided with the person standing next to her in the dark who screamed that something was attacking her and the next instant there was a mad scramble for the exit.

When the guide switched the torch back on Marion found herself surrounded by strangers, all with a look of embarrassment on their faces. Claire was nowhere to be seen. Then her mother spotted her on the other side of the vault. Shaking with a mixture of fear and relief, the little girl explained that when the light went out a hand had gripped hers and led her to the far end of the vault. She knew it wasn't her mother's hand, but she had been too frightened to cry out. Asked how she knew it wasn't her mother's hand, she replied, 'Because it had claws.'

## GREYFRIARS GRAVEYARD

> Greyfriars is the most haunted spot in the country's most haunted city.
>
> *The Weekly News*

Greyfriars is known locally as a 'thin place', a site where the veil between this world and the next is believed to be so fragile that spirits can pass through it. Its reputation presumably grew from the fact that it was the site of mass graves following the great plague of 1568 when countless thousands of diseased corpses were flung into a huge pit and from the fact that it was the custom to display the heads of executed criminals on its gate posts. A grisly lot, the Scots.

Twelve hundred survivors of the Covenanter movement (Scots

*Twelve hundred survivors of the Covenanter movement were imprisoned in the Covenanters' Prison. . . many of them never emerged again*

Presbyterians) were imprisoned in the Covenanters' Prison on the orders of Charles II after their defeat at the Battle of Bothwell Brig and many of them starved to death or died from disease. Of the remainder many thousands were executed by the King's Advocate, 'Bloody' George Mackenzie. Mackenzie was buried in Greyfriars in 1691 within sight of the Covenanters' Prison and the graves of those he had condemned to death. Not surprisingly perhaps, this inspired a host of macabre ghost stories including one in which 'Bloody' Mackenzie's coffin is said to move within the tomb, known as the Black Mausoleum, because he is restless and tormented in death.

Mackenzie had company for Christmas in 1879 when the city council disinterred hundreds of rotting corpses from St Giles' cemetery and unceremoniously dumped them in nearby Greyfriars. Visitors who climb the hill to look down on the town are unaware that they are actually standing on a mountain of dead bodies.

## SPIRITS PUT TO THE TEST

> . . . hauntings do not just happen. It is not merely by chance that you are there when the ghost walks. A physical presence is needed not only to see the apparition but perhaps to cause it to appear.
>
> Antony D. Hippisley Coxe, *Haunted Britain*, 1973

With so many spirit sightings it was inevitable that sooner or later the parapsychologists would investigate Edinburgh's hottest spots.

The most serious study was conducted in the vaults off South Niddry Street by a team headed by Dr Richard Wiseman, who measured the magnetic fields, light levels, air temperature and movement. Members of the public were invited to visit the vaults while the experiment was in progress and to write down their experiences.

*The Black Mausoleum (on the right), which hides its dark character during daylight*

The usual 'disturbances' were duly reported. These perhaps predictably included strange odours and the sense of being watched, but Dr Wiseman's team attributed these to imperceptible changes in the atmospheric conditions.

> These alleged hauntings do not represent evidence for 'ghostly' activity, but are instead the result of people responding – perhaps unwittingly – to 'normal' factors in their surroundings.
>
> *British Journal of Psychology*, 2003

Such mundane explanations do not, however, explain many visitors' often violent reactions to the atmosphere in the 'haunted vault' off Niddry Street or indeed to the Black Mausoleum which is situated in Greyfriars Graveyard, neither of which were investigated by the scientists, something which is beginning to look more and more like an oversight.

Nor do these environmental changes take any account at all of the physical marks, scratches, bruising and torn-out hair, which have been reported to the tour operators by so many visitors. The following accounts are just a small sample of those received.

## EYEWITNESS ACCOUNTS

We had not been in the Black Mausoleum long when we started hearing knocking noises coming from beneath us, which steadily grew louder and seemed to move up and round the walls. I was standing at the back and I felt the temperature drop, even though it was a very warm night. I started physically shaking, even though I was wearing several jumpers, and had pins and needles in my feet and arms. I then felt myself go freezing cold and the next thing I remember is waking up lying on the ground. My friend had also collapsed. The next morning, I woke up to find that I had three deep scratches on my stomach – there is no way this could have been caused by my falling, as I was wearing several layers. My friend Lewis also had scratches on his arm.

I decided to go back again, this time with a group of different friends. I experienced the same sensations – the feeling of cold, pins and needles, and shaking, followed by the inevitable black-out and scratches on my arms the next morning.

Camilla Davidson

On my first tour I was part of the 'mass poltergeist attack' where the whole tour heard knocking and both myself and another girl fainted. The second time I heard knocking again and again I fainted. I felt something kneel beside me, actually touching my leg. I was terrified and was crying, but felt I was unable to open my eyes.

Debbie Stephen

As you might know there were a number of attacks/strange happenings on the 10 o'clock tour last Saturday. Two men and a woman collapsed and remained unconscious for a minute or so, while people inside heard weird noises. Being a huge sceptic I find it hard to believe these people could have been actors. If they were, then they were damn good. To be honest, while standing inside in the back, I felt something like cold spots on my legs. That's when I left . . .

Jeroen Remmerswaal

I thought you might like to add this experience to your archive, as I was so spooked I'm afraid I fled without really speaking to any of your colleagues. I'd been on the tour the previous August and experienced a feeling like something placing its hands on my chest and pushing me gently backwards inside the Covenanters' Prison, and then I'd been the centre of a cold spot inside the mausoleum. Again when we went inside the prison, I felt the sensation of being pushed backwards.

Without warning something tugged on the end of my watch strap, hard. I was wearing a jacket that covered my watch, and my arm was wrapped around my friend. If it was someone trying to mess about, for them to have found their way inside the cuff of my jacket and then found the end of my watch strap, without either myself or my friend feeling something, would have been impossible.

After this, we went to the bar, where the spookiest thing of all happened. Over a hefty dose of whisky, we watched scratches that tingled like nettle rash come up on the first two knuckles of both of my hands – my friend had hold of my hand and would have known if anything had scratched me or I had scratched myself.

No offence, but I'm not going on that tour again. Twice was enough, I think a third time might be chancing my luck!

Alix Cavanagh

I felt as if the temperature was gradually falling – nothing unusual there, it being the middle of January. However, another member of the tour ran out stating she simply 'needed to leave'.

Once she had gone someone began pulling at my hair. There was no one behind me and I knew those around me couldn't be doing it – they were too far forward. It was a repeated insistent tugging. A few days afterwards the back of my head felt incredibly cold and the hair began falling out from a very concentrated area – the area I felt that had been pulled at.

Louise Wright

I hit a cold patch that chilled me to my very bones. A woman grabbed my left arm and then the cold hit us both really hard as if the wind had become a 'being' or a 'wall'. She panicked and ran from the place. I noticed that I was swaying and when I looked around at the silhouettes, everyone was swaying . . . The lady behind me was swaying so much she grabbed me to stop herself from passing out.

Jenny Bosson

Standing at the back of the Black Mausoleum I kept feeling someone, or should it be something, breathing in my face. This was a little unnerving as everyone was facing the front of the mausoleum!

Christine Hornsby

I felt frozen solid all over the whole time, i.e. I couldn't move and I don't think it was just fear because I tried to move my hand and I couldn't. All I can remember doing is praying to God that nothing would touch me, and that I've never felt so scared in my entire life.

Josh Blinco

I felt a sensation of extreme cold, dizziness and nausea. I put this sensation down to nerves. It was only when I returned to my hotel that I noticed a series of deep and increasingly painful scratches on my back, abdomen and chest.

Kenny J Gray

I distinctly felt a man's hand grab my arm twice. Something brushed past me and hit me on the elbow and it punched my sister on the back. Later she was complaining of a sore back and we discovered scratch marks.

Debbie Reid

Suddenly my husband moved away from me. As I tried to pull him back he stiffened and then began to wobble. He shakily told me something had 'run up and down his back'. When we finally left the tomb he was visibly shaken.

Helen Davidson

After being in the tomb for a couple of minutes I started to hear heavy scratching noises at the back. I saw a girl looking up at the exact same time to the exact same spot as if listening to the scratching as well. Back on the Royal Mile I saw the girl again, and she described the exact same location (at the back and top of the tomb) and the same sounds (heavy scratching). It certainly freaked me out.

Sandy Hager

Two pictures that I took in the Covenanters' Prison had 'orbs' on them. However, the strangest thing happened when we got back to our hotel room. My wife had five or six large scratch marks on her back, like she had been clawed by something. They were in a 'v' shape. The next morning they were completely gone.

Richard Torble

I suddenly began to cry and feel an overwhelming feeling of sadness. The closer we got the worse I became and I was sobbing so hard I was almost unable to breathe. It was the most awful feeling of sadness, grief and despair that I have ever felt. I have never cried like that before in my whole life and never want to again.

Kathryn, Sheffield

One of our friends was standing next to me in the Black Mausoleum and started hyperventilating about two minutes into us being there. He told me he had seen a ghost inside. He'd actually looked him in the face. He described him as a man with blue eyes and a cloak. He said he felt the most sad and then the most scared he has ever felt in his life. He felt incredibly cold from the inside – the cold sensation had started in his feet and worked its way up through his body.

Name withheld

I still felt quite happy when we entered the Covenanters' Prison. It wasn't until I got into the Black Mausoleum itself that I began to feel uneasy. I felt that someone or something was looking right at me. As I turned to look I saw what can only be described as a hooded figure with a featureless face and a couple of inches shorter than me.

B Johnson, Coventry

I was standing just inside the crypt and my feet just froze, they went completely numb and I felt a freeze climb my legs. I had to keep stepping from side to side, moving out of the cold spot, but it followed me as I moved around. Later when I stepped back inside so I could have a picture taken I felt a burning sensation on my neck. I noticed my mate was totally pale. He finally asked if I felt anything strange and I described what I felt. He said that, at the time of the photo being taken, he saw a halo that appeared around my neck and shoulders. He then looked at the back of my neck and noticed it was all red and scratched.

Alan Smith

. . . the next morning after the tour my girlfriend found a series of scratches on her chest. They were very red and fine, quite angry-looking. From memory there were at least three main scratches (each consisting of three to four scratch lines), perhaps more. They certainly weren't done by human hand as they were too close together, more like a tiny cat's paw. The scratches were long too, trailing up to 30–40 centimetres in length.

Alan Maxwell

As I was entering the 'prison' a woman next to me took a photo. When the flash went off there was what I would describe as a ghost. It was a young girl (maybe 8 or 9 years of age) and she was just standing in front of this tree in what looked like a white or a white lace dress . . . I only wish it showed up on the digital camera but of course it didn't.

Dan Dickens

One of the tour party commented to one of the team that she could see 'a black mass' in the rear corner of the Mausoleum. Interestingly the EMF [Electro Motive Force] showed a large rise in activity in the area where the mass was seen. When the person said she could no longer see it, the readings dropped back to normal. A separate team member was approached and told by another tour party member that she had been touched on the back of the neck . . . however, no one was behind her at the time. Another mentioned that he was experiencing numbness in his feet and pins and needles down one side, and yet another reported seeing 'rapidly moving lights' on the wall. Sam also reports being scratched by something across her right hand, but inside her clothes, not through them!

UK Paranormal Investigator

We're never going in there again. Ever.

William Jones

Other visitors complained of feeling gripped around the ankles by an ice-cold band as if they were experiencing what it had felt like to be shackled to the wall in the Covenanters' Prison. Dozens reported that their cameras malfunctioned in certain sites but not in others, while those who managed to capture images of floating balls of light and luminous shapes sent copies to the tour agency and to magazines to prove their claims.

## GHOST TOURS

There are currently six separate tour operators offering guided ghost walks of the city and they are all doing a roaring trade. Evidently Edinburgh is a city of spirits and not all of them are bottled. I caught up with Jan-Andrew Henderson, author of the most comprehensive book on haunted Edinburgh, entitled *Edinburgh – City of the Dead*. He is also the founder of the appropriately named Black Hart Tours.

Jan-Andrew once lived in the midst of haunted Edinburgh in a house on the edge of Greyfriars Graveyard and he became fascinated by the history and the distinctive atmosphere of the place. Dissatisfied with the sensationalistic nature of other books on the subject and frustrated by the lack of credible evidence, he decided to trace as many eyewitnesses as he could and record first hand the stories of people who had taken his tour and who claimed to have had a brush with the shadow people and lived to tell the tale.

*How did your fascination with Edinburgh's hidden history, if I can call it that, begin?*

Like many locals, I didn't have a huge interest in Edinburgh history – or any sort of history – until I got a job as a tour guide. Then, because I wanted to be good at it, I began to dig up little-known things and fascinating facts about Edinburgh's past. Then Scotland's past. Now I love all kinds of history, especially the little-known stuff.

*What is the legend behind the Black Mausoleum and the Mackenzie poltergeist?*

Because I run a walking tour, the area we cover isn't very large, so we stick mainly to the Royal Mile. It was the heart of Edinburgh for thousands of years, and so every inch has history. The Black Mausoleum and the Mackenzie poltergeist are different. The poltergeist has only appeared in the last seven years, so it doesn't have much of a legend. People think it is the ghost of George Mackenzie, but there's actually no evidence for that. It's called the Mackenzie poltergeist because the first reported attack took place on the steps of George Mackenzie's tomb. But most of the attacks after that took place in a fairly nondescript tomb, which is now known as the Black Mausoleum.

The Black Mausoleum seems to differ from Edinburgh's other haunted locations for two reasons. One is the frequency of the poltergeist sightings. The other is the severity of the incidents. The period between the first recorded sightings in 1999 and the present has seen over 350 documented 'attacks' in the Black Mausoleum and Covenanters' Prison. Of these attacks, an astonishing 150 have caused the witness to collapse.

*Jan-Andrew Henderson*

There have been sightings of a white figure, unexplained smells and auditory anomalies – including knocking noises under the ground and inside the tomb itself. Dead animals are found, unmarked, in front of the Black Mausoleum. The area has been exorcized twice – both times unsuccessfully.

Poltergeist activity has been reported in four different houses around the graveyard and a large fire broke out in the residences behind George Mackenzie's tomb in 2002.

*I don't know what the Mackenzie poltergeist really is. I don't know if it's a supernatural entity, a pheromone cloud, a demon or a set of psychosomatic and hysterical reactions. All have been suggested. But I*

*King's Advocate George Mackenzie was the scourge of the Covenanters. He doesn't seem to be resting on his laurels: his alleged ghost is one of the best-documented poltergeists ever*

*know it has become the best-documented supernatural case of all time and probably the most conclusive.*

Let me put it this way – if the Mackenzie poltergeist isn't a genuine supernatural entity then I don't think there's any such thing. Not anywhere in the world.

*What manner of experiences have been reported?*
Hot spots. Cold spots. People overcome with sorrow. People feeling suddenly nauseous. People are punched, pushed, bitten, burned and have their hair and clothes pulled by something they can't see. Often they feel something under layers of clothes. All have marks to prove it. People falling unconscious. Cameras failing to work. Strange sounds and smells. Auditory anomalies. Spectral voices. One or two people have claimed to be temporarily possessed. Others find the disturbances continue back at their hotel or home. Many feel nothing at all and then discover marks on their body when they leave the tomb.

*Have you been unnerved by the experiences that have been reported to you or by the atmosphere of the place? And what effect did it have on you living in proximity to the graveyard? Or have you become immune over time? Your attitude seems to be a challenge to it to show itself.*
I've never been unnerved by it. I think it's great. I'm deeply sceptical of traditional 'ghosts' and feel sure there is a rational explanation – even if I don't have one. But I find the things that happen in the graveyard fascinating rather than scary. I was actually quite surprised that living in a graveyard with such a haunted reputation didn't faze me. Maybe that's why I'm so determined to be sceptical. If I really did think the place contained a violent supernatural entity, I'd probably find it hard to turn off the lights at night.

*What was the most disturbing and convincing case that you have heard about or experienced connected with the City of the Dead?*
I've heard many eyewitness accounts, seen the strange marks and witnessed people collapse. But the most convincing thing I saw involved an animal. I saw a bird sitting on the grass just outside the Black Mausoleum, staring into the tomb. It was so transfixed it let me walk right up, kneel beside it and even touch it. It simply refused to take its eyes off the tomb entrance – though it was broad daylight and I could see there was nothing inside. Assuming it couldn't fly, because it was young or injured, I stood up and stepped back.

As I did the bird shot backwards, almost as if it had been kicked.

Then it twisted in the air and flew off. I have never seen an animal act that way. And unlike any incident involving a human – it simply couldn't be faked. Something in that empty tomb terrified it to the point where it couldn't move.

*Have you seen the bruises, bites, scratches and other injuries that people claim to have sustained during the tour?*

I have, because I used to be a tour guide. I also have a number of pictures – though not nearly as many as I should have.

In October 2003 my house overlooking the graveyard burned down, destroying most of my records. I lost five years' worth of letters, photographs, records and statements concerning the Mackenzie poltergeist as well as every possession I had in the world. None of the surrounding properties were damaged and an official cause for the fire has not been established. Fortunately, I had saved most of the sightings and eyewitness accounts on a computer in another building – about the only thing that did survive. I live somewhere else now.

*You devised a test to weed out spurious claims. Can you describe that please?*

We've tried different things. Taking people into the wrong tomb or describing a fictional 'symptom' of the poltergeist attack to see if people then claim it has happened to them. Unfortunately, there's no foolproof test that anyone can devise.

If there really is a poltergeist, there's no reason such an entity couldn't take its cue from us and move tombs or do exactly what we're describing.

*Have psychic mediums ever been on the tour and if so, did they claim to have been able to identify the restless spirit responsible for these phenomena?*

We've had lots and they described different things. One or two have sensed children and another couple, a tall figure. Most, however, simply claim to sense a presence that is powerful and malevolent.

*What has been your impression of the 'witnesses' you interviewed? Were they genuinely shaken? Were they credible?*
Again, there has been a huge range. Some seem far too gullible or just plain weird to be taken seriously. But there are others I simply couldn't imagine making stuff up or being over-imaginative. Sensible, intelligent older men and women, who don't even believe in the paranormal.

*Despite your own experiences, such as the inexplicable fire at your former home and having taken the witness statements, you remain unconvinced. Is that true, or is it that you reserve judgement and don't want to put a name to something you haven't seen with your own eyes?*
Pretty much the latter. That's just the kind of person I am.

I don't believe in God for the same reason – no matter how many people tell me they've been touched by Him. I want empirical evidence before I say: 'Yes, that's a supernatural entity.' The problem is I haven't got empirical evidence for any other explanation. But something odd is certainly going on there.

## GHOSTS OF EDINBURGH – THE OLD TOWN

Jan-Andrew kindly offered to act as our tour guide of Edinburgh's Old Town.

The following entries are taken from his definitive guide, *Edinburgh – City of the Dead* (Black and White Publishing) and these are reprinted by kind permission of the publishers.

### EDINBURGH CASTLE

The castle is haunted by several apparitions. This is hardly surprising given its history of conflict and the fact that there has been some sort of fortification on Castle Rock since prehistory.

John Graham of Claverhouse is said to haunt the castle. He was known as 'Bloody Clavers' because of his ruthless persecution of Covenanters in the 17th century – along with his accomplice 'Bloody' George Mackenzie.

When James II of Scotland was deposed, Claverhouse made a momentous about-turn and raised a Catholic highland army to fight for his king. He was killed leading a magnificent highland charge at the Battle of Killiekrankie in 1689 and, because of this, is better known in Scots lore as 'Bonny' Dundee. He was first seen in the castle on the night of his death by Lord Balcarres, who was in charge of the castle's Jacobite prisoners, and has appeared periodically from then on.

That same year the Duke of Gordon, governor of the castle, stabbed his steward for bringing news of his family's death. The unfortunate man now wanders the walls. Some employees are just impossible to get rid of.

The castle, it seems, is afflicted with all sorts of military-themed spooks. Phantom drumming was first heard in 1650 and the castle was taken by Oliver Cromwell's forces soon after – leading to the idea that this was a portent for disaster. In later sightings the drummer is sometimes invisible, sometimes headless and was last reported in the 1960s.

The ramparts also boast ghostly bagpiping and the invisible marching of massed men. The dungeons are said to be plagued by the ghosts of prisoners held during the Napoleonic Wars and blue orbs have been captured on film.

The castle is also haunted by Janet Douglas, Lady Glamis. A member of the Douglas family, long distrusted by the Stuart kings, she was accused of witchcraft on a trumped-up charge and burned at the stake in 1537 in front of her husband and son. A busy ghost, she also manages to find time to haunt Glamis Castle in Angus.

## THE LAWNMARKET

Site of Edinburgh's last public hanging in 1864. There is a legend of a *Marie Celeste*-style house here. In the 18th century one of the flats was suddenly abandoned in panic, right in the middle of a dinner party. The exit was so hasty that half-eaten food was left on the table, though those who fled did lock the door behind them – a door that was never reopened. I must admit this bit of the legend puzzles me. If the door was never unlocked again, how do we know what was left on the table?

By the 19th century the story had passed into lore with Robert Chambers writing, 'No one knows to whom the house belongs; no one ever inquires after it, no one living ever saw the inside of it, it is a condemned house.' Unfortunately it really was condemned and no longer exists.

## CITY CHAMBERS, ROYAL MILE

Underneath are the remains of Mary King's Close, the famous haunted street.

## THE SCOTSMAN HOTEL, NORTH BRIDGE

Formerly the *Scotsman* newspaper office, which seemed to have a whole plethora of ghosts. In 1990 a security guard ran into an employee who he knew to be dead. In 1994 a page-make-up artist, working in the basement, came across a door he had never seen before. Upon entering he stumbled upon a phantom printer sporting old-fashioned clothes and beard and carrying antiquated printing plates. The building was also haunted by a blonde woman who would vanish any time a member of staff came over to ask what she wanted. Apparently, there is also a phantom forger. Then again, you can't believe everything you read in the press.

## THE SOUTH BRIDGE

Vaults inside the bridge are said to be haunted by a faceless man and a mischievous poltergeist.

## WHISTLE BINKIE'S BAR, NIDDRY STREET

This bar, refashioned out of 19th-century converted bridge vaults, is haunted by a long-haired gentleman in 17th-century attire. He is called 'the Watcher' but no one has ever seen his face. This bar and the storerooms of South Bridge shops are also home to an entity known as 'the Imp'. This mischievous creature stops clocks, slams doors and moves objects. Sightings began in the early 1990s and continue to this day.

*In the* Scotsman *building, it's best not to look behind mysterious doors*

## ST MARY'S STREET

Haunted by the victim of an apparently motiveless murder. A young woman was killed here in 1916 by an assailant who leapt out of a doorway, stabbed her and ran off, without robbing her or molesting her in any other way. She is still seen occasionally, her clothes spattered with blood, an understandably astonished expression on her face.

## THE MUSEUM OF CHILDHOOD, ROYAL MILE

The area behind this building is said to ring with the voices of crying children late at night. During the plague years, an outbreak occurred in a nearby nursery, which was sealed up with the children and mothers inside.

## CHESSELS COURT

Site of Deacon Brodie's last botched robbery at the Edinburgh Excise Office. In the late 19th century, the tenements that stand there were haunted by a woman wearing a black silk veil – identified as an occupant who had recently hanged herself.

## THE CANONGATE, ROYAL MILE

Haunted by a burning woman. She was the daughter of an influential family in the 18th century but had the misfortune to fall pregnant by a servant. A minister was called to deliver the last rites to the girl, which he objected to, since she looked perfectly healthy. He was given money and threatened to keep his mouth shut.

Later that day the girl was killed when an 'accidental' fire mysteriously burned the house down. The house was rebuilt but caught fire again many years later.

In the heart of the conflagration the girl appeared, screaming, 'Once burnt, twice burnt, the third time I'll scare you all!' The third fire has, so far, not occurred.

## QUEENSBERRY HOUSE, CANONGATE

Haunted by a kitchen boy who was roasted and eaten by James Douglas, the lunatic Earl of Drumlanrig – son of the Duke of Queensberry. At the time the Duke was arranging the union of Scottish and English parliaments in 1707 – an act so loathed by the Edinburgh people that they rioted in the streets and cursed his house.

### HOLYROOD PALACE, ROYAL MILE

This has an excellent class of ghost – being haunted by Mary Queen of Scots, her husband Lord Darnley and her secretary David Rizzio – all of whom came to violent ends. Lowering the tone is the naked ghost of Bald Agnes, who was stripped and tortured in 1592 after being accused of witchcraft.

### THE COWGATE

Site of the 'Cleansing of the Causeway' in 1524 – Scotland's largest street fight in which hundreds of participants were killed. The Cowgate was the birthplace of Walter Scott and James Connolly, the Irish republican leader. The area is haunted by an unnamed man with rope burns round his neck.

### WEST BOW (VICTORIA STREET)

Anderson's Close, demolished in 1827, was the home of Major Thomas Weir (The Wizard of the West Bow). It was also 'Stinking Close' and after repeated sightings of spectres came to be known as 'Haunted Close'.

The West Bow is also haunted by a phantom coach and the ghost of a sailor named Angus Roy. Crippled on a voyage in 1820, he settled in this area and spent the next 20 years there until his death. He longed for the sea and was tormented by local children who mimicked his severe limp. He is still seen occasionally, dragging his injured leg behind him. It's a shame he picked such a steep street to haunt.

### GRASSMARKET

This was the site where Covenanters were executed and a circular monument set into the ground commemorates these tragic events. It was also the place of public hangings and the cleverly named Last Drop pub is behind the spot.

The White Hart Inn, where the mass murderers William Burke and William Hare reputedly picked up victims in the 1820s, still stands here. The area is haunted by a woman with a burned face and the phantom coach that gallops down the West Bow sometimes carries on through the Grassmarket.

### BELL'S WYND

In 1780 a tenant in one of the tenements, George Gourly, repeatedly approached his landlord with what he thought was a reasonable request. His family was growing and he wished to rent the empty flat below his.

His landlord Patrick Guthrie always said no, but refused to give a reason for the rebuttal. In frustration Gourlay broke into the flat and found a ghostly female figure standing in the middle of the room. He was so frightened that he reported what he had done to the procurator fiscal.

An investigation discovered the corpse of Patrick Guthrie's wife in the empty flat. He had killed her when he found out she'd been having an affair.

### GEORGE IV BRIDGE

Number 21 is 'The Elephant House' where *Harry Potter and the Philosopher's Stone* was written.

Bridge vaults under the National Library of Scotland are haunted by an unidentified highland chief. When he was spotted by librarian Elizabeth Clarke in 1973, she noticed that his hands were manacled. The bridge vaults were used in the 19th century to imprison debtors.

### BEDLAM THEATRE, FOREST ROAD

Near the site of a former asylum. Haunted by a shadowy figure that flits through the theatre.

# UNINVITED GUESTS

There was once a time when any self-respecting ghost would haunt only the grandest of stately homes. But times change, and today even ghosts must settle for what they can get. It's quite a comedown from country house to council house, so perhaps that's why the poltergeists of Prial Avenue in Lincoln, England, are so tetchy.

It seems that Lincoln city council has been inundated with requests from tenants demanding to be relocated to escape spectral squatters who have made their lives a living hell.

Jade Callaby, a 26-year-old single mum, suffered six years of unexplained paranormal activity in her Prial Avenue property. It began with kettles, TVs and toasters switching on by themselves and with objects disappearing from one room only to turn up in another. But then the curious incidents became less playful and more disturbing. Jade and her 9-year-old daughter, Courtney, were startled out of their sleep night after night by loud banging noises. They also claim to have seen shadows when no one else was present in the house.

In desperation Jade called in a priest to 'bless' the house, but the unsettling incidents continued. She was forced to ask the council to relocate her.

'It's been absolutely terrifying,' she told a local reporter. 'Kettles and vacuum cleaners have turned on and off by themselves, cups have moved, dark shadows have appeared and darkened rooms, and my daughter has been woken up by the sound of heavy breathing in front of her face – but nobody was there. I used to try to explain things away, but now I believe – and I'm not staying there another night.'

Lincoln housing official John Morris admitted that Prial Avenue is not the only area of the city to be plagued by ghosts. 'There have been reported cases of haunted council houses in the past, but there has never been any tangible evidence of haunting.' During my research I discovered that, during the Second World War, Prial Avenue and the surrounding streets were decimated by a German air raid in which many residents were killed in their sleep. In the early hours of 8 May 1941, a bomb blew the fronts off four houses, leaving a hole large enough to accommodate two double-decker buses standing one on top of the other. At Westwick Gardens a bomb demolished the back wall of a house, killing a baby and its father. The back garden adjoined Prial Close, where an elderly woman was killed the same night. All these events might account for the hauntings in that area.

## THE FORMER TENANT

In March 2000, a paranormal investigation group calling themselves the Ghost Club were invited to a two-bedroom council flat in Woolwich, south London. The tenant, a young mother with a baby daughter, had complained of being tormented by noises, shadows and inexplicable activity. She was so distressed by these disturbances she had told the council that she was willing to move to a smaller flat if necessary.

The hauntings had begun with seemingly insignificant signs, such as her daughter appearing to react to an unseen presence, and the cat running away as if it had been frightened. Then the young woman heard footsteps in an empty room above and a shuffling sound outside her bedroom door, as though someone was pacing restlessly in the hall. She heard the bed creaking as if someone was getting in beside her, and one night the duvet was pulled off. The atmosphere in her daughter's room was often icy and there was a cold draught at the bottom of the stairs. The woman also sensed that someone was watching her from the bottom of the stairs when she walked up to her flat.

There could be a rational reason for all these incidents, but it is harder to explain what happened next. One evening, the young woman walked into her bedroom and saw the shadow of a man in the corner. This shadowy presence had substance and she could see that he was wearing a suit. He was a black man, between 30 and 40 years of age, and he appeared to be asleep. He only disappeared after she repeatedly looked away to see if she was imagining the vision. Another night she woke to see a man standing in the corner of the room, before fading away; whether or not it was the same man, she couldn't say.

At this point she became convinced that the house was haunted and decided to contact the previous tenant to see if she had experienced the same feelings. The tenant, who had lived in the flat for eight years, admitted experiencing a constant feeling of being watched. She said she had found her small son talking to an invisible presence he called Peter; the child had also been given to screaming for no apparent reason. His toy car would shoot across the room on its own and the dog would growl unaccountably at the bottom of the stairs. At first, the woman suspected that the presence might be the spirit of her dead father, but then the feelings became so unsettling and unpleasant that she knew it couldn't be him. Other people saw things too: the brother of a friend of hers visited the flat in 1992 and mentioned seeing the shadow of a man in the hallway.

The Ghost Club asked a psychic to check out the house. He wasn't told any specific details about the sightings or the sounds and he had no prior knowledge of the history of the house, but as soon as he entered he felt he was being watched. He identified the presence as male and traced it to the right-hand corner of the bedroom, where the shadow of the man had been seen. He then entered the child's room and felt that the presence had a connection with a child.

On 6 July, members of the Ghost Club returned with a number of psychics, who picked up on several things they could not have known about in advance. In the bathroom, they sensed that two previous female tenants had suffered miscarriages; this was subsequently confirmed. In the child's room, they picked up on the presence of a man in black, a sense of panic and someone screaming for help.

At 11 pm that night, all the visitors to the house heard the sound of footsteps running down the hallway. The group decided to disperse throughout the house and see what impressions they could pick up. One of them had the strong sense that a man had carried on abusive relationships with the women, one of whom had murdered him. According to one of the psychics, his ghostly presence in the bedroom was because he had lived next door and entered the flat from a balcony that led to the bedroom window.

Following the investigation the female tenant was rehoused and, according to members of the Ghost Club, her personality has undergone a significant change.

She is no longer depressed, but happy and relieved to be away from the oppressive atmosphere and out of reach of whatever, or whoever, remains trapped in that house.

## THE SHADOW IN THE CELLAR

In May 2001, Steven LaChance, a single father of three living in Union, Missouri, was desperate to find a new home for his family, as the lease on their apartment was about to expire. He had answered many adverts for rental properties, but had found nothing suitable; time was running out. Then he received a phone call from an elderly woman who said she was holding an 'open house' for an old property she wanted to rent. From the moment Steven saw it, he knew it was the perfect home for his family – at least that is what it appeared to be in daylight. It was a white, weather-boarded house with three bedrooms and a basement – plenty of space for a growing family.

Steven's eagerness to move in led him to dismiss the warning signs suggesting that all might not be right with his new home. The first indication that something sinister was lurking in the shadows came when the landlady asked to meet him in a local restaurant to sign the contract and take the deposit. Why, he wondered, hadn't she invited him to the house? Steven noticed she seemed very relieved to get the property off her hands. This struck him as odd because the house was very attractive, with charming original features and was in good condition for its age.

However, from the very first day there were indications all was not well. Pictures fell repeatedly from their hooks even though they had been hung securely, local people crossed the street to avoid walking in front of the house, and neighbours ignored Steven's greetings as though shunning the property and its new inhabitants. The first sign of a malevolent presence came when Steven's youngest son ran screaming from the basement, claiming that something had chased him and that it was 'big'. Steven was alarmed to see a pool of urine at the boy's feet. The child was clearly terrified and nothing his father could say would persuade the child that he had imagined it.

Nothing unusual occurred for a few days, then the family came home to find that all the lights in the house were on even though they had turned them off before going out. There was a noticeable chill in the air in the living room, despite the fact it was midsummer. The next evening, the family discovered what was causing the unexplained disturbances. As they sat watching TV with their backs to the kitchen, a figure appeared in the doorway. The body seemed to form out of a swirling black mist and Steven could hear laboured breathing. Fortunately, the children were glued to the TV, so only Steven saw it. Then the figure vanished. Steven had been planning to take the children to their grandmother's house the next day, but he suddenly felt as though it would be a good idea to leave straightaway!

As the children calmly filed out of the house, unaware of why their father had changed his plans, they heard a wail welling up. It was so loud that the neighbour's dogs began to bark. As the family drove away, the youngest son blurted out that the 'basement monster' was watching them from an upstairs window. Steven glanced back to see the same figure he had seen only moments earlier.

A week later, Steven returned from a business trip, collected the children from their grandmother and returned to the house. He told himself that whatever he thought he had seen and experienced was unlikely to recur, but that didn't prevent him from suffering a sleepless night or two.

He called the landlady and tried to sound as casual as he could while probing for information about former tenants. There had been a young woman who moved away suddenly after claiming that her dead father had called on her. She left her belongings in the shed and refused to return to collect them. Another tenant had departed in the middle of the night. He too had abandoned his belongings, which were still in the garden shed.

## A Malevolent Presence

That should have been enough to encourage the family to move out, but they hoped that things would quieten down. But it was not to be; the disturbances became more violent and life-threatening. One evening, doors began to bang. Steven assumed his children were the cause, but the younger two were in bed and his daughter was in another part of the house. Then the building began to shake, the temperature dropped and a terrible stench wafted through the rooms. In rising panic, Steven struggled to reach his children, but their bedroom doors were locked. He somehow found the strength to break down the doors and, as he fled into the street with his children, was certain that the malevolent presence was behind them. Once in the car, they drove down the street, then pulled over and looked back. They could see a black shadow moving from room to room upstairs as though it was searching for the occupants.

The children never returned to the house, but Steven had to do so in order to collect their clothes and possessions. But he didn't go alone. On one occasion his brother accompanied him and took a photograph of Steven in the basement. It was an odd thing to do, Steven thought, but maybe his brother wanted something to remind the family of the time they had lived in a haunted house – not that they were ever likely to forget! When the photograph was developed, Steven was not alone in the picture. There, standing behind him, was the shadowy figure of a man dressed in old-fashioned clothes, an angry expression on his face.

The family were more than relieved to have escaped and wanted to forget the whole business, but Steven's brother was curious about the history of the house and its previous inhabitants. He scoured the internet for details and discovered that a Civil War hero, Major General Eugene Asa Carr, had once lived there. The Major's photograph was the spitting image of the malevolent figure who had stood behind Steven in the basement. But the Major had been a hero and there was no mention of what might have caused him, if indeed it was him, to haunt the house. Maybe some spirits simply can't accept that they are dead.

## HAUNTED HOTELS

In the 19th century, Virginia City in Nevada was a centre for silver prospectors who had struck it rich and were looking for a wild time. A hundred years later, there was little for tourists to do in the town aside from window shopping, drinking at the many saloons or taking in a show at the Opera House. When Janice Oberding checked into the Silver Queen Hotel after an evening at the theatre, she was ready for a good night's sleep. But in the early hours of the morning she was awoken by a couple arguing in the room next door. The man's voice was raised so loud that Janice could hear it through the wall; she could also hear the woman begging him for forgiveness. Then the man became physically abusive and pushed the woman against the wall. Janice was about to call the desk clerk, but she remembered that in such a small hotel there was unlikely to be anyone on duty at that hour. She would have called the sheriff, but didn't have a mobile phone, so she determined to make a complaint in the morning. The verbal abuse and the crying continued and then there was silence. It was now past 3 am and Janice was finally able to sleep.

After breakfast Janice reported the row to the manageress, only to be told that the room next to hers was unoccupied. The manageress said the disturbance had been caused by the resident ghosts. Years ago, a man had murdered his girlfriend in that room. If Janice didn't believe it, the manageress said, she would show her. When the two women searched the room they found it empty, but for a decorator's ladder and some paint pots.

At the Balsams Hotel in Dixville Notch, New Hampshire, a female resident woke one morning to see a dripping wet, naked man standing at the foot of her bed. She drowsily assumed it was her husband emerging from the shower; she called out to him, but her husband was sleeping next to her. He woke just in time to corroborate her story. The next instant, the naked figure vanished. It is said that in the 1930s, a band leader who was staying in that room had drowned in a nearby lake.

## THE GHOST BOOK

Hotels are required to keep a register of their guests, but one hotel in Bisbee, Arizona, keeps a register of its ghosts too.

The Copper Queen Hotel has a long and eventful history dating back to 1902. Hotel staff are happy to share this colourful past with inquisitive guests, many of whom book in for that very reason. The desk clerk relates how he heard a woman's voice in the elevator when he was the only person in it at the time. If you ask nicely, he will open the ghost register – a record of the activities of the non-paying residents who checked out a hundred years ago. The entries describe many seemingly insignificant but unsettling incidents, such as a child's soft toy playing hide and seek with its owner, and the inexplicable failure of cameras and mobile phones in certain 'dead spots'. There have been various sightings of a ghostly boy called Billy who has been seen jumping on a leather couch in the lobby, decades after he was found drowned in a nearby river. Some guests have reported encountering a bearded man in a top hat, who leaves behind a trail of cigar smoke; other male guests claim to have been 'interfered with' by the ghost of a prostitute who is said to have committed suicide in the hotel.

All told, there are said to be 16 spirits haunting Bisbee, enough to encourage a local historian to organize a ghost tour of the town conducted from the driving seat of a second-hand hearse.

## THE MANY GHOSTS OF THE MYRTLES MANSION

The old plantation mansions of the Deep South, particularly those in Louisiana, have a singular atmosphere, shrouded as they are in Spanish moss and veiled in creeping fog seeping in from the bayou. Of all the houses in St Francisville, the Myrtles mansion (built in 1796 for Deputy Attorney General David Bradford) is considered to be one of the most haunted in the United States. However, in their enthusiasm to find wraiths under every bed some ghost hunters have mistakenly attributed too many spooks to the site, which is now doing a thriving trade as a historic guesthouse.

Nevertheless, several guests have spoken of being approached by slaves and domestic servants who ask what they can do for the guests, before fading in front of their eyes. A gateman quit the guesthouse after welcoming a lady in a white dress, who walked up to the house and promptly disappeared through the (closed) front door! In the evening the piano has been heard to play one melancholy chord over and over again, but no one is seen sitting at the keyboard.

One visitor, Stacey Jones, founder of the Central New York Ghost Hunters group, enthused, 'It is a spectacular place to stay, if you keep an open mind. While taking the guided tour, I saw what looked like a heavyset African-American woman wearing an apron walk by the door, on the porch. Thinking it was a worker in period dress, I peeked out and no one was there.' Stacey's friend, a devout sceptic, apparently had a distressing experience when lying in bed that night. Pinned down by unseen hands, she was unable to move or cry out. Eventually, the unseen presence tired of the game and released her.

## Fictitious Phantoms

While there is no shortage of spirits on the 240 hectare (600 acre) plantation and some claim that ten murders have been committed there, only one killing has been confirmed.

A former slave named Chloe is said to have been hanged for the murder of three children, whose ghosts have been seen playing on the veranda. Both Chloe and her crimes are now believed to be nothing more than morbid fancies – even though at least one house guest has claimed to have seen her. In the late 1980s, Frances Myers was staying in one of the downstairs rooms when she awoke to find a black woman in a long dress standing beside her bed. The apparition was wearing a green scarf or shawl around her head and holding a candle which emitted a faint glow. Frances screamed and hid under the covers; when she looked again, the ghost was gone. It may be that she saw 'Chloe's Ghost', the spirit whose blurry shadow is seen on one of the postcards sold on the site. But a close look at the photograph reveals the face of a much older woman than the one Frances described.

Children's voices have been heard throughout the house and a little girl with golden ringlets and wearing a Victorian-era dress has been sighted peering through the window of the games room. This room was used as a makeshift infirmary during the yellow fever epidemic that claimed several of the former owner's children.

The only murder to have been substantiated is that of attorney William Winter, who was shot by an unnamed assassin in 1871 as he stood on the side porch. Legend has it that Winter dragged himself to the staircase, where he expired in his wife's arms. Guests and guides claim to have heard his footsteps echoing in the hall as he staggers up the steps; they also say they have heard him give his last dying gasp, but the fact is that William Winter died where he fell. The assassin escaped on horseback and was never brought to trial. Winter's wife died of a broken heart seven years later, aged 44.

While legends of the ghostly inhabitants may be greatly exaggerated, the house seems to have been cursed from the moment the first nails were put in.

## Yellow Fever

The mansion's first owner sold the plantation, which was then known as Laurel Grove, for several hundred barrels of flour. At the time flour was in short supply and he hoped to make a fortune by selling it on, but the flour was never delivered and he died an embittered man. The next owner was distraught with grief when his children succumbed to yellow fever during an epidemic that scourged the region. Unable to remain in the house, he sold it to the wealthy Stirling family, who rebuilt it, doubling its size by adding a southern extension and introducing many imposing features, including a front gallery 32 m (107 ft) long. After furnishing the rooms with European art and antiques, they renamed the estate the Myrtles.

But four years later the master of the house died, leaving the property to his formidable wife, Mary. Four of the couple's children had died young and their eldest son died the same year as his father. It is thought that these may be the spirits who haunt the house to this day, reliving happier times of wealth and privilege. The dark days at the end of the Civil War saw the house and plantation looted by federal troops; after the Confederacy surrendered to the Union in 1865, the family fortune was rendered worthless. Following a succession of owners, the house passed to a family whose son had drowned during a storm.

## Chloe the Slave

In the 1950s the house was sold to a widow, Marjorie Munson, and that is when the ghost stories began. Marjorie was tormented by unexplained occurrences and asked her neighbours if any of them had heard if the house was haunted. There was a local legend of an old woman in a green bonnet, but she had no name; it was only when James and Frances Kermeen purchased the house in the 1970s that the legend of Chloe the slave was born. It was said that Chloe wore the green headband to cover a gaping wound where her ear had been cut off as punishment for eavesdropping. Even more lurid and fanciful was the tale of how the slave had been abused by her master (in truth, a man known to have been uncommonly kind to his servants) and then abandoned. She was said to have sought revenge by poisoning his three children, a crime for which she was hanged by her fellow slaves. In fact, two of the children she was accused of killing died several years apart and the third was not even born at the time of the alleged crime. Exhaustive research by historian David Wiseheart failed to find any record of a slave by the name of Chloe. Other graphic crimes said to have been committed on the plantation were equally without foundation.

## Blood on the Floorboards

Of the six murder victims named in previous histories of the house, one was found to have died of yellow fever (not stabbed to death over a gambling debt, as local legend would have it); the tale of three Union soldiers who were shot during a looting spree was also exposed as a complete fallacy. In echoes of numerous other ghost stories, it was said that their bloodstains on the floorboards could not be scrubbed clean, but no account of their murder could be found in the local newspapers or military archives. The story of the fifth 'victim', a caretaker killed during an attempted burglary in 1927, may have been inspired by the murder of a local man in another building on the plantation around the same time.

## The Haunted Mirror

Even though many of the ghosts have been dispatched by diligent research, some enthusiasts remain stubbornly devoted to the mansion's reputation and point to the 'haunted mirror' as evidence of its supernatural cachet.

Photographs of this antique-looking mirror appear to show a cluster of phantom hands imprinted behind the glass. When this was pointed out to the present owners, they had the glass professionally cleaned, but the prints could not be erased. They replaced the glass and still the prints were seen when the guests had their snapshots developed. The latest theory is that the impressions are flaws in the wood which appear in the shape of handprints when the flashlight catches the indentations.

It would seem that the only certain way to evaluate the paranormal quotient of the Myrtles is to check in and see what happens. Is anyone brave enough to check in and take their chances?

## IN THE STILL OF THE NIGHT

The Myrtle mansion is an essential stopover for any serious ghost hunter, but there's another haunted plantation house that is off the official tourist map. Legendary country music singer Loretta Lynn was raised a God-fearing Christian in the mountains of Kentucky, but she is not ashamed or afraid of her psychic abilities, which she believes she inherits from her mother. When she was living with her first husband and feeling homesick, she would often sense when a letter from home was about to be delivered and what its contents would be, as though she could read her mother's thoughts while she was writing it. Loretta also experienced several premonitions, including one where she saw her father lying in a casket the day before she heard he had died. Many years later, when she visited her childhood home in Butcher Hollow, she saw his ghost sitting on the front porch.

Then in the late 1960s, after becoming an internationally famous country music star, Loretta was driving though Tennessee, house-hunting with her husband, when they took a wrong turn and came upon a historic plantation house in Hurricane Mills. They were so enamoured with the house that they bought the nearby town as well!

However, shortly after they moved in, strange and unsettling things occurred. Doors would open and close by themselves, a woman in period clothes would appear in the children's bedroom and the sound of a woman walking up the stairs in high heels could be heard in the still of the night. Loretta believes the sounds were made by a woman in white who she saw standing on the second-floor balcony, wringing her hands and sobbing. She is said to be the ghost of Beula Anderson, the wife of a former owner of the plantation who died days after losing her newborn child. Both mother and child are buried near the house.

The sound of rattling chains has also been heard from the slave pit, a cellar where slaves were confined for disobeying their white owners, and shadows have been seen moving through the upstairs rooms, where cold spots have been felt by believers and non-believers alike. The singer's personal assistant has reported hearing noises when she was staying alone in the house. But not all the house guests are mere shadows. Both Loretta and her granddaughter have been woken several times in the night by a man in black standing at the foot of their bed – and it wasn't Johnny Cash! When Loretta's son Jack went to sleep with his boots on, the spectre of a confederate soldier tried to remove them, as if to say, 'a Southern gentleman is never too drunk or too tired to take his boots off in the house'. The family later learnt that a number of rebel soldiers had been buried on their land after a fire-fight during the Civil War. Sadly, Jack later drowned in the river that runs through the plantation, a tragedy his grandmother had foreseen, but was powerless to prevent.

Despite its tragic past, Loretta has learned to live with the former inhabitants of her home and doesn't mind sharing it with them: 'As long as you're good to ghosts, they'll be good to you. I don't make them mad.'

## THE NIGHT VISITOR

When terminally ill or elderly people move into a hospice, they don't expect to leave alive. Perhaps that is why some of them remain within its walls after they die. The Homestead Nursing Home in New Jersey is one such place. It eventually closed and was converted into an apartment block, but those who lived there swore they were visited by the ghosts of former patients.

As a teenager, Markus Misery (his real name) was fascinated rather than frightened when told the history of the building into which his family had just moved. He would explore the crawl spaces in the basement, where he found artefacts including dental records and receipts for food supplies. But nothing untoward happened until, years later, Markus returned home from serving in the army. In bed one night he experienced deep sleep paralysis, a natural phenomenon attributable to extreme fatigue. It is quite common and occurs when a person wakes from a deep sleep to find himself unable to move or cry out because his body has become rigid, even though his mind is alert. This state has given rise to the myth of the 'night hag', who sits astride the sleeper and sucks the breath of life from his body until he struggles to wake and cast her off. It's a form of nightmare, but it seems very real at the time as it is accompanied by pressure on the chest which feels as though something or someone is pinning the sleeper down.

Markus was evidently exhausted after the physical trials of army training, but the 'night hag' experience cannot account for what happened next. On more than one occasion he felt someone climb into bed next to him and, although fear forced him to keep his eyes shut, he felt as if someone was staring at him face to face. Even when he heard a high-pitched screaming in his ear, he screwed up his eyes as tight as he could. This occurred once a month until Markus became used to it and eventually opened his eyes – but there was nothing to see.

## A Figure at the Window

Then one evening Markus was standing in the driveway waiting for his friends when he happened to look up at his room and saw a figure standing in the window. It was a grim-faced old woman with long, white hair; she was wearing a nightgown. The friends saw her too. This was the first of several appearances witnessed by Markus and other visitors to the building. When Markus eventually married, his wife, who had no knowledge of the uninvited guest, saw the old woman in the window and asked who she was. 'That's Mrs Kennedy,' Markus told her, for by now he knew the old woman's identity. He had been told her name by the daughter of a neighbour who, as a child, had often seen the old woman watching her while she played in the street.

After Markus left home and his parents moved to an apartment on the lower floor, a succession of tenants moved in – and out – citing the apparition as their reason for vacating early. A curious footnote to this story is that one day, when Markus was showing photos of his old home to work colleagues, one of them recognized the building as the former care home where her mother had worked. One of her patients had been Mrs Kennedy.

## HOTEL CALIFORNIA

There is nothing spookier than a derelict mental hospital – other than a haunted one. Among the more imposing of such institutions is Camarillo State Mental Hospital in California which opened in 1936 and was home to 7,000 patients, many of them violent. The hospital was reputed to be haunted by several former inmates, some of them as young as 11 years old. Many of them had allegedly been subjected to electro-shock therapy and heavy sedation. It is rumoured that abuse was endemic and several patients had been murdered by their fellow inmates. The combination of violent death, routine brutality, mind-altering drugs and mental illness is thought to account for the uncommonly large number of disturbed souls said to be haunting the corridors of this creepy facility. It is believed to have been the inspiration for the Eagles' 1976 hit 'Hotel California' (whose guests can check out anytime, but can never leave. . .).

Female cleaners have reported seeing disembodied legs in the stalls of the men's toilets. Other people have been roughly manhandled by invisible hands, and had their hair pulled and their shoulders gripped and shaken. The figure of a man has been seen entering the women's restroom dressed in the tan jumpsuit that patients were required to wear to distinguish them from the staff. When Sheryl Downey, a nurse, called out to him he ignored her and went inside, so she called a co-worker, who found the room empty. The co-worker couldn't account for the sudden disappearance, as there were no windows or exits, but when he reported this to Sheryl he saw the man standing behind her – then the man vanished.

A more humane regime was introduced at the start of the 1990s, but the facility finally closed in 1997. Still, the building retained a disturbing influence over visitors, including film crews who used it as a movie location. Actors and technicians complained of nausea, dizziness, splitting headaches and fatigue as well as an uncomfortable feeling of being watched. Tools disappeared only to reappear in locked rooms, objects fell to the floor while no one was within reach and there were sightings of a woman in white drifting through the abandoned wards and the spirit of an old woman near the bell tower. But perhaps saddest of all is the ghost of an old man who has been seen sitting at a bus stop outside the hospital, waiting for a ride that never comes.

## GHOSTS OF NEW YORK

New York might seem to be too modern and bustling a city to offer ghosts the eerie quiet they seem to crave, but the Big Apple's skyscrapers and apartment blocks were erected on the site of former saloons, Prohibition-era speakeasies and paupers' cemeteries known as potter's fields (800,000 paupers are buried in the Bronx alone). So you just have to know where to look and which areas to stake out to catch the dead at play.

The Old Merchant's House at 29 East 4th Street is now a well-preserved museum with many interesting artefacts, but it is a melancholy place to visit after dark. For it is then that the hapless spirit of Gertrude Tredwell, spinster daughter of a wealthy businessman, walks the empty rooms. Gertrude gave birth to an infant out of wedlock and was forced to live an unhappy existence in the shadow of her domineering father.

According to the *New York Times*, the 19th-century townhouses in Bay Ridge, Brooklyn, are haunted by several restless souls who pace the corridors in the early hours, their shadows passing across the frosted glass panels in the front doors of the second-floor apartments.

One tenant told reporters of the night she woke to see a figure hovering over her bed and of another occasion when she felt the ice-cold touch of phantom fingers on her back.

In a Chelsea tenement, a young golden-haired girl in a lacy dress gave the living tenant's heart a jump start when he turned over in bed to see her kneeling in prayer with her hands clasped and her head looking heavenward. As he reached to touch her hair, she vanished. The next night a man – perhaps her father – appeared in the air above a sleeping tenant and the following night the ghost of a middle-aged woman was seen staring at a blank TV screen in the same apartment, but vanished the instant the light was switched on.

Even paranormal investigators get the creeps in Bay Ridge. Arthur Matos of the Eastern Paranormal Investigation Centre confessed to being too scared to be left alone in an apartment where he had recorded the sound of a little girl humming and a husky disembodied voice asking, 'What's that?'

## Looks Like Teen Spirit

The Upper West Side is host to fashionable spooks, such as the Kurt Cobain lookalike in ripped jeans and grunge shirt who materialized in Ellen Giglio's apartment. He strolled across the room and melted into the wall. When Ellen described the youth to the building's superintendent he didn't doubt her story for a moment. He recognized the young man as a previous tenant who had jumped to his death from the roof wearing the very same clothes Ellen described.

The inhabitants of Morningside Heights are decidedly more retro – both the living and the dead. A demolition man and blogger who uses the moniker Bald Punk doesn't scare easily, but he resents having to share his Budweiser with an uninvited guest whose sad eyes and cadaverous features elicit pity rather than terror. But even a hard man can get shaken up when a spook drains away before his eyes, as this sad-eyed spectre did after wandering around the apartment in a fuzzy blue cloud.

## The Big Apple's Big Names

The Big Apple has its share of notable historical apparitions, too. The city's last Dutch colonial governor, Peter Stuyvesant (nicknamed Peg-Leg Pete after the wooden prosthesis replacing his amputated right leg) has been sighted hopping down the dimly lit alleys of the East Village and around St Mark's in the Bowery.

The Morris-Jumel Mansion at 65 Jumel Terrace was built in 1765 for British colonel Roger Morris and it is the oldest house in Manhattan. It is rumoured to be haunted by the ghost of its former mistress, Eliza Jumel, who glides through the rooms in a purple dress checking that windows and doors are locked. There's also the restless spirit of a young suicide victim – a servant girl who jumped from an upstairs window – and a soldier of the American Revolution whose portrait hangs on display.

The spirit of author and wit Mark Twain is thought to hang out in a 19th-century brownstone building at 14 West 10th Street, where he lived briefly at the beginning of the 20th century. However, the building has a more sinister reputation on account of the 22 violent deaths that have occurred there in more recent years, giving rise to the unenviable nickname 'The House of Death'.

## Spirits in a Bottle

These sites don't welcome paranormal investigators or curious tourists, but if you're looking for atmosphere there are plenty of bars where you can sit over a drink as you wait for sightings of spirits of a different kind. The intimidating spectre of Welsh poet Dylan Thomas has been seen brooding at his favourite corner table at the White Horse tavern in the West Village, where he allegedly drank himself to death in 1953.

The Bridge Café at 279 Water Street under the Brooklyn Bridge is reputedly haunted by pirates who once frequented the oldest drinking den in 'New Amsterdam'. The 19th-century Landmark Tavern on 46th Street boasts the ghosts of a Confederate soldier and an Irish serving girl, while the Manhattan Bistro on 129 Spring Street was the site of a vicious murder when a young girl, Emma Sands, was dropped down a well in what is now the basement. Her alleged murderer, Levi Weeks, was not convicted and Emma is believed to be unable to rest until he confesses to the killing.

Then there is the Chelsea Hotel (immortalized in song by Lou Reed and Leonard Cohen), where the belligerent spirit of Sid Vicious taunts the guests; and Chumleys, a speakeasy at 86 Bedford Street, where John

Steinbeck, William Faulkner and F. Scott Fitzgerald enjoyed a snifter. It is also said to be haunted by Henrietta Chumley, wife of the former owner, who drinks Manhattans with lonely barflies. Another incorporeal presence in that district of the city is Thomas Jefferson's former vice president, Aaron Burr, who still frequents the quaintly named restaurant One If By Land, Two If By Sea in Barrow Street. Aaron has been seen in the company of his daughter, Theodosia, who drowned off the coast of North Carolina en route to visit her father. The building stands on the site that once was their carriage house. Female customers at the restaurant have been robbed of their earrings by the mischievous Theodosia, and plates have been sent flying by her intemperate father, who once killed a political rival in a duel.

## Showbiz ghosts

The Dakota Building at Central Park West has a morbid fascination for many, as it was both the location of John Lennon's murder and the setting for Roman Polanski's horror movie *Rosemary's Baby*. The exclusive apartment block is also known for being haunted by the spirit of a young man and a girl in turn-of-the-century dress, while Lennon's restless spirit has been sighted near the grimly named Undertaker's Gate.

The theatres of Times Square and Broadway are crowded with ghosts of performers and backstage staff. The Belasco Theatre is said to be haunted by the ghost of its eponymous owner, who died in 1931, but who returns to shake a clammy hand with unsuspecting thespians. The Public Theatre occasionally plays host to the spectre of Washington Irving, author of *The Legend of Sleepy Hollow*; and the Palace Theater in midtown Manhattan is believed to be inhabited by more than a hundred different ghosts, which surely qualifies it as one of the most haunted buildings in New York. Judy Garland's ghost has been sighted standing by a private entrance and the vague impression of a little girl has been seen on the balcony, as has that of a small boy near the mezzanine. A phantom female cellist has been seen practising after hours in the orchestra pit and a haunting piano refrain has been heard in the auditorium, even though the piano lid is always locked when the instrument is not in use. Perhaps the most unsettling spirit is that of an acrobat who fell to his death during a performance. To see him is to be forewarned of one's own death.

Performers and backstage staff at the New Amsterdam Theatre at 214 West 42nd Street have reason to leave immediately after the evening's entertainment. This is when the ghost of Olive Thomas, a Ziegfeld Follies chorus girl, can be encountered drifting through the auditorium, a blue bottle clutched in her shadowy hand. It is thought to be the bottle of syphilis medicine prescribed for her unfaithful alcoholic husband, from which she drank a fatal dose when his womanizing had become too much for her to bear.

One of the more bizarre residents of New York is buried in the grounds of St Paul's Chapel on Broadway and Fulton Street. English actor George Frederick Cooke died in September 1811, but he was interred without his head which he donated to science in payment of medical bills. His skull was subsequently used in several productions of Hamlet, although it's not known if it was acknowledged in the programme. Cooke's headless ghost is said to haunt the burial ground.

## More City Spirits

Finally, most impressive of all is the derelict King's Park Psychiatric Center on Long Island, with its dozens of century-old buildings that housed the seriously disturbed and criminally insane. From its abandoned buildings, shrieks and screams can be heard by those brave enough to venture within earshot.

If you imagine that you can avoid bumping into the spirits of the old city by sticking to the modern tourist sites, think again. Some visitors to the Empire State Building in Lower Manhattan have seen more than a spectacular panorama from the viewing gallery. A young woman in 1940s clothes has been heard to say that she can't live without her fiancé, who has been killed in the war. She has been seen to throw herself off the observation platform, in spite of the high safety barriers (which were not in place till after the Second World War). There's no need to rush to see this performance, as she repeats it every night.

## HAUNTED LONDON THEATRES

While stately homes and castles are still the most popular 'haunt' for restless spirits, theatres must surely rank in the top five. As every theatre-goer knows, it's hard to get an actor to leave the stage after the final curtain – but it's even more difficult when they are dead!

London lays claim to being the most haunted big city in the world. The cluster of theatres concentrated in the West End date back to the Elizabethan era, so it's not surprising that there are reputed to be hundreds of deceased actors, directors and backstage employees who refuse to leave the spotlight.

### Out for the Count

In 1878, actor-manager Sir Henry Irving acquired the lease of the Lyceum Theatre in the Strand and brought in his business manager, Bram Stoker. In his office, over a seven-year period, Stoker wrote much of *Dracula* and, like many literary and artistic figures of the 19th century, is believed to have indulged in opium to stimulate his imagination. Opium is said to stimulate the psychic senses, or Third Eye, located in the pineal gland near the centre of the brain. This produces melatonin, a hormone that affects sleep patterns. Under the influence of drugs, Stoker's intense brooding on the dark subject matter of his novel and his research into the myth of vampirism over such a protracted period may have created the etheric equivalent of a wormhole through which spirits pass from their dimension to our own. That's a theory put forward by psychic investigator Becky Walsh and her team, who held a vigil in the upper circle bar in 2005. They sensed a 'sweeping energy' which left them all feeling nauseous and which they attributed to a past resident having dabbled in the occult.

Stoker's ghost has not been seen in the theatre, although an assistant manager reported being surprised by a man who walked out of a solid wall near the grand circle, tipped his hat and bid the startled employee 'good morning' before vanishing.

The ghost of a grey lady has been seen by several staff members and their descriptions of her bear an uncanny resemblance to the photograph of actress Ellen Terry which hangs in the box office. Ellen's spirit was seen by an employee at an hour when the building would have been empty. She was dressed in a grey cloak and ignored his pleas to stop, so he followed her down a corridor until she disappeared into the solid wall at the far end.

## The Show Must Go On

When the Queen musical *We Will Rock You* was packing them at the Dominion Theatre, Tottenham Court Road, the spirit of rock star Freddie Mercury was seen by several employees. Cast member Jenna Lee James claims to have felt Freddie pass through her as she was singing one of his songs, while Ian John Shillito, stage manager and co-author of *Haunted West End Theatres*, remembers sensing a presence while cueing the show. He then saw Freddie watching from the wings and criticizing aspects he didn't approve of!

The aptly named Phoenix Theatre in Charing Cross Road is rumoured to be haunted by the ghost of musical star Stephanie Lawrence, who is best remembered for creating the roles of Pearl in *Starlight Express* and Mrs Johnstone in the musical *Blood Brothers*. She died in November 2000, but deputy stage manager Richard Kingcott 'saw' her 12 years later, standing in a doorway of the set in her costume as if awaiting her entrance. At first Kingcott thought nothing of it, as he had been accustomed to seeing her there when she was alive, but he then realized that of course she was dead.

Stephanie isn't the only cast member Kingcott has witnessed returning to the scene of a former triumph. On several occasions, when a character known as Eddie has been on stage, Kingcott has felt a presence behind him. He believes it is that of a young cast member who died tragically while essaying the role. Stage manager and psychic investigator Becky Walsh also sensed a presence behind her when she worked at the Phoenix. It only occurred when the character of Eddie was on stage and usually when an understudy was taking the role, which suggested that the young actor who had died was checking out his replacement.

Becky gave a detailed description of the young man to the company manager, who confirmed that it was an accurate description of the youth who had died while playing the part of Eddie.

It is ironic that the Fortune Theatre in Covent Garden was haunted by a ghost during a long-running production of the supernatural thriller *The Woman in Black*. The most unnerving aspect was that the real apparition and the stage spectre looked uncannily alike, prompting other cast members to do a double-take. Natalie Block, an usher turned actress who had taken the role of the ghost, saw her doppelgänger on several occasions. Natalie was sitting at the back of the dress circle during a performance when she noticed a grey shadow in box A. She turned away, thinking it was a trick of the light, but when she looked again the shadow had form. It was a woman sitting motionless watching the play, wearing a turn-of-the-century corseted dress with her hair done in a fashionable Victorian style. Natalie looked away, wondering if the vision would have vanished when she looked back, and sure enough the box was empty.

When the theatre management heard about the sighting they immediately saw the opportunity for publicity and informed the press that a real ghost was watching the show. Natalie had also sensed an oppressive atmosphere in the small hospitality room attached to box A and smelt perfume and pipe smoke in other parts of the building. She claims that while she was on stage she had seen a 'moving darkness' in the wings and that the young male lead had experienced considerable anxiety as he watched her walk off stage into the outstretched arms of the ghost! Natalie insists she saw nothing on that occasion, but felt her skin crawl when she was told about it later.

## The Ballet Ghost

The Palace Theatre on Shaftesbury Avenue is home to a curious apparition – the torso of a ballerina which emerges from the floor of the stage to perform an arabesque. It is believed to be the world famous ballet dancer Anna Pavlova, who appeared regularly on the bill when the theatre was known as the Palace of Varieties. The reason why only her upper body is seen is that, in Pavlova's time, the stage was at a lower level.

## The Aristocrat and the Clown

The oldest theatre in the West End is the Theatre Royal, Drury Lane, which is thought to date back to the 17th century. Perhaps unsurprisingly it is considered to host more ghosts than its neighbours. Its most famous inhabitant is an 18th-century aristocrat known to past and present members of the cast and crew as the 'Man in Grey'. This gentleman always appears in a powdered wig and a tricorne hat, immaculately attired in a jacket, cloak and riding boots and carrying a sword. He is believed to be the ghost of a murder victim whose remains were discovered bricked up within the building, a knife protruding from his ribs.

His manifestation during rehearsal is possibly the best-documented sighting of its type, as he was witnessed by the entire cast. Unfortunately, no one had the presence of mind to ask for his autograph!

Those suffering from coulrophobia (fear of clowns) would do well to avoid visiting the Theatre Royal, as the mischievous spirit of Joseph Grimaldi, the 'father' of modern clowns, has an unnerving habit of appearing behind members of the audience dressed in full white face make-up. There is surely only one thing more scary than a clown close up and that's a dead clown breathing down your neck! Grimaldi has been credited with guiding nervous actors through their paces, but is less gracious with the more experienced members of the company. Many have complained of being kicked by an invisible mischief-maker and theatre legend has it that the head of the old joker has been seen to manifest in the mirror of his old dressing room, to the consternation of any poor actor who happens to be applying his make-up at the time.

## Willy Wonka's Ghost

The Aldwych Theatre in Drury Lane was built by actor-manager Seymour Hicks and opened in 1905. In the 1920s it became famous for presenting a series of popular comedies known as the *Aldwych Farces*, but there have been few laughs for the staff who have complained of poltergeist activity such as doors opening unaided, the sound of a woman weeping and spirit lights or orbs floating through the auditorium. As might be expected, the turnover in staff is uncommonly high.

When psychic Becky Walsh investigated the Aldwych, she 'saw' clairvoyantly the image of a gentleman dressed in what she described as a Willy Wonka-style costume with a top hat and cane. She sensed that the ghost's manner of dress was not in keeping with the period, but reflected instead his eccentric fashion sense and style. She had the impression that he had been a wealthy entrepreneur who had renovated the theatre and considered it his 'baby'. She believed that at some point he had sold the theatre and she was watching him walking from the building for the last time. She reported her findings to the management, who produced a photograph of Seymour Hicks dressed in what can only be described as a Willy Wonka costume of the kind worn by Johnny Depp in the Tim Burton movie, *Charlie and the Chocolate Factory*.

## The Old Vic

The Old Vic derives its name from the Royal Victoria Coffee and Music Hall established in 1880 by social reformer Emma Cons. Miss Cons is said to haunt the theatre along with her niece Lilian Baylis, who took over the management of the theatre when her aunt died in 1912. Lilian has been seen on the balcony of the upper circle staring wistfully out of the window at the garden across the road.

The lady with bloodstained hands who has been seen by many over the years is thought to be the spirit of a Shakespearean actress reliving her role in 'the Scottish play'. (The title of *Macbeth* is never to be mentioned backstage for fear of bringing a curse on the production.)

One evening, stage doorman Ned Sego saw the actress on the second floor as he was checking the building was empty before locking up for the night. He assumed she was an actress because she was wearing period costume and looked as solid as the rest of the company he had just seen leave the theatre, but as he followed closely behind her down the stairs to the exit she disappeared through a bricked-up doorway which must have been the exit in former times. Ned admitted that at that moment his heart stopped.

After the First World War the company was performing *Julius Caesar*; it featured a cast that had been assembled in some haste as several leading players had died in the Spanish Flu epidemic of 1918. On the opening night, some members of the company asked the director who the 'extra' was in the orchard scene. The director didn't recognize the man so he asked a friend, who unhesitatingly identified him as Eric Moss, the actor who had taken the part of Brutus before succumbing to a fatal bout of the flu.

## Les Misérables

During its hundred-year history, the Queen's Theatre in Soho, London has produced a number of ghost stories. Chief electrician Mike Cordina spotted what he thought was a contractor passing through the upper circle of the auditorium after everyone had gone home. The exits were locked and chained, leaving only the stage door unlocked, so Mike was concerned that the man, who had short grey hair and was dressed in a long grey coat with velvet lapels, would lose his way looking for a way out. He called out to him, but the man continued walking and disappeared round a corner – literally, it seems, for as soon as Mike rounded the corner he came to a solid, blank wall. The stranger was nowhere to be seen.

Other members of staff have reported seeing the same figure when the building was known to be empty, and Becky Walsh has sensed the presence of a male spirit standing behind her when working as a member of staff at the theatre. On that occasion she mentally asked the spirit to identify himself and was told clairvoyantly that he had worked in the office situated through a door at the back of the auditorium. This was curious because there was no door there. A week or so later, Becky happened to see an old photograph of the theatre and there was indeed a door precisely where the ghost had described it.

## The Strangler Jacket

The Duke of York's Theatre in Saint Martin's Lane is home to the ghost of another actor-manager, Violet Melonette, who died in 1935. She has been sighted in the audience on a number of occasions, although it's not known if she voiced her opinion of the show she was watching or simply gave patrons the cold shoulder. The theatre, which opened in 1892, also houses a singular item of macabre memorabilia – a lady's bolero jacket that has been known to drive its wearers to question their own sanity. It originally belonged to Victorian actress Edith Merryweather, who was allegedly drowned by a jealous lover. It is said that the jacket was bought on a market stall and worn by various actresses, all of whom complained of feeling constricted, to the extent that the garment quickly acquired the name 'the Strangler Jacket'. Subsequently, actresses refused to wear it. In an effort to allay their fears, the wife of the then producer volunteered to try it on. She reluctantly admitted that it seemed to contract as soon as she buttoned it up, making it hard to breathe. On handing the jacket back to the wardrobe mistress, the producer's wife saw a look on the poor woman's face that made her wish she had taken the story more seriously. For on the producer's wife's neck, clear for all to see, was a red band of welts such as might have been made by a strangler's hands.

## The Spook with Chubby Cheeks

The 300-year-old Theatre Royal, Haymarket, is reputed to be haunted by comic actor-manager John Baldwin Buckstone, whose disembodied voice and footsteps have been heard in what was once his dressing room. The late Margaret Rutherford (cinema's original Miss Marple) and her dresser once spent the night in that very room and claim to have seen Buckstone's spirit enter, only to vanish before their eyes.

In 1949, Sir Donald Sinden was appearing in a play with Sir Ralph Richardson when he and actress Gillian Howell saw a man in a long, grey Victorian morning coat standing near Richardson's dressing room. The man looked pensive and was staring out of the window. He had his back to them so they both assumed that it was Richardson; they greeted him as they passed on their way to the stage, but received no reply. A few minutes later, as they waited in the wings, they saw Richardson on stage, so Sinden rushed back up the stairs to check, but the mysterious figure had vanished. More recently, Dame Judi Dench saw a man in a long tailcoat hurrying ahead of her along the corridor from the stage to the auditorium, but when she turned the corner she came to a dead end and he was nowhere to be seen.

The ghost may have been Buckstone, who was also seen by the theatre's master carpenter one night long after the evening performance had finished. The phantom was dressed in a cloak and top hat, but what is particularly significant about this sighting is that the witness remarked on the spirit's solidity and that it vanished in front of him. This gave the carpenter such a fright that it made him physically ill. The carpenter recalled that the ghost had been smiling and had 'chubby cheeks' and he identified the spectre as Buckstone from a photograph in the archives.

Sometimes the spooks are not so solid. One staff member was pursued by two shadows as she walked down a backstage passageway. One was her own; but the other continued past her when she stopped to see who was following her.

Stage doorman Brian Russell believes he made physical contact with a ghost when he went under the stage to turn off the lights and collided with what he described as an 'electric energy' so strong that it made him nauseous.

## HAUNTED HOTEL

In three days of fighting at the battle of Gettysburg in July 1863, a battle that was to mark the turning point in the American Civil War, 53,000 men lost their lives. The scale of the slaughter surpassed even that of the bloodiest days on the Somme during the First World War. No wonder then that visitors to the site have sworn that they have seen spectral soldiers wandering the battlefield as disorientated as the day they were killed. Some say it is the most haunted place in America.

On the first day of the battle rebel snipers were able to pick off retreating Union soldiers from their vantage point in the Farnsworth House on Baltimore Pike. The house, still pockmarked with bullet holes, is now a small hotel where guests have awoken in the night to find an indistinct figure at the end of their bed. Odder still was the occasion when a local radio station set up an outside broadcast from the Farnsworth House only to have the power and telephone lines cut

*Dead soldiers lie on the battlefield of Gettysburg, July 1863*

out. A local psychic, who was on site to give impressions to the listeners, heard disembodied voices warning their comrades that 'traitors' were around and he suddenly realized that the sound engineers were dressed in blue shirts and blue jeans – the same colour as the Union uniforms of the Civil War.

Several tourists have approached the park rangers over the years to ask the identity of a ragged, barefooted man dressed in a butternut shirt and trousers with a large floppy hat who appears at the rock formation known as the Devil's Den. He always says the same thing, 'What you're looking for is over there,' while pointing north east towards the Plum Run, then promptly vanishes. The description fits that of the Texans who were a rag-bag unit feared for their fighting spirit.

At the wooded end of the Triangular Field, site of Colonel Chamberlain's heroic bayonet charge which drove Confederate troops off the hill known as Little Round Top, visitors have documented chaotic paranormal activity including phantom musket fire and drum rolls. Shadowy rebel sharpshooters have been seen taking cover among the trees, but whenever the ghost hunters enter the field to record these phantom figures their cameras malfunction. There appears to be some form of electromagnetic disturbance hanging like a pall over the field; even photographs of the area taken from the outside looking in are either fogged or fail to develop. One possible explanation is that it is a mass of residual personal energy discharged into the atmosphere following the violent death of so many soldiers.

Several visitors have regaled their fellow travellers with tales of having heard musket fire from Little Round Top and even having smelt acrid clouds of cordite and cannon smoke. In fact, it is known that on the third day of the battle the sound of the massed cannons was so loud that it could be heard in Washington, 80 miles away. But the most unearthly episode must have been that experienced by a group of volunteer re-enactors who worked as extras on the epic recreation of the battle for the movie *Gettysburg* in 1993. During a break in the filming the group were admiring the sunset from Little Round Top when a grizzled old man approached them in the uniform of a Union private. He smelt of sulphur, which was used in gunpowder of the period, and his uniform was threadbare and scorched, unlike those of the extras. The man handed out spare rounds and commented on the fury of the battle. It was only later when they showed the rounds to the armourer that they learnt these were authentic musket rounds from the period.

The battle was finally decided by a single suicidal assault, the infamous attack known as Pickett's Charge, in which 12,000 Confederate infantry marched shoulder to shoulder across an open field only to be massacred by massed cannons and musket fire. In that single, fatal hour 10,000 were killed and with them died General Robert E. Lee's hopes of victory. Park rangers have witnessed many apparitions in the field after visiting hours including an unidentified mounted officer and another who was the image of General Lee. Local residents have maintained that on warm summer evenings they have encountered cold spots while out walking which transformed their breath to mist.

## THE TOWN TOO TOUGH TO DIE

They called Tombstone, Arizona, 'The Town Too Tough To Die' and it appears that certain of its most notorious inhabitants are equally reluctant to go quietly. The town is now preserved as a national museum with many of the old buildings lovingly restored to their former rickety glory and stocked with original artefacts from its violent past including the hearse that transported bodies to Boot Hill, the hangman's noose and the honky-tonk piano which accompanied many a bar-room brawl. Some say that if you stay after closing time you can hear the piano playing 'Red River Valley', the cowboys' favourite tune, and hear the echo of their raucous laughter.

Some of the meanest gunfighters of the old West did their hardest drinking and gambling in the town's notorious Bird Cage Theatre which took its name from the 14 cribs suspended from the ceiling in which 'painted ladies', dressed in exotic feathers, would swing. The Bird Cage also served as a saloon where the cowboys and card sharps took their pleasure with women who could out-drink and out-cuss the best of them. Arguments were settled with a six gun and the loser was buried on Boot Hill, so named because many of its residents died with their boots on.

The streets of Tombstone were the setting for numerous showdowns, the most famous being the gunfight at the OK Corral when Marshal Wyatt Earp, his brothers and their consumptive trigger-happy friend Doc Holliday faced down the Clanton and McLaury gang, three of whom were killed. In the aftermath, the surviving Clantons and their friends took their bloody revenge. Virgil Earp was shot in the back while playing pool in the Bird Cage and his dying words are said to echo there after dark.

The tour guides are fond of telling visitors that as many as 31 ghosts are thought to haunt the saloon which was the site of 26 killings – a fact borne out by the 140 bullet holes that can be seen peppering the ceiling. The spook most frequently seen in the saloon is a stagehand dressed in black striped trousers, wearing a card dealer's visor and carrying a clipboard. He is said to appear from nowhere, walk across the stage

*Tombstone, 1885. The town suffered two major fires in 1881 and 1882. Those, with the decline in the silver mines, meant that by the mid-1880s the place was virtually abandoned*

and exit through the facing wall. Tourists have also reported seeing the ghost of a young boy who had died of yellow fever in 1882 and heard an unidentified woman sighing plaintively as if pining for her lost love. Others have commented on how impressed they have been by the authenticity of the actors' clothes in the gambling parlour and the dancehall, only to be told that the museum doesn't employ actors, nor does it ask its staff to dress in period costumes.

Since it is a museum, no one is allowed to smoke inside the buildings but nevertheless visitors will often remark on the strong smell of cigar smoke which lingers round the card tables and some have spoken of the delicate scent of lilac perfume in the backstage bathroom. Equally odd is the $100 poker chip which mysteriously appeared on the poker table one day then promptly vanished after being locked away in a desk before turning up in a filing cabinet some days later. And this is not the only object which appears and disappears to the bewilderment of the museum staff. The ghosts seem to enjoy playing hide and seek with small but significant items which they know the staff will notice if they are missing or out of place. Furniture has moved by itself and one member of the museum staff was physically attacked by a mischievous spirit who hit the tour guide on the back of the knee, causing him to fall to the floor. Anyone who doubts that there is a physical presence in the old saloon only has to put his hand in the notorious 'cold spot' and feel the contrast with the warm air surrounding it to sense a distinct chill in the atmosphere.

Over the years several ghost hunters have attempted to capture the ghosts on film, but their cameras have malfunctioned as if triggered by an influx of energy as ghosts appear. Unattended still cameras have fired off exposures by themselves and have altered focus in the middle of shooting before resetting themselves correctly. However, it seems the ghosts can register on electrical equipment if their emission is strong enough. Small balls of light have been captured on film floating up from the floor and a face has been seen in the large painting which hangs

*Virgil Earp's last words echo down the ages; the Bird Cage Theatre in 1946*

behind the bar. One female member of staff who works in the gift shop on the ground floor of the Bird Cage Theatre swears she once saw on a security monitor a lady in a white dress walking through the cellar at closing time when all the visitors had left.

## Tombstone's Spooky Sites

Other haunted sites in Tombstone include Nellie Cashman's Restaurant, where customers and employees have reported seeing dishes crash to the floor, and Schiefflin Hall where rowdy town council meetings were held in the 1880s. At the Wells Fargo stage stop ghostly drivers and phantom passengers have been seen alighting from a spectral stagecoach on their way to the Grand Hotel – renamed Big Nose Kate's after its most famous owner, a prostitute who enjoyed a volatile relationship with its most famous resident, Doc Holliday, who lived in room 201. Residents and tourists have also reported seeing a man in a black frock coat who starts walking across the street but never appears on the other side and traffic often stops for a woman in white who committed suicide after her child died of fever in the 1880s.

The town's tour guides thought they had heard and seen it all until recently when they were shown photographs taken by visitors on two separate occasions. Both were taken at the same spot on Boot Hill and at first sight they appeared to be typical snapshots of their relatives standing in front of the gravestones, but on closer inspection the first subject was shadowed by the faint but unmistakable image of a cowboy in period costume. However, there was nothing discernible of this phantom figure below the knee. In the second shot, taken by someone unconnected with the first tourist, their friend or family member smiled from the photo unaware that behind them could be seen a ghostly pair of cowboy boots and the lower part of their owner in precisely the spot where the legless cowboy had been seen in the first photograph. It may be that the film or exposure setting on the first camera was less sensitive to residual personal energy and so captured the cowboy's upper half which would be the stronger emanation, while the second camera captured the fainter portion only.

## A GLIMPSE INTO THE PAST

For over a century, tourists have been allowed access to enjoy the elegant palace and gardens of Versailles, near Paris, where Louis XVI and his queen Marie Antoinette lived in splendour just prior to the French Revolution. However, few can have seen as much of the palace's past glories as Eleanor Jourdain and Anne Moberly did in the summer of 1901.

Miss Moberly, aged 55, was the head of a women's residential hall at Oxford University and 35-year-old Miss Jourdain had been offered a post as her assistant. It had been Miss Jourdain's idea to invite Miss Moberly to spend part of the summer vacation touring France with her in the hope of becoming better acquainted while she considered the offer. Both were the daughters of Anglican clerics and not given to a belief in the supernatural, but what they saw on their visit to Versailles on 10 August shook their faith and forced them to question their beliefs.

They began with a tour of the main palace and then decided to walk to the Petit Trianon, one of two smaller palatial buildings in the grounds where the ill-fated Marie Antoinette retreated to escape the formalities of the court. It was a pleasantly warm day with barely a cloud in the sky, cooled by a soft freshening breeze – ideal walking weather, in fact – but after strolling through a large formal garden and a glade the ladies lost their way. Perhaps they had been distracted in the course of conversation, or had misread their guidebook, but whatever the reason, they now found themselves at the Grand Trianon, the palace built for Louis XIV.

Unperturbed, they consulted their Baedeker guide, which offered an alternative route to the smaller building by way of a lane which lay ahead of them. Neither lady remarked on the fact that they appeared to be the only visitors in this part of the grounds, although it struck them both as very strange considering how popular Versailles was with tourists at that time of the season. But Miss Jourdain did think it odd when her companion did not take the opportunity to ask directions from a domestic servant who was leaning out of the window of a building shaking the dust from a bed sheet. It later transpired that the older

*The entrance to the palace of Versailles*

woman had not seen the servant. In fact, when they compared notes some months later they discovered that their shared experience differed in small but significant details.

The end of the lane divided into three paths and it was here that the English visitors came upon two men dressed in green coats and three-cornered hats whom they assumed were gardeners. One of the men offered directions in such a gruff, offhand manner that Miss Jourdain felt the need to ask again, but she received the same response. Looking around for a more civil guide she caught sight of a woman and a young girl standing in the doorway of a cottage and thought it odd that they should be dressed in such old-fashioned clothes. She later learnt that Miss Moberly had not commented on it because she hadn't seen the women – nor, for that matter, had she seen the cottage.

It was at this point that both women began to sense a change in the atmosphere. They were overcome by a profound sense of melancholy and a detachment from reality as if they were sleepwalking through a particularly lucid dream. Miss Moberly was later to describe the atmosphere as 'unnatural' and distinctly 'unpleasant': ' . . . even the trees behind the building seemed to have become flat and lifeless, like a wood worked in tapestry. There were no effects of light and shade, and no wind stirred the trees. It was all intensely still.'

The atmosphere was unusually oppressive as they came to the edge of a wood in front of which was a pillared kiosk, intended perhaps for tired visitors who wished to sit and shield themselves from the sun. But neither lady felt disposed to do so when they caught sight of the face of a man in a cloak who was seated nearby. Both women sensed a shiver of repulsion as they looked on the swarthy, malevolent features. But was he looking at them or through them? Neither said a word, but instead debated whether to take the left- or right-hand path. While they were considering what to do a handsome-looking young man, his face framed in black ringlets, appeared in period costume complete with buckle shoes, a cloak and wide-brimmed hat and he advised them to take the path to the right through the wood. An instant later he was gone, but his directions had proven correct. As they emerged from the trees they saw the Petit Trianon in the clearing and approached it

*A cottage built for Queen Marie Antoinette in the vast gardens of Versailles, as part of the rustic village, or 'petit hameau'*

with a palpable sense of relief. It was then that Miss Moberly spotted a rather pretty fair-haired young woman in period costume sketching near the terrace. She was attired in a low cut white dress with a full skirt, a light-coloured scarf around her shoulders and a wide-brimmed hat to shield her pale skin from the sun. There was something about this artist that predisposed Miss Moberly to dislike the woman, but she couldn't put her feelings into words. Curiously, her companion made no comment as they passed and it was only weeks later that Miss Jourdain admitted that she hadn't seen anyone sketching in the garden. The oppressive stillness returned as they toured the outside of the house but swiftly evaporated when they encountered a French wedding party in modern dress near the entrance whom they joined for a tour of the rooms.

## Sense of Foreboding

Neither lady spoke of their experience until a week later when Miss Moberly was overcome with the same stifling sense of foreboding that she had sensed at the kiosk while recalling her experiences in a letter to her sister. At this she turned to Miss Jourdain and asked if the younger woman thought that the palace might be haunted. 'Yes I do,' replied Miss Jourdain. The two women then shared their recollections of that day. It was only later that they learnt that 10 August had been a significant day in French history for it was the day that revolutionaries marched on Versailles and seized the royal family. Had the two women unconsciously tapped into a residual memory of that pivotal day in the minds of those who had been present and sensed the approaching threat? And could it have been Marie Antoinette herself that Miss Moberly had seen sketching in the garden of the Petit Trianon? Miss Jourdain determined that another visit to Versailles was called for. Her second outing proved no less remarkable.

On a chilly, damp day in January 1902 she returned to Versailles and immediately set off in search of the Hameau, a model peasant village where Marie Antoinette had amused herself play-acting an idyllic rustic life with her friends. As she neared the site Miss Jourdain was again overcome with a sense of unreality, as if she was sleepwalking through someone else's dream. When she came in sight of the Hameau she passed two labourers in hooded cloaks who were gathering lopped branches and loading them into a cart. When she turned to observe them more closely they had gone. In the model village she was overwhelmed by an oppressive atmosphere and was tempted to turn back, but decided to press on as she suspected this might be her last opportunity to get to the bottom of the mystery. Eventually she emerged into a wooded park where she wandered a labyrinth of paths screened by dense hedges. The only person she saw there was an elderly gardener, but she heard the rustle of silk dresses which she thought impractical in wet weather and overheard the excited chatter of women speaking French. Occasionally she thought she could hear faint strains of chamber music although there were no musicians in sight. On returning to the main palace she asked the tour guides if there were any actors on the grounds in historical costume, or musicians, and was informed that there were neither.

Determined to verify what they had seen, Miss Jourdain and Miss Moberly embarked on a thorough examination of all the documents they could find relating to the palace during the period immediately prior to the Revolution. What they found appeared to validate their experiences. They traced a plan of the grounds which showed a cottage precisely where Miss Jourdain had said she had seen it, although nothing remained by 1901. They also found proof that there had been a pillared kiosk at the spot where they had observed the malevolent looking man who answered the description of the Comte de Vaudreuil. He had betrayed the queen by fooling her into permitting the staging of an anti-royalist play which had incited disaffected elements within the court to join the revolutionaries. As for the costumed figures, they identified the men in the three-cornered hats and green coats as Swiss Guards and the young man with black curls who had offered directions near the kiosk as the messenger who had hurried to warn the queen of a mob marching on the palace. This incident occurred on 5 October 1789, the same day that a cart had been hired to carry firewood from the park near the Hameau. If Miss Moberly and Miss Jourdain had indeed tuned in to this particular day it would explain why all the men they had seen on that hot day in August were dressed in autumnal clothes and why the two women had been oppressed by a sense of foreboding.

## Published, and Damned

Convinced that they had experienced a genuine glimpse into the past – a phenomenon known as retrocognition – the two ladies decided to publish their story. The resulting account, modestly titled *An Adventure* (1911), became an instant sensation and has remained a hotly debated issue ever since. Sceptics have argued that the women had mistaken actors in period costume for genuine spectres and in evidence of this offer Philippe Jullian's biography of turn of the century poet Robert de Montesquiou. Jullian notes that de Montesquiou and his friends often amused themselves by dressing in period costume and rehearsing historical plays in the grounds of Versailles and that Marie Antoinette was a prominent character. Although a perfectly rational scenario, this does not explain why Miss Jourdain did not see the domestic servant shaking a cloth from the window or the lady sketching in the garden, both of whom were observed by Miss Moberly. Neither does it explain the appearance of the woman and girl at the doorway of the cottage which had long been demolished, nor does it account for the kiosk which had also gone by 1901. Miss Moberly and Miss Jourdain were equally adamant that the handsome young messenger and the men collecting fallen branches had vanished within moments of being seen and could not have had time to move on in so short a time.

Unfortunately, both women naively willed the copyright to a sceptical friend, art historian Dame Joan Evans, who subscribed to Philippe Jullian's rational explanation of events. Consequently, Dame Joan Evans refused to allow the book to be reprinted after the authors' death, but a century later their story continues to be cited as one of the most compelling cases of retrocognition.

Such episodes are very rare, but perhaps they are not as uncommon as one might imagine. In 1926, two English ladies shared a similar experience. They took a walking tour of the villages near their new home to familiarize themselves with the area when they came upon a large Georgian house in substantial grounds surrounded by a wall. But when they made enquiries as to the owner and its history none of the locals knew which house they were talking about. Intrigued, on their next outing the ladies retraced their steps but found only a vacant plot with no sign of the house.

## THE GHOSTS OF GLASTONBURY

Glastonbury is one of the most sacred and mysterious sites in Britain, and of great spiritual significance to mystically minded Christians and pagans alike. Legend has it that King Arthur and Queen Guinevere are buried within the ruins of Glastonbury Abbey and that the Holy Grail, the chalice from which Jesus is said to have drunk on the night before his crucifixion, is hidden nearby. But of all the legends associated with Glastonbury the most extraordinary and controversial is that concerning the discovery of the ruins of the abbey itself.

In 1907, architect and archaeologist Frederick Bligh Bond (1864–1945) was appointed director of excavations by the Church of England and charged with the task of unearthing the abbey ruins which several previous incumbents had spent their lives searching for in vain. The work was unpaid, but Bligh had a thriving architectural practice in Bristol and he viewed the search for the abbey as an almost mystical mission. He was confident that he would succeed where the others had failed for he believed that he had an uncommon advantage over his predecessors.

His interest in paranormal phenomena had led him to join the Society for Psychical Research through which he had met Captain John Allen Bartlett, an eager advocate of automatic writing. Together the two men took up pen and paper in the hope of pinpointing the location of the ruins by tapping into what Jung had called the Collective Unconscious.

The quality of the messages they received swiftly persuaded them that they were in communication with separate discarnate personalities, quite possibly the ghosts of long dead monks who had lived in the monastery.

At the first session, which took place in November 1907, the two men sat opposite each other across an empty table in reverent expectation.

Bartlett took the part of the medium and Bond the 'sitter'. This involved Bond asking the questions while placing two fingers on the back of Bartlett's hand to make a connection with the spirits.

'Can you tell us anything about Glastonbury?' asked the architect, to which an invisible force answered in a legible scrawl by animating Bartlett's hand: 'All knowledge is eternal and is available to mental sympathy.'

The connection had been made and information as to the location of the chapels and other buried structures was freely given in a mixture of Latin and English by a dis embodied spirit who identified himself as a 15th-century monk named Brother William (possibly William of Malmesbury).

To Bond and Bartlett's delight the 'monk' and his companions, known as 'The Watchers', supplied very detailed information regarding

*The ruins of Glastonbury Abbey*

the location of the abbey's foundations. When the excavations started, often the workmen would simply have to dig a few feet down to hit the precise spot, after which the archaeologists would move in and begin sifting the soil for artefacts. Needless to say, Bond's benefactors were beside themselves and the full extent of the ancient site was revealed over dozens of sessions during the next five years.

By 1917, Bond felt justly proud in having uncovered one of Britain's most sacred sites and decided to tell his story in print. But when *The Gates of Remembrance* was published in 1918, the Church condemned it and strenuously denied that anything other than conventional methods had been used to unearth the abbey. In an effort to distance themselves from Bond they terminated his employment, banned him from ever setting foot within the grounds again and ordered that his guidebook to Glastonbury be removed from the shelves of the gift shop.

Since that time the occult significance of the abbey's location has been argued over by scholars who believe that it was intentionally built on an ancient pagan site to conform to an alignment of stars. Bond's communications with 'Brother William' appear to confirm this.

> . . . our Abbey was a message in ye stones. In ye foundations and ye distances be a mystery – the mystery of our faith, which ye have forgotten and we also in ye latter days.
>
> All ye measurements were marked plain on ye slabbes in Mary's Chappel, and ye have destroyed them. So it was recorded, as they who builded and they who came after knew aforehand where they should build. But these things are overpast and of no value now. The spirit was lost and with the loss of the spirit the body decayed and was of no use to (us).
>
> There was the Body of Christ, and round him would have been the Four Ways. Two were builded and no more. In ye floor of ye Mary Chappel was ye Zodiac, that all might see and understand the mystery. In ye midst of ye chappel he was laid; and the Cross of Hym who was our Example and Exemplar.

## GHOSTS OF THE LONDON UNDERGROUND

The London Underground, or the Tube as it is known to the commuters who use it, shuts down not long after midnight, which is a likely relief to its many late-night workers. Many employees fear they will meet more than muggers, drug addicts and drunks if they work the 'graveyard shift'.

When the original underground tunnels were excavated during the Victorian era several historic graveyards were destroyed to make way for the network, and it is believed that their inhabitants were none too pleased at having their eternal rest disturbed. Other historic sites including gaols, paupers' graves and, most significantly, 17th-century plague pits were wilfully destroyed in the name of progress.

During the construction of St Pancras Station the church complained that the reburying of caskets at the site of an old cemetery was being carried out in haste and with disrespect for the dead. As recently as the 1960s the construction of the new Victoria line had to be delayed when a boring machine tore through a plague pit, unearthing the corpses and traumatizing several brawny navvies.

If you add to this the number of poor souls who have committed suicide by throwing themselves under trains and those who have perished in disasters, you have a real-life ghost train experience waiting for the unwary traveller.

### ALDWYCH

This station was built on the site of the Royal Strand Theatre and was said to be haunted by the ghost of an actress who hungers for applause. Closed in 1994, Aldwych had a higher than average turnover of cleaning and maintenance staff as dozens refused to work there after being confronted by a 'figure' which suddenly appeared on the tracks inside one of the approach tunnels without warning.

### BANK

When Bank station was built, workmen are said to have disturbed the restless spirit of Sarah Whitehead, known locally as the 'Black Nun'.

*Merchant seaman and tea planter turned actor, William Terriss or 'Breezy Bill' as he was known, was stabbed to death by a deranged and out-of-work actor in December, 1897*

In life she was the sister of a bank cashier who had been executed for forgery in 1811. She acquired her nickname from the commuters who saw her dressed in black waiting, every evening for 40 years until her death, outside the bank where he had worked.

### COVENT GARDEN

Staff at Covent Garden demanded a transfer to another station in the 1950s after a tall Edwardian gentleman in a frock coat, top hat and wearing opera gloves appeared unannounced in their restroom. It is thought that he might be the actor William Terriss, who was stabbed to death outside the Adelphi Theatre in the Strand in 1897. The station was built on the site of a bakery which the actor patronized en route to rehearsals.

### ELEPHANT & CASTLE

After closing time, when the station falls silent, the night staff have reported hearing phantom steps, inexplicable rapping sounds and doors banging shut. It is believed the platforms are haunted by the ghost of a traveller who was in such haste that he tripped and fell under an oncoming train.

### FARRINGDON

Of all the London Underground stations, Farringdon is the one to avoid if you are travelling alone. It is the haunt of the 'Screaming Spectre', a vengeful young apprentice hat maker who was murdered in 1758 by her master and his daughter.

### HIGHGATE

Highgate underground station is in the vicinity of the famous cemetery of the same name, a place that guarantees some serious spectral activity. Contrary to popular belief, ghosts do not linger around their graves as they do not want to be reminded that they are dead or how they met their end. Instead they 'commute' to where they can relive their routine lives and for many recently deceased Londoners this means their home, office and the Tube network. And you thought the trains were overcrowded with the living!

Curiously, local residents claim to be able to hear the sound of trains running through an abandoned and overgrown cutting that was intended to connect with the Northern line when the station was extended in 1941.

### SOUTH KENSINGTON

The only reported sighting of a ghost train was made by a passenger in December 1928. The commuter claimed to have heard the screech of its brakes and to have seen a phantom figure dressed in an Edwardian smoking jacket and peaked cap clinging to the side of the engine just moments before it was swallowed up in the darkness of the tunnel.

## GHOST FLIGHT

Executives of American carrier Eastern Airlines were literally haunted by their past when they decided to reuse parts salvaged from a crashed Tristar Lockheed L-1011 to repair other planes in their fleet. Their troubles began in December 1972 when Flight 401 fell out of the sky over the Florida Everglades claiming more than 100 lives including the pilot, Bob Loft, and flight engineer, Don Repo.

Within months of the crash, members of the cabin crew were reporting sightings of both men on their flights and these were augmented by sightings from passengers who had been disturbed by faint but full-length figures, subsequently identified as Loft and Repo from their photographs. One female passenger became hysterical when she saw the man in the seat next to her disappear. He had looked so pale and listless that she had called an attendant to see if he was ill. The attendant arrived just in time to see the man disappear before her eyes. He had been dressed in an Eastern Airlines uniform and was later identified from photographs as Don Repo.

On several occasions the pair have taken an active interest in the flight. A flight engineer was halfway through a pre-flight check when Repo appeared and assured him that the inspection had already been carried out. One particularly persuasive account was recorded by a vice president of Eastern Airlines who had been enjoying a conversation with the captain of his Miami-bound flight from JFK until he recognized the man as Bob Loft. Needless to say, the apparitions played havoc with the schedules. When the captain and two flight attendants saw Loft fade before their eyes they hastily cancelled the flight.

Usually the pair appear simply to check that all is well but on one particular flight they intervened to prevent a potentially fatal accident. Flight attendant Faye Merryweather swore she saw Repo looking inside an infrared oven in the galley and called the flight engineer and the co-pilot for assistance. The engineer immediately recognized Repo's face, then they heard him say, 'Watch out for fire on this airplane.' The warning proved timely. During the flight the plane developed serious engine trouble and was forced to land short of its destination. The oven was subsequently replaced to appease the cabin crew, who were becoming increasingly unsettled by such incidents.

This and other episodes are a matter of record in the files of the Flight Safety Foundation and the Federal Aviation Agency. The former investigated several incidents and concluded: 'The reports were given by experienced and trustworthy pilots and crew. We consider them significant. The appearance of the dead flight engineer [Repo] . . . was confirmed by the flight engineer.'

The airline responded to the intensifying interest in their planes by refusing to co-operate with anyone other than the airline authorities. It appears they have learnt the true meaning of 'false economy'. The story inspired a bestselling book, *The Ghost of Flight 401*, by John G. Fuller and a 1978 TV movie of the same name starring Ernest Borgnine and the then unknown Kim Basinger.

## HAUNTED HOLLYWOOD

> What the average man calls Death, I believe to be merely the beginning of Life itself. We simply live beyond the shell. We emerge from out of its narrow confines like a chrysalis. Why call it Death? Or, if we give it the name Death, why surround it with dark fears and sick imaginings? I am not afraid of the Unknown.
>
> Rudolph Valentino

Living legends die hard, particularly those whose larger-than-life personalities dominated the silver screen in Hollywood's heyday. Hollywood Memorial Cemetery (recently renamed Hollywood Forever) is the oldest graveyard in Tinseltown and is reputed to be uncommonly active as far as spectral sightings are concerned. The cemetery backs on to Paramount Studios which is said to be haunted by the ghosts of its most enduring stars, Douglas Fairbanks and Rudolph Valentino, who do not seem content with merely revisiting the scene of their past glories. Curiously, the ghosts do not appear during the day while filming is taking place, but instead wait until the sound stages are quiet and the crew are preparing for the next day's shoot. The most remarkable incident occurred one evening when a technician fell 20 ft from a lighting gantry and was apparently saved from certain death by a spectral Samaritan who broke his fall. He seemed to hover in the air just inches from the ground for an instant, before dropping to the floor, unharmed, in full view of his startled colleagues.

On another occasion two property men suspected their colleagues of playing a practical joke after chairs that they had stacked in a corner of a storeroom mysteriously returned to the centre. They decided to stay overnight in the hope of catching whoever was responsible and that night, to their horror, they heard scraping sounds and saw the furniture moving around the room by itself. The following night they plucked up sufficient courage to attempt another vigil, but the phenomenon did not recur. Evidently the spirits were satisfied that their presence had been acknowledged.

At Culver City Studios, carpenters speak in whispers of a grey figure dressed in a jacket and tie and sporting a fedora hat who walks right through them and disappears through a door in the facing wall. From the description he appears to be the restless spirit of former studio boss Thomas Ince, who is credited with establishing the studio system and creating the role of the producer. He died in suspicious circumstances aboard a yacht owned by William Randolph Hearst in 1924. It is rumoured that the rabidly jealous newspaper tycoon was trying to shoot Charlie Chaplin at the time but killed Ince by mistake.

For a generation of silent movie fans Rudolph Valentino personified the 'Latin lover' and after his death at the age of 31 he became the most active ghost in Hollywood. His spirit glides elegantly through the rooms of his former mansion, the Falcon's Lair, gazing longingly from a second-floor window and visiting the horses in the stables. Staff

Marilyn Kills Self

Found Nude In Bed ...

Hand on Phone ...

Took 50 Sleep Pills

Begin Her Tempestuous

MARILYN DEAD

*Newspapers proclaiming the death of Marilyn Monroe, 6 August 1962*

at Paramount studios have sworn they have seen 'the Sheik' admiring the stock in the costume department and walking soundlessly through Studio Five where he lived every man's fantasy, seducing beautiful female film stars and being handsomely paid for doing so. Curiously, his fans appear equally persistent. The ghost of a lady admirer in a veil is often seen bringing phantom flowers to the star's tomb at the Hollywood Forever cemetery.

Another haunted studio is Universal, which was the setting for the original silent version of *Phantom of the Opera* (1925) starring horror screen legend Lon Chaney Sr whose spirit has been seen scampering along the catwalks and gantries with his cape billowing behind. Chaney, who died in 1930, was known as 'the man of a thousand faces' because of his uncanny ability to transform himself – by aid of make-up and acting – into all manner of the most hideously deformed characters.

TV's original Superman, actor George Reeves, is said to have shot himself at his Beverly Hills home in 1959, three days before his wedding, because he could not cope with being typecast. His friends and family maintain that he was murdered.

Visitors to the house have reported sensing his apparition dressed in his Superman costume.

Another mysterious murder/suicide was that of Thelma Todd who appeared with silent comedy stars Laurel and Hardy, and Buster Keaton. She managed to make the transition to sound pictures but died in 1935 in the garage of her beachside café on the Pacific Coast Highway, near Malibu. The police suspected a suicide, but there were bloodstains which were never satisfactorily explained. The present owners of the property claim to have seen her ghost on the premises and to have smelt exhaust fumes in the empty garage.

The Vogue Theatre, Hollywood Boulevard, is said to be haunted by a projectionist who collapsed and died in the projection booth, a maintenance engineer, and a schoolteacher and her pupils who were burned to death when their school, Prospect Elementary, which had previously occupied the site, was destroyed in a blaze. The theatre had been a regular venue for studio broadcasts but there have been so many instances of (paranormal) interference with electrical equipment that TV companies are reluctant to hire the theatre anymore.

Other haunted Hollywood locations include the Roosevelt Hotel in which several stars made their second home. Guests have frequently

*Bette Davis is said to haunt the rooms of Los Angeles' Colonial Building, where she lived for many years*

complained of hearing a clarinet playing in the early hours only to be told that it is the resident ghost of screen star Montgomery Clift, who had stayed at the hotel during the filming of *From Here To Eternity* and had to learn the instrument to secure the role that earned him his third Academy Award nomination. Guests at the time had complained of the unsociable hours he chose to practise and they are continuing to complain long after his death.

More unsettling is the case of the haunted mirror which used to take pride of place in a room Marilyn Monroe had stayed in. Long after Marilyn's death a cleaner suffered the shock of seeing Monroe's face appear in the mirror, forcing the management to remove it and hang it in the hallway. But the ghost reappeared in the mirror whenever a guest paused to check their appearance and it has since acquired a reputation as 'the ghost glass'.

Some ghosts had too good a time during their life to waste the afterlife wailing and moaning. Writer, director and *bon vivant* Orson Welles continues to enjoy brandy and cigars at his favourite table in Sweet Lady Jane's Restaurant in Hollywood. Fellow diners, the living ones that is, regularly comment on the smell of cigar smoke but the maître d'hôtel refuses to give a refund.

Actor Hugh Grant is said to have heard the ghost of Bette Davis sobbing and moaning as it sweeps through the luxury apartments in Los Angeles' Colonial Building where she used to live, while another larger-than-life actress, comedian Lucille Ball, is said to haunt her home at 100 North Roxbury Drive; windows have been broken in the Ball house, furniture has moved of its own accord and shouting has been traced to an empty attic. But if the new owners were thinking of calling in the ghostbusters they might want to think again. *Ghostbusters* star Dan Ackroyd may have been fearless when facing spooky special effects on the big screen but in real life he admits to being unnerved when he realized he was sharing his bed with the ghost of Mama Cass Elliot, one-time member of 60s singing group The Mamas and the Papas. 'A ghost certainly haunts my house. It once even crawled into bed with me. I rolled over and just nuzzled up to whatever it was and went back to sleep. The ghost also turns on the Stairmaster and moves jewellery across the dresser. I'm sure it's Mama Cass because you get the feeling it's a big ghost.'

One would imagine that behind the walls of their luxury homes Hollywood's celebrities would enjoy peace and privacy, but the home of actress Elke Sommer and husband Joe Hyams was a living hell to rival anything seen on screen in *The Amityville Horror*. On several occasions the couple and their dinner guests witnessed the spectre of a middle-aged man in a white suit passing through the rooms. The couple were repeatedly forced to flee from the choking fumes of fires which spontaneously and inexplicably broke out at all hours of day and night. Fire Department investigators made a thorough examination of the luxury property on several occasions with particular attention paid to the attic where the conflagrations had begun, but they could find no physical cause for the blazes such as faulty wiring, and expressed disbelief that the fires could have caught hold in that part of the house as there was no inflammable material to feed the flames. Dissatisfied, the couple called in the American Society for Psychical Research who documented a catalogue of anomalous incidents, but they could not appease the spirits. Sommer and Hyams were finally forced to sell their dream home before it burned down with them inside. It was subsequently sold no less than 15 times with many owners living there for less than a year.

But arguably the most disturbing Hollywood haunting was that experienced one evening in the 1960s by the late Sharon Tate, actress wife of film director Roman Polanski. Tate was in her bedroom when she saw the spectre of a 'creepy little man', as she later described him, enter her room and appear to search for something. She recognized him as the former owner of the house, Paul Burn, a theatrical agent who had shot himself in the upstairs bathroom after the break-up of his marriage to actress Jean Harlow. When Tate fled from the room she came face to face with a second apparition at the foot of the stairs. It was the spirit of a woman who was tied to a pillar with her throat cut. Tate's screams echoed round the walls for it was her own ghost. Shortly afterwards the house became the scene of a sickening ritual murder when Tate was killed by members of the so-called 'Manson Family', who tied her to the staircase and slashed her throat.

## THEIR FINAL BOW

Hollywood is not the only place to be haunted by dead celebrities whose egos were too large to go quietly. Flamboyant entertainer Liberace (1919–87) reputedly haunts Carluccio's restaurant off the Las Vegas strip which he once owned and where he still demands that his presence is acknowledged. Regular customers recall the time when the lights failed and all power to the kitchen was cut off until someone remembered that it was Liberace's birthday. After they had drunk to his memory the power came back on. But unfortunately that is not the extent of his activities. Several female patrons swear they have been on the receiving end of the former owner's mischievous sense of humour – they claim to have been locked in the cubicles in the powder room by an unseen hand.

Elvis Presley, arguably the biggest star of all, is clearly not yet ready to bow out gracefully. Las Vegas stagehands have reported seeing the portly apparition in his trademark white sequined suit taking a final bow at the venue he made his own in the early 1970s, the Hilton Hotel. Elvis has also been seen revisiting scenes of his former glory, specifically the former RCA recording studios off Nashville's Music Row where the mere mention of his name is answered by falling ladders, exploding light bulbs and odd noises echoing through the sound system.

Not all the apparitions in Las Vegas are those of the entertainers who lived like kings in the 24-hour pleasure palaces. The town's most notorious resident was Mobster 'Bugsy' Siegel who is credited with turning the desert town into the gambling capital of America. On 20 June 1947, Bugsy was 'whacked' by disgruntled business associates who accused him of overspending their ill-gotten gains and skimming some off the top for himself. He has been sighted mooching about his favourite casino in the Flamingo Hotel in Vegas dressed in a smoking jacket and grinning from ear to ear, as well as in the presidential suite which he had made his home. He has also been spotted running and ducking to avoid imaginary bullets at his girlfriend's mansion in Beverly Hills, the scene of his murder, although he was shot while seated on the sofa. Perhaps it is his guilty conscience which pursues him into the afterlife.

## SPOOKED CELEBRITIES

Some people can take spirits in their stride while others need to sleep for weeks afterwards with the light on. Oddly enough it's usually the action hero types who discover that their fearless on-screen persona deserts them when faced with the inexplicable.

Jean-Claude Van Damme, 'the Muscles from Brussels', admits he was spooked the night he came face to face with a ghost in his bathroom mirror. 'I suddenly felt very cold. I turned round and thought: "I've had a vision or something." It was blue and white and had a very smoky body. Since that moment I've believed in ghosts.'

Movie star Nicolas Cage, who has cultivated an edgy, unpredictable screen persona in such films as *Face Off*, *Windtalkers* and *Lord of War*, admits he was freaked by a phantom intruder at his uncle Francis Ford Coppola's home. 'I was living in the attic, and there were bats there between the walls – you could hear the scratching. One night I was not quite asleep when the door in front of my bed opened and there was this pitch-black silhouette of a woman with big hair. I thought it was my aunt coming to say goodnight. So I said, "Goodnight", and it didn't say anything. Then it moved towards me and my body froze up and I let out this blood-curdling scream and threw my pillow at it. Then it disappeared. Now, am I saying I saw a ghost? I still don't know. But I saw something that freaked me out.'

*The Matrix* star Keanu Reeves may have been a messianic hero who saved the world in cyberspace, but he can still wake up in a sweat when haunted by nightmares of a real ghostly encounter during his childhood. 'I was living in New Jersey when I saw and felt this ghost. I remember just staring at this suit which had no body or legs in it as it came into the room before disappearing. It was a double-breasted suit in white, and I looked at my nanny who was just as shocked as me. I just couldn't get back to sleep afterwards, and I still see the figure in my dreams and nightmares.'

Richard Dreyfuss, star of *Jaws* and *Close Encounters of the Third Kind*, was wide awake when he encountered the spook that cured him of his cocaine habit. 'I had a car crash in the late 1970s, when I was really screwed up, and I started seeing these ghostly visions of a little girl every night. I couldn't shake this image. Every day it became clearer and I didn't know who the hell she was. I had no kids, I was a bachelor. Then I realized that kid was either the child I didn't kill the night I smashed up my car, or it was the daughter that I didn't have yet. I immediately sobered up. I still don't get it, but, hey, it did the trick.'

## Life Imitating Art

Even horror movie queens are unnerved when they meet the real thing, as *Scream* star Neve Campbell discovered when she bought her Hollywood home without checking its history. 'Someone was murdered in my house six years before I bought it. I had friends round and I left them in the living room to go in the kitchen and they both thought I had just walked back in again. But I hadn't, so what they saw was the woman who was murdered. The previous owner had an exorcist come in, but I don't think it worked.'

Rumour has it that celebrity ex-couple Ethan Hawke and Uma Thurman were forced to abandon their 18th-century dream home in Sneden's Landing, New York, only months after they had moved in, because of inexplicable incidents. It appears that they were too scared to describe what they had seen and experienced even after retreating to the safety of their old Manhattan apartment.

Rock star Sting was driven to call in professional ghostbusters when he discovered that his family were sharing their north London home with mischievous spirits. 'Ever since I moved there, people said things happened – they were lying in bed and people started talking to them, or things went missing. I was very sceptical until the night after my daughter Mickey was born. She was disturbed and I went to see her. Her room is full of mobiles and they were going berserk. I thought a window must be open, but they were all shut. I was terrified.' It seems exorcists did the trick as Sting and his kids now sleep soundly without unwanted interruption.

The late John Entwistle, bass player with the Who, enjoyed playing the role of the lord of the manor at his 19th-century country estate and was evidently prepared to share it with the previous resident. 'A lot of weird things have happened in the 22 years I've been here. Among them are sightings of a lady in 19th-century clothes walking the grounds, and the camera of an uninvited photographer falling apart. Most recently I was having trouble locating a recording of Keith Moon pounding out a never-used Who song, and so I asked my friendly ghost for a helping hand. A few hours later, when I was about to give up the search, the tapes spontaneously fell off a shelf behind me revealing the Moon recording which had been hidden behind them. I used it.'

One would think that living in a converted church would guarantee peace and quiet but Tim Robbins, star of the supernatural drama *Jacob's Ladder* and writer-director of the (ironically) titled *Dead Man Walking*, was evicted from his home, a former chapel, by decidedly unholy spirits. 'It was in Los Angeles, 1984. I had just moved into a new apartment in a converted church. I had two cats. I came home one night – everything was still in boxes – it was dark and the cats were terrified. There were clearly spirits in the room. Then I looked on the wall and there were cockroaches all over it. I moved out the next day.'

John Lennon's widow Yoko Ono discovered a 'lost' Lennon song without supernatural assistance but when the surviving Beatles came to finish it they sensed the presence of the author overseeing the production. Paul McCartney and John Lennon were volatile soulmates and successful songwriting partners during the Beatles' heyday until their acrimonious split in 1970. So it is perhaps not unexpected that the surviving members sensed the late Lennon's presence in the studio when they reformed to record John's *Free As A Bird* using his unfinished demo. McCartney has said, 'There were a lot of strange goings-on in the studio – noises that shouldn't have been there and equipment doing all manner of weird things. There was just an overall feeling that John was around.'

## Celebrity Séance

Dave Grohl of rock band the Foo Fighters was sceptical when it came to the subject of the supernatural until his wife, Jennifer, persuaded him to join her in a séance. She had sensed unseen presences at their Seattle home and was determined to discover their cause. Grohl remembers, 'Jennifer asked if there were any spirits in the house. The glass on the Ouija board spelled out: "Y-E-S". I was just looking at Jennifer and she wasn't moving at all. The glass was travelling without her pushing it. Jennifer then asked, "What happened here?" The glass spelled out: "M-U-R-D-E-R-E-D". I asked who was murdered and got the reply: "M-Y-B-A-B-Y".'

The couple has since learnt that according to a local legend, a Native American baby was murdered there by its mother and buried in a well. The Grohls believe that it is her restless spirit which haunts their house grieving for the child and pleading with the present owners to give it a proper burial. But it's not just Hollywood celebs and rock stars who admit to being spooked. Princess Stephanie of Monaco has confessed to having written a song with her dead mother, Princess Grace, who had died in a car accident in 1982. 'I found I'd written my own song and recorded it without really being present to the whole thing. Something was telling or guiding me to sit down and just write. I grabbed a pen and pad and the words came flowing out. I can't explain it, but I don't feel as if I wrote them. The words just came into my head as if someone on the other side was writing them down for me.' Her second album contained 'Words Upon The Wind', a song dedicated to her mother. According to her daughter, Princess Grace reappeared when Stephanie succumbed to stage fright during a French TV broadcast. 'Without my mother's help, I could never have done it. I was so petrified that I couldn't speak. Yet as soon as I got in front of the cameras, I could hear my mum telling me to relax and to just remember everything that she had always told me.'

# CHAPTER NINE

# GHOST HUNTERS

Fancy a spot of ghostbusting? This chapter tells you all you need to know, including a close look at serious spook hunters' essential equipment.

Shortly before his death, ghost hunter Harry Price was asked to write an account of his most extraordinary encounter with the spirit world. The article was published posthumously in the *Australian Herald* on Saturday, 3 April 1948:

HARRY PRICE – GHOST HUNTER

> Many times have I been asked for my 'best ghost story': for the most thrilling and sensational incident in a lifetime's inquiry into the unknown and the unseen. I have investigated hundreds of alleged haunted houses, sometimes, as at Borley Rectory, with exciting results. I have attended thousands of séances, many of them in my own laboratory, in an attempt to pierce the 'iron curtain' that separates this world from the next. I have sat in poltergeist-infested homes, in which objects have been

*Harry Price, ghost hunter extraordinaire*

flying about – objects which no human hands could possibly have propelled. I have seen crude limb-like materialisations form under my eyes when experimenting with the Schneider mediums. I have shivered as I watched the mercury fall during a séance, when normally the air should have become warmer. But only once have I seen what YOU would call a ghost – a solid three-dimensional spirit from, apparently, the other side of that 'iron curtain' I have just mentioned.

On November 8, 1937, a few days after I had broadcast a talk on haunted houses, a woman rang me up to tell an extraordinary story. She explained that she was the wife of a hop broker and had a large house in the South of London. Some years previously she had met a middle-aged widow who attended the same church. The widow, a French-woman, had been married to a British officer who was killed in 1916, leaving her with a young daughter, Rosalie. The widow determined to bring up her child in England, and made her home in London.

The child, Rosalie, was never strong. In 1921, when she was six, she contracted diphtheria and after a few days' illness [she died]. The mother, whom I will call Madame Z. was heart-broken. She became ill with grief and nearly died. And then came the miracle.

One night, early in 1925, when Madame Z. was lying awake in bed, she thought she heard her dead child's voice calling 'Mother'. She nearly swooned with fear and delight at the thought that her girl had 'come back' and was still near her. She called her daughter by name but there was no reply. Next night and on many succeeding nights Madame Z. heard that same word 'Mother' coming out of the darkness in the same loving, lisping voice that was so dear and so familiar to her. Gradually, she thought she could see in the dim obscurity of her bedroom the fluorescent outline of her child. She put her arm out of bed, she said, and her hand was clasped by that of Rosalie. After that, the visits became more frequent; the 'spirit' more human, and mother and child even talked a little. That was the story told by the woman who rang me up. She added that in 1928 she persuaded Madame Z. to visit her home in order to see whether Rosalie could be induced to 'appear'.

The experiments were successful and, in six months the child was materialising, regularly, in the home circle, every Wednesday night. I was invited to attend one of these séances. I was surprised when I was told that I could take charge of the séance, search the rooms, search the sitters, control anything and everything. The one condition was that I had to ask permission to do anything during the actual sitting, in order to avoid shock to Rosalie or her mother. This was reasonable. I accepted. The séance was fixed for December 15, 1937. After I had had supper with the family I began my search of the house, a large detached building. I examined every room. I sealed all external doors and windows. I removed most of the furniture from the séance room (the drawing room), examined the bare boards of the floor, sounded the distempered walls and ceiling, blocked up the chimney with newspapers, and finally sprinkled starch powder in front of the fireplace and locked door in order to register any possible foot or hand marks. Then I sealed the door and windows with adhesive tape and screw-eyes and drew the heavy curtains across the windows. A mouse could not have entered that room undetected. We were ready for the séance. It was 9.10 p.m. when I finished the job, watched – not without amusement – by the broker and his wife, his daughter, her boyfriend, and Madame Z. With myself, these formed the sitters. I then searched them. No one was concealing anything. In the centre of the room I placed six heavy mahogany chairs in a circle. We sat down. My host switched off the lights. The séance began.

Suddenly, Madame Z. gave a choking sob and murmured 'My darling!' I was warned that Rosalie was present. At the same moment I sensed that something was before me and that the distressed mother was fondling her child. Then something brushed my left hand; it felt soft and cool. I did not move, but asked permission to touch the figure. Permission was given, and I stretched out my arm, which came into contact with the nude and living body of a little girl, about three feet seven inches tall. I stroked her cheeks and rested my hand on her chest. I could feel her heart beating and could hear her breathing. Then with both hands I felt her hair, long and soft, falling over her shoulders. By this time most of the sitters were distressed.

I got permission to examine the child be means of some luminous plates. I found that Rosalie was a well-formed little girl with dark, intelligent eyes, which gazed into mine without flinching. I received permission to speak to the figure. I hesitated, and finally said:

'Where do you live, Rosalie?' (No answer)

'What do you do there?' (No answer)

'Do you play with other children?' (No answer)

'Have you any toys there?' (No answer)

'Are there any animal pets?' (No answer)

Rosalie simply stared, and did not seem to understand what I was saying. I asked her a final question: 'Rosalie, do you love your mummy?' I saw her expression change and her eyes light up. 'Yes,' she lisped.

Rosalie had barely uttered this single word when Madame Z. gave a cry and clasped her 'daughter' to her breast. Our luminous plates were removed and the séance was over. Rosalie had gone. We sat for fifteen minutes, then the light was switched on. I found all my seals and controls intact. After thanking my hosts I left – not nearly as sceptical as I was a few hours before. I was impressed, puzzled, and almost convinced that survival of human personality had been demonstrated.

I asked for another sitting, in my own laboratory, with a different group of observers. This was promised, but before it could be arranged Madame Z. went to visit her old home in Paris. This was at the end of August, 1939. She was apparently engulfed by the war and nothing has been heard of her since.

## MOST HAUNTED

Belief in ghosts and the paranormal has soared in recent years thanks largely to the success of the worldwide syndicated television series *Most Haunted*. The ground-breaking show which is avidly watched by millions in countries as far apart as Australia, Poland, Canada, Ukraine and Israel, investigates a wide variety of allegedly haunted sites in Britain and the USA using state-of-the-art audio-visual equipment (including night-vision cameras) to record paranormal activity which lends the footage a *Blair Witch Project* feel. The show has attracted a cult following with fans getting together to hold *Most Haunted* parties when they draw the curtains, light candles and gather around the TV to share the shivers. The programme's website has recorded 30 million hits and 50,000 fans of all ages regularly apply for tickets whenever a live broadcast is announced.

*Psychic Derek Acorah 'saw' a Jacobite army in an area where it had not been known the Jacobites had actually been*

The producers shrewdly assembled an investigative team of specialists from diverse disciplines to put their collective insights and experiences in perspective. Celebrity psychic Derek Acorah and psychic artist Brian Shepherd are complemented by historian Richard Felix and parapsychologist Dr Ciaran O'Keeffe. The idea is that if Derek psychically channels information of which Richard was previously unaware but is later able to confirm through research then it lends credibility to the claim that Derek made a genuine connection with the spirit world. Such an incident occurred at Sandbach Old Hall in Cheshire. Derek was adamant that he could 'see' Scottish soldiers fighting with swords at the site although Richard, who was an expert on the Jacobite rebellion, was equally adamant that Bonnie Prince Charlie's troops had not penetrated that far south. Subsequent research proved Derek correct: 1,500 soldiers under Lord George Murray had taken a detour to Sandbach to avoid clashing with the garrison at Manchester. As Richard said, 'If even I didn't know that at the time, how could Derek have known?' Derek's heightened sensitivity to the highly charged atmosphere and occasional 'possession' by the resident spirits must have convinced some of the most sceptical viewers of the existence of unseen presences.

Derek was a reluctant convert to mediumship even though he was just 'knee-high' when his grandmother overheard him talking to the ghost of his grandfather. Over the course of the next 30 years he developed a gift for psychometry (being able to 'read' impressions imprinted on personal objects by their previous owners), a talent he demonstrated to remarkable effect on an early TV series *The Antiques Ghost Show*. He attributes the uncanny accuracy of his 'readings' to his spirit guide 'Sam' who acts as intermediary between himself and the many disembodied intelligences who seek to communicate.

Psychic artist Brian Shepherd works in much the same way. When he arrives at a location he will walk around it until he feels drawn to a particular spot. Then he opens up to whatever presences may be near and lets his drawing implement glide across paper. He says when the connection is strong it is as if he is being guided. At first he has a sense of a person, then their features appear as if he is building an identikit from

*When TV's* Most Haunted *team went to Warwick Castle to try and see its ghost, Sir Fulke Greville, footsteps were heard and one of the team was possessed by a spirit, causing him to shout at those around him*

a given description. Invariably it's just a head, the rest of the figure being blurred. He chooses to work in charcoal because it is more immediate than colour, which he would have to think about and that would risk constricting the flow of images. At the Black Swan Inn at Devizes in Wiltshire he 'saw' a man with a bulbous nose sitting by the bar wearing a hat. When he showed the finished sketch to the landlady she burst into tears as she recognized him as the ghost she had been seeing over the years. Sometimes he appeared so solid that she has asked the bar staff why they haven't served him yet.

The locations for *Most Haunted* are kept secret from the psychics so that they cannot be accused of having researched the site prior to filming. In fact, the producers go to great lengths to ensure that Derek cannot be unduly influenced by knowing the location in advance. He is not given the name of his hotel until 24 hours before filming and that can be up to 45 minutes' drive from the location.

There are more than 10,000 locations in the UK which have been officially registered and documented as sites of alleged hauntings and probably the same number again could have been registered, but for one reason or another their owners decided not to publicize the presence of their uninvited guests. One would imagine that such a large number of locations would mean that the production team would be spoilt for choice, but they have limited themselves to those claiming recent sightings which had been verified by several witnesses. Although it is primarily an entertainment programme, the *Most Haunted* team take the show very seriously and zealously guard their integrity. They go to enormous lengths to rule out physical causes for what might appear to be paranormal activity during filming. Before each show the technical team scours the site for electromagnetic anomalies using an EMF meter so that fluctuations during filming can be compared to the baseline measurement. Temperature readings are also taken which are compared with those made with a directional laser thermometer during the broadcast. Temperature changes are a positive indicator of a spectral presence. At Bodelwyddan Castle in Wales, for example, the presenter Yvette Fielding felt the spirit of her grandmother grasp her hand. The thermal-imaging camera showed Yvette's hands were blue while everyone else's hands were red.

The team also performs a lengthy and thorough walk-through of the building to check for creaky floorboards, doors that might swing open with a draught, the noise level and vibrations caused by passing traffic or a railway line, loose pipes and even insect infestation. During their initial research they became aware that owners of commercial premises seemed suspiciously eager to discover that they might have resident ghosts as it makes for great publicity. In fact, they resisted a request from a major broadcaster to fake paranormal activity using special effects then admit what they had done at the end of the show. Their response was that even if nothing happened during filming it would still be riveting viewing to see how a paranormal investigation is conducted and to watch the team both in front of and behind the cameras dealing with the 'scare factor'.

Surprisingly, it is the male members of the team who seem to be most sensitive to atmosphere. It's probably because they feel they have to laugh off the very idea of ghosts and so are unnerved when their preconceptions are shaken. Several crew members dropped out, including one of the big beefy riggers who ran the cabling, because they couldn't face their fears. 'They're all cocky when they arrive,' says Yvette, 'but at 2 am, when they have to de-rig in the pitch black, it's a different matter. I've seen huge guys walking hand in hand across a graveyard in the dark – it was quite sweet really.' Yvette herself is often torn between her desire for something uncanny to happen and her own fear of being spooked. 'I always say I want something to happen so we can capture it on camera – but when it does, I can't tell you how scared I am. Words can't describe it.'

The producers decided from the outset that watching Derek and the team sitting in hushed expectation in a single room would make for dull viewing so they only investigate locations where sightings have been made in at least three areas. Over the course of six series they have braved all-night vigils in damp underground tunnels, an isolated lighthouse, a prison, several treacherous towers, various ruined castles, country houses and windswept hillsides, all in pitch darkness and bitter cold.

And their verdict? Everyone involved, both in front of and behind the camera, admits to having seen or sensed inexplicable changes in atmosphere, to have heard strange unearthly sounds, to have smelt strong scents with no obvious source, to have been pushed, scratched and physically attacked by an unseen presence and to have been very, very scared indeed. The only contentious element is how they interpret their experiences. The team and crew are divided between those who blame spirits and those who suspect there might be another explanation such as an electromagnetic force field which scientists claim can cause headaches, auditory hallucinations and even the feeling of being watched in susceptible individuals.

Recently an ex-member of the group cast doubt on the validity of the evidence and the nature of the experiences shared by certain members of the team, but his colleagues have dismissed such claims out of hand.

## IS YOUR HOUSE HAUNTED??

Have you ever sensed an invisible presence in your home as if someone was watching you, or perhaps seen something moving out of the corner of your eye? Maybe you've felt a touch like cobwebs on your face or a gentle pressure on your hair as if someone had laid an invisible hand on your head? Have you been kept awake at night by inexplicable sounds, smelt strange scents like perfume or tobacco, or perhaps you have a 'cold spot' in your house or flat which makes you uncomfortable when you approach it? If so, your home may be haunted, but there could also be a natural explanation for some of these anomalies and you need to be able to eliminate these before embarking on a paranormal investigation, as they can be expensive.

All houses are subject to 'settling' as the timbers in the roofing, joists and floors expand and contract with changes in temperature and these can cause creaks and groans that may be unsettling if you're a nervous and imaginative type. In very old buildings, rats and mice can be a source of scratching sounds, particularly at night when they scurry through the pipes, ventilation system and between the walls, foraging for food.

These are all obvious sources of unnerving sounds, but far less known is the fact that even such seemingly genuine sensations such as spectral caresses can be caused by fluctuations in your own energy field, or aura. Certain acutely sensitive individuals can be affected by the weather, particularly low pressure. Animals have an innate sense of an approaching storm or even rain as the atmospheric pressure changes under the gathering clouds. People can share this sensitivity but usually to a lesser degree and can become tired or develop headaches as a result. In extreme cases they may become depressed due to the change in pressure. Psychics can actually see an inverted funnel of mental energy pressing down on the head of a depressed person as their thoughts turn inwards instead of radiating outwards. For this reason, anyone who senses subtle pressure which they suspect may be caused by phantom fingers or the presence of spirits should first ask themselves if these sensations could originate within themselves. You can do this by relaxing into a light meditative state or trying automatic writing in which you can ask a direct question regarding the source of these sensations. Even 'cold spots' can have a rational explanation. Most houses have a spot where dampness can accumulate and this is to do with geological factors or the presence of an underground stream or pipes. A cold spot does not necessarily signify an evil presence, nor does a fall in air temperature which can trigger a fear response in the body.

If you have eliminated all rational explanations and are keen to carry out a scientific investigation into possible paranormal activity, you will need to buy or hire certain items of equipment which no self-respecting ghost hunter can afford to be without.

The most essential item is an EMF meter which measures fluctuations in the electromagnetic field. Orthodox science considers these to be a natural phenomenon, but paranormal researchers believe these disturbances to be proof of the presence of ghosts. A normal EMF reading is between 0.5 and 1.5 milligauss so anything above this could be significant, especially if the reading fluctuates. It is important to be aware that domestic appliances such as fridges and microwaves and faulty wiring can cause unusually high readings.

If you still think you may have an uninvited presence in your home do not assume it to be malevolent. It is far more likely to be a loved one or friend who merely wants to assure you that they are well or to pass on information regarding your current circumstances or something they left unsaid. If so, you can communicate safely with them by using the exercise on page 434–5, or you can contact a medium. It is extremely rare to be plagued by a poltergeist (for which there is usually a rational explanation) or a spiteful spirit, so don't lose any sleep over it. If you suspect you have an unwanted presence, you can clear the property yourself or call in an experienced psychic who will exorcize it for you.

If you decide to do it yourself, you may find a spot of research at your local library to be useful in uncovering the history of the house and the area. Crimes, disasters and accidental deaths are usually recorded in the local paper or parish records. Maintain a detached attitude so that you are not unduly influenced by what you read. It is better to attempt communication first and then research the records to validate or dismiss what you have learnt from the spirit.

## HOW TO SEE A GHOST

We are surrounded by spirits but unless you are acutely sensitive (psychic) you will be insensible to their presence. However, you can raise your awareness through meditation and exercises such as the one described below.

It is very important, though, that you protect yourself against mischievous and malevolent spirits as well as the strong possibility of self-deception, by grounding and centring yourself before attempting all psychic work, and remembering to close down at the end of each session.

### Invoking Protection

- Stand with your arms by your side and establish a steady natural rhythm of breathing. With each in breath you will feel reinvigorated and with each exhalation you will dispel tension.

- When you feel suitably relaxed, visualize sending fibrous roots of etheric energy into the ground from the soles of your feet to anchor yourself. Then imagine a small sphere of white light hovering over your head. Bring it down through the top of your head and see it pass through your body to the floor so that you now stand in a protective tube of light which radiates outwards, dispelling the darkness and charging the air around you with divine energy. If you wish, you can invoke protection from whichever source you feel is right at this moment. 'The Lord's Prayer' would be suitable for a Christian, the invocation of the four archangels for the occultist. Do whatever feels right for you. You are now grounded and centred in yourself. Nothing can disturb you and nothing can invade your sacred space.
- If you live in an old house you can tune into the residual impressions of the previous residents using the following exercise. Otherwise you will need to find a suitable place such as an old church or hospital where you can sit for an hour or so in comparative peace.
- Keeping your eyes open, still your mind by focusing on your breath. Let your thoughts subside so that you settle into a passive state, receptive to the subtle impressions around you.
- Begin by making physical contact with the place. Stand with your back to a wall and take several deep breaths. If you are a natural medium you might be able to sense or see something straight away. If not, put your hands on something that will have absorbed an impression such as a chair, or church pew. Sit quietly. You may feel cold, heat or a tingling in your fingers. The atmosphere may also change in a subtle but significant way as you become sensitized.
- Next, heighten your sense of smell. If you are outdoors expand your awareness by centring on the scent of the grass, flowers

and the soil. Hospitals will have their own distinct smells and churches too will have retained the smell of incense, flowers and polished wood.

- Now raise your awareness to the sounds that surround you and then see if you can go beyond those to the vibrations at higher frequencies. To do this, listen acutely to your watch or a clock. Home in on the ticking to the exclusion of everything else.
- Finally, soften your gaze so that any reflected light, such as through a stained glass window or off a polished surface, has a mildly hypnotic effect. Look beyond the light into the middle distance and see if you can detect a shape or figure. If not, look away into a dark corner and see if you can detect any movement in the shadows.
- If you are anxious for any reason, you can ask your inner guides or guardian angel to draw near, to isolate you from any disturbing influences in the atmosphere. You can help the process by stimulating your third eye. Simply make gentle, circular movements with your index finger in the centre of your forehead until you feel a tickling sensation. You are now open to the more subtle impressions in the atmosphere.
- Remember to close down and ground yourself when you have finished by counting down slowly from ten to one, stamping your feet and ritually rinsing your hands in cold water, anointing your face with cold water or discussing what you plan to do with the rest of the evening with your companions.

## SPEAKING WITH SPIRITS?

If we are surrounded by spirits – both malevolent and benign – how can we distinguish between those who wish us well and those who would do us harm? It is a popular misconception that spirits are summoned at the request of the medium and because of this many people still believe that spirit communication is wrong because it disturbs the peace of the departed. In fact, the reverse is true. Spirits come only when they have something that they are desperate to impart to the living and they use a medium because most of us are not receptive to direct communication.

- For this exercise you will need a photograph of the deceased and, if possible, one of their personal possessions such as a watch or a ring. Take the photograph in one hand and the memento in the other. Make yourself comfortable, close your eyes and focus on your breath.
- Begin by drawing a circle of soft golden light around you to raise your awareness to a higher level and exclude any unwelcome influences. Now sensitize yourself to the residual vibrations in the personal object by centring your awareness in that hand. You should feel a warmth or a tingling sensation. If your psychic awareness is becoming more attuned you may even have a vision of the person you want to communicate with.
- If not, open your heart centre by imagining a small pulsating sphere of green light growing in intensity as you go into a deeper state of relaxation. Sense your heart centre softening and envisage the person you want to communicate with emerging from the light.
- If that person does not appear you may see your inner guide instead. If so, you can ask it to help you find the person you want to communicate with. Do not be surprised if they appear as they were when they were younger or in an idealized form as this is a projection of their self-image.
- However, you may not receive a visual communication. Instead you might have a sense of that person in the room, or hear their voice in your inner ear. If it is a lady you may have a scent of their perfume. If it is a man who smoked you may become aware of the smell of their favourite tobacco.

When you are ready to return to waking consciousness close down, clear the aura and ground yourself using the techniques previously described.

## THE GHOST HUNTER'S TOOL KIT

You don't need expensive equipment if you're starting out as an amateur ghost hunter. Initially all you need is a digital camera or a 35 mm autofocus camera with flash, loaded with 400 ASA film for interior shots and 800 ASA film for exterior work. Although 35 mm film is sometimes considered technically redundant, serious paranormal researchers and certain professionals such as forensic photographers still use it because the images are more difficult to manipulate than digital and therefore less likely to have their authenticity questioned. However, digital cameras have one major advantage. Their memory cards offer a far larger photo capacity than film (for example an 8Mb memory card can store over one hundred pictures) and the unwanted shots can be erased and the card reused. Digital enables you to take dozens of pictures in sequence without worrying that you are using up valuable film. When you want something more serious you might consider a motion sensor scouting model mounted on a tripod which takes a series of pictures automatically when the sensor is triggered. But make sure it is fitted with infrared bulbs so that you can shoot in the dark.

Ghosts don't generally pose for pictures so although a succession of still shots will capture the trail of a moving spirit, a camcorder would be more practical. Again, ensure the model you choose has an infrared nightshot feature for recording without a light source rather than a night-vision scope which has serious drawbacks, including the risk it poses to the user when flash guns are in use. When choosing a camcorder don't forget to budget for an infrared light extender which increases the camcorder's night vision range from 10–100 ft.

For the audio aspect (such as electronic voice phenomena) choose a digital DAT recorder with an external multi-directional microphone. A cassette recorder will create too much mechanical noise and its dynamic range is extremely limited. When it's quiet you won't hear much above the hiss and motor hum. An external microphone minimizes the amount of machine noise picked up by the mike and is of infinitely superior quality. If you invest in a digital recorder with a voice activation feature you won't have to spool through hours of silence to locate the recording you want.

An essential piece of equipment is the electromagnetic field detector which measures fluctuations in the electromagnetic field. Models vary in sensitivity and range from 3–25 ft depending on the price. Most have either an LED or audible alarm to notify the user that they have a reading. This can be helpful if you are working mostly in the dark. Commercial contact thermometers can be useful in measuring cold spots. Alternatively, remote thermometers can scan several rooms at the same time while you monitor them from a central location.

Motion detectors are absolutely essential and surprisingly inexpensive. They produce an audible signal whenever an infrared beam is broken. You may also want to consider non-essential items such as walkie-talkies, and heavy duty torches (with a red filter to reduce glare), plus notebooks to record EMF, temperature readings and details of where and when the photos or camcorder footage was taken. It is easy to forget where and what was taken in all the excitement and this will devalue your evidence. And, finally, don't forget to pack lots of spare batteries as ghosts have a knack of draining power, so leaving you literally in the dark.

## HOW TO CONDUCT A GHOST HUNT

You can conduct a ghost hunt in your own home or at a suitable site such as an old church, theatre, public house or battlefield. Remember, if you are investigating a site that is not your own home or on public land you will need to ask the owner's permission. Ghost hunts are best conducted by a small group who can verify each other's findings. Also, it is much more fun to work with others. If you work on your own there will be no one to verify your findings and act as a witness and if you fall in the dark there will be no one to call on for help.

### Choosing a Location

Graveyards are to be avoided. Ghosts tend to linger in locations where they lived or where they died and rarely where their body is buried. They do not associate themselves with their physical shell and many believe they are still alive.

*Harry Price's 'ghost-hunting' kit – a far cry from the intricate electrical instruments used today*

Graveyards can also induce a morbid turn of mind in those who are sensitive to atmosphere and it is necessary for serious investigators to maintain an objective, scientific approach. On a purely practical level, graveyards tend to generate a confusion of residual energies due to the number of bodies buried there over the centuries and these energies can also be mixed with those who have mourned their passing. It is better to choose a location where you are likely to pick up isolated individual impressions and where there is a minimal risk of being overwhelmed by paranormal activity and discarnate entities.

## Invoking Protection

It is strongly advisable to begin every investigation with a prayer or invocation for protection whether you are religiously observant or not. Such rituals serve to ground and centre you so that you will not be easily disturbed by experiences which may or may not have a supernatural origin. You can imagine drawing a circle of white light around you and/or invoking protection from the four archangels (see pages 432–4:

Invoking Protection), a religious figure or your spirit guides. Take what you are doing seriously and show respect for the dead otherwise you risk a psychic attack – one you cannot see and whose strength and nature you cannot determine.

If it is an interior location you will need to conduct a thorough preliminary walk-through in daylight to establish EMF and temperature baselines. You will need to take readings near domestic appliances so that you are not fooled by any abnormal readings in these areas during the actual investigation. Although it may seem obvious, it is surprising how many ghost hunters forget in their eagerness to check for loose latches on doors and windows and for draughts which can cause creaking doors or chill winds. You will also have to take practical steps such as noting where there are steps or other potential hazards so that you don't stumble over them in the dark.

Remember also to take sample photos of the area in good light so that you can identify where significant readings, sightings and sounds took place. When all of these precautions and preliminary checks have been completed, it is recommended that you bait a spirit trap with a personal object associated with the history of the individual in a sealed room. Choose a room that has seen activity in the past, or is most likely to register activity. The object can be placed on a sheet of plain paper and an outline drawn around it so that it will be seen if it is moved by unseen hands. Alternatively, you could place the object on a dusting of flour or talcum powder so that you can rule out a draught which would disperse the flour or a cat which would leave paw prints. Then mount a lock-off camera with a motion sensor on a tripod and point it at the object. If you want to guarantee no one will tamper with the experiment you can set up a separate motion detector as an alarm then seal the room from the outside with tape. You can now explore the rest of the site with a camcorder, still camera, EMF and temperature equipment, leaving the locked room until last.

When you are finished, it is important that you close down by asking for the blessing of the divine on the location, on those spirits which linger there and on all those involved in the investigation. Thank the angels or spirit guides whose presence you invoked at the beginning and then ground yourself by drinking cold water, rinsing your hands and talking aloud about what you plan to do with the rest of the evening or the next day. Do not be tempted to begin analyzing the data, but start fresh the next day. This will ensure you view the material with detachment and that you do not carry a residue of emotional energy from the site.

# AFTERWORD

> Behind every man now alive stands 30 ghosts, for that is the ratio by which the dead outnumber the living.
>
> Arthur C. Clarke, *2001: A Space Odyssey*

There is a saying I have heard often when talking to the various psychics and paranormal researchers I have worked with and interviewed over the past 30 years or more. 'For those who believe, no proof is necessary; for those who don't, no proof is enough.'

It is my understanding that the spirit world and the physical world co-exist and that we can all glimpse this other dimension, this other reality because we are all psychic to various degrees. Clairvoyants and mediums are different from the average person only in that they are aware that they possess this innate ability, or sensitivity, and have chosen to develop it by being uncommonly receptive to these subtle impressions from the 'other side' and trusting in their intuition.

Others may glimpse the inhabitants of this other reality under certain conditions without having made a conscious effort to do so. In this book I have given numerous examples of both and hope that it has provided those who believe in ghosts with much to support and justify their convictions and for those who did not believe, with sufficient grounds to question their doubts and reserve judgement until they see a ghost for themselves!

Those who deny the possibility of the supernatural do so partly out of fear and partly on principle, believing that the logical and scientific mind should discount what they consider to be nothing more than an irrational superstition. They argue, and with some justification, that the presence of ghosts has never been proven and that other paranormal phenomena have not been replicated under laboratory conditions. However, heightened states of consciousness and the incorporeal cannot be measured, recorded or filmed. Brain waves and heart rates can be measured, but thoughts and emotions cannot. It is the same with ghosts which appear to be either our disembodied consciousness or residual emotions in the ether.

However, most us cannot live in a world of spirits and the supernatural because we need to be grounded in the 'real' world to fulfil our responsibilities and in doing so we find stability and a certain security. That is both understandable and desirable, but if we live entirely in the material world which is by nature transient and superficial, then we are sleepwalking through life and oblivious to the multi-dimensional world in which we exist.

Believing in ghosts and other manifestations of the supernatural and paranormal is not, therefore, an escape from reality as the sceptics would have us believe, but quite the opposite. It is to truly see what wonders and potential dangers we live amongst.

Having explored many aspects of the paranormal and written several books on the subject, I thought I had the paranormal pretty well sussed, as they say. I had my beliefs, based largely on personal experience and those of psychics and mediums I had worked with, but also my doubts about other aspects, specifically spirit photography. Until that is, a member of my family happened to mention having seen a photograph that her teenage daughter had taken at a children's birthday party in 2005. It had been passed around the group of friends all of whom remarked on the presence of a little girl in Victorian dress who could be seen peeping out from under the legs of one of the children. This was not the typical faint blurry image one associates with alleged 'ghost photos', but a sharp unmistakable image of a little girl with blond ringlets who nobody could identify. It had been a small party in a private house so there was no chance for an uninvited guest to sneak in unnoticed. Everyone in the photo knew one another, with the exception of the unidentified child. What is even more remarkable is that when the photograph had been taken, one of the children had run screaming from the room and had to be comforted by her mother. It wasn't until the photograph was developed that the hosts understood the reason for her fear. The distressed girl must have seen the ghost.

So, I no longer dismiss the possibility of such phenomena out of hand, although I maintain a healthy scepticism with regard to some of the more dramatic claims.

> It is wonderful that five thousand years have now elapsed since the creation of the world, and still it is undecided whether or not there has ever been an instance of the spirit of any person appearing after death. All argument is against it; but all belief is for it.
>
> Samuel Johnson, *The Life of Samuel Johnson*

# INDEX

# PICTURE CREDITS

*Corbis:* 12, 15, 39, 52, 82, 84, 86, 91, 95, 109, 115, 123, 133, 135, 146, 150, 195, 221, 223, 245, 248, 250, 256, 268 (2), 270, 272, 281, 288, 291, 305, 322, 325, 341, 390, 394, 397, 398, 403, 412, 427
*Shutterstock:* 23, 35, 155, 176, 191, 227
*Jeff Danalek:* 25
*Michael Ebbs USA www.photoreciprocity.ifp3.com:* 29
*Getty:* 30, 156, 170, 178, 228, 410
*Amanda Keeys:* 32
*Mary Evans:* 47, 237, 243 (2), 250, 260, 422, 426, 438
*Topfoto:* 88, 93, 97, 137, 168, 201, 203, 285, 310
*Science Photo Library:* 116
*Rex:* 131, 275
*Bill Stoneham:* 185
*Flickrname: fat ballerina:* 339
*Flickrname: Gunnella:* 342
*Flickrname: craigjam:* 358
*Jan-Andrew Henderson:* 351

We have made every effort to contact the copyright-holders of the photographs and illustrations within this book. Any oversights or omissions will be corrected in future editions.

'Beneath the tides of sleep and time
Strange fish are moving.'
Thomas Wolfe